The Geopolitics of Resource Wars

A wealth of natural resources such as oil or diamonds should, in theory, favour a country's economic and social development. And yet, from the oil fields of the Persian Gulf to the diamond mines of West Africa, millions of people in resource-rich countries have seen their lives devastated as a result of exploitative commercial relations, corrupt governance and war. Going beyond conventional arguments of resource competition over scarce resources, this book examines the 'resource curse' affecting many resource-dependent countries and the spaces of (mis)governance shaping the violent geopolitics of many raw materials.

Highlighting the multiple forms of violence accompanying the history of resources exploitation and current business practices supporting predatory regimes, insurgent groups and terrorists, this book provides fresh and in-depth perspectives on so-called 'resource wars'. The book includes conceptual chapters (Philippe Le Billon, Rick Auty) and covers a wide range of case studies including the geopoiitics of oil control in the Middle East, Central Asia and Colombia (Fouad El-Khatib, Sarah O'Hara, Shannon O'Lear and Leslie Wirpsa), spaces of governance and 'petro-violence' in Nigeria (Michael Watts) and 'blood diamonds' and other minerals associated with conflicts in Sierra Leone and the Congo (Marilyn Silberfein, Kevin Dunn).

This book is a special issue of the journal *Geopolitics*.

Philippe Le Billon is Assistant Professor at the University of British Columbia with the Department of Geography and the Liu Institiute on Global Issues. A former Research Associate at the International Institute for Strategic Studies and the Overseas Development Institute, he is the author of *Fuelling War: Natural Resources and Armed Conflicts*.

Books of Related Interest

Constructing Post-Soviet Geopolitics in Estonia
Pami Aalto, University of Tampere

From Geopolitics to Global Politics: A French Connection
Jacques Lévy, Reims University (ed.)

Geopolitics at the End of the Twentieth Century:
The Changing World Political Map
Nurit Kliot, Haifa University and David Newman,
Ben Gurion University of the Negev (eds)

The Changing Geopolitics of Eastern Europe
Andrew H. Dawson and Rick Fawn, University of St Andrews (eds)

Boundaries, Territory and Postmodernity
David Newman, Ben Gurion University of the Negev (ed.)

The Marshall Plan Today: Model and Metaphor
John Agnew and J. Nicholas Entrikin, University of California,
Los Angeles (eds)

Geopolitics and Strategic History, 1871–2050
Colin S. Gray, University of Reading and Geoffrey Sloan,
Britannia Royal Naval College

11 September and Its Aftermath: The Geopolitics of Terror
Stanley D. Brunn

THE GEOPOLITICS OF RESOURCE WARS

RESOURCE DEPENDENCE, GOVERNANCE AND VIOLENCE

Edited by

PHILIPPE LE BILLON

FRANK CASS

LONDON • NEW YORK

First Published 2005 by Frank Cass, an imprint of Taylor & Francis
2 Park Square, Milton Park, Abingdon, Oxon OX14 4RN

Simultaneously published in the USA and Canada
by Frank Cass
270 Madison Ave, New York NY 10016

Frank Cass is an imprint of the Taylor & Francis Group

Transferred to Digital Printing 2005

Typeset in Times New Roman by Taylor & Francis Books

British Library Cataloguing in Publication Data
A catalogue record for this book is available from the British Library

Library of Congress Cataloging in Publication Data
A catalog record for this book has been applied for.

ISBN 0-714-65604-6

Contents

The Geopolitical Economy of 'Resource Wars'

PHILIPPE LE BILLON

Introduction

Natural resources have gained a new strategic importance in wars. With the withdrawal of Cold War foreign sponsorship in the late 1980s, local resources have become the mainstay of most war economies. Beyond financing war, natural resources have been depicted as an important motive of several wars in the 1990s, from the Iraqi invasion of Kuwaiti oilfields, to civil wars fuelled by diamonds in West Africa. While much attention had been previously devoted to the risk of armed conflicts resulting from the vulnerability of supply of 'strategic resources' for major powers or environmental scarcity in poor countries, most resource-related wars in the 1990s have opposed domestic or regional politico-military entrepreneurs over locally abundant and internationally valuable resources, such as oil, timber, or diamonds. In this light, some interventions by regional powers have been tainted by the 'lust' for valuable resources, as with the Ugandan or Zimbabwean military deployment in the Democratic Republic of Congo.[1] Speaking of the 'poisonous mix' of diamonds and greed fuelling the war in Sierra Leone, UN Secretary-General Kofi Annan even suggested that 'when a whole Guinean battalion [of peacekeepers] on its way to Sierra Leone – 900 men with Armoured Personal Carriers – said they were disarmed [by rebels], you wonder … Did they sell them?'[2]

This introductory essay examines the geopolitical economy of so-called 'resource wars', that is, armed conflicts revolving 'to a significant degree, over the pursuit or possession of critical materials'.[3] The term 'resource war' itself emerged in the US in the early 1980s in reference to perceived Soviet threats over US access to Middle Eastern oil and African minerals.[4] Beyond this conventional geopolitical and strategic perspective on resource competition, this essay argues that the significance of resources in wars is largely rooted in the political and economic vulnerabilities of resource dependent states. This essay stresses the links between (mis)governance, conflicts, and the historical legacy of the social construction and exploitation of 'resources' by imperial powers, as well as the current multiscalar practices of the global political economy in which commodity and financial flows are

rarely matched with informational and 'ethical' ones. Resources have
specific historic, geographic, and social qualities participating in shaping the
patterns of conflicts and violences. The discursive construction and
materiality of oil and diamonds, for example, entail distinct social practices,
stakes, and potential conflicts associated with their territorial control,
exploitation, commercialization, and consumption. Among these qualities,
their territorialization as well as physical, economic and discursive
characteristics come to define resources both materially and socially in
dialectic relationships with institutions and practices. As pointed out by
Kevin Dunn in the case of Central Africa, 'the material aspects of a war
economy are intrinsically linked to its discursive production'; whereby
perceptions of threats, sectarian identity politics and spaces of (in)security
inform and reflect the so-called 'greedy' dimensions of (violent) resource
extraction and trade.[5] The crucial interplay between specific institutions,
spaces of governance and resources also needs to be stressed, as
demonstrated by Rick Auty and Michael Watts in this volume. In this regard
the understanding of so-called 'resource curse' and 'resource wars' needs to
give consideration to both the forms of power exercised in the 'pre-resource'
era, as well as the specific ways in which different resources define specific
'political idioms' and influence social and political outcomes.

This study focuses on the relative importance of the materiality of
resources and their geography *vis-à-vis* the type and course of conflicts. The
following section briefly reviews the evolution of geopolitical perspectives
on resource competition. The third section examines the political economy
of resource dependence in relation to the causes of conflict. The fourth
section demonstrates the importance of different resources in financing
armed conflicts, with the fifth section stressing the complicity and
responsibilities of businesses in this regard. The sixth section outlines
different geographies of 'resource wars' according to the characteristics of
resources. In conclusion, the study briefly considers regulatory initiatives
brought to bear on belligerents and businesses to prevent 'resource wars'.

The Geopolitics of Resource Competition

Resources have provided some of the means and motive of global European
power expansion, while also being the focus of inter-state rivalry and
strategic denial of access. Western geopolitical thinking about resources has
been dominated by the equation of trade, war, and power, at the core of
which were overseas resources and maritime navigation. During the
mercantilist period of the fifteenth century, trade and war became intimately
linked to protect or interdict the accumulation of 'world riches', mostly in
the form of bullion, enabled by progress in maritime transport and upon

which much of the balance of power was perceived to depend.[6] For example, the decision to pursue 'commerce warfare', in effect piracy, by French military engineer Vauban aimed, but failed, at precipitating the downfall of English and Dutch power by targeting their maritime trading.[7] Writing on the wake of the three consecutive wars between the English and the Dutch in the seventeenth century, John Evelyn commented that,

> Whoever commands the ocean commands the trade of the world, and whoever commands the trade of the world commands the riches of the world, and whoever is master of that commands the world itself.[8]

Since sea power itself rested on access to timber, naval timber supply became a major preoccupation for major European powers from the seventeenth century onwards. Besides motivating overseas alliances, trade, or even imperialist rule, England in particular pursued a policy of open sea 'at all costs' that led to several armed interventions in the Baltic; a situation that would bear similarities with the case of oil in the twentieth century.[9] With growing industrialization and increasing dependence on imported materials during the nineteenth century, western powers intensified their control over raw materials, leading along with many other factors such as political ideologies to an imperialist 'scramble' over much of the rest of the world.[10] Late imperial initiatives also influenced the Prussian strategy of consolidating their economic self-sufficiency through a resource access provided by a 'vital space', or *Lebensraum*, while the potential role of railways to enable land-based transcontinental control of resources raised a threat to maritime-based power, giving way to the idea of 'Heartland' developed by Halford Mackinder. The significance of imported resources, and in particular oil, during the First World War reinforced the idea of resource vulnerability, which was again confirmed during the Second World War.[11]

Strategic thinking about resources during the Cold War continued to focus on the vulnerability of rising resource supply dependence, and to consider the potential for international conflicts resulting from competition over access to key resources.[12] In their search for resource security and strategic advantage, industrialized countries continued to take a diversity of initiatives (on the vulnerability of western energy supply, see Susanne Peters in this volume), including military deployment near exploitation sites and along shipping lanes, stockpiling of strategic resources, diplomatic support, 'gunboat' policies, proxy wars or *coup d'état* to maintain allied regimes in producing countries, as well as support to transnational corporations and favourable international trade agreements.

Geopolitical discourses and practices of resource competition were not only defined at an international scale but as well as at a sub-national one, especially in reference to the territorial legacy surviving the decolonization process and its implications in terms of resource control (see the discussion of secessions, below). By the 1970s, concerns also came to encompass the potential threat of political instability resulting from population growth, environmental degradation, and social inequalities in poor countries, leading to a redefinition of national security.[13] The ensuing concept of 'environmental security' emerged to reflect ideas of global interdependence, illustrated through the debates on global warming, environmental 'limits to growth', or political instability associated with environmental scarcity in the South (for a critique, see Simon Dalby's *Environmental Security*).[14] Traditional western strategic thinking remained, however, mostly concerned with supply vulnerability within the framework of the two blocs, notably about Soviet threats over the western control of oil in the Persian Gulf or 'strategic minerals' in Southern and Central Africa.[15] The decolonization process, the 1956 Suez crisis, the 1973 Arab oil embargo, and the 1979 Iranian revolution also clearly focused western strategic concerns on the part of western governments as well as resource businesses, over domestic and regional political stability and alliances.[16] The end of the Cold War and disintegration of the Soviet empire, and the Iraqi invasion of Kuwait further reinforced this view. Although the security of supply continues to inform governmental and corporate decisions in the management of several minerals, in particular with regard to high-tech and radioactive materials, oil stands apart in terms of global strategic importance.[17]

As more attention was again devoted to the internal mechanisms of wars in the early 1990s, a view emerged that a new and violent scramble for resources amongst local warlords as well as regional and international powers was becoming 'the most distinctive feature of the global security environment'.[18] Noting the growth of mass consumerism and the 'economization' of international affairs in the 1990s, political scientist Michael Klare associates 'resource wars' with a combination of population and economic growth leading to a relentless expansion in the demand for raw materials, expected resource shortages, and contested resource ownership.[19] Asia's growing mass consumerism and energy demand, for example, are of specific concern for the militarized control of the South China Sea and Spratly islands. The control of the oil and pipelines in the Caspian region is another, as illustrated by Shannon O'Lear and Sarah O'Hara in this volume. If market forces and technological progress can mitigate some of these problems, Klare remains essentially pessimistic given the readiness of countries claiming resources or importing them, especially the US, to secure their access to resources through military force, and given the political instability of many producing regions. Indeed, the strategic military posturing of the US in the Arabian Peninsula, the maritime deployment of the US-led Multinational Interception Force enforcing UN sanctions on Iraq, as well as the US military occupation of Iraq and the deployment in Central Asia give to the geopolitics of oil in this region a strong military tone.

While the Persian Gulf area has received most attention as a prominent terrain for 'resource wars' due to foreign oil supply interests, tensions and civil unrest in the region also testify in part to the problems of the historical trajectories as well as political economy and governance of resource-dependent countries.

The Political Economy of Resource Dependence

In the aftermath of the Second World War and decolonization, much hope was placed in the promise that extractive sectors would assist poor countries in developing economically and politically.[20] The successful development path of countries benefiting from rich natural endowments, such as Australia, Canada and the US frequently served to justify these views; even though development largely preceded and enabled the relatively positive role of mineral resources, for example, and most poor countries have been facing vastly different domestic and international contexts in which resources may contribute to their development.[21] Since the oil shocks of the 1970s, resource wealth appears to have left large numbers of people in developing countries worse off than otherwise. Resource-dependent countries tend to have lower social indicators and their states tend to be more corrupt, ineffective and authoritarian and, to prioritize military expenditures.[22] They also appear to be amongst the most conflict-ridden countries.[23] Although some argue that these problems characterize all poor countries and that resource dependence is simply a symptom of economic underdevelopment, others believe that a rich resource endowment is more a curse than a blessing.[24]

Well-managed resources can prove a valuable development asset, but resources can also prove a source of vulnerabilities and 'excesses' negatively influencing the domestic politics and economy of exporting countries, as well as foreign relations.[25] Of 'strategic' importance to domestic or foreign economic and political concerns, resource access and exploitation can become highly contested issues. Because of their territorialization, resources generate more territorial stakes than many other economic sectors, centred on the definition of political boundaries and local representation or alliances with foreign powers. Exportable on the international market, resources give rise to stakes over access and control of *filières* or commodity networks, trading routes, and markets. Generating large financial rents, the control of resources often provides a crucial link between the economy and politics, in particular through relations of co-

optation or patronage that often come to replace the taxation/representation
nexus, while the impact of resources on development is itself highly
sensitive to the institutional context in which they are exploited.

Through patronage or coercion, large resource revenues can 'pay for
stability' and maintain a generally autocratic, stable political order. Yet
political transition imposed by ageing leaders, domestic or international
pressure for democratization, and economic downturns affecting key resource
sectors, can all represent major challenges to such regimes, which are
generally characterized by the low accountability of élite groups. Arguably,
political development comes in large part through the taxation of society by
authorities. As noted by Mick Moore, many poor and conflict-affected states,

> live to a high degree on 'unearned income' – mainly mineral resources
> and development aid – and correspondingly face limited incentives to
> bargain with their own citizens over resources or to institute or respect
> democratic processes around public revenue and expenditure.[26]

Respectively, people and informal business groups lightly or not taxed by a
government relying on resource rents, would be less concerned by a
government's lack of accountability and legitimacy than heavily taxed ones;
thereby being less motivated to promote political changes. Rulers can play
on this by ignoring corruption and leaving most of the economy to become
informal. Mobutu did precisely that when urging citizens to 'fend for
yourselves' and to 'steal a little in a nice way', without aiming to become
rich overnight or to transfer funds overseas; a 'policy' that became
popularly known as 'Article 15' of the Zairian constitution and served as a
justification for all forms of trafficking.[27] These policies reflected as much
Mobutu's pragmatism in the face of an economic meltdown, as the
instrumentalization of disorder by local political and economic actors.[28]
Smuggling and the unofficial economy did provide the marginalized
population in general and the political opposition with an alternative
political economy that delayed political polarization, but they also further
weakened the fiscal base of the state apparatus, and promoted corruption or
demobilization among officials.[29]

A resource-rich economy thus facilitates the formation and viability of
politically underdeveloped rule; although resource wealth may neither be
necessary nor sufficient. Dangerously remaining at the core of political
institutions while being eroded by reserve depletion, corruption,
mismanagement or falling prices, resource rents ultimately risk leading to
political instability and conflicts.

In a worst case scenario, resource revenues monopolized by a corrupt
élite or squandered by mismanagement justifiably feed grievances amongst
marginalized groups, while resentment may also easily grow out of other

resource-related issues, such as pollution, labour conditions, or the social inequity frequently accompanying resource exploitation.[30] Competing businesses convinced of their own powerlessness assert their neutrality and continue to serve as intermediaries between local actors and global consumers; leaving a wide gap of accountability that an economically disempowered population cannot easily fill. Importing countries too often accommodate or even support predatory states, as long as access to cheap or strategic resources is secure. As resources become depleted, prices collapse, or corruption-weary businesses leave, and the legitimacy and capacity of local rulers are further eroded. Disavowed by their population, rulers face the challenge of political change and the temptation of their own radicalization. At this juncture, violence and exclusionary identity politics become seductive means of empowerment and survival for most parties.

As natural resources gain in importance for belligerents, so the focus of military activities becomes centred on areas of economic significance. This has a critical effect on the location of military deployment, type of conflict, and intensity of confrontations.[31] Complementing guerrilla strategies of high mobility, concentration of forces, and location along international borders, rebel groups seek to establish permanent strongholds or areas of 'insecurity' wherever resources and transport routes are located. Government troops generally attempt to prevent this by extending counter-insurgency to these areas, occasionally displacing and 'villagising' populations. In many cases, however, government troops join in the plunder. Distinctions between soldiers and rebels then often become blurred, as both groups entertain the same economic agendas, occasionally co-operating to keep trading routes open and to maximize gains while minimizing their costs. As demonstrated by the coalition formed by many elements of the Sierra Leone Army and the rebel Revolutionary United Front in 1997, both groups can also have similar social backgrounds, similar grievances towards the traditional ruling élite and a shared goal of empowerment through force. Beyond politico-military entrepreneurs turning into warlords and building their power in part out of the (violent) control of valuable resources, many ordinary people may also use violence as a deliberate means of accessing resources, thereby increasing the spatial and social diffusion of a conflict.[32]

History as well as political culture, institutions, the individual personality of leaders and the availability of weapons intervene at least as much as the political economy of natural resources *per se* in these conflicts and their violent escalation, but the exploitation of nature represents a source of power and conflicts that should not be ignored. Just as important, different resources present to belligerents different opportunities of financing or profiteering from war.

Resource Opportunities and War

During wars, economically motivated violence among rebels will be more likely when the potential rewards are great and when 'natural resources can be exploited with minimal technology and without the need to control the capital or machinery of the state'.[33] As Rick Auty demonstrates in this volume, some resources, in other words, are more accessible than others to rebels, offering the ability to scale-up and profit from their military operations. The geographical location, concentration, and the mode of exploitation influence the lootability of a resource. In terms of location, a resource close to the capital is less likely to be captured by rebels than a resource close to a border inhabited by a group lacking official political representation. Accordingly, resources are close or distant from the centre of power, in both geographical and political terms. Resources are also more likely to be looted if they are spread over a larger territory than a small area that can be more easily defended. *Point resources* are spatially concentrated in small areas and include mainly resources that can be exploited by capital-intensive extractive industries, such as deep-shaft mining or oil exploitation, and which generally employ a small workforce.[34] *Diffuse resources* are spatially spread over vast areas and often exploited by less capital-intensive industries. These include alluvial gems and minerals, timber, agricultural products, and fish. This concentration is determined both in terms of spatial spread, and mode of exploitation and control. In short, the risk of looting is higher when resources are located at the periphery of domestic control and in proximity to foreign markets.

Highly valuable and easily mined through artisanal means, alluvial diamonds are particularly accessible to rebel groups. The control of the most prolific diamond areas of Sierra Leone generated tens of millions of dollars for the RUF in the 1990s. In eastern Democratic Republic of Congo (DRC), several rebel factions operate as intermediaries for the control of the diamonds by Ugandan interests, while the government has granted the Zimbabwean military some of the best diamonds concessions in return for its support.[35] In Angola, diamonds exploitation provided several hundred million dollars in net revenue to the UNITA rebel movement of Jonas Savimbi during the 1990s.[36] If the Angolan government wanted to control diamonds, it had to secure a monopoly of access over a vast territory in remote regions. Even though the major mines are concentrated in the north-east, alluvial diamonds can be found in many river-beds over a huge territory covered by bush, facilitating guerrilla activities, and are accessible to a large number of firms and even small groups of *garimpeiros* – freelance diggers.[37] Although diffuse by geography and mode of production, the tight control exercised by UNITA over *garimpeiros* and mines in some regions is such that diamonds can also be considered as a point resource with regard to the concentration of profits. If diamonds had been found only in Kimberlite pipes, as in Botswana, access to diamonds by UNITA would have been complicated, not to say impossible. In Namibia, many diamonds are found on vast beaches, thereby constituting lootable diffuse resources. Recognizing the problem, colonial authorities defined the area as *Sperrgebiet* or 'Forbidden Zone' and drastically enforced access rules to prevent theft. Yet the open terrain of the deserted coast offered no cover to a guerrilla force. As stated by a former SWAPO fighter, now Director of Mines, 'We could not have operated there, the South Africans would have simply bombed us.'[38]

The lootable character of diamonds does not only concern rebels. Ruling élites have also developed modes of appropriation detached from the legal and institutional apparatus of the state, often by creating parallel mechanisms of involvement and control in the private or informal diamonds sector. In Sierra Leone – a case examined by Marilyn Silberfein in this volume – the RUF rebel movement referred in its propaganda to former Presidents Siaka Stevens and Valentine Strasser, arguing that 'when a valuable gemstone is found [Presidents] jump into a plane and shoot off to Europe to sell the diamonds trusting no one but themselves'.[39] While also motivated by private gains, such a mode of appropriation nevertheless retains important political dimensions.[40] As such, diamonds have long influenced both the militarization of diamond-producing regions and half of the main producing countries of alluvial diamonds have been embroiled in diamonds-related wars. Furthermore, the high value, durability, transportability, and anonymity of diamonds have made it a convenient financial instrument for terrorist groups such as Al Qaeda.[41]

Besides diamonds, many other 'small' strategic or valuable metals, such as gems, cobalt, coltan, gold, and silver have similar lootable characteristics. Sapphires and rubies have provided the Khmer Rouge in Cambodia and the Karen in Burma with significant revenues during the early 1990s. In Afghanistan, the late Massoud's United Front commander earned annually around $50 million from the control of emeralds and lapis lazuli.[42] Gold is also mined with minimal investments and easily transported and traded. In Zaire/DRC, diamonds and other valuable minerals such as gold are located in alluvial deposits covering thousands of square kilometres and open to illegal exploitation and clandestine trading. The great distance from Kinshasa, the proximity of 'smuggling markets', for example in Burundi, and the possibility of artisanal mining have long provided a favourable context for the illegal exploitation and trafficking of gold in the eastern part of the country. The mining and trafficking of alluvial gold in the hilly terrain of south-eastern Kivu sustained Laurent Kabila's rebel movement, the *Party Révolutionnaire du Peuple*, between the late 1960s and the creation of the AFDL in 1996.[43] Gold continues to sustain the numerous armed groups operating in this region, from Rwandan troops to local 'Mayi-Mayi' self-defence units. New minerals have also appeared on the balance sheet of 'war economies' as new demand increased their value, as with coltan (columbite-tantalite) a metal ore from which tantalum is extracted for use in mobile phones. Coltan allowed armed groups such as the Mayi-Mayi to prosper and, along with predation upon the general population, to transform themselves from self-defence militias into self-interested criminal bands.[44] While supposedly allied with the government in Kinshasa, most of the trade was directed towards rebel-controlled areas and Rwanda and Uganda, thereby requiring collusion between opposing sides.

Not all minerals are as lootable as diamonds or coltan. Others, like copper and oil, require large-scale infrastructures and involve a minimum of approval or accounting by recognized authorities for international trading. While this means that these resources are less lootable by rebel groups, highly centralized control by the ruling élite enables state looting on a grand scale. Furthermore, revenues can still be generated by rebels groups through extortion: oil and gas, for example, can remain 'extortable' by even lightly-armed rebel units due to vulnerability of their onshore installations, such as pipelines, or staff – giving way to a militarization of production and transport. Thad Dunning and Leslie Wirpsa discuss in this volume the case of Colombia, where most of the oil is inland and shipped through pipelines. In that country, the oil sector is alleged to pay annually, mostly through their subcontractors and local officials, a total of $100 million per year in protection rent to guerrilla groups, while major oil companies pay $250 million to the government through a 'war tax' set up in 1992.[45] When located offshore, this sector is largely insulated from threats of violence by insurgent movements, unless the armed opposition holds airborne weapons or at least marine commandos – as was the case when the South African Defence Force supported UNITA. Rather than the inaccessible production sites, the sites of state power – such as the capital and presidential palace – become the target of rebel control. In Nigeria, however, protests and kidnapping – which are part of the 'petroviolence' discussed by Michael Watts in this volume – have been staged on oil platforms demonstrating the local agendas at work. In 1998, about 100 youths occupied a Chevron platform to protest against environmental and distributional issues and demand monetary compensation and jobs, leading to a joint police and navy operation which resulted in the death of two protesters. In 1999, a small commando of the 'Enough is Enough in the Niger River' group kidnapped three staff and hijacked an helicopter on a Shell platform, later releasing them for a ransom. In some instances of kidnapping, companies had reportedly not paid protection fees in advance to the 'right people'.[46]

Forest products, mostly in the form of timber, are probably the most common resource fuelling wars. The first reason, besides the relatively widespread world-wide distribution of forests, is that insurgents have repeatedly used forests as refuge from government armies. Many rebel groups have thus taken advantage of this location to engage in racketeering or set up logging businesses. Although the difficult control of forests increases the lootability of this sector, the bulkiness of logs and the need for roads or river rafts provide a greater opportunity for the control of transport and trading. Participation in logging operations requires extremely 'porous borders' or the complicity of neighbouring authorities. As a Thai general commented about the conspicuous nature of imports into Thailand from Khmer Rouge areas in Cambodia: 'We are talking about logs, not toothpicks'.[47] Under-funded or financially self-interested army units deployed for counterinsurgency purposes, but also high-ranking government officials frequently join in the business or authorize loggers to operate in rebel-controlled areas in exchange for bribes.[48] The lootability of timber thus often rests on a high degree of collusion between rebels, governments, and businesses. Finally, the logging industry also tends to be risk-prone in order to access increasingly rare and valuable old growth 'timber', as demonstrated by the presence of international companies in the disputed areas of Liberia, West Papua in Indonesia, or the Cabinda enclave in Angola.

Agricultural commodities can also be the objects of mass-scale looting and sustained extortion. Following the resumption of the war in DRC in 1998, coffee and cattle were among the main commodities 'systematically drained' from areas controlled by Burundian, Rwandan, and Ugandan forces and their local ally the Rally for Congolese Democracy.[49] These forces not only conducted organized large-scale confiscation of the stockpiles of local companies, but also looted banks and dismantled some factories, while individual soldiers stole savings from Congolese citizens. In Colombia, a prominent form of 'mafia violence' focusing on extortion of coffee producers and cattle-rustling took place alongside politically motivated violence.[50] Even marine resources by foreign fishing fleets can be looted. Thai fishing vessels plundered Cambodian territorial waters during the transition period that followed the withdrawal of Vietnamese troops in 1989, often with the authorization of local strongmen and military units also controlling the smuggling of consumer goods and timber. Similarly in Somalia, fishing vessels from neighbouring countries, Europe, Pakistan, Korea, and Japan operated in Somali territorial waters under licence from Mogadishu warlords or Somaliland authorities.[51]

Beyond the political economy of resource-dependence and its commercial or strategic value for foreign interests, the specific characteristics of a resource as well as its location thus come to define its accessibility by belligerents, rebels and government officials alike, and thereby its contribution to prolonging wars. War commodities may prolong wars by providing a financial support to the weaker side enabling it, and possibly motivating it, to fight longer militarily. Resource revenues can also create a financial incentive for opposing armed groups to settle into a 'comfortable conflict stalemate' that is mutually beneficial and relatively non-threatening in order to control, produce or market resources. By providing political networks of support, including 'private resource diplomacy', resources can also prolong conflicts. UNITA's diamonds not only allowed the rebel movement to buy arms, but also secured diplomatic and logistical support from regional political leaders, while the hope of securing oil reserves in case of an electoral or military victory by UNITA pushed some western companies to support the rebel movement until the early 1990s. In this regard, bilateral actors may be inclined to accommodate commercial interests benefiting their corporations, and commodity revenues may also decrease the potential leverage of donors to exercise pressure on the warring parties in favour of a negotiated settlement. Finally, access to commodity revenues can act as a divisive factor among domestic and international players. Resource wealth can prolong conflict by weakening the application of a cease-fire or peace agreement by local commanders who stand to lose financially from resources under their control, hence potentially leading to a factionalization of movements along lines of commercial interests. Examining the differential impact of specific commodities on the duration of 15 conflicts according to their lootability and obstructability, Michael Ross finds support for the hypothesis that lootable commodities and, to a lesser extent, obstructable (or extortable) commodities, prolong war by financing the weaker side of a conflict, and creating discipline problems.[52]

Although resource wealth tends to prolong wars, it can also shorten them in several ways. First, it can produce an overwhelming concentration of revenues in the hands of one party, as oil did for the Angolan government. The government's consequent ability to rearm and reorganize allowed it to mount a decisive military campaign between 1999 and 2002 against UNITA, while the rebel movement could not easily sell its diamond stock or trade it for weapons in part due to a more effective UN sanction regime.[53] Second, a government's greater access to resources can motivate rebel groups to defect to the government and provide an incentive in peace negotiations, or even lure rebel leaders to the capital to allow their capture. Local commanders or movements eager to protect their commercial interests may strike a peace agreement with the government, as occurred within several armed groups in Burma. Economic sanctions and the cooperation of neighbouring countries in closing their borders to rebel trade, as well as trust-building mechanisms around wealth-sharing agreements can be essential in this regard (see below). Finally, the control of commodity revenues can create problems of trust and discipline within movements, with fragmentation often affecting rebel movements as a result of the 'bottom up' direction of resource flows (i.e., from local units to headquarters).[54]

It does not follow, however, that a war would be less violent in the absence of resources. On the contrary, belligerents lacking access to resources may intensify predation and abuses on populations, while large-scale revenues can allow belligerents to shift from a war of terror on civilians to a conventional type of conflict. Yet, as the extreme violence and widespread abuses by the RUF and UNITA against populations exemplifies, violence towards civilians has many other motives than purely economic ones. It remains the case that resources will tend to prolong and intensify conflicts and if, in this regard, a resource-rich environment is generally propitious to financing rebellion, opportunities for armed groups will also depend on the practices and complicity of businesses.

The Responsibility and Complicity of Resource Businesses

Belligerents generally require business intermediaries to access commodity, financial, or arms markets. A wide variety of commercial operators intervene in resource-based war economies, from 'barefoot local entrepreneurs' to international brokers, and from international contraband networks to major transnational corporations – resources thus often come to participate in the growing 'contraband capitalism' characterizing the 'wild zones' of the world.[55] Some businesses simply attempt to cope with a degrading political and security context, others see in such a context the possibility of a competitive advantage. This role varies from simple economic intermediaries to complex forms of influence, including political and military support. Antagonisms between private and public foreign interests can emerge. In the late 1970s and 1980s, for example, US oil companies defended by Cuban troops fiscally supported the Angolan communist regime condemned and fought by the US administration.[56]

Businesses, from petty gems traders to oil majors, often refrain from having a direct role in resource-fuelled wars, limiting involvement to the collateral impact of operations in 'intrinsically unstable areas'.[57] Oilman and now US Vice-President Dick Cheney even argued that 'the problem is that the good Lord didn't see fit to put oil and gas reserves where there are democratic governments', brushing aside the role of oil in dampening democracy, and the role of companies in sustaining this pattern.[58] As oil expert Thomas Waelde observes from the history of the oil industry, 'at the beginning of most corporate or individual successes … was usually some bold, rarely very ethical, exploitation of commercial opportunities blocked to competitors by politics'.[59] Oil businesses engaging with 'pariah states' can access markets denied to other companies eager to protect their good name, or legally barred by unilateral sanctions. The presence of British company, Premier Oil, in Burma supported a democratically illegitimate and coercive regime through both financial and private diplomatic means, even if its Chief Executive Officer (CEO) justifies the company's engagement by declaring that, 'If Burma is ever to rejoin the human race, our nationalization programme for staff will have prepared the country.'[60] Similarly, Unocal, a US energy company also present in Burma, long courted the Taliban in Afghanistan until its pipeline project was terminated in 1998 by US military retaliation against Al Qaeda bases in the country for the terrorist attack on the US embassy in Kenya.[61]

Countries in conflict also constitute a valuable 'niche market' for businesses whose competitive advantage lies in their risk-taking mentality, political acumen, or connections with security services. At best, these 'pioneers' of the international economy help to provide local jobs, humanitarian assistance, and tax revenue much needed for social services. At worst, opportunistic 'bottom-feeders' directly support war criminals in their financial and arms dealings. Often, the margin is small between these two categories as the operational environment is an invitation to much compromise. Junior companies in particular seek out markets characterized by high political risks or legal barriers, creaming off easily accessible resource reserves or preparing the ground for investment by larger businesses. Referring to mining deals in the DRC, a Swiss-based mining entrepreneur argued: 'if you want big finds, you should go to countries that are not popular.'[62] The company's strategy is also 'going to places where Americans cannot go', namely, for oil operations in Sudan.[63] But to access and secure resources in these 'unpopular places', businesses often associate themselves with dubious brokers or private military corporations. In other cases, resource businesses directly deal with arms dealers paid by belligerents through natural resource concessions or mortgaged resource production. In Liberia, several logging companies exported from the port of Buchanan controlled by Charles Taylor in the early 1990s and were reportedly 'responsible for the logistical aspects of many of [Taylor's] arms deals', including 'onward shipment of weapons to Sierra Leone'.[64]

Business interests also 'invest' in rebel factions in the perspective that they could control resource areas in the near future, even if they also pay the government to keep options open. Discreet relations or support to armed opposition movements also provide companies with 'insurance' against political changes. During the Algerian war of independence, the Italian oil company ENI reportedly supplied money and arms to FLN in return for future 'considerations'.[65] Western businessmen did the same with Savimbi in Angola during the 1980s.[66] From late 1996, many foreign companies supported the Rwandan and Ugandan-backed *Alliance des Forces Démocratiques pour la Libération du Congo* (AFDL) as it gained control of eastern and southern Zaïre, including key mining sites.[67] In Liberia, Charles Taylor rapidly gained the recognition and payment of 'taxes' by major businesses, including a subsidiary of Firestone owning a major rubber plantation, not only as a protection racket, but also to restart production.[68] Some companies may even appear rather progressive as a result. Shell, for example, has long sought contacts with separatist groups in West Papua, currently under contested Indonesian rule; and such a move may have enticed the government in Jakarta to consider further political and fiscal devolution for the province.[69]

Geographies of 'Resource Wars'

The conjunction of the geopolitics of resource competition, the history and political economy of resource exploitation, as well as the financial opportunities afforded in part by businesses to belligerents, is critical to the analysis of the geographies of 'resources wars'. This section outlines the comparative geographies of warlordism, *coup d'état*, secession, and foreign intervention in relation to the characteristics of resources. Four broad categories of resources are distinguished, according to their relative concentration of access, expressed in terms of 'point' or 'diffuse' resources (as presented above), and to their relative location *vis-à-vis* the government, expressed in terms of 'proximity' or 'distance'. *Proximate resources* are close to the centre of power (i.e., firmly under the control of the government) and less likely to be captured by rebels than those close to a border region inhabited by a group lacking official political representation. *Distant resources* are located in remote territories along porous borders, or within the territory of social groups politically marginalized or in opposition to the extant regime (i.e., under tenuous or controversial control of the government).

Based on these categories, specific resources are more likely to be associated with specific types of conflicts (see Table 1). The argument is not that oil will systematically be associated with conflicts taking the form of secession or *coup d'état*, for example, but that resources provide a context for political mobilization as well as the motivations, strategies, and capabilities of belligerents. If the characteristics of a commodity influence the motives of conflicts and balance of opportunities between opposing parties, complicity between members of supposedly opposing groups,

TABLE 1

RELATION BETWEEN THE CHARACTERISTICS OF RESOURCES
AND TYPES OF CONFLICTS

Characteristics	Point	Diffuse
Proximate	*Coup d'état*/foreign intervention	Peasant/mass rebellion
Distant	Secession	Warlordism

corruption, and involvement of government officials or agencies in the illegal economy, frequently blur the boundaries of these neat categories.

While rebel movements generally attempt to overthrow the incumbent regime, the existence of lootable resources, such as diffuse resources distant from the centre of power, can provide an economically viable fallback position in case of failure. Since these resources, such as timber or alluvial diamonds in border or remote regions, can be more easily exploited and marketable by illegal groups, they are more likely to be associated with economically viable forms of warlordism. This relationship is further consolidated if the resource is 'illegal' either at a national level (such as with illegal logging or mining) or global level (such as with narcotics). Rebel groups thereby create areas of *de facto* sovereignty imposed through violence and shaped in part by criminal and commercial opportunities such as mining areas, forests, or smuggling networks. However, diffuse and proximate resources involving large numbers of producers – such as cash crops near the provincial or national capital – are more likely to be associated with rioting and support or participation in mass rebellions. Again, the issue is not that coffee, for example, is never associated with secession or with coercive forms of warlordism, but that the geopolitical economy of a natural resource can inform both the possibilities of political mobilization and the war economy of the armed movement.

Highly coercive forms of warlordism are less likely to be economically viable with diffuse but labour-intensive resources, such as cash crops and drugs. Rather, participatory forms of rebellions are more likely to be sustained because of the need for a large volume of labour input and the difficulty of controlling workers over vast areas. Conditions of slavery and control of labour through hostage-taking can be imposed over short periods but like most predatory war economies, they can rarely be sustained over the long term. As such, the armed faction is likely to act as a 'protector' towards local populations, even if more in the sense of a Mafia group than a welfare state. This is the case of FARC guerrilla units in Colombia that provide protection to peasants on land holding and on minimum prices for both agricultural products and coca, against the *latifundistas*, paramilitary, and army.[70] While there has been more recently a drift towards more criminal activities, maintaining a balance of threats and economic incentives motivating peasant production was key to the viability of the revolutionary movement since its inception in the 1950s during the period of *'Violencia'* that opposed conservative and liberals. Similarly, the expansion of the New People's Army (NPA) in the Philippines in the 1970–80s largely came from a 'symbiotic' relation with a peasant population whose subsistence agriculture was threatened by agribusinesses, logging companies, or hydropower projects.[71] Like the FARC, the NPA provided in many respects an alternative to the regime of Ferdinand Marcos that had lost all legitimacy and even presence among rural communities.[72] Yet both movements obtained the majority of their support and funding from taxation and extortion schemes over drug trafficking and cattle ranches for the FARC, and plantations, logging, and mining for the NPA.

Point resources that are either close to the centre of control, such as offshore oil, or located in areas with historic claims for political autonomy, are likely to result, respectively, in coup attempts and secessionist wars. Point resources, such as oil or deep-shaft minerals, are generally less lootable than diffuse resources, such as cash crops and alluvial minerals, and often depend on international political recognition for mobilizing investors and accessing markets. As such, they are much more accessible to governments than to rebel movements. In the case of high-investment energy and minerals, rebels can at best disrupt government revenues or racket-exploiting companies if the infrastructures are vulnerable to attacks, such as pipelines or railways, or staff can be threatened or kidnapped. In the absence of alternative sources of finance and political basis for secession, the best option left to an armed opposition movement is to rapidly capture the state through a *coup d'état* in the capital city. This is particularly the case when resources are largely beyond the reach of a poorly armed rebel movement, such as with offshore oil.

The wars in the Republic of Congo (Brazzaville) in 1993–4 and 1997 between the main competing politicians – Sassou Nguesso, Lissouba, and Kolelas – were clearly a struggle for state power exacerbated by the control of an offshore oil sector representing 85 per cent of export earnings. The fact that these wars took the shape of a coup attempt in the capital city was in this respect characteristic. Yet Lissouba's government should have rapidly won the war through its control of the oil rent and associated military power. In fact, the war in 1997 dragged on for five months before being brought to a conclusion in favour of Nguesso by the military intervention of the Angolan government, an ally of the former President eager to protect its claims over the oil-rich enclave of Cabinda and prevent the use of Congo as a platform for UNITA diamonds-for-arms deals.

Destroying a large part of the capital and leaving thousands dead, this stalemate resulted from several factors. Firstly, a large part of the army did not engage in the conflict, while others supported Nguesso, their former patron and ethnic affiliate. Secondly, both contenders benefited from access to the oil rent as Nguesso was allegedly favoured over Lissouba by the French oil company dominating the sector and parallel channels supported Nguesso's arms purchase.[73] Finally, at street level, the conflict rapidly changed nature as the different militias supporting politicians benefited from the looting of the capital city. Urban youths on all sides instrumentalized and even appropriated the political conflict to contest the legitimacy of a corrupt political élite that had dominated and plundered the country for more than 30 years.[74] Looting became known as 'killing the pig' or 'Nkossa [oilfield], everyone his share'.[75] This form of justification echoed the devastating looting of the Liberian capital Monrovia in 1996, when NPFL fighters hijacked their leaders' military offensive, renaming it 'Operation Pay Yourself' and seeing it as form of compensation for years of fighting 'without compensation from their leaders'.[76]

Finally, point resources distant from the centre of power, for geographic or political reasons, are more likely to be associated with armed secession. The relationship is, of course, not exclusive: secessionist groups also tax logging activities if given the opportunity, and oil deposits will not automatically transform local people into armed secessionists. Yet because point resources often necessitate sovereign rights to be accessed by opposition groups, these are more likely to lead to secession than warlordism. Unable or unwilling to gain control over the existing centre of power, secessionist movements have an interest in asserting sovereign claims over the lucrative periphery they claim as theirs. Furthermore, while diffuse resources often provide local economic opportunities, including through illegal practices, point resources tend to have a low local employment rate with little scope to set in motion the type of class-based mass rebellion or 'peasant wars' examined above. In the 1990s, no less than ten secessionist movements were active in regions with large resource endowments (see Table 2). Most secession or decolonization attempts have a pre-existing historical basis, yet these movements have often been at least reinforced by the socio-economic and political transformations affecting resource-rich regions and by the resource stake, not to mention immediate financial opportunities.

The economic and social changes associated with the development of Western Sahara's important phosphate industry, for example, laid ' the basis for the rise of a modern nationalist movement, setting its sights on the creation of an independent nation-state'.[77] As Saharawis recognized in this economic bonanza the prospect of an economically viable or even

TABLE 2

SECESSIONIST/NATIONALIST MOVEMENTS AND MAJOR RESOURCES
IN THE 1990s

Movement	Country	Major resources
BRA	Bougainville (Papua New Guinea)	Copper
FLEC	Cabinda enclave (Angola)	Oil
FLNKS	New Caledonia (France)	Nickel
FRETILIN	East Timor (Indonesia)	Oil
GAM	Aceh (Indonesia)	Gas
OPM	West Papua (Indonesia)	Copper, gold, gas
PDK, PUK	Kirkuk region (Iraq)	Oil
POLISARIO	Western Sahara (Morocco)	Phosphates
SPLA	South Sudan (Sudan)	Oil
Uygur (various)	Xinjiang (P.R. China)	Oil and gas

prosperous country, the simplistic assumption that Morocco was after their new-found mineral wealth served to mobilize armed resistance. Secessionist armed movements can also (re)emerge around the socio-environmental impacts or wealth redistribution associated with the commercial development of resources. In Sudan, political manoeuvres by the northern-dominated government in Khartoum to control oil resources located in the south participated in re-igniting the war in 1983. These manoeuvres included toponymic and administrative reshuffling in favour of the north, but also the exclusion of southerners from decision-making and technical training, the replacement of southern army units by northern ones in the main oilfield area, and the relocation of the oil refinery to the north.[78] As commented by a Nuer fighter about the renewed conflict after the first phase of the war for self-determination of southern Sudan between 1955 and 1972, 'We fought for seventeen years without even knowing of the true wealth of our lands. Now that we know the oil is there, we will fight much longer, if necessary!'[79] The Sudanese People's Liberation Army now prioritizes the destruction of government-controlled oil installations in the south of the country to assert their rights over this territory, improve their bargaining with the northern government, and racket oil businesses.[80] Secessionism in Aceh was historically rooted in the existence of an independent sultanate until the Dutch militarily defeated it in the late nineteenth century. Yet the formation of the Aceh Freedom Movement (GAM) coincided with the exploitation of major gas reserves in the early 1970s and GAM's 'Declaration of Independence' in 1976 specifically claimed that $15 billion in annual revenue was exclusively used for the benefit of 'Javanese neo-colonialists'.[81] Land expropriation and exploitation of other resources, such as timber, by businesses dominated by Javanese ownership and labour forces further exacerbated the conflict.[82]

Similarly, as with some other parts of Papua New Guinea, the island of Bougainville has a history of separatism based on geographical and identity distinctiveness. Yet local politicians' demands for, and obtaining of, 'special status', including favourable funding allocations during the period of transition to independence, clearly related to the economic significance of the island's gold and copper mine in Panguna.[83] The secessionist agenda set again in 1989 by Francis Ona, was clearly related to the impacts of copper mining, compensation and closure of the mine, as well as a 'Government of PNG [that] is not run to safeguard our lives but rather to safeguard the few rich leaders and white men'.[84] Ona, a former mine surveyor, is a local dweller but not title-holder of the mining lease area. As such he had little say in the allocation of a new trust fund set up in 1980 by the mine to compensate local communities. Although Ona's agenda 'is most reasonably understood as part of his conflict with his own relatives in the kind of land dispute ... characteristic of [local] Nasioi culture', his analysis nevertheless resonated throughout the local Nasioi community, especially as repression by PNG forces started. The war lasted until 1998 when the Bougainville Revolutionary Army signed a peace declaration, shortly after the 'scandal' of hiring Sandline mercenaries had brought down the Prime Minister of PNG in 1997 and following a conflict resolution bid by Australia and New Zealand.[85]

Most recently, the presence of large oil reserves around Kirkuk in northern Iraq significantly heightened the stakes around the creation of an autonomous Kurdish state in that region during the invasion of Iraq by US-led forces. It was clear for the Turkish government that large oil revenues falling under Kurdish control would constitute a threat to the territorial and political integrity of Turkey.[86]

Because of the current reluctance of the international community to reshape international borders, nationalist claims need to be backed by historical sovereign rights. Such rights afforded East Timor to regain its independence from Indonesia in 1999. Ironically, this was made possible by Australia's military intervention, one of the few countries that had officially recognized Indonesia's illegal sovereignty, in part to settle territorial claims over petroleum resources in the Timor Sea.[87] A similar problem of sovereignty continues to prevail over the exploitation of phosphate and exploration of oil in Western Sahara by foreign companies. Authorized by the Moroccan government, these ventures are deemed illegal by the UN Legal Affairs Office in recognition of the claims for sovereignty supported by the Front POLISARIO.[88]

Finally, foreign interventions, through a support of local insurrections, *coup d'état*, or annexation by military force, have been frequently associated with resource-linked 'geopolitical economic' interests. External actors have intervened in secessionist attempts by manipulating local political identities to access resources. In the late nineteenth century, the discovery of gold and diamonds in the newly created Boer republics in South Africa led to both stronger resistance to annexation by Britain and a massive influx of British prospectors. The refusal of Boer authorities to grant political rights to these British '*uitlanders*' (outlanders) led British entrepreneurs such as De Beers founder, Cecil Rhodes, to arm British settlers' militias taking part in the Boer War.[89] The French government, seeing its resource interests threatened by the war of independence in Algeria, organized in 1957 the institutional secession of resource-rich Sahara in the south, placing it along with parts of Mauritania and Mali under the direct control of Paris through the '*Organisation Commune des Régions Sahariennes*'. In response, the FLN placed the territorial integrity of the country on top of its cease-fire negotiation agenda with the French to ensure its control of the Saharan resources.[90] Despite its political character, the Biafran secession in Nigeria and its repression by the government, were largely motivated by local oil reserves. French oil interests supported the Biafra secession attempt and the Nigerian army started fighting in July 1967, 'more than a month after the declaration of independence but only days after Shell … agreed to pay its royalties to Biafra rather than Nigeria'.[91] Within the turmoil of Belgian Congo's independence, Anglo-Saxon and Belgian commercial interests, eager to secure their hold on copper mines in the province of Katanga, supported a secession led by Moise Tshombe, leading to military clashes between corporate-funded foreign mercenaries and UN troops supporting the unity of the country.[92] Noting the growth of mass consumerism and the 'economization' of international affairs in the 1990s, political scientist Michael Klare fears that such resource-driven interventions will increase in the coming decades.[93]

The resource dimension of foreign military intervention can also be associated with dilemmas between economic interests and strategic objectives. US dependence on oil, including major imports from Iraq, clearly demonstrate this. Asked about Weapons of Mass Destruction and the 'double-standard' of US intervention between Iraq and North Korea, US Deputy Secretary of Defense, Paul Wolfowitz, argued in reference to the lack of US and international economic leverage on Iraq that, 'The most important difference between North Korea and Iraq is that economically, we just had no choice in Iraq. The country swims on a sea of oil'.[94] The (tacit) US support for a coup by business leaders and military officers against democratically-elected President Chavez on 12 April 2002, also demonstrated tensions between US dependence on Venezuelan oil and its distrust for Chavez.[95]

Yet, as the Russian military campaigns in Chechnya or US military deployment and interventions in the Persian Gulf or assistance to the Colombian military to protect oil pipelines demonstrate, the resource dimensions of foreign interventions are often integrated into broader geopolitical discourses and practices of hegemony and resistance. The war in Iraq in 2003 is again a major case in point, with pro-war advocates stressing that the US-led 'liberation' was about freeing Iraqi people so that they can finally enjoy the benefits of their oil wealth, while anti-war advocates stress the economic and strategic motives of this 'invasion' and the bias held by the Bush administration in favour of American oil interests (see Le Billon and El Khatib in this volume). Similarly, the Rwandan, Ugandan and Zimbabwean military and associated commercial activities in the DRC not only represented vested financial interests, but a mix of domestic security interests (including that of the intervening governments) and pursuit of regional hegemony. Such pursuit was not only carried out through the association of force and commerce, but also the redefinition of (local) identities, with the debate over a definition of Congolese nationality excluding or including 'Rwandans' and 'their' access to land and mineral resources.[96]

Conclusion

The geopolitics of natural resources has long been a strategic concern for both exporting and importing states. Western powers' concerns over 'resource wars' have been largely put at ease with the end of the Cold War and greater flexibility of international trade, even if their continued supply dependence, rising demand for raw materials, and recent armed confrontations and instability in key areas such as the Persian Gulf, continue to place this item on their geopolitical agenda. But this apparent progress has not resolved and may even have aggravated several other strategic issues about resources, this time mostly of concern to exporting countries.

The first issue relates to the political economy and governance of resource-dependent countries, many of which face a similar pattern of growth collapse, corruption, and delegitimated state authority. Given the importance of natural resources in the economy or the economic potential of many developing countries, the issue of translating resource exploitation into political stability and economic development will remain central in the years to come, often for entire regions.

The second issue relates to the scale and number of economic, environmental or socio-cultural conflicts related to resource exploitation that increasingly oppose local populations, business interests, the state, and global environmental and human rights networks.[97] While most conflicts are either peacefully negotiated or limited to social protest movements and small-scale skirmishes, in other cases customs of violence and a radicalization of ideologies turned them into full-scale civil wars. Organized opposition to processes of globalization unaccountable to local interests and growing demand for raw materials could increase such adversarial politics and the need for more effective dialogue.

The third, and often related strategic issue is that natural resource revenues have become the economic mainstay of most wars in the post-Cold War context. Accessible and internationally marketable resources such as diamonds and timber, not to mention drugs, have played a significant role in conflicts in at least 20 countries during the 1990s. This is not to argue that those wars are only financed or motivated by the control of resources, but that resources figure prominently in their agendas, at least economically. Given the concentration of wars in poor countries with few foreign-earning sources, resources are likely to remain the economic focus of most belligerents in years to come. Even if 'conflict resources' come under greater regulatory pressure, there is a likelihood that criminal networks and unscrupulous businesses will pursue trading, especially those already involved in arms trafficking.

This introductory essay has examined some of the causes and processes relating to these three issues. The cases examined here suggest that the vulnerability of populations and need for political and economic accountability in resource management should be taken seriously at both local and international levels. There is no simple and comprehensive measure that can reduce the prevalence of conflicts in resource-dependent countries, but several factors can assist in this regard. The specificities of resources and licit character of their trade demand a new type of engagement and set of regulations on the part of businesses and policy-makers to tackle their contribution to war economies. The Security Council, governments, business associations, and advocacy non-governmental organizations (NGOs) have been developing an array of rules, investigations, sanctions, and implementation measures targeted at specific commodities over the past few years, and these initiatives need support and encouragement.[98] Most noticeably, diamonds have been the targets of unprecedented regulatory measures that, however, in the absence of sustained monitoring efforts will most probably remain plagued by difficulties inherent to the physical and market specificities of this commodity. In other cases, vested commercial and geopolitical interests, constrained as well as by the potential humanitarian impact on the targeted 'conflict resource', have continued to refrain from the use of sanctions, with mixed effect.

Beyond targeting the access of belligerents to resource revenues, three areas are particularly important: fair and more stable prices for resources; tighter domestic and international regulation of resource-derived revenues focusing on transparency; and a change in the culture of impunity in international resource trade. In the first case, producing countries and the international community should consider how revitalized commodity agreements and complementary mechanisms such as insurances might improve revenue flows to producing countries and contribute to positive economic and political improvements. Accordingly, revisiting pricing mechanisms should take place in tandem with an international framework for the regulation of resource revenues, which would seek not only greater stability in revenues, but also greater transparency, and increased accountability to local populations. Finally, international instruments used to prevent or terminate conflicts financed by natural resource exploitation would move from 'shaming' international actors to formalizing sanctions, against individuals as well as corporations. These measures will take time to develop. In the interim, confronted with the likelihood of continued resource-fuelled wars, the international community should seek to develop and apply frameworks through which the 'economic demobilization' of combatants could break the current pernicious relationships between natural resources, underdevelopment, and armed conflict.

NOTES

1. *Report of the Panel of Experts on the Illegal Exploitation of Natural Resources and Other Forms of Wealth of the Democratic Republic of Congo*, S/2001/357 (New York: United Nations Security Council 2001).
2. Barbara Crossette, 'U.N. Chief Faults Reluctance of U.S. to Help in Africa', *New York Times*, 13 May 2000.
3. Michael T. Klare, *Resource Wars: The Changing Landscape of Global Conflict* (New York: Henry Holt 2001), p.23. The paper concentrates on extractive resources such as oil, minerals, and timber legally traded on international markets, and excludes drugs as well as water. On water and conflicts, see Kevin Freeman, 'Water Wars? Inequalities in the Tigris-Euphrates River Basin', *Geopolitics*, Vol.6, No.2 (2001), pp.127–40; Tony Allan, *The Middle East Water Question: Hydropolitics and the Global* (London: I.B. Tauris 2000).
4. See Michael T. Klare, 'Resource Wars', *Harper's*, Jan. 1980, pp.20–23; National Strategic Information Centre white paper cited in Wilson Clark and Jake Page, *Energy, Vulnerability, and War. Alternatives for America* (New York: Norton, 1981), p.95.
5. Kevin Dunn, 'Identity, Space and the Political Economy of Conflict in Central Africa', *Geopolitics*, Vol.6, No.2 (Autumn 2001), p.56.
6. Ian O. Lesser, *Resources and Strategy* (Basingstoke: Macmillan 1989) p.9.
7. Raymond Aron, *Peace and War* (London: Weidenfeld and Nicolson 1966) pp.244–5.
8. John Evelyn, *Navigation and Commerce* (1674); cited in Aron (note 6) p.245.
9. Lesser (note 6) pp.11–12.
10. On the case of Africa, see Thomas Pakenham, *The Scramble for Africa: White Man's Conquest of the Dark Continent from 1876–1912* (London: Weidenfeld and Nicolson 1991).
11. Hitler's party programme demanded as early as 1920, 'land and territory for the sustenance of our people, and the colonisation of our surplus population'. Cited in http://www.yale.edu/lawweb/avalon/imt/proc/judnazi.htm; Lesser (note 6).
12 Hanns W. Maull, *Raw Materials, Energy and Western Security* (Basingstoke: Macmillan 1984); Arthur H. Westing (ed.), *Global Resources and International Conflict: Environmental Factors in Strategy Policy and Action* (Oxford: Oxford University Press 1986).

13 Lester R. Brown, *Redefining National Security* (Washington DC: Worldwatch Institute 1977); Richard H. Ullman, 'Redefining Security', *International Security*, Vol.8, No.1 (Summer 1983), pp.129–53; Jessica T. Mathews, 'Redefining Security', *Foreign Affairs*, Vol.68, No.2 (Spring 1989), pp.162–77.

14. World Commission on Environment and Development, *Our Common Future* (Oxford: Oxford University Press 1987); Norman Myers, *Ultimate Security: The Environmental Basis of Political Stability* (New York: W. W. Norton 1993) pp.17–30; for a comprehensive critique of this concept, see Simon Dalby, *Environmental Security* (Chicago, IL: University of Minnesota Press 2002).

15. James E. Sinclair and Robert Parker, *The Strategic Metals Wars* (New York: Arlington House 1983); Oye Ogunbadejo, *The International Politics of Africa's Strategic Minerals* (London: Frances Pinter 1985); Ruth W. Arad (ed.), *Sharing Global Resources* (New York: McGraw-Hill 1979).

16. Bruce Russett, 'Security and the Resources Scramble: Will 1984 be Like 1914?' *International Affairs*, Vol.58, No.1 (Winter 1981–82), pp.42–58.

17. Ewan W. Anderson and Liam D. Anderson, *Strategic Minerals: Resource Geopolitics and Global Geo-economics* (Chichester: Wiley 1998).

18. Kofi Annan, *The Causes of Conflict and the Promotion of Durable Peace and Sustainable Development in Africa* (New York: United Nations 1998) para.14; William Reno, *Warlord Politics and African States* (Boulder, CO: Lynne Rienner 1998), Klare (note 3) p.213.

19. Klare (note 3) pp.10, 23, 25.

20. Canada and the US provided examples of success and led to the staple theory of growth, see Harold A. Innis, *Essays in Canadian Economic History* (Toronto: University of Toronto Press 1956); and Douglas C. North, 'Location Theory and Regional Economic Growth', *Journal of Political Economy*, Vol.63 (April 1955).

21. For a comparative historical study of the contribution of mining sectors to development, see Thomas M. Power, *Digging to Development? A Historical Look at Mining and Economic Development*, Oxfam America Report (New York: Oxfam 2002).

22. On the manipulation of resource sectors, see Robert H. Bates *Markets and States in Tropical Africa: the Political Basis of Agricultural Policies* (Berkeley, CA: University of California Press, Berkeley 1981); Raymond L. Bryant and Michael J.P. Parnwell (eds), *Environmental Change in South-East Asia: People, Politics and Sustainable Development* (London: Routledge 1996). On the characteristics of oil and mineral dependent states, see Michael L. Ross, 'Does Oil Hinder Democracy?', *World Politics*, Vol.53 (April 2001), pp.325–41; and Michael L. Ross, *Extractive Sectors and the Poor*, Oxfam America Report (New York: Oxfam 2001).

23. Paul Collier, 'Economic Causes of Civil Conflict and Their Implications for Policy', in Chester A. Crocker, Fen Osler Hampson and Pamela Aall (eds), *Turbulent Peace: The Challenges of Managing International Conflict* (Washington DC: United States Institute for Peace Press, 2001).

24. Alan H Gelb (ed.), *Oil Windfalls: Blessing or Curse* (Oxford: Oxford University Press 1989); Richard M. Auty, *Sustaining Development in Mineral Economies: the Resource Curse Thesis* (London: Routledge 1993); Michael L. Ross, 'The Political Economy of the Resource Curse', *World Politics*, Vol.51, No.2 (January 1999), pp.297–322.

25. For a discussion of the 'excesses' of authority and connections with the West on the underdevelopment of Africa, see James D. Sidaway, 'Sovereign Excesses? Portraying Postcolonial Sovereigntyscapes', *Political Geography*, Vol.22 (2003), pp.157–78.

26. Michael P. Moore, 'Political Underdevelopment. What Causes Bad Governance?' *Public Management Review*, Vol.3, No.3 (2001), pp.385–418.

27. Cited in Kisangani N.F. Emizet, *Zaire After Mobutu: A Case of a Humanitarian Emergency*, Research for Action No.32 (Helsinki: WIDER 1997) p.35.

28. Patrick Chabal and Jean-Pierre Daloz, *Africa Works: Disorder as Political Instrument* (Oxford: James Currey 1999).

29. Crawford Young and Thomas Turner, *The Rise and Decline of the Zairian State* (Madison WI: University of Wisconsin Press 1985); Emizet (note 27) p.39.

30. On the cases of Liberia and Sierra Leone, see Stephen Ellis, *The Mask of Anarchy. The*

Destruction of Liberia and the Religious Dimension of an African Civil War (London: Hurst 1999); William Reno, *Corruption and State Politics in Sierra Leone* (Cambridge: Cambridge University Press 1995); Paul Richards, *Fighting for the Rain Forest. War Youth and Resources in Sierra Leone* (Oxford: James Currey 1996).

31. Philippe Le Billon, 'The Political Ecology of War: Natural Resources and Armed conflicts', *Political Geography*, Vol.20, No.5 (2001), pp.561–84.
32. David Keen, *The Economic Functions of Violence in Civil Wars*, Adelphi Paper No.320 (Oxford: Oxford University Press for the IISS 1998) p.45.
33. Keen (note 32) p.41.
34. Richard M. Auty (ed.) *Resource Abundance and Economic Development* (Oxford: Oxford University Press 2001).
35. *Report of the Panel of Experts on the Illegal Exploitation of Natural Resources and Other Forms of Wealth of the Democratic Republic of Congo*. S/2001/357 (New York: United Nations Security Council 2001).
36. Philippe Le Billon, 'Angola's Political Economy of War: The Role of Oil and Diamonds 1975–2000', *African Affairs*, Vol.100, No.398 (Jan. 2001), pp.55–80.
37. Filip de Boeck, 'Domesticating Diamonds and Dollars: Identity, Expenditure and Sharing in Soutwestern Zaire (1984–1997)' *Development and Change*, Vol.29, No.4 (1999), pp.777–810.
38. Interview with Kennedy Hamutenya, Ministry of Mines and Energy, Ottawa, April 2002.
39. Strasser was alleged to have gone to Sweden to sell diamonds.
40. François Misser and Olivier Vallée, *Les Gemmocraties: L'Economie Politique du Diamant Africain* (Paris: Desclée de Brouwer 1997) pp.7–8.
41. Global Witness, *For a Few Dollars More: How Al Qaeda Moved into the Diamond Trade* (London: Global Witness, April 2003).
42. Françoise Chipaux, 'Des Mines d'Emeraude pour Financer la Résistance du Commandant Massoud', *Le Monde* 17 July 1999.
43. Elizabeth Heath, 'Kabila, Laurent-Désiré', available through <http://www.africana.com>.
44. Stephen Jackson, *Fortunes of War: Structures and Dynamics of the Coltan Trade* (London: Overseas Development Institute 2001) p.17.
45. 'Petroleum Companies Hire Army to Curb Terrorism', *Crime and Justice: The Americas* 9/5 (1996).
46. Interview with James Fennel, ArmorGroup, London, Jan. 2002.
47. Global Witness, *Corruption, War and Forest Policy. The Unsustainable Exploitation of Cambodia's Forests* (London: Global Witness 1996).
48. On the case of Cambodia, see Philippe Le Billon, 'The Political Ecology of Transition in Cambodia 1989–1999: War, Peace and Forest Exploitation', *Development and Change*, Vol.31, No.4 (2000), pp.785–805.
49. UN Expert Panel Report, S/2001/357 (New York: United Nations Security Council 2001), p.8.
50. Frank Safford and Marco Palacios, *Colombia: Fragmented Land, Divided Society* (Oxford: Oxford University Press 2002).
51. 'BCCP Urges Warlords To Stop Depleting Somalia's Marine Resources', *Africa News Service*, 23 Feb. 2000.
52. Michael Ross, 'Oil, Drugs, and Diamonds: How Do Natural Resources Vary in their Impact on Civil War?', in Karen Ballentine and Jake Sherman (eds), *Beyond Greed and Grievance: The Political Economy of Armed Conflict* (Boulder: Lynne Rienner, 2003).
53. After disengaging in late 1997 from the richest mines due to a combination of political compromise, loss of regional allies, and military pressure, UNITA also faced many difficulties to exchange its diamonds for arms and logistical support due to an increasingly effective sanction regime. Ironically, UNITA's diamonds wealth in the early to mid-1990s may have encouraged its leadership to pursue a bold but ultimately self-defeating conventional warfare strategy that the rebel movement was not able to sustain (see Assis Malaquias, 'Diamonds Are a Guerilla's Best Friend: the Impact of Illicit Wealth on Insurgency Strategy', *Third World Quarterly*, Vol.22, No.3 (2001), pp.311–25).
54. In contrast, when resources follow a top-bottom flow within the movement – which tended

to occur during the Cold War through foreign sponsorship – leaders can maintain a greater degree of control over their allies and subordinates, see Keen (note 32).

55. Timothy W. Luke and Gerard Toal, 'The Fraying Modern Map: Failed States and Contraband Capitalism', *Geopolitics and International Boundaries*, Volume 3, No.3 (Winter 1998), pp.14–33.

56. Kenneth A. Rodman, *Sanctions Beyond Borders. Multinationals Corporations and U.S. Economic Statecraft* (Lanham, MA: Rowman and Littlefield 2001) pp.137–42.

57. Interview, Thai and Belgium gems traders, 2001 and 2002; Shell (2000), *Operating in Politically Sensitive Regions*, <http://www.shell.com/royal-en/content/0,5028,25547-51060,00.html>.

58. Dick Cheney was Chairman of oil company Halliburton, cited in *Petroleum Finance Week*, 1 April 1996. Ironically, this would include the US and the state of Texas in particular.

59. Thomas Waelde, 'Legal Boundaries for Extraterritorial Ambitions', in John V. Mitchell (ed.), *Companies in a World of Conflict: NGOs, Sanctions and Corporate Responsibility* (London: Royal Institute of International Affairs and Earthscan, 1998), p.178. For a story of the oil industry, see Daniel Yergin, *The Prize: The Epic Quest for Oil, Money and Power* (New York: Simon and Schuster, 1991).

60. Statement by Charles Jamieson, CEO of Premier Oil, Brussels, 21 Nov. 2000.

61. Ahmed Rashid, *Taliban. Islam, Oil and the New Great Game in Central Asia* (London: Tauris 2000) pp.174–5.

62. Cited in Pierre Baracyetse, 'L'Enjeu Geopolitique des Sociétés Minières Internationales en République Démocratique du Congo (ex-Zaire)', Dec. 1999, <http://www2.minorisa.es/inshuti/minieres.htm>.

63. Interview with company official, Nov. 2001.

64. Report of the UN Panel of Experts concerning Sierra Leone, S/2000/1195 (New York: United Nations Security Council 2001), para.215.

65. Cited in Ali Aïssaoui, *Algeria: The Political Economy of Oil and Gas* (Oxford: Oxford University Press 2001) p.49.

66. Fred Bridgland, *Jonas Savimbi: A Key to Africa* (Hodder and Stoughton, London 1988).

67. Jean-Marie Balancie and Arnaud de La Grange, *Mondes Rebelles. Guerres Civiles et Violences Politiques* (Paris: Michalon 1999) p.420.

68. Marc-Antoine de Montclos, 'Libéria: des Prédateurs aux "Ramasseurs de Miettes"', in François Jean and Jean-François Rufin (eds), *Economies des Guerres Civiles* (Paris: Hachette, 1996), p.281.

69. Interview, anon. human rights activist, 2000.

70. Alain Labrousse, 'Colombie-Pérou: Violence Politique et Logique Criminelle', in François Jean and Jean-Christophe Rufin (eds), *Economie des Guerres Civiles* (Paris: Hachette, 1996), p.386.

71. Maj. Rodney Azama, 'The Huks and the New People's Army: Comparing Two Postwar Filipino Insurgencies', <http://www.globalsecurity.org/military/library/report/1985/ARS.htm>.

72. Carl H. Lande, 'The Political Crisis', in John Bresnan (ed.), *Crisis in the Philippines. The Marcos Era and Beyond* (Princeton, NJ: Princeton University Press, 1986), p.133.

73. Roland Pourtier, '1997: Les Raisons d'une Guerre "Incivile"', *Afrique Contemporaine*, No.186 (1998), pp.7–32; interview with Pascal Lissouba, London, Jan. 2002. Controlling the north of the country, Nguesso could also have benefited from logging revenues of timber exports via Gabon and Cameroon (*La lettre du Continent*, 13 Jan. 2000).

74. Pourtier (note 73) p.7.

75. Nkossa was the name of an oilfield recently awarded to French oil company Elf Aquitaine. Rémy Bazenguissa-Ganga, 'Les Milices Politiques dans les Affrontements' *Afrique Contemporaine*, No.186 (1998), p.52.

76. Cited in Ellis (note 30) p.108.

77. Tony Hodges, *Western Sahara: The Roots of a Desert War* (Westport, CN: Lawrence Hill 1983) p.vii.

78. Peter Nyot Kok, 'Adding Fuel to the Conflict: Oil, War and Peace in the Sudan', in Martin Doornbos et al. (eds), *Beyond Conflict in the Horn* (London: James Currey, 1992),

pp.104–13.
79. Cited in Sharon E. Hutchinson, *Nuer Dilemmas: Coping with Money, War, and the State* (Berkeley, CA: University of California Press 1996) p.9.
80. Interview with SPLA official, Nairobi, Nov. 2001.
81. Nazaruddin Sjamsuddin, 'Issues and Politics of Regionalism in Indonesia: Evaluating the Acehnese Experience', in Lim Joo-Jock and Vani (eds), *Armed Separatism in Southeast Asia* (Singapore: Institute of Southeast Asian Studies, 1984).
82. 'Aceh: Ecological War Zone', *Down To Earth*, No.47 (November 2000).
83. The mine began production in 1972, independence was obtained in 1975. See John Connell, 'The Panguna Mine Impact', in Peter Polomka (ed.), 'Bougainville Perspectives on a Crisis', *Canberra Papers on Strategy and Defence* 66/43; Stephanie Lawson, 'Ethno-nationalist Dimensions of Internal Conflict – The Case of Bougainville Secessionism', in Kevin Clements (ed.), *Peace and Security in the Asia Pacific Region* (Tokyo and Palmertson North: United Nations University and Dunmore,1993), p.66.
84. Cited in Polomka (note 82) p.8. See also Volker Boge, 'Mining, Environmental Degradation and War: The Bougainville Case', in Mohamed Suliman (ed.), *Ecology, Politics and Violent Conflict* (London: Zed Books, 1999), pp.211–28. .
85. Karl Claxton, 'Bougainville 1988–98', *Canberra Papers on Strategy and Defence*, No.130 (1998).
86. Hoomani Peimani, 'Turks Threaten: 10,000 Fighters in Kirkuk', *Asia Times*, 21 Dec. 2002.
87. Brian Dubois, 'The Timor Gap Treaty – Where to Now?', *Briefing Paper No.25* (Oxford: Oxfam Community Aid Abroad, 2000).
88. Kamal Fadel, 'Will UN Stop Morocco's Violations of International Law?', *Self-Determination Conflict Watch* 2/7, 13 March 2002.
89. Thomas Pakenham, *The Boer War* (London: Weidenfeld and Nicolson, 1997).
90. Aissaoui (note 65) p.47–9.
91. Alexander A. Arbatov, 'Oil as a Factor in Strategic Policy and Action: Past and Present', in Westing, *Global Resources and International Conflict* (Oxford: Oxford University Press 1986), p.34.
92. Balancie and Delagrange (note 67).
93. Klare (note 3).
94. Cited by George Wright, 'Wolfowitz: Iraq War Was About Oil', *Guardian*, 4 June 2003.
95. In 2001, 13 per cent of US oil imports came from Venezuela. See 'Country Analysis Brief – USA', *Energy Information Administration*, May 2002.
96. Interview with Prof. Séverin Mugangu, Université Catholique de Bukavu, April 2002.
97. Al Gedicks, *Resource Rebels: Native Challenges to Mining and Oil Corporations* (Cambridge, MA: South End Press 2001).
98. Philippe Le Billon, Jake Sherman, Marcia Hartwell, *Controlling Illicit Resource Flows to Civil Wars: A Review and Analysis of Current Policies and Legal Instruments* (New York: International Peace Academy 2002).

Natural Resources and Civil Strife: A Two-Stage Process

RICHARD M. AUTY

The Structure of the Study

The link between natural resource abundance and the propensity for civil strife is now well established. For example, de Soysa reports that civil strife is strongly associated with natural resource abundance, and particularly with mineral exports.[1] He finds no evidence that civil strife is related to resource paucity. Collier concurs and finds civil strife is strongly positively linked to primary exports.[2] The corollary is that grievance is not a significant cause of conflict because it creates problems of co-ordination and dealing with free riders. Collier also finds that civil strife is positively linked to economic decline (a growth collapse) as a result of which a relatively large young male population (aged 15–25) with little education seeks immediate financial reward through conflict. However, Collier finds that civil strife is not linked to ethnic heterogeneity or inequitable distribution of income, even though 'civil wars create economic opportunities for a minority of actors even as they destroy them for the majority'.[3]

Collier recognises that natural resources are not the only geographical factor at work: relative location plays a role in terms of whether armed groups can control not only territory but also communications, legal or illicit, to the outside world. He concludes that disputed territory with porous national borders feeds civil strife. Le Billon echoes the importance of relative location.[4] He uses the proximity of the natural resource to the geographical centre of political power to identify susceptibility to conflict and also the type of conflict. Where the resource is close to the centre of power, violence is more likely to take the form of a political coup to replace the government and control the rent. In the case of remoter resources, violence is more likely to take the form of either political secession or war-lordism. Le Billon also notes a second neglected geographical theme, namely how the socio-economic linkages associated with different natural resources influence conflict. Elsewhere, Ross also explores the link between the ease with which resources can be looted and whether conflicts are separatist or non-separatist in nature.[5] This strand of research can, in turn, be related to the work of Mikesell and Murphy who link the aims of disaffected social groups to the likelihood of accommodation or secession.[6]

This article elaborates on this research theme by identifying a two-stage process that links natural resources to civil strife. It uses the staple trap model of resource-driven economic development to explain growth collapses in resource-abundant countries, which appear to be a necessary pre-condition for civil strife, but not a sufficient condition. The study therefore goes on to identify two basic properties of natural resources related to civil strife, namely the pattern of socio-economic linkages produced by the commodity and the mobility ('lootability' in the terminology of Ross) of the resource rent.[7] The socio-economic linkages may be either 'point source', which means they are concentrated on a handful of economic agents, like large-scale mining, or they may be diffused among many agents, like peasant crops. The former are more likely to engender conflict. Mobility is positively linked to the commodity value/weight ratio and to location adjacent to remote porous national borders. The thesis of the article is that the risk of civil strife is highest when:

- Economic growth has collapsed,
- The resource generates point socio-economic linkages,
- The commodity has a high value/weight ratio and/or
- Production occurs adjacent to porous national borders.

The article draws upon large databases, notably those of the World Bank,[8] to quantify the scale of key parameters such as gross domestic product (GDP) growth rates, size of the natural resource rents, revenue streams and relative transportation costs that are associated with different types of natural resources. This limits reliance on subjective interpretation and also facilitates inter-country comparison, which distinguishes characteristics that a country shares with other groups of countries from idiosyncratic characteristics, and thereby allows country case-studies to be linked to general models, and vice versa.[9]

The study is structured as follows. The next section, applies the staple trap model to explain the counter-intuitive negative relationship that emerged after the 1960s between natural resource abundance and growth in per capita GDP. The model shows that resource-rich countries tended to spawn predatory political states that distorted their economies and rendered them vulnerable to growth collapses. Yet many such countries avoided conflict so section three examines why concentrated or 'point source' socio-economic linkages are associated with heightened risk of civil strife in a collapsed economy. Section four analyses how high commodity value/weight ratios accelerate rent mobility and also funnel rent into concentrated forms, even from commodities with diffuse linkages, to sustain conflict in *remote* regions. Section five explains how proximity to porous national borders creates anomalies by boosting the mobility of rents for even low-value bulky commodities. Section six summarizes the conclusions and draws some policy implications.

Growth Collapses in Resource-Abundant Countries: Causes and Characteristics

In 1960 the average per capita GDP of the resource-rich developing market economies was more than 50 per cent above that of the resource-poor countries, but by the early 1990s the resource-poor countries had closed the gap.[10] This reflected the emergence of a counter-intuitive outcome during the 1970s whereby the per capita GDP of the resource-poor countries grew faster than that of the resource-rich countries. Table 1 compares the GDP growth of countries, classified into six groups according to their natural resource endowment, before and after the period of oil shocks, 1974–85, and the associated global economic instability. The basic criteria for classification draw upon a recent UNU/WIDER study and comprise country size (using GDP in 1970 as an index of domestic market potential for industrialization) and cropland per capita in 1970. Most countries fall into the small resource-abundant category so this is further sub-divided by identifying the mineral economies (with 40 per cent or more of their exports in either oil or ore). The table shows that during the years 1974–85 all four sets of resource-abundant countries experienced a growth collapse and also that the mineral economies subsequently showed least resilience.

Sachs and Warner confirm the disappointing economic growth in the resource-abundant countries.[11] Elsewhere, they link the growth collapses to Dutch disease effects arising out of policy failure.[12] Sachs subsequently shows that resource-abundant countries require a politically unpopular large depreciation of the real exchange rate in order to diversify their economies competitively and thereby sustain economic growth.[13] This article provides more details of this process. It identifies two basic causes of the recent inferior economic performance of the resource-rich countries, namely that the natural resource endowment conditions the type of political state and also the nature of the development trajectory.

The Resource-Poor Countries' Higher Propensity to Engender Developmental States

Resource-poor countries are more likely to engender a 'developmental' political state than resource-rich countries. A developmental political state

TABLE 1

NATURAL RESOURCES, ECONOMIC GROWTH, INVESTMENT EFFICIENCY AND
POPULATION 1960–97

Resource endowment category	Invest-ment (% GDP)	GDP growth (%/year)	ICOR	PC GDP GDP (%/year)	Population growth (%/year)
Small non-mineral resource-rich					
1960–73	14.8	4.2	3.5	1.6	2.6
1973–85	20.5	3.4	6.9	0.7	2.7
1985–97	21.9	3.5	6.0	0.9	2.6
Small oil-exporting resource-rich					
1960–73	24.5	6.6	3.7	4.0	2.6
1973–85	31.0	6.5	5.7	2.3	4.2
1985–97	23.9	1.9	12.4	-0.7	2.6
Small ore-exporting resource-rich					
1960–73	17.5	4.9	5.7	2.2	2.7
1973–85	21.8	3.0	7.3	0.1	2.9
1985–97	17.1	2.3	7.5	-0.4	2.7
Large resource-rich					
1960–73	20.3	5.4	4.0	2.7	2.7
1973–85	21.8	3.1	7.1	0.7	2.4
1985–97	20.1	4.0	5.0	1.9	2.1
Small resource-poor					
1960–73	18.8	6.1	3.2	3.5	2.6
1973–85	24.8	4.0	6.2	1.8	2.2
1985–97	23.0	4.4	5.2	2.4	2.0
Large resource-poor					
1960–73	17.7	5.0	4.2	2.4	2.6
1973–85	25.5	5.8	4.4	3.7	2.1
1985–97	26.3	6.0	4.4	4.7	1.3

Source: World Bank, *World Development Indicators 2001* (Washington DC: World Bank).

is one that has sufficient autonomy to pursue a coherent economic policy *and* which uses that autonomy to raise long-run social welfare. Two basic variants of the developmental state are identified in Table 2, namely the benevolent autonomous state and the consensual democracy. The former is strongly associated with the successful resource-poor countries of East Asia, the latter with resource-poor Mauritius and also with three rare examples of successful resource-rich countries, namely Botswana, Malaysia and post-Pinochet Chile. More usually, resource-rich countries engender factional or predatory states.

Table 2 incorporates the natural resource endowment into Olson's typology of political states in order to generate a dynamic model of resource-driven political change.[14] The incentive for a government to provide public goods and to encourage wealth generation as opposed to capturing and distributing rents increases not only, as Olson observed, with

TABLE 2
TYPOLOGY OF NATURAL RESOURCE ENDOWMENT, POLITICAL
STATE AND SOCIAL SANCTIONS

Olson typology	Model typology	Autonomy of state	Aims of state
Roving Bandit			
Resource-rich	Violent predator	High	Pillage
Resource-poor	Violent predator	High	Pillage
Stationary Bandit			
Resource- rich	Predatory autonomous state	High	Sustainable rent-seeking
Resource-poor	**Benevolent autonomous state**	Moderately high	Public goods > rent-seeking
Oligarchy			
Resource-rich	Ethnic/Military/landed faction	Moderately high	Sustainable rent-seeking
Resource-poor	Industrial/Military faction	Moderate	Public goods + modest rent-seeking
Democracy			
Resource-rich	Polarised democrracy	Dominant faction controls	Redistribute > grwoth
Resource-poor	**Consensual democracy**	Consensus controls	Growth with redistribution

Note: Developmental political states are identified in bold.

the extension of the encompassing interest of the state over a greater fraction of economic agents (running from the top to the bottom of Table 2), but also with *decreasing* access to natural resource rents. Consequently evolution down the typology in Table 2 proceeds faster for resource-poor countries than for resource-rich countries. The rationale can be illustrated by assuming there are two sources of income available to governments, resource rents and returns to investment. High-rent and low-rent countries yield contrasting incentives for governments. The government in the high-rent country will find it easier to satisfy its financial needs by capturing the rents than by investing to generate wealth so that the latter will be neglected in favour of the former. Effort will therefore be diverted into the political process by which rents are extracted (termed rent-seeking behaviour), which entails lobbying politicians and creates scope for corruption, and away from measures to raise productivity, like improving institutions. Indeed, effective institutions may be regarded as an impediment to rent-seeking behaviour because they increase government accountability and promote competition, both of which shrink rent-seeking opportunities.

In contrast, limited natural resource rents strengthen the incentive for governments of resource-poor countries to boost output in order to advance their interests: they maximize their remuneration by making the most of national output. Resource-poor countries also experience minimal Dutch disease effects (the contraction of competitive agriculture and manufacturing during a resource boom) so they are less likely to experiment with closed trade policies than resource-rich countries, and where they do they abandon them earlier (personal communication from A. M. Warner, based on the Sachs and Warner model).[15] This is because it is transparent at a relatively low level of per capita income that the resource sector is too small *vis-à-vis* the rest of the economy to support slow-maturing infant industry or a bloated government bureaucracy.[16] Nor can the competitive manufacturing sector that resource-poor countries depend upon to earn foreign exchange provide subsidies for the protected sector because the fraction of rent on labour-intensive manufacturing is less than in the case of natural resources. Finally, lower natural resource rents reduce the scope to sustain flawed policies. In sum, resource paucity places a premium upon the efficient use of scarce resources and encourages the political state to nurture efficient investment to raise output.

Diverging Development Trajectories

Resource-poor countries are not only more likely to foster political states that promote competitive economic growth, but the pattern of structural change is characterized by an early start on competitive industrialization. This triggers an expansion of labour-intensive manufacturing, much of it for export, which promotes virtuous interlocking economic and social circles that sustain rapid and equitable economic growth. The competitive industrialization model explains the superior performance of the resource-poor countries (column 1 of Table 3). In contrast, resource-rich countries depend for longer on commodity exports so that diversification into competitive manufacturing is postponed compared with resource-poor countries.[17] The staple trap model summarizes the development trajectory of resource-rich countries (columns 2–5 of Table 3). The staple trap model is elaborated below to show how growth collapses occur in resource-rich countries and the implications of a collapse for conflict.

Resource abundance lengthens dependence on primary product exports compared with resource-poor countries, which delays competitive industrialization and this has three adverse consequences. First, economic diversification must initially occur into other primary products and this may prove difficult for the smallest resource-rich economies whose natural resource endowment is likely to be skewed towards one or two viable commodities.[18] Second, slow industrialization retards urbanization and

TABLE 3

STYLISED FACTS MODELS OF THE POLITICAL ECONOMY OF THE NATURAL RESOURCE ENDOWMENT AND ECONOMIC GROWTH

Model	Competitive industrialization		Staple trap		
Natural resource endowment	Poor	Abundant diffuse	Abundant diffuse	Abundant point ore	Abundant point oil
Pre-conditions					
Political state	Autonomous benevolent	Consensual democracy	Oligarchy/Predatory	Oligarchy/Predatory	Autonomous paternalist
Income rich 1/5: poor 1/5a	4.0–9.0	7.0–16.0	5.0–33.0	9.0–32.0	12.0–20.0
Obsolete capital stock	Low	Low	Low/High	Low/High	Low/High
Policy					
Reform response	Early	Early	Postponed	Postponed	Partial
Trade policy	Open	Open	Closed	Closed	Open
Incentive bias towards	Comparative advantage	Comparative advantage	Rent–seeking	Rent–seeking	Neutral/Public sector
Capital build-up					
Genuine saving	Strongly positive	Moderately positive	Low/Negative	Low/Negative	Negative
Produced	Rapid rise >24%GDP	Slower rise >20%GDP	Slow rise >20%GDP	Slower rise +<20%GDP	Rapid rise >25% GDP
Human	Virtuous circle	Slower virtuous circle	Lagged + skewed	Lagged + skewed	Rapid + ineffective
Social	Transaction improving	Transaction improving	Transaction repressing	Transaction repressing	Feudalistic
Economic outcome					
ICOR 1985–97	4.8	5.5	6.0	7.5	12.4
Dutch disease effect	Negligible	Small	Strong	Strong	Strong
Diversification	Competitive widening	Slow competitive widening	Retarded/Regressive	Regressing	Mono-product
Resilience to shocks	Robust	Robust	High vulnerability	High vulnerability	Financial cushion
PCGDP growth (%)	Sustained: 2.5–4.0	Sustained: 1.0–2.5	Erratic: 0.5–1.5	Boom + bust: (0.5)–2.0	Boom + decline: (0.4)–4.0
Examples					
Classic	South Korea	Malaysia	Ghana	Bolivia	Saudi Arabia
Classic	Singapore	Thailand	Argentina	Zambia	Nigeria
Anomalous	Bangladesh	Myanmar	Costa Rica	Botswana	Oman

Source: R.M. Auty, *Resource Abundance and Economic Development* (Oxford: Oxford University Press, 2001).

therefore the passage through the demographic cycle. The final column of Table 1 shows the delayed deceleration of population growth in the resource-rich countries, especially the smaller (and less industrialized) countries. This causes the ratio of dependants/workers to stay high for longer than in resource-poor countries (Table 4). For example, the ratio of dependants to workers for oil-rich Angola increased from 0.8 to 1.0 between 1965–95 whereas that for South Korea fell from 0.9 in 1965, just two years after that country embarked on the competitive industrial model growth trajectory, to 0.4 by 1995. Consequently, in resource-rich countries that lack developmental governments, consumption expenditure absorbs a higher share of domestic GDP so that the rise in saving and investment is retarded compared with resource-poor countries, as shown in the first column of Table 1.[19] Third, investment efficiency declines (Table 1, column 3) as resources are extracted from the competitive primary sector and sunk in the burgeoning inefficient protected sector so that per capita GDP growth slows or turns negative (Table 1, column 4). Fourth, the rapid expansion of labour-intensive manufacturing that initially characterizes the competitive industrialization model of resource-poor countries is omitted so that surplus labour persists and depresses the wages of the poor. Fears of rising income inequality and mounting unemployment, especially among the younger population, put pressure on governments to provide jobs by forcing industrialization and over-expanding government employment.[20]

Forced industrialization by infant industry protection has three principal flaws for economic development. First, it creates contrived rents (arising from government abuse of its power to create monopolies for favoured associates). The typically predatory and factional governments of the resource-rich countries deploy these rents with minimal transparency (Table 2) so that they degenerate into a corrupt rent-dispensing mechanism that further distorts the economy in an *ad hoc* and cumulative fashion. Second, infant industry tends to be capital-intensive and creates few jobs, causing governments to subsidize still more non-productive employment, thereby further expanding the parasitic protected sector. Gelb *et al.* model such a policy and their simulations use empirically plausible data that suggest that within a decade the efficiency of capital can be depressed below the level required to sustain economic growth.[21] Third, protected industry supported by rents takes decades to mature instead of the five to eight years considered the maximum if the benefits of infant industry support are to compensate for the costs of that support.[22] This imposes increasing demands on the primary sector for transfers and foreign exchange that outstrip the natural resource rents and absorb the return to capital so that incentives and competitiveness in the primary sector are both undermined.[23] The result is an economy locked into a *staple trap* in which a protected sector comprizing slow-

TABLE 4
DEPENDANT/WORKER RATIOS, SELECTED COUNTRIES 1965-95

	1970	1980	1990	1998
Conflict Africa				
Angola	0.82	0.87	0.95	1.02
Congo D.R.	0.88	0.93	0.98	1.00
Sierra Leone	0.79	0.84	0.87	0.97
Conflict Asia				
Cambodia	0.84	0.82	0.73	0.84
Myanmar	0.81	0.80	0.76	0.56
Philippines	0.92	0.86	0.78	0.72
Conflict Latin America				
Bolivia	0.86	0.87	0.84	0.80
Colombia	1.00	0.89	0.72	0.64
Peru	0.91	0.88	0.78	0.67
Successful Resource-rich				
Botswana	1.11	1.10	0.98	0.86
Chile	0.82	0.73	0.59	0.56
Malaysia	0.97	0.85	0.74	0.66
Resource-poor				
China	0.80	0.78	0.55	0.48
Mauritius	0.96	0.74	0.57	0.50
South Korea	0.87	0.71	0.52	0.41

Source: World Bank, *World Development Indicators 2001* (Washington DC: World Bank).

maturing industry and bloated public services depends on increasing subsidies from a commodity-producing sector with diminishing incentives, whose share in GDP declines due to waning competitiveness and long-term structural change.

The economy is increasingly distorted and the political state is further corroded so that social tensions rise even as the economy weakens. Income inequality intensifies because the persistence of surplus labour depresses the wages of the poor, while the slow accumulation of skills sustains the wage premium on higher skills. Birdsall *et al.* and Wood and Berge confirm that resource-rich economies accumulate skills more slowly than resource-poor ones.[24] Moreover, the inequitable distribution of income combines with slower urbanization and delayed passage through the demographic cycle to retard the accumulation of social capital and stop per capita incomes from rising to levels where pressures for greater political accountability and democracy are accommodated, as occurs in the competitive industrial model associated with the resource-poor countries.

In summary: the pursuit during the 1950s and 1960s of policies that encouraged state intervention to force industrialization in order to reduce dependence on primary products became corrupted and weakened the economy. The presence of greater rents in the resource-rich countries sustained such policies for longer than resource-poor countries (which, as noted earlier, quickly abandoned them as impractical) so that the economic distortion and political corruption were therefore greater than in the resource-poor countries. It is ironic that this cumulative economic distortion occurred even as co-ordinated action among primary product producers to raise commodity prices triggered price shocks that severely tested the resilience of such weakened economies in the 1970s. Subsequent reform of the collapsed resource-rich economies has proved protracted leaving many of them, consistent with Collier,[25] with high population growth, low skills, inadequate employment and a motive to wrest natural resource rents by force. These growth collapses are the first stage of the transition to conflict. The next three sections examine the second stage and explain why some natural resources appear more likely to trigger civil strife than others.

Point versus Diffuse Socio-Economic Linkages

Point Resource Linkages Concentrate Rents and Heighten Economic Distortion

The potential for economic distortion, and therefore for a growth collapse, is greater with 'point' natural resources, like minerals, than with resources with diffuse socio-economic linkages like peasant crops (compare Column 4 with Column 2 in Table 3). This is because mining is usually highly capital-intensive and employs much foreign capital but only a small, albeit well-paid workforce. As a result, final demand linkage (i.e., domestic spending by capital and labour) is modest. Moreover, the productive linkages are limited because mine inputs are usually imported due to their specialized nature, while the higher value-added stages of mineral processing are frequently located at the market.[26] This leaves corporate taxes plus any resource rent that the government secures through royalties or special taxation as the sector's principal contribution to the economy.[27]

The extreme concentration of the rents on the government heightens the risk that the rents will not be effectively deployed for reasons that the staple trap model explains. Moreover, governments are less likely to treat windfall revenues as temporary than are private agents such as farmers, so they tend to spend the revenues too quickly and this distorts the economy.[28] In contrast, the export of peasant cash crops *within a developmental political state* is more conducive to economic development because the rents are diffused across a wider set of domestic economic agents.[29] Moreover, there is evidence that social capital tends to accumulate faster with diffuse socio-economic linkages than with point linkages.[30]

The higher rent of oil-rich countries (Table 5) increases the subsidies available to the protected sector, so that the distortion of the political economy is the greater. The resource rents facilitate a relaxation of market discipline that compounds distortions within the economy and creates social entitlements that are then politically difficult to reform when the rents decline. Table 5 shows that small mineral economies and especially the oil-exporters have the highest rents in relation to GDP (data available for 1994 only) but the slowest per capita GDP growth 1985–97. The rents consolidate the power of the political élite during booms, but such political states become brittle if the rents contract. Lacking the political legitimacy with which to undertake necessary reforms, these political states resort to repression to stay in power. Ross shows that relative to developing countries as a whole the governments of oil-rich countries function with limited democratic accountability, low political contestability and greater vulnerability to military overthrow.[31] Once a growth collapse has occurred, an expansion of the rents may only exacerbate economic distortion and heighten political tension rather than provide an opportunity to facilitate reform, as Angola illustrates.[32]

Angolan Oil Rents Nourish a Stationary Bandit Political State that Postpones Reform

The abrupt withdrawal of Portuguese settlers when Angola achieved independence in 1975 inflicted a severe negative economic shock. GDP

TABLE 5

SHARE OF RENTS IN GDP, SIX NATURAL RESOURCE ENDOWMENT CATEGORIES 1994 (%)

Resource Endowment	Pasture and cropland	Minerals	Total rent	Per capita GDP growth (%/year)
Resource Poor[1,2]				
Large	7.3	3.2	10.5	4.7
Small	5.4	4.4	9.8	2.4
Resource Rich				
Large	5.8	6.9	12.7	1.9
Small, non-mineral	12.9	2.5	15.4	0.9
Small, hard mineral	9.6	7.9	17.5	-0.4
Small, oil exporter	2.2	19.0	21.2	-0.7
All Countries	8.8	6.3	15.1	

Source: Derived from World Bank, *World Development Indicators 2001* (Washington DC: World Bank).
   1 Resource-poor = 1970 cropland/head < 0.3 hectares.
   2 Large = 1970 GDP > $7bn.

halved when the settlers left but per capita incomes then held steady at around $700.00 (in US$ 1997), despite the maladroit implementation of central planning by the MPLA government. Exploration lifted Angolan oil reserves to 5.4 billion barrels by 2000.[33] Oil production began to expand in the mid-1980s and almost tripled during 1985–97 (Table 6) to reach 735,000 barrels per day in 2000. It is projected to rise to 2.5 million per day by 2015.[34] The main oil fields are offshore and thereby protected from guerrilla activity. When the Cold War ended, expanding oil rents therefore provided the Luanda-based MPLA government with an opportunity to extend law and order into rebel-held areas, stabilize the economy, support economic reform and raise per capita incomes.[35]

Instead, the oil rents replaced the lost geopolitical rent and perpetuated a predatory (stationary bandit) political state (Table 2). Although economic reform commenced in 1991, repeated attempts to stabilize the economy failed, mainly because the government and an urban élite of wealthy families prospered without reform. In addition, reform was poorly sequenced, rested on inadequate institutions and was buffeted by renewed civil war. Periodic surges in inflation brought sharp swings in policy. The real exchange rate was erratic: it appreciated by 85 per cent in 1993, then declined by 87 per cent in 1994 only to rebound by 216 per cent in 1995, halve in 1996 and then double in 1997.[36] This instability deterred efficient investment, but a well-connected élite prospered by capturing in the early-1990s small and medium state enterprises that were privatised, and by running monopolies or oligopolies on imports. Control of these markets conferred control of prices and profits so that the élite was indifferent to exchange rate swings and inflation, and the need for reform.

TABLE 6

SCALE OF OIL RENT AND STRUCTURE OF ANGOLAN ECONOMY 1985–99
(% GDP)

	1985	1986	1987	1988	1989	1990	1991	1992	1993	1994	1995	1996	1997	1998	1999
Oil Rent	12.3	15.8	17.8	22.1	20.2	20.3	18.9	44.2	42.2	62.1	55.9	45.1	46.0	39.5	41.9
Agriculture	13.6	14.4	12.9	15.9	19.2	17.9	24.0	10.1	11.6	6.6	7.5	7.1	9.0	13.0	6.9
Industry	43.3	34.1	41.3	39.4	39.0	40.9	33.3	53.2	51.2	66.8	64.4	67.8	60.8	55.7	77.1
Manufac-turing	9.7	10.9	7.3	8.2	6.1	5.0	6.2	5.0	5.7	4.9	3.9	3.4	4.4	6.3	3.5
Services	43.2	51.5	45.9	44.7	41.8	41.3	42.6	36.6	37.2	26.4	28.2	25.1	30.2	31.3	16.3
Oil output (000 bl/d)	230	280	350	450	455	475	495	550	505	610	585	610	670	645	575
Crop output index	96	108	102	109	99	96	104	111	108	137	132	134	129	158	143

Source: World Bank, *World Development Indicators 2001* (Washington DC: World Bank); BP, *BP Statistical Review of World Energy 2001* (London: BP, 2001).

Ironically, although the oil rents doubled their share of GDP (Table 5), this did not avert chronic budget deficits. One important cause of the deficits was military spending which ballooned to $500m annually, one-fifth of the oil rent. A second cause was public sector subsidies that conferred a large fraction of the rent on the wealthy through personal allowances. The fiscal debt was monetized, which perpetuated both over-valuation of the exchange rate and inflation. Meanwhile, civil service remuneration was slashed and payment arrears accumulated so that government services deteriorated. This merely encouraged state governors to compensate by abusing their power and extracting revenues from the local people. Both military officials and civil servants reportedly colluded with rebel UNITA forces and mercenaries in mutually beneficial deals for personal enrichment.[37]

The mismanagement of the oil rents caused Angola's per capita GDP to decline by two-thirds.[38] Even as the well-connected élite prospered, Dutch disease effects weakened the competitiveness of the non-mining tradable sectors like agriculture and manufacturing. The share of agriculture and manufacturing was already only one-quarter of GDP in the mid-1990s, barely half the size of comparator countries and yet it contracted to one-eighth of GDP by the late 1990s (Table 5). The decline in agriculture was associated with a sharp jump in the rate of urbanization from one-fifth to one-third between 1980–99.[39] By the late 1990s the Luanda enclave contained one-third of the urban population, but absorbed 86.5 per cent of the expended government budget.[40] The rise in urbanization was associated with the flight from rural conflict rather than with rising living standards so that the demographic transition was still postponed and population growth remained high, averaging 3 per cent between 1980–99.[41] This perpetuated a high dependency/worker ratio (Table 4) and chronic under-employment, especially among the youth of the country.

Angola illustrates how, in the absence of a developmental political state a substantial rise in natural resource rents may not only fail to rekindle economic growth, but also exacerbate economic and social malaise, encouraging violent contests for political power. In such circumstances, the oil rents provided an attractive target for disaffected groups and the availability in remote eastern Angola of a second source of lucrative rents – alluvial diamonds – sustained a military challenge to the MPLA government. A critical characteristic of alluvial diamonds is the ease with which they are extracted and transported, i.e., the mobility of the rents. But the smuggling of the alluvial diamonds to western markets transformed the diffuse linkages (and their potentially benevolent effects) into linkages with point source features, reflecting the concentration of control on the smuggling agencies. These rents fed war-lords and secessionist movements, as the next section shows.

High Value/Weight Ratios: Alluvial Diamonds and Drugs

The significance of the value/weight ratio of different natural resource commodities has been neglected in the literature on natural resources and conflict. Table 7 compares the price per kilo of a number of commodities. It identifies sharp differences between bulk commodities like copper, oil and sugar on the one hand, which are relatively unlootable, and 'conflict' commodities such as alluvial diamonds and cocaine on the other. The latter exhibit low production costs and high prices (due to cartels or other supply constraints) confer exceptionally high rents that are insensitive to even significant rises in production costs or transport costs.

Diamonds and Conflict in Angola

Diamond rents sustained the UNITA rebels in eastern Angola when the geopolitical rents provided by Cold War funding declined in the late 1980s. Angola is the fourth largest diamond producer with around 11 per cent of global reserves with a quality second only to that of Namibia.[42] The diamonds are produced from alluvial deposits scattered across 300,000 km^2 in the north-east of the country and from kimberlite deposits under more capital-intensive large-scale development. Rents comprise around 60 per cent of the price for capital-intensive diamond mines in Botswana and significantly more for labour-intensive alluvial diamond production.[43] According to Cockburn, global diamond production is estimated at 24 tonnes annually, worth $7bn prior to polishing and $50bn retail.[44] Over half the diamonds originate in Africa; Gujarat cuts 90 per cent of stones; Antwerp handles 80 per cent of sales; and the US provides 48 per cent of

TABLE 7
COMPARATIVE PRICES, SELECT COMMODITIES (CURRENT US$/KILO)

	1970	1980	1990	1998
Copper	1.42	2.18	2.66	1.65
Diamonds[a]	n.a.	n.a.	n.a.	292,000.00
Gold	1,157.40	19,457.20	12,329.53	9,458.5
Oil	0.01	0.27	0.17	0.10
Coffee	1.15	3.47	1.97	2.98
Sugar	0.08	0.63	0.28	0.20
Coca[b]	n.a.	n.a.	1.25	1.40
Cocaine[c]	n.a.	40,000.00	16,000.00	14,000.00

Source: World Bank, *World Commodity Markets*, Vol.7, No.2 (1999) (Washington DC: World Bank), except
    [a] A. Cockburn, 'Diamonds: The Real Story', *National Geographic*, Vol.202, No.3 (2002), pp.2–35;
    [b] 'The Andean Coca Wars', *The Economist*, 4 March 2000, pp.25–7;
    [c] 'The War on Drugs', *The Economist*, 2 September 2000, pp.52–4.
Figures in constant 1996 dollars.

demand (Japan 19 per cent). UNITA was able to smuggle diamonds through Zambia and Namibia into the de Beers diamond syndicate. It generated revenues averaging $600m annually during 1993–97, triple the diamond revenues under government control, although the gap narrowed sharply through the late 1990s.[45]

The Bicesse Accords of 1991 brought peace to Angola ahead of elections in 1992. UNITA lost the election and restarted the war. The 1992 offensive pushed UNITA to the peak of its power, when it controlled 90 per cent of the country's diamond production and 70 per cent of Angolan territory, leaving just Cabinda and the coastal strip in MPLA control along with some of the provincial capitals.[46] The Lusaka agreement of 1994 brought four more years of uneasy peace during which UNITA revenues eased back to average $480m. However, UNITA forces also supported themselves by using forced labour in farming and by extortion. This corroded the loyalty of UNITA's natural supporters, namely those alienated by the Luanda government. Consequently, UNITA relied heavily upon diamonds and proved vulnerable when renewed MPLA campaigns in 1998 wrested control of some of its fields.[47] In addition, the international community tightened surveillance of diamond exports, froze UNITA financial assets and imposed travel restrictions. UNITA was driven back into its Moxico Province where its leader was killed in 2002.

The Angolan experience suggests that, once started, conflict may follow a distinctive pattern in which rebel groups initially fight each other to establish a local monopoly of power that permits the desired level of looting.[48] Once the monopoly is established, the rebel group may have little to gain from achieving peace, especially in an ethnic duopoly, as opposed to an ethnically more fractional society. However, it also shows that the international community may be able to exert pressure on rebel groups because their income depends on gaining access to legitimate international markets or to shadow markets in the case of drugs.

Cocaine and Conflict in Remote Andean Regions

The global trade in illicit drugs is estimated by the United Nations at $400bn, equivalent to one-twelfth of world trade. Gross profit margins of up to 300 per cent insulate traffickers from seizures, believed to comprise over one-third of cocaine and one-tenth for heroin,[49] and also from fluctuating crop prices and courier charges.[50] In the case of narcotics, rebels frequently seek to gain control of remote territory in which illicit crop production can thrive. Collier notes that in Latin America, rebel groups that initially claimed to fight over grievances have frequently evolved into drug baronies. In such cases, efforts to restrict access to international markets merely intensify the shortage of the product and thereby drive up the returns.

Consequently, such action may have a perverse or counter-productive effect on rebel incentives.

Some 75–80 per cent of cocaine production is believed to emanate from South America and much of it is flown from northern Colombia to the North American market via Florida, Mexico and the Bahamas. Cocaine production entails a substantial weight loss, around 200–fold, so that it has a very high price/weight ratio (Table 7). The wholesale price for South American cocaine was $11,000–20,000/kg, with a street value at least twice this.[51] Cocaine production comprises 95 per cent of the value added along the production chain and coca leaf a mere 5 per cent. The bulk of the revenue from the commodity chain therefore exhibits point source linkages, being concentrated on some 80–240 coca processing organizations, typically comprising twenty operatives, aged 25–40 with no criminal record, and linked to legitimate businesses.[52]

Coca production expanded rapidly within the Andes from the 1970s in response to an explosion in cocaine demand, especially from the US. Thereafter, chronic economic growth collapses in mineral-rich Bolivia and Peru rendered coca an attractive crop for poor farmers in the central Andes valleys.[53] Coca is hardy and once planted it can be cropped three to four times annually for up to ten years. Yields of 750 kgs per hectare enable a typical 5 hectare coca holding to produce 3500 kgs annually. Leaf prices during the 1990s generated a return of up to $1,500/hectare that made it more profitable than legal crops like cocoa and maize. Coca was estimated to occupy 300,000 hectares of land by the late 1980s, mostly in Peru (60 per cent) and Bolivia (30 per cent).[54] Although US-backed government campaigns reduced coca production in the 1990s in Bolivia and Peru, this was offset by a rise in Colombia to 122,500 hectares.[55]

The manufacture of coca leaves into cocaine takes place mainly in empty jungle regions in the east of Colombia. Most Colombian coca and cocaine is produced in the south, remote from Bogota in the Andes, and under the control of the FARC, which protects and taxes the cultivators, earning an estimated $500 million annually that supports 17,000 guerrillas.[56] Cementing a culture of lawlessness, cocaine is believed to finance right-wing militias. In addition, large investors like British Petroleum (BP), with oil fields 100 kms east of Bogota, are vulnerable to extortion to protect their pipelines. Drug money has also fed guerrilla activity outside Colombia: in the 1980s and 1990s, Sendero Luminoso was based in the isolated coca-growing highlands of Peru, where it offered peasants protection from the authorities in exchange for funds for its terrorist campaign.

The UN estimated that cocaine generated 6 per cent of Peruvian GDP, 7 per cent for Colombia and 9 per cent for Bolivia in the early 1990s, prior to the relocation of coca leaf production. Despite some positive effects on the balance of payments and remote rural economies, drug money imposes substantial negative externalities.[57] It inflates domestic prices and pushes up the exchange rate, leading to Dutch disease effects. In addition, the drug trade evades legitimate government income, sales and export taxes that are imposed on legal trade. The drug barons launder earnings in 'legitimate' investments such as real estate, imported luxury goods and legal businesses – driving up prices. Moreover, drug production can corrupt the courts, police and politicians because drug wealth creates the incentive to buy state passivity when economic austerity imposes salary freezes on public sector workers. Landowners seek to minimize their workforce, which they view as a potential threat in the lawless countryside, by favouring ranching over crops, despite higher returns from crops.[58] The net result is reduced employment, under-investment in infrastructure and poor market access for small farmers, which sustains a vicious circle of inadequate opportunity, illicit activity and violence.

Porosity of Remote National Borders: Some Anomalies

The mobility of natural resource rents is not just a function of the concentration of the socio-economic linkages and the value added/weight ratio but also of proximity to porous borders. Cambodia illustrates how the natural resource rents of even products like timber, with low value to bulk ratios, can generate relatively mobile rents under such circumstances. During the 1990s, Cambodian politicians and the military associated with each of the main political parties expanded logging to secure rents with which to consolidate their power. The two parties formed a coalition government in the mid-1990s that allocated 7 million hectares of forest to private concessions without adequate capacity to oversee the system. Bribery at all levels of government diminished regulation and increased the commercial (and associated political) trans-border logging sales for the military, business and peasant farmers. Deals were struck between 'hostile' armies, including factions of the Khmer Rouge, and also with military and political agents in Thailand and Vietnam.[59]

The International Monetary Fund (IMF)[60] estimates that logging reached 2 million cubic metres annually in Cambodia 1995–98, a rate capable of eliminating capacity for sustainable timber production by 2003. A sustainable level of forest rents for the government is estimated at 1 per cent of GDP, one-tenth of all current government revenue. The actual level of logging in the mid-1990s is calculated to have lost the government revenue equivalent to 3.5 per cent of GDP annually. As with Angolan diamonds, but not with Andean drugs, foreign intervention proved effective at stemming abuse. International lenders made government loans conditional on improved forest management and a reduction in the armed forces. Foreign aid comprised $500m annually (half total public revenue) so this sanction exerted effective pressure and annual timber production fell to 15 per cent of its previous level, allowing recovery in forest reserves.

Conclusions

The association between natural resources and conflict appears to reflect a two-stage process. The staple trap model demonstrates that resource-rich countries tend to spawn predatory political states that distort the economy and create four of Collier's conditions for civil strife, namely: a growth collapse, low educational attainment, a large cohort of unemployed young males and high resource dependence. However, these conditions characterize the resource-rich countries as a group, and yet most have avoided civil strife. Consequently, as Le Billon[61] suggests, the risk of conflict is mediated by the properties of the natural resource.

This article suggests that the risk of conflict is higher for resources that engender point socio-economic linkages (like minerals) because they concentrate rents on the government and thereby corrode the political economy. High-rent commodities like oil sustain such corrosion for longer than low-rent commodities and elicit military challenge from disenchanted groups. In addition, diffuse natural resource commodities with high value in relation to weight (like drugs and diamonds) entail transport logistics that strongly concentrate the socio-economic linkages within the higher added value section of the commodity chain. The rents so captured support secessionist regimes and/or war-lords located in remote regions. Finally, proximity to a porous national border also enhances rent mobility. Moreover, porous national borders that are remote can permit even low value/weight products like timber to generate mobile rents. Significantly, alluvial gems and drugs create point linkages and have a high value to weight that renders most national borders porous. Ross confirms that these commodities exhibit the highest incidence of conflict.[62]

The conflict relationships analysed in this article are probabilistic ones rather than deterministic, however, so that there are anomalies. For example, Botswana shows that conflict is not inevitable with point source rents. This implies some scope to adopt policies to limit adverse effects, whether through successful domestic pressure for greater political accountability or external pressure as with Angolan diamonds. For example, the international community can demand standard codes of transparency regarding the transfer of rents from multinational corporations to government agencies. It can also seek to close off the options for rebel goods to access markets by increasing the risks of seizure and thereby lowering the real return to rebels. This may have an especially beneficial outcome because loot-driven wars collapse when starved of funding. Collier reports that loot-driven wars don't appear to carry a high probability of re-ignition, in contrast to the expectation for civil strife that is driven by grievance that echoes across generations and even centuries. The Angolan case supports these hypotheses, although the issue of the risk of re-ignition remains to be tested. Drug-fuelled conflicts appear more amenable to policies targeted at the market rather than at earlier stages in the supply chain, however.[63]

ACKNOWLEDGEMENTS

The author gratefully acknowledges helpful comments from Philippe LeBillon and two anonymous referees.

NOTES

1. I. De Soysa, 'The Resource Curse: Are Civil Wars Driven by Rapacity or Paucity?' in M. Berdal and D.M. Malone (eds), *Greed and Grievance: Economic Agendas in Civil Wars* (London: Lynne Reinner, 2000), pp.113–35.
2. P. Collier, 'Doing Well out of War', in M. Berdal and D.M. Malone (eds), *Greed and Grievance: Economic Agendas in Civil Wars* (London: Lynne Reinner, 2000), pp.91–111.
3. Ibid., p.91
4. P. Le Billon, 'The Political Ecology of War: Natural Resources and Armed Conflicts', *Political Geography.* Vol.20 (2001), pp.561–81.
5. M. Ross, 'Oil, Drugs and Diamonds: How Do Natural Resources Vary in their Impact on Civil War?', paper produced for the International Peace Academy on Economic Agendas and Civil Wars, 2002.
6. M.W. Mikesell and A.B. Murphy, 'A Framework for Comparative Study of Minority-Group Associations', *Annals Association of American Geographers,* Vol.81, No.4 (1991), pp.581–604.
7. Natural resource rent is the residual after deducting all costs of production by an efficient world producer, including a risk-related return on investment, from the natural resource revenue. It can be regarded as a gift of Nature because production would continue in the absence of such rent.
8. World Bank, *World Development Indicators 2002* (Washington DC: World Bank 2002).
9. R.M. Auty, 'Third World Response to Global Processes: The Mineral Economy', *Professional Geographer,* Vol.43 (1991), pp.68–76.
10. R.M. Auty, *Resource Abundance and Economic Development* (Oxford: Oxford University Press 2001a), p.5.
11. J.D. Sachs and A.M. Warner, 'Economic Reform and the Process of Global Integration', *Brookings Papers on Economic Activity* 1 (1995a), pp.1–118; J.D. Sachs and A.M. Warner, *Natural Resource Abundance and Economic Growth* (Cambridge, MA: HIID mimeo, 1997).
12. J.D. Sachs and A.M. Warner, *Natural resources and economic growth* (Cambridge, MA: HIID mimeo, 1995).
13. J.D. Sachs, 'Resource Endowments and the Real Exchange Rate: A Comparison of Latin America and East Asia', in T. Ito and A.O. Krueger (eds), *Changes in Exchange Rates in Rapidly Developing Countries* (Chicago, IL: University of Chicago Press, 1999), pp.133–53.
14. M. Olson, *Power and Prosperity: Outgrowing Communist and Capitalist Dictatorships* (New York: Basic Books 2000).
15. J.D. Sachs and A.M. Warner (note 12).

16. R.M. Auty (note 10).
17. M. Syrquin and H.B. Chenery, 'Patterns of Development, 1950 to 1983', *World Bank Discussion Paper* 41 (Washington DC: World Bank, 1989).
18. R.M. Auty and R.F. Mikesell, *Sustainable Development in Mineral Economies* (Oxford: Clarendon Press 1998).
19. D.E. Bloom and J.G. Williamson, 'Demographic Transitions and Economic Miracles in Emerging Asia', *The World Bank Economic Review*, Vol.12 (1998), pp.419–55.
20. D. Lal and H. Myint, *The Political Economy of Poverty, Equity and Growth* (Oxford: Clarendon Press 1996).
21. A.H. Gelb, J. Knight and R. Sabot, 'Public Sector Employment, Rent Seeking and Economic Growth', *Journal of Economic Literature*, Vol.101 (1991), pp.1186–99.
22. A.O. Krueger and B. Tuncer, 'An Empirical Test of the Infant Industry Argument', *American Economic Review* Vol.72 (1982), pp.1142–52.
23. R.M. Auty (note 10).
24. N. Birdsall, T. Pinckney and R. Sabot, 'Natural Resources, Human Capital and Growth', in R.M. Auty (ed.), *Resource Abundance and Economic Development* (Oxford: Oxford University Press, 2001), pp.57–75; A. Wood and K. Berge, 'Exporting Manufactures: Human Resources, Natural Resources, and Trade Policy', *The Journal of Development Studies*, Vol.34, No.1 (1997), pp.35–59.
25. P. Collier (note 2), pp.91–111.
26. R.M. Auty, *Resource-Based Industrialization: Sowing the Oil in Eight Exporting Countries* (Oxford: Clarendon Press 1990).
27. M.J. Woolcock, J. Isham and L. Pritchett, 'The Social Foundations of Poor Economic Growth in Resource-Rich Countries', in R.M. Auty (ed.), *Resource Abundance and Economic Development* (Oxford: Oxford University Press, 2001), pp.76–92.
28. A.H. Gelb and Associates, *Oil Windfalls: Blessing or Curse?* (New York: Oxford University Press 1988).
29. R.E. Baldwin, 'Patterns of Development in Newly Settled Regions', *Manchester School of Social and Economic Studies*, Vol.24 (1956), pp.161–79; D.J. Bevan, P. Collier and J.W. Gunning, 'Consequences of a Commodity Boom in a Controlled Economy: Accumulation and Redistribution in Kenya', *World Bank Economic Review*, Vol.11 (1997), pp.489–513.
30. M.J. Woolcock *et al.* (note 27).
31. M. Ross, 'Does Oil Hinder Democracy?', *World Politics*, Vol.53, No.3 (2001), pp.325–61.
32. R.M. Auty, 'Transition Reform in the Mineral-rich Caspian Region Countries', *Resources Policy*, Vol.27, No.1 (2001), pp.25–32.
33. British Petroleum, *BP Statistical Review of World Energy 2001* (London: BP 2001).
34. 'War-torn Angola on Brink of Great Expansion of Oil Output', *Financial Times*, 7 January 2000.
35. R. Aguilar, *Angola's Incomplete Transition*, UNU/WIDER Discussion Paper 47 (Helsinki: UNU/WIDER, 2001).
36. Ibid., p.7.
37. J.H. Sherman, 'Profits Versus Peace: The Clandestine Diamond Trade in Angola', *Journal of International Affairs*, Vol.53, No.2 (2000), pp.699–719.
38. P. Le Billon, *A Land Cursed by its Wealth? Angola's War Economy 1975–99*, Research in Progress 23 (Helsinki: UNU/WIDER, 1999).
39. World Bank, *World Development Indicators 2001* (Washington DC: World Bank 2001).
40. LeBillon (note 38).
41. World Bank (note 39).
42. 'Angolan diamonds', *The Economist*, 14 Sept. 1996, p.92.
43. Auty and Mikesell (note 18).
44. A. Cockburn, 'Diamonds: The Real Story', *National Geographic*, Vol.202, No.3 (2002), pp.2–35.
45. Sherman (note 37) p.707.
46. Ibid.
47. Ibid.
48. Collier (note 2) pp.91–111.

49. 'Illicit Drugs Trade is Put at $400 Billion', *Financial Times*, 26 June 1997.
50. 'The Andean coca wars', *The Economist*, 4 March 2000, pp.25–7.
51. Ibid.
52. 'Colombia: A New Class of Trafficker', *The Economist*, 11 Sept. 1999, p.66.
53. Auty and Mikesell (note 18).
54. D.K. Whynes, 'The Colombian Cocaine Trade and the War on Drugs', in A. Cohen. and F.R. Gunter (eds), *The Colombian Economy* (Boulder, CO: Westview, 1993), pp.329–52.
55. The Economist (note 50).
56. The Economist (note 50).
57. L. Kamas, 'Dutch Disease Economics and the Colombian Export Boom', *World Development*, Vol.14 (1986), pp.1177–98.
58. J. Heath and H. Binswanger, 'Natural resource degradation effects of poverty and population growth are largely policy-induced: The case of Colombia', *Environment and Development Economics*, Vol.1 (1996), pp.65–83.
59. P. Le Billon, 'The Political Ecology of Transition in Cambodia 1989–1999', *Development and Change*, Vol.31 (2000), pp.785–805.
60. IMF, *World Economic Outlook: October 2000* (Washington DC: International Monetary Fund 2000).
61. Le Billon, 'The Political Ecology of War' (note 4), pp.561–81.
62. M. Ross (note 5).
63. D.E. Boom and S.M. Murshed, 'Globalisation, Informalization and Criminalization and North–South Interaction', in S.M. Murshed (ed.), *Globalization, Marginalization and Development* (London: Routledge, 2002), pp.35–46.

Resource Curse? Governmentality, Oil and Power in the Niger Delta, Nigeria

MICHAEL WATTS

The most dangerous level of primary commodity dependence is 26% of GDP. At this level the otherwise ordinary country has a risk of conflict of 23%. By contrast, if it had no primary commodity exports (but was otherwise the same) its risk would fall to only one half of one per cent.

Paul Collier[1]

The oil-impedes-democracy claim is both valid and statistically robust; in other words oil does hurts democracy ... There is at least tentative support for three causal mechanisms that link oil and authoritarianism: a rentier effect ... a repression effect ... and a modernization effect.

Michael Ross[2]

A year prior to the events of 11 September 2001, the US Department of State in its annual encyclopaedia of 'global terrorism' identified the Niger Delta – the ground zero of Nigerian oil production – as a volatile breeding ground for militant 'impoverished ethnic groups' for whom terrorist acts (abduction, hostage-taking, kidnapping and extra-judicial killings) were part of their stock in trade.[3] A Central Intelligence Agency (CIA) report concurred, alerting the American stenographers of power to the possibly apocalyptic consequences of 'environmental stresses' on 'political tensions' in the region.[4] Nigeria – the thirteenth largest producer of petroleum and an archetypal oil nation for whom petroleum products accounts for 80 per cent of government revenues, 95 per cent of export receipts, and 90 per cent of foreign exchange earnings – provides at least 5 per cent currently of US daily consumption (and over 10 per cent of US imports), and West African fields now exceed the volume of US imports from Saudi Arabia.[5] The Petroleum Finance Company (PFC) acknowledged the enhanced significance of Nigerian oil in a March 2000 presentation to the US Congressional International Relations Committee Sub-Committee on Africa, taking particular note of the strategic value of West African oil whose high quality and low cost 'sweet' reserves – including new offshore, deepwater discoveries – demanded substantial foreign investment. Not surprisingly, in the wake of the Al Qaeda attacks, the crisis in Venezuela, and now the Iraq war, the West African 'new Gulf oil states'[6] have emerged, as the Institute for Advanced Strategic and Political Studies observed in January 2002, as 'a priority for US national security'.[7] In the last year, the ugly footprint of Africa's black gold – in Gabon, Angola, Equatorial Guinee – has been rarely off the front pages. Oil and blood, as Jon Anderson says, are ubiquitous.[8] Political Islam, in the popular imaginary, has added an extra *frisson* to this ugly pairing, namely oil terrorism: the 'nightmare', as the *New York Times* noted, of 'sympathizers of Osama Bin Laden sink[ing] three oil tankers in the Straits of Hormuz'.[9]

The *geist* of oil has been central to the history and mythos of the modern world. The great Polish journalist Kapuscinski noted as much in his marvellous meditation on oil-rich Iran: 'Oil creates the illusion', he noted, 'of a completely changed life, life without work, life for free ... The concept of oil expresses perfectly the eternal human dream of wealth achieved through lucky accident ... In this sense oil is a fairy tale and like every fairy tale a bit of a lie.'[10] It is this deceit, one might say, that currently confounds oil producers in West Africa, and Nigeria in particular. The fact that perhaps $50bn of the total of $270bn oil revenues that have flowed into the Nigerian exchequer since 1960 should have 'disappeared', speaks powerfully to the deception at the heart of Nigeria as an oil nation.

It is no accident, then, that Robert Vitalis, in an exceptionally valuable reinterpretation of the early history of oil in the Middle East, could suggest that the rapid, complete and irreversible rise of American dominance in Saudi Arabia (corporate investment in what he calls 'white supremacy' and the 'ascriptive hierarchy' known as racism) has so much light to shed on why 'the Niger Delta is currently in crisis'.[11] And indeed it is. The Niger Delta is located at the crossroads of contemporary Nigerian politics – it was the epicentre of voting fraud in the April 2003 elections – and yet is virtually ungovernable. Since 12 March 2003, escalating violence between ethnic communities (Ijaw, Urhobo and Itsekiri in particular) in the creeks around Warri has led to over 100 deaths and the devastation of eight communities. President Obasanjo's deployments of notoriously corrupt security forces to the Delta prompted further violence and threats by Ijaw militants to detonate 11 occupied oil installations. On 19 March 2003 all of the oil majors withdrew staff and closed operations, with the consequence that production has dropped by 817,000 barrels per day (40 per cent of national production).

Marginalized and excluded from the benefits of oil, the Niger Delta stands at the confluence of four pressing political flashpoints in the current political economy of Nigeria. First, the efforts led by a number of Niger Delta states for 'resource control', in effect expanded access to and control over oil and oil revenues. Second, the struggle for self-determination of minority people and the clamour for a sovereign national conference to rewrite the constitutional basis of the federation itself. Third, a crisis of rule

in the region as a number of state and local governments are rendered
helpless by militant youth movements, growing insecurity and ugly intra-
community, inter-ethnic and state violence. And not least, the emergence of
a South-South Alliance linking the hitherto excluded oil-producing states
(Akwa Ibom, Bayelsa, Cross River, Delta, Ondo and Rivers) in a bulwark
against the ethnic majorities (the Hausa, the Yoruba and the Ibo). Standing
at the heart of Alliance politics is the dispute between the federal state and
the littoral states over offshore oil revenues.[12] Oil is the theatre of conflict
within which Nigerian politics is currently beingplayed out.

In virtue of the geo-strategic significance of oil to contemporary
capitalism – and to US hegemony in particular – it is perhaps no surprise
that the relations between natural resources, and oil in particular, and
economic growth, democracy, and civil war should have emerged as an
object of substantial scholarly attention, not least by economists and
political scientists.[13] None other than Jeffrey Sachs and the International
Monetary Fund (IMF) have entered into the fray positing a strong
association between resource-dependency, corruption and economic
performance. Sachs and Warner argue that one standard deviation increase
in the ratio of natural resource exports to gross national product (GNP) is
associated with a decrease of just over 1 per cent in the growth rate
(irrespective of the endogeneity of corruption, commodity price variability
and trade liberalization).[14] Leite and Weidemann of the IMF believe that for
fuels the figure is 0.6 per cent and due 'entirely to the indirect effect of
corruption'.[15] Michael Klare sees oil as a dwindling resource – and a key
strategic one – that will be increasingly generative of inter-state conflict (see
also Homer-Dixon) and associated with what he calls the 'economization'
of international security affairs.[16] This line of argument developed by Paul
Collier of the World Bank, using resource dependency as a way of thinking
about rebellion, especially in Africa, sees oil as central to the economics of
civil war. It permits, indeed encourages, extortion and looting through
resource predation (at least up to the point where 26 per cent of gross
domestic product (GDP) is dependent on resource extraction). It is the
feasibility of predation that determines the risk of conflict. Rebels predate
through secession. For Collier the risks are greater from resource
dependency than from ethnic or religious diversity. For Michael Ross oil is
a 'resource curse' due to its *rentier effect* (low taxes and high patronage
dampen pressures for democracy), its *repression effect* conferred by the
direct state control over sufficient revenues to bankroll excessive military
expenditures and expanded internal security apparatuses, and a
modernization effect, namely the 'move into industrial and service sector
jobs render them less likely to push for democracy'.[17] Ross inventories a
number of 'factors' peculiar to oil (employment and linkage effects, its

territorial and enclave properties and so on) but such qualities are less unique to oil than to extraction, and as a consequence his analysis resembles a sort of commodity determinism confirming perhaps Coronil's point that 'Oil, more than any other commodity, illustrates both the importance and the mystification of natural resources in the modern world.'[18] But if oil hinders democracy (as though copper might liberate parliamentary democracy?), one needs to surely appreciate the centralizing effect of oil and the state in relation to the oil-based nation-building enterprises that are unleashed in the context of a politics that predates oil.

Much of this resource politics work is deeply problematic. It either elides the purported effects of oil with incumbent politics, or as Collier's work illustrates, presumes a predation-proneness for what is in fact the dynamics of state and corporate enclave politics.[19] Collier's analysis assumes that oil can be predated because of asset specificity and because of choke point that can be looted.[20] But it is not clear how oil can be looted (as opposed to say diamonds) and what difference its specific qualities make for rebellion or conflict in general. But what is distinctive about oil is its enclave character and the fact that there are certain tactical points (nodes in the commodity chain as Le Billon puts it[21]) for holding up supply (oil flow stations, pipelines). Collier, for example, has little to say about the rebel organization and the forms of mobilization and how oil enters into them (other than the presumption of funding rebel organization in ways that have to be documented). What is striking in all of this resource-politics scholarship is the almost total invisibility of both transnational oil companies (which typically work in joint ventures with the state) and the forms of capitalism that oil or enclave extraction engenders. My analysis charts the relations between oil and violence but does so through examining how forms of governable spaces are shaped and recreated out of what Dean calls authoritarian governmentality.[22] Rather than seeing oil-dependency as generative of predation or as a source of state power through its security apparatuses, I explore how oil capitalism (what I call petro-capitalism) produces, from the realities of forms of rule and political authority into which it is inserted, specific sorts of what I, following Rose, call 'governable space' (that is a specific configuration of territory, identity and rule). I focus on three such spaces – chieftainship, the space of indigeneity, and the nation – each of which is associated with conflict and violence.[23] In contrast to Collier and others, I seek to trace the variety of violences engendered by oil (not just civil war or rebellion), to elaborate the ways in which resources, territoriality and identity can constitute forms of rule (or unrule), and to understand the genesis of violence associated with the differing sorts of governable or ungovernable spaces.[24] These spaces are sorts of enclaves in which, contra Ross and Collier, oil capital is an active presence.

Petro-capitalism, in my analysis, operates through a particular sort of 'oil complex' (a unity of firm, state [and its security forces], and community) that is territorially constituted through oil concessions. This complex is generative of substantial unearned income and strong centralizing effects at the level of the state (it is, in other words, a particular fiscal sociology).[25] The presence and activities of the oil companies as part of the oil complex, constitute a challenge to customary forms of community authority, inter-ethnic relations, and local state institutions principally through the property and land disputes that are engendered, via forms of popular mobilization and agitation. These political struggles are animated by the desire to gain access to (i) company rents and compensation revenues, and (ii) federal petro-revenues by capturing rents (often fraudulently) through the creation of new regional and/or local state institutions. The oil complex (as a static institutional description) and petro-capitalism (as a dynamic set of forces) refigure differing sorts of governable spaces in which contrasting sorts of identities, and forms of rule come into play. In some cases youth and generational forces are key, in some cases gender, the clan or the kingdom or the ethnic minority (or indigenous peoples). In other instances local governmental authorities or electoral wards may be crucibles within which oil politics are generated.[26]

My analysis emphasizes the *simultaneous* production (and reworking) of differing forms of pre-existing rule and governable space consequent upon the insertion of centralized oil revenues (unearned income) into the Nigerian political economy. What concerns me is the simultaneity of different 'scale politics' to use the language of Neil Smith.[27] Each scale – each governable space – is the product of the oil complex and petro-capitalism, but these spaces curiously work against, and often stand in direct contradiction to, one another. There are obvious slippages between these spaces. A youth within a system of Chiefly rule can and often is a member of an ethnic minority; politicized ethnic minorities may become or self-identify as nations. But all of these idioms of political identification (and for me spaces of rule) are inseparable from, and is some profound way shaped by, the political economy of oil. Chieftainship, ethnic minority, and nation represent ways of exploring what I call 'governable spaces': particular politics of scale which are more or less coherent, more or less stable, more or less violent. Standing at the centre of each governable space is a central contradiction: at the level of the oil community, the overthrow of gerontocratic authority but its substitution by a sort of violent youth-led Mafia rule. At the level of the ethnic community is the tension between civic nationalism and a sort of exclusivist militant particularism. And at the level of the nation one sees the contradiction between oil-based state centralization and state fragmentation, as oil becomes a sort of generalized equivalent put to the service of massive corruption. I have tried to root these contradictions in the double-movement of petro-capitalism which is generative of an authoritarian governmentality constituted by the three forms of governable space that I have described.

There is a deliberate irony in my deployment of the term 'governable space' in that the Foucauldian project, from which it is derived, is often chided for its panoptical sense of closure, its overwhelming aura of domination, whereas my account of Nigeria reveals ragged, unstable, perhaps *ungovernable*, spaces that hardly correspond to the well-oiled machine of disciplinary and bio-power. Such is, in my book, the heart of the so-called crisis of the post-colonial state in Africa. It is in this sense that I invoke the idea of 'economies of violence' – rather than a resource curse – to characterize governmentality and rule in contemporary Nigeria. I seek to shed rather different light on why, as Achille Mbembe puts it, 'regions at the epicenter of oil production are torn apart by repeated conflicts'.[28]

A Note on Governmentality and Governable Space

> *Governmental thought territorializes itself in different ways ... We can analyze the ways in which the idea of a territorially bounded, politically governed nation state under sovereign authority took shape ... One can trace anomalous governmental histories of smaller-scale territories ... and one can also think of these [as] spaces of enclosure that governmental thought has imagined and penetrated ... how [does it] happen that social thought territorializes itself on the problem of [for example] the slum in the nineteenth century?*
>
> Nikolas Rose[29]

I am taking the idea of governmentality from the work of Michel Foucault for whom it implies an expansive way of thinking about governing and rule in relation to the exercise of modern power.[30] Government for Foucault referred famously to the 'conduct of conduct', a more or less calculated and rational set of ways of shaping conduct and of securing rule through a multiplicity of authorities and agencies in and outside the state and at a variety of spatial levels. In contrast to forms of pastoral power of the Middle Ages from which a sense of sovereignty was derived, Foucault charted an important historical shift, beginning in the sixteenth century, toward government as a right manner of disposing things 'so as to not lead to the common good ... but to an end that is convenient for each of the things governed'.[31] The new practices of the state, as Mitchell Dean says, shape human conduct by 'working through our desire, aspirations, interests and beliefs for definite but shifting ends'.[32] Unlike the new governance literature of Putnam[33] and others for whom governance is the self-organizing networks that arise out of the interactions between a variety of organizations and agencies, govermentality for Foucault refers not to sociologies of rule but, to quote Rose, to the:

> studies of stratums of knowing and acting. Of the emergence of particular regimes of truth concerning the conduct of conduct, ways of speaking truth, persons authorised to speak truth ... of the invention and assemblage of particular apparatuses for exercising power ... they are concerned with the conditions of possibility and intelligibility for ways of seeking to act upon the conduct of others.[34]

It was Foucault's task to reveal the genealogy of government, the origins of modern power, and the fabrication of a modern identity. The conduct of conduct – governmentality – could be expressed as pastoral, disciplinary or as bio-power. Modern governmentality was rendered distinctive by the specific forms in which the population and the economy was administered, and specifically by a deepening of the 'governmentalization of the state' (that is to say how sovereignty comes to be articulated through the populations and the processes that constitute them). What was key for Foucault was not the displacement of one form of power by another, nor the historical substitution of feudal by modern governmentality, but the complex triangulation involved in sustaining many forms of power put to the purpose of security and regulation.[35]

Governing, that is to say what authorities wanted to happen in relation to what problems and objectives and through what tactics, can be assessed through the 'analytics of government', in other words the processes by which we govern and are governed within different regimes, the conditions under which they emerge, operate and are transformed.[36] Dean notes that there are four dimensions to government so construed. The first he calls *forms of visibility* (the picturing and constituting of objects). The second is the *techne of government* (through what means, mechanism, tactics, and technologies is authority constituted and rule accomplished). Third, the *episteme of government* (what forms of thought, knowledge, expertise, calculation are employed in governing and how is form given to what is governable). And fourth, *forms of identification* (the forming of subjects, selves, agents, actors, in short the production of governable subjects).

On this theoretical canvas, I seek to explore the relations between two interrelated aspects of governmentality.[37] One is what Foucault explicitly refers to as relations between men and resources (in my case, people and oil in the Niger delta) as an expression of his complex notion of the governance of things. As he put it:

> On the contrary, in [the modern exercise of power], you will notice

that the definition of government in no way refers to territory: one governs *things*. But what does this mean? I think this is not a matter of opposing things to men, but rather of showing that what government has to do with is not territory but, rather, a sort of complex composed of men and things. The things, in this sense, with which government is to be concerned are in fact men, but *men in their relations, their links, their imbrication with those things that are wealth, resources, means of subsistence, the territory with its specific qualities, climate, irrigation, fertility, and so on; men in their relation to those other things that are customs, habits, ways of acting and thinking and so on; and finally men in relation to those still other things that might be accidents and misfortunes such as famines, epidemics, death and so on ...* What counts is essentially this complex of men and things; property and territory are merely one of its variables.[38]

The other aspect, taken from Rose's notion of 'governable spaces' as they emerge from the four analytics of government detailed above. For Rose, governable spaces, and the spatialization of government, are 'modalities in which a real and material governable world is composed, terraformed, and populated'.[39] The scales at which upon government is 'territorialized' – territory is derived from *terra*, land, but also *terrere*, to frighten – are myriad: the factory, the neighbourhood, the commune, the region, the nation. Each of these governable spaces has its own topology and is modelled, as Rose puts it, through systems of cognition and remodelled through government practice in a way that frames how such topoi have emerged: the social thought and practice that has territorialized itself upon the nation, the city, the village or the factory.[40] The map has been central to this process as a mode of objectification, marking and inscribing but also as 'a little machine for producing conviction in others'.[41] But in general it was geography that formed 'the art whose science was political economy'.[42] Modern space and modern governable spaces were produced by the biological (the laws of population which determine the qualities of the inhabitants) and the economic (the systems of the production of wealth). Governable spaces necessitate the territorializing of governmental thought and practice but are simultaneously produced as differing scales by the 'cold laws of political economy'.[43]

Petrolia: The Oil Complex and the Niger Delta

One of the great deltaic regions in the world, the Niger delta is a vast sedimentary basin constructed over time through successive thick layers of sediments dating back 40–50 million years to the Eocene epoch. An immense coastal plain covering almost 70,000 square kilometres, its geographical perimeter extends from the Benin river in the west to the Imo river in the east and from the southernmost tip at Palm Point near Akassa to Aboh in the north where the Niger River bifurcates into its two main tributaries. A classic arcuate delta, typically below the 15 metre contour across its entire extent, the delta is also endowed with very substantial hydrocarbon deposits (31.5 billion barrels according to the Organization of Petroleum Exporting Countries (OPEC)). Crude oil production in the Niger delta currently runs at 2.18 million barrels per day, accounting for over 90 per cent of Nigerian foreign exchange earnings. To say that Nigeria as the largest producer of petroleum in Africa is heavily dependent upon the oil sector is a massive understatement. Post-colonial Nigeria is a mono-economy, much more an export dependency than it ever was in the colonial period.

It is difficult to estimate the current population, but since the 1960s, population has been growing at about 2.7 per cent per annum and the population of Delta, Rivers and Bayelsa States is in excess of 7 million. The settlement pattern is largely nucleated and rural, typically occupying isolated dry sites within the deltaic swamps. Farming systems are predominantly peasant, characterized by small land parcels, short-fallow systems of cultivation, and diversified forms of rural livelihood including hunting and fishing. The delta is a region of astonishing ethic and linguistic complexity. While there are five major linguistic categories (Ijoid, Yoruboid, Edoid, Igboid and Delta Cross), each embraces an enormous profusion of ethno-linguistic communities. The history of the delta is in some respects captured in this linguistic and cultural complexity since pre-colonial trade across the region was linked to a social division of labour rooted in occupation and micro-ecology. Early European explorers commented upon the trans-deltaic trade networks, but these transactions were radically compromised by the Portuguese in the fifteenth century, and subsequently by the French, Dutch and British slavers. The rise of the so-called legitimate trade of the nineteenth century – the genesis of rubber and cocoa which displaced slavery after abolition – shaped, under British auspices, the creation of the Oil Rivers Protectorate in which a vital commercial life flourished. The establishment of the Nigerian colony and the imposition of Indirect Rule in the early 1900s initiated a process of profound political change through the warrant chief system, yet at the same time economically marginalized the multi-ethnic communities of the Delta.[44] Indeed, in the transition to Independence in the 1950s, the so-called ethnic minorities voiced their concerns to the Willink Commission in 1955, that they were positioned outside a federation dominated by three ethnic majorities (the Hausa, the Yoruba and the Ibo) that constituted 70 per cent of the population. What was true under colonialism became more so in the post-colonial oil era.

The onset of commercial petroleum production in 1956 in the delta – discovered in Oloibiri in Baylesa State – seemed to hold out the promise of rapid development for the hitherto neglected ethnic minorities. But the presence of the transnational oil companies in joint ventures with the Nigerian State (the Nigerian National Petroleum Company, NNPC) presided over enormous environmental despoliation and a crisis of forms of traditional livelihood. By the 1970s and 1980s, a number of ethnic communities had begun to mobilize against the so-called 'slick alliance' of oil companies and the Nigerian military. A foundational role was played in the 1990s by Ken Saro-Wiwa and the Ogoni people, a small ethnic group of 400,000, who established a political movement (MOSOP) and a Bill of Rights to challenge both Shell for environmental compensation and the Nigerian state for direct control of 'their oil'. Saro-Wiwa and the MOSOP leadership were hung by the Nigerian military in 1995, but their legacy was the proliferation of 'many Ogonis' as more minorities (the Adoni, the Itsekiri, the Ijaw for example) organized precisely as MOSOP fell into decline amidst internal political bickering and acrimony. Women's groups – building upon a longer history of political mobilization[45] – have been at the forefront of the oil struggles, recently gaining international attention by occupying a Chevron oil refinery and demanding company investments and jobs for indigenes.[46] A 1997 co-ordinated protest by 10,000 youths at Aleibiri to end Shell's activities, captured much of these post-MOSOP energies. At the same time, by 1998–99, the mobilization of the Ijaw in particular, building upon the struggles of the Ijaw Youth Council, the Ijaw National Council and the Movement for the Survival of the Ijaw Ethnic Nationality against the Abacha junta, had devolved into the so-called 'Egbesu wars' – named after an Ijaw cult – marking a period of deepening political disorder across the Delta.[47]

Let me say a brief word about oil and its relationship to Nigerian political economy.[48] Nigeria is a multi-ethnic state, and a former British colony until 1960. Colonial indirect rule imposed a 'decentralized despotism',[49] orchestrated through regional rule by the powerful ethnic (and regional) majorities. The backbone of each region was an export commodity and a government Market Board. At Independence, Muslim northerners sustained a fragile hegemony over a highly charged multi-ethnic polity and it was into this weak federal system that commercial oil production was inserted. The break up of the federation in 1967 (following a succession of military coups) was detonated by a civil war (1967–1970) prompted by the secession by Biafra (the former eastern Region), a conflagration that was in no small measure a reflection of the new saliency of oil politics. In the wake of the oil boom of 1973, black gold provided the material and fiscal basis for ambitious modernization and for autocratic state-led development. Nigeria became, in short order, an oil nation. Oil unleashed a rapid state-led industrialization project articulated through fiscal linkages and a vast investment of petro-dollars. Oil production in Nigeria has always been a joint venture, currently 16 oil majors bound by joint operating agreements to determine the distribution of royalties and rents. Oil, one might say, created a form of state-landed property.[50] But what began as a boom and untempered ambition in the 1970s ended with the bust in 1985, and its attendant austerity and World Bank adjustment programmes. In 1999 after a terrifying period of military authoritarianism under Sani Abacha, Olesegun Obasanjo became the first democratically elected President in two decades, inheriting an economy in shambles, vast political and economic resentments by ethnic minorities, and the prospect of building a democracy on the backs of long-standing regional, ethnic and religious frictions.

I want to make four fundamental points about the political economy of oil. The first is that oil capitalism operates through what I call an 'oil complex' involving: (1) a statutory monopoly over mineral exploitation (the 1946 Solid Minerals Law, and 1969 Petroleum Law);[51] (2) a nationalized oil company (NNPC was set up in a phase of state indigenization in 1971) that operates through joint ventures (memoranda of understanding) with oil majors who are granted territorial concessions (blocs);[52] (3) the security apparatuses of the state (working synergistically with those of the companies themselves) protecting costly investments and ensuring the continual flow of oil; and (4) an institutional mechanism (in Nigeria called the 'derivation principle' and the Distributable Pool Account (DPA) formed in 1966, later renamed as the Federation Account in 1979) by which federal oil revenues are distributed to the states and producing communities, and not least the oil-producing communities themselves.[53] In Nigeria this marked, as oil revenues grew, the rise of fiscal centralism and a shift from derivation (which plummeted from 100 per cent to 3 per cent) to a Federation Account (i.e., a centrally controlled account which dominated the allocation of federally collected revenues).[54] Much can be said about this complex – which has parallels in Indonesia and Venezuela – but it provides the setting, at once institutionally dense and politically cogent, within which new governable spaces are manufactured.[55] Central to the oil complex is its enclave character, the extent to which it is militarized as a national security sector, and a dominant fiscal sociology, namely the massive centralizing consequences of vast unearned income, flowing to the federal exchequer, derivative of the alliance of state and capital. As Wirpsa and Dunning show in this volume, the oil complex often has associated with it, in the name of the 'economization' of security affairs, a panoply of paramilitary, mercenary, security and other militarized agents. As anyone who has spent any time in or around oil installations – whether Warri or Midland, Texas – it is saturated with all manner of actual and symbolic violence, and the stench of security and surveillance.

Oil matters profoundly, and this is the second point, to the character and dynamics of Nigerian development. Oil is a biophysical entity (fluid, subterranean, and enclave in character); it is also a commodity that enters the market with its price tag, and is the bearer of particular relations of production. And not least it has its fetishistic qualities, it is the bearer of meanings: a harbinger of El Dorado and unprecedented wealth, avarice and power. Not unexpectedly oil crops up constantly in the popular imagination;[56] its evil powers ('the devil's excrement'), its ability to corrupt, and so on. Only in these three ways can we understand Coronil's claim that 'oil illustrates the importance and the mystification of natural resources in the modern world'.[57] My third point about oil is that Nigerian oil-fuelled capitalism, petro-capitalism, contains a double movement, a contradictory unity of capitalism and modernity. On the one hand oil is a centralizing force, one that rendered the state more visible (and globalized), and permitted, that is to say financially underwrote, a process of secular nationalism and state building. On the other, centralized oil revenues flowing into weak institutions and a charged, volatile federal system produced an undisciplined, corrupt and flabby oil-led development that was to fragment, pulverize, disintegrate and discredit the state and its forms of governance. It produced conditions which challenged and undermined the very tenets of the modern nation-state. Coronil dubs this conundrum 'the Faustian trade of money for modernity' which in Venezuela brought 'the illusion of development'.[58] In Nigeria it brought illusion too but more importantly it produced forms of governable spaces that question Nigeria itself, that generated forms of rule, conduct and imagining at cross purposes with one another, antithetical to the very idea of a developed modern nation-state that oil represented.

Economies of Violence and Governable Spaces

Let me now turn to these governable spaces, which I shall refer to as the space of chieftainship (the politics of youth and gerontocratic rule in an oil-producing community), the space of indigeneity (the politics of ethnic mobilization as a basis for civic nationalism), and the space of the nation-state (the politics of nation-building and citizenship). I want to think about the genesis of differing sorts of governable spaces in Nigeria as part of a larger landscape of what Dean calls 'authoritarian governmentality', that is to say an articulation of generalized uses of the instruments of repression with bio-politics (as he says, 'it regards its subjects capacity for action as subordinate to the expectation of obedience').[59] These spaces and forms of power emerge from the oil complex as part of an overarching logic of petro-capitalist development, that is to say a particular sort of extractive development generative of differing sorts of scale, or the 'politics of scale' as Neil Smith calls it. Oil violence is generated by the evil twins of authoritarian governmentality and petro-capitalism.

The Space of Chieftainship

Nembe community[60] in Bayelsa State stands at the originary point of Nigerian oil production. In the 1950s, the Tennessee Oil Company (a US company) began oil explorations there but oil was not found until much later when Shell D'Arcy unearthed the Oloibiri oil field in Ogbia. Subsequent explorations led to the opening of the large and rich Nembe oil fields near the coast in the Okpoama and Twon-Brass axis. Currently the four Nembe oil fields produce approximately 150,000 barrels of high quality petroleum through joint operating agreements between the Nigerian National Petroleum Company (NNPC), AGIP and Shell. If Nembe is the ground zero of oil production, it is also a theatre of extraordinary violence and intra-community conflict, the result of intense competition over political turf and the control of benefits from the oil industry. The violence can be traced back to the late 1980s when the Nembe Council of Chiefs acquired power from the then King, Justice Alagoa Mingi IX, to negotiate royalties and other benefits with the oil companies. The combination of youth-driven violence and intense political competition has transformed Nembe's system of governance and set the stage for further challenges to the traditional authority of chieftainship.[61]

Oil became commercially viable in the 1970s, but to grasp its transformative effects on Nembe politics and community – that is to its genesis as a distinctive governable space – requires an understanding of chieftainship in the Delta. Indirect rule in the colonial period certainly left much of the Niger Delta marginalized and isolated, but it also, in the name of tradition, built upon and frequently invented chiefly powers of local rule which in the Nembe case were grafted onto a deep and complex structure of kingship and gerontocratic rule. To understand the dynamics of Nembe as a governable space one needs to recall that land lay in the hands of customary authorities (notwithstanding the fact that the 1969 Petroleum Law granted the state the power to nationalize all oil resources). Land rights and therefore claims on oil royalties were from the outset rooted in the *amayanabo* (king), and derivatively the subordinate powers, namely the Council of Chiefs and the Executive Council. Historically, the Nembe community possessed a rigid political hierarchy consisting of the *amayanabo* presiding over in descending order the Chiefs (or heads of the war canoe houses[62]) elected by the entire war canoe houses constituted by their prominent sons. Although the Chiefs were subservient to the *amayanabo*, they acted as his closest advisers, supported the *amayanabo* in the event of military threat, and in turn were responsible for electing the *amayanabo* from the Mingi group of Houses, or the royal line. The current Nembe Council of Chiefs is the assemblage of the recognized Chiefs of Nembe 'chalked' by the King.[63]

In 1991, the Nembe monarch's ineffectiveness in dealing with the oil companies led to a radical decentralization of his powers to the Council of Chiefs, headed by Chief Egi Adukpo Ikata. In so far as the Council now dealt directly with Shell, and handled large quantities of money paid by the oil companies, competition for election to the Council intensified as various political factions struggled for office. By 2000, the Council had expanded from 26 to 90 persons. Coeval with the evisceration of kingly powers, the deepening of the Council mandate, and the expansion of the Council members, was a subtle process of 'youth mobilization'. In an age-graded society like the Nembe Ijaw, youth refers to persons typically between their teens and early forties who, whatever achievements they may have obtained (university degrees, fatherhood and so on), remain subservient to their elders. Central to any understanding of the emergence of a militant youth in Nembe town was the catalytic role played by a former company engineer with Elf Oil Company named Mr Nimi B.P. Barigha-Amage. He deployed his knowledge of the oil industry to organize the youths of the Nembe community into a force capable of extracting concessions from the oil companies in essence by converting cultural organization into protection services. Chief Ikata was quick to exploit the awareness and restiveness of the youths to pressure Shell into granting community entitlements. A pact between Chief Ikata and the young engineer was in effect instituted: the engineer supplied the youths with information regarding community entitlements, and the Chief deployed his knowledge of military logistics to organize the shutting down of flow stations, the seizure of equipment and sabotage.[64]

Armed with insider knowledge of the companies and an understanding of a loosely defined set of rules regarding company compensation for infringements on community property, Barigha-Amage pushed for the creation of youth 'cultural groups' which gradually, with the support of some members of the Council of Chiefs, were the intermediaries with oil companies and their liaison officers, and manipulated the system of compensation in the context of considerable juridical and legal ambiguity. Liaison officers, colluding with community representatives, invented ritual or cultural sites that had ostensibly been compromised or damaged by oil operations, for which monies exchanged hands. As the opportunities for appropriating company resources in the name of compensation became visible through the success of the cultural groups, other sections of the youth community began to organize in turn around clan and familial affiliations. In 1994, for example, a group called 'House of Lords' (*Isongoforo*) was created by a former university lecturer, Lionel Jonathan, and a year later in 1995 Mrs Ituro-Garuba, wife of a well-placed military officer, established *Agbara-foro*. Inevitably, with much at stake financially, and control of the space between community and company in the balance, conflicts within and among youth groups proliferated and deepened. In turn, growing community militancy spilled over into often violent altercations with the much detested mobile police ('Mopos') and local government authorities. The regional state and governor attempted to intervene as conditions deteriorated but a government report, on which such action was predicated, was never released for political reasons. A subsequent banning of youth groups had, as a result, no practical effect.[65]

Slowly, the subversion of royal authority, the strategic alliances between youth and chiefs, and the growing (and armed) conflict between youth groups for access to Shell resulted in the ascendancy of a highly militant *Isongoforo*. In an environment of rampant insecurity and lawlessness, occupation and closure of flow stations, and tensions between the companies, the service companies and local security forces, *Isongoforo* were provided 'stand by' payments by the companies, that is to say hired for protection purposes, and at the same time colluded with the community liaison officers to invent compensation cases. *Isongoforo* occupied the centre of a new governable space which they ruled through force rather than any sense of consent or customary authority. This 'mafiosi' was funded by the large quantities of monies that they commanded from the companies, and by the arms with which they controlled. This volatile state of affairs collapsed dramatically as local resentments and struggles proliferated. In February 2000 a 'Peoples Revolution' overthrew *Isongoforo*, ostensibly precipitated by the humiliation of the Council of Chiefs at the hands of Shell (backed by the intimidating *Isongoforo* forces). The Chiefs now orchestrated the occupation of flow stations and undermined the powers of *Isongoforo* by recruiting and supporting other youth groups. By May 2000 *Isongoforo* had been sent into exile but they were promptly replaced, in the wake of the return of Barigha-Amage as High Chief of Nembe, by his own 'cultural group' *Isenasawo/Teme*. *Teme* instituted a rule of terror and chaos far worse than their predecessors. It too proved unstable in the context of excessive youth mobilization and split into two factions, producing in short order a number of 'counter coups' and much bloodshed. A government Peace Commission was established in January 2001 in a desperate effort to bring peace to one of the jewels in the oil-producing crown.[66]

Much of this later violence (after 1996) was largely beyond the control of the relatively weak local state authorities because of its concurrence with the 1999 elections in which some of the key youth leaders were expected to deliver votes for the incumbent gubernatorial race. In the creation of what in effect was a sort of vigilante rule, there were complex complicities between chiefs, youth groups, local security forces, and the companies. The occupation of oil flow stations (for purposes of extortion) were often known in advance and involved collaboration with local company engineers; youths were *de facto* company employees providing protection services, and local compensation and community officers of Shell and AGIP produced fraudulent compensation cases and entitlements. Nembe, a town with its own long and illustrious history and politics, had become a sort of company town in which authority had shifted from the king to warring factions of youth who were in varying ways in the pay of, and working in conjunction with, the companies. The Council of Chiefs stood in a contradictory position, seeking to maintain control over revenues from the companies and yet intimidated and undermined by the militant youth groups on whom they depended. In the context of a weak and corrupt state and strongly polarized social class forces, the genesis of this power-nexus bears striking resemblances to the genesis of the Mafia in nineteenth-century Sicily.[67] Privatized violence and the deployment of youth for protection services – involving collusion and fraud between all parties – were central to the disorder of the reconfigured space of chieftainship.

What I have described is the displacement of a specific form of power (chieftainship) by a governable space of civic vigilantism, a sort of thickening of civil society that does not necessarily imply the basis of the kind of governance put forth by Putnam[68] and others. Civic powers have expanded by overthrowing a territorial system and a gerontocratic royal order. Youth mobilization – whose political affiliations and ambitions in any case were complex because they reflected an unstable amalgam of clan, family and local electoral loyalties – had thrown up an identity and subjectivity that was indisputably revolutionary, representing an unholy alliance between civic organizations (presenting themselves as cultural organizations) and private companies. Rule in Nembe is a realm of privatized violence; force presiding over consent. Government here turns on what Foucault calls men in their imbrication with wealth and resources – the government of men and things, as opposed to territory.[69] It is institutionalized through forms of calculability, *techne*, and visibility that emerge from the legal and company dispositions to regulate local populations backed up by the forces of what one might call civic repression. The governable subject is *de facto* a sort of company employee, and cultural categories serve as the form by which this company rule is experienced – violent youth groups – but in a way that renders the space increasing *ungovernable*.

The Space of Indigeneity

The Niger delta is a region of considerable, perhaps one should say bewildering, ethno-linguistic complexity. The eastern region, of which the delta is part, is dominated statistically by the Ibo majority, but there is a long history of excluded ethnic minorities in the delta dating back at least to the 1950s when the Willinck Commission took note of the inter-ethnic complexity of the region. Throughout the colonial period prior to the arrival of commercial oil production, there had been efforts by various minorities, who saw themselves as dominated by the Ibo, to establish Native Authorities of their own. In the 1960s, prior to the outbreak of civil war, two charismatic local figures, both Ijaw – Nottingham Dick and Isaac Boro – declared a Delta Republic, a desperate cry for some sort of political inclusion that lasted a mere 12 days. Isaac Boro and the ill-fated Delta Peoples Republic in 1966 was the forerunner of what is now a prairie fire of ethnic mobilization by the historically excluded minorities – now tagged as 'indigenous' in order to capture the political and legal legitimacy conferred by the International Labour Organization of the United Nations (ILO169).[70] The paradigmatic case in the delta is the struggle by Ken Saro-Wiwa and the Movement for the Survival of the Ogoni People (MOSOP). Their case reveals a rather different sort of governable space, one marked by ethnic subjects and indigenous territory.

The Ogoni are typically seen as a distinct ethnic group, consisting of three sub-groups and six clans dotted over 404 sq miles of creeks, waterways and tropical forest in the north-east fringes of the Niger Delta. Located administratively in Rivers State, a Louisiana-like territory of some 50,000 sq. kilometres, Ogoniland is one of the most heavily populated zones in all of Africa. Indeed the most densely settled areas of Ogoniland – over 1,500 persons per sq. km. – are the sites of the largest wells. Its customary productive base was provided by fishing and agricultural pursuits until the discovery of petroleum, including the huge Bomu field, immediately prior to Independence. Part of an enormously complex regional ethnic mosaic, the Ogoni were drawn into internecine conflicts within the delta region, largely as a consequence of the slave trade and its aftermath, in the period prior to arrival of colonial forces at Kono in 1901. The Ogoni resisted the British until 1908 but thereafter were left to stagnate as part of the Opopo Division within Calabar Province.[71] As Ogoniland was gradually incorporated during the 1930s, the clamour for a separate political division grew at the hands of the first pan-Ogoni organization, the Ogoni Central

Union, which bore fruit with the establishment of the Ogoni Native Authority in 1947. In 1951, however, the authority was forcibly integrated into the Eastern Region. Experiencing tremendous neglect and discrimination, integration raised long-standing fears among the Ogoni of Ibo domination.[72] Politically marginalized and economically neglected, the delta minorities feared the growing secessionist rhetoric of the Ibo and consequently led an ill-fated secession of their own in February 1966. Ogoni antipathy to what they saw as a sort of internal colonialism at the hands of the Ibo, continued in their support of the federal forces during the civil war. While a Rivers State was established in 1967 –which compensated in some measure for enormous Ogoni losses during the war – the new state recapitulated in microcosm the larger 'national question'. The new Rivers State was multi-ethnic but presided over by the locally dominant Ijaw, for whom the other minorities felt little but suspicion and sometimes contempt.[73]

During the first oil boom of the 1970s, Ogoniland's 56 wells accounted for almost 15 per cent of Nigerian oil production[74] and in the past three decades an estimated $30bn in petroleum revenues have flowed from this Lilliputian territory. It was, as local opinion had it, 'Nigeria's Kuwait'. Yet according to a government commission, Oloibiri, where the first oil was pumped in 1958, has no single kilometre of all-season road and remains 'one of the most backward areas in the country'.[75] Rivers State saw its federal allocation fall dramatically in absolute and relative terms. At the height of the oil boom, 60 per cent of oil production came from Rivers State but it received only 5 per cent of the statutory allocation (roughly half of that received by Kano, Northeastern States and the Ibo heartland, East Central State). Between 1970 and 1980 it received in revenues one-fiftieth of the value of the oil it produced. Few Ogoni households have electricity, there is one doctor per 100,000 people, child mortality rates are the highest in the nation, unemployment is 85 per cent, 80 per cent of the population is illiterate and close to half of Ogoni youth have left the region in search of work. Life expectancy is barely 50 years, substantially below the national average. If Ogoniland failed to see the material benefits from oil, what it *did* experience was an ecological disaster – what the European Parliament has called 'an environmental nightmare'. The heart of the ecological harms stem from oil spills –either from the pipelines which criss-cross Ogoniland (often passing directly through villages) or from blow outs at the wellheads – and gas flaring. As regards the latter, a staggering 76 per cent of natural gas in the oil-producing areas is flared (compared to 0.6 per cent in the US). As a visiting environmentalist noted in 1993 in the delta, 'some children have never known a dark night even though they have no electricity'.[76] Burning 24 hours per day at temperatures of 13–14,000 degrees Celsius,

Nigerian natural gas produces 35 million tons of CO_2 and 12 million tons of methane, more than the rest of the world (and rendering Nigeria probably the biggest single cause of global warming). The oil spillage record is even worse. There are roughly 300 spills per year in the delta and in the 1970s alone the spillage was four times greater than the much publicized Exxon Valdez spill in Alaska. In one year alone almost 700,000 barrels were soiled according to a government commission. Ogoniland itself suffered 111 spills between 1985 and 1994.[77] Figures provided by the NNPC document 2676 spills between 1976 and 1990, 59 per cent of which occurred in Rivers State,[78] 38 per cent of which were due to equipment malfunction.[79] Between 1982 and 1992, Shell alone accounted for 1.6 million gallons of spilled oil, 37 per cent of the company's spills world-wide. The consequences of flaring, spillage and waste for Ogoni fisheries and farming have been devastating. Two independent studies completed in 1997 reveal the total of petroleum hydrocarbons in Ogoni streams at 360 – 680 times the European Community permissible levels.[80]

The hanging of Ken Saro-Wiwa and the Ogoni nine in November 1995 – accused of murdering four prominent Ogoni leaders – and the subsequent arrest of 19 others on treason charges, represented the summit of a process of mass mobilization and radical militancy which had commenced in 1989. MOSOP necessarily built upon previous cultural and political organizations like the Ogoni Klub and Kagote (both élite organizations) and, most especially, the founder of modern Ogoni politics, Naaku Paul Birabi, who established in 1950 the Ogoni State Representatives Association (OSRA) to promote Ogoni interests in the new eastern Region Government. The civil war hardened the sense of external dominance among Ogonis. A cultural organization called Kagote which consisted largely of traditional rulers and high-ranking functionaries, was established at the war's end and in turned gave birth in 1990 to MOSOP. A new strategic phase began in 1989 with a programme of mass action and passive resistance on the one hand and, on the other, a renewed effort to focus on the environmental consequences of oil (and Shell's role in particular) and on group rights within the federal structure. Animating the entire struggle was, in Leton's words, the 'genocide being committed in the dying years of the twentieth century by multinational companies under the supervision of the Government'.[81] A watershed moment in MOSOP's history was the drafting in 1990 of an Ogoni Bill of Rights.[82] Documenting a history of neglect and local misery, the Ogoni Bill took the question of Nigerian federalism and minority rights head on. Calling for participation in the affairs of the republic as 'a distinct and separate entity', the Bill outlined a plan for autonomy and self-determination in which there would be guaranteed 'political control of Ogoni affairs by Ogoni people ... the right to control and use a fair proportion of Ogoni economic resources ... [and] adequate representation as of right in all Nigerian national institutions'.[83] In short the Bill of Rights addressed the question of the *unit* to which revenues should be allocated – and derivatively the rights of minorities.[84] At the heart of Saro-Wiwa's political vision was an Ogoni state.

In spite of the remarkable history of MOSOP between 1990 and 1996, its ability to represent itself as a unified pan-Ogoni organization remained an open question. There is no pan-Ogoni myth of origin (characteristic of some delta minorities), and a number of the Ogoni subgroups (clans) engender stronger local loyalties than any affiliation to Ogoni 'nationalism'. Gokana clan, for example, was the most populous and well-educated and its élites wielded disproportionate influence in Ognoi. Conversely, the Eleme clan-head did not even sign the Ogoni Bill of Rights and Eleme's leading historian has argued that they are not in fact Ogoni. In 1994 Eleme leaders proposed the creation of Nchia state which comprised non-Ogonis from Bonny, Andoni, Opobo and Etche, thereby turning their backs on Saro-Wiwa's goal.[85] Furthermore, the MOSOP leaders were actively opposed by elements of the traditional clan leadership, by prominent leaders and civil servants in state government, and by some critics who felt Saro-Wiwa was out to gain 'cheap popularity'.[86] Some Ogoni notables (Edward Kobani and Dr Leton) aspired to participate in conventional politics by running for the two major parties rather than assisting in the birth of a nation. MOSOP moreover was a political movement of the élite led by the élite. MOSOP was not in fact a mass movement and both youth and women were not represented on MOSOP's first steering Committee. Gradually the youth wing of MOSOP, which Saro-Wiwa had made use of, emerged as militants but the leadership were often incapable of controlling them. MOSOP in short was wracked by tensions. There were as Okonta says 'cracks in the pot'. The movement dramatically unravelled along class, gender, generational and clan lines.

What sort of articulation of indigenous identity and political subjectivity did Saro-Wiwa pose? What sort of governable space did it represent? It was clearly one in which territory and oil were the building blocks upon which ethnic difference and indigenous rights were constructed. And yet it was an unstable and contradictory sort of articulation. First, there was no simple sense of 'Ogoniness', no unproblematic unity, and no singular form of political subject (despite Saro-Wiwa's claim that 98 per cent of Ogonis supported him). MOSOP itself had at least five somewhat independent internal strands embracing youth, women, traditional rulers, teachers and Churches. It represented fractious and increasing divided 'we', as the splits and conflicts between Saro-Wiwa and other élite Ogoni confirms.[87] Second, he constantly invoked Ogoni culture and tradition, yet he also argued that war and internecine conflict had virtually destroyed the fabric of Ogoni society by 1900.[88] His own utopia then rested on the reinvention of Ogoni culture and suffered like many reinventions from a quasi-mythic reading of the past, and of Ogoni ur-history. Third, ethnicity was the central problem of post-colonial Nigeria – the corruption of ethnic majorities – and for Saro-Wiwa its panacea (the multiplication of ethnic minority power). To invoke the history of exclusion and the need not simply for ethnic minority inclusion as the basis for federalism, led Saro-Wiwa to ignore the histories and geographies of conflict and struggle among and between ethnic minorities. Saro-Wiwa's brilliance then was in the face of élite opposition (and his own marginal position in the 1980s) to make MOSOP a green, indigenous movement (with international backing and visibility) and to take the movement to the poor and the young to secure a powerful identity. Saro-Wiwa's crowning moment of glory was Ogoni national day on 4 January 1993, when he presided over the birth of the Ogoni flag, the Ogoni anthem and the National Youth Council of the Ogoni People.

Paradoxically Ogoni/MOSOP surfaced as a foundational indigenous movement even though its significance as an oil-producing region was diminishing. By the late 1990s moreover, as a movement it had fallen apart and inter-group struggles deprived it of much of its previous momentum and visibility. But it gave birth to what one might call indigenous movements among oil-producing communities. The same forces have spawned a raft of self-determination indigenous movements among Ijaw (INC, IYV), Isoko (IDU), Urhobo (UPU), Itsekiri (INP), Ogbia (MORETO), among others.[89] MOSOP itself fell apart precisely as these other movements gained power. Since the return to civilian rule in 1999, there has been a rash of such minority movements across the Delta calling for 'resource control', autonomy and a national sovereign conference to rewrite the Nigerian constitution. At the same time the Delta has become ever more engulfed in civil strife: militant occupations of oil flow stations, pipeline sabotage, intra-urban ethnic violence, and of course the near-anarchy of state security operating in tandem with company security forces.[90] The shock troops of many of these indigenous movements are youth and women, and the multiplication of ethnic youth movements is one of the most important political developments in contemporary Nigeria. And it is here that the politics of oil-producing communities meet up with the politics of oil-producing indigenous groups.

What does the Ogoni case reveal, then, as a form of governable space? Oil entered an already fraught multi-ethnic polity in which a sort of Ogoni proto-nationalism had emerged from the experience of colonial exclusion and what they saw as subjection to locally dominant ethnic minorities like the Ijaw. Birabi's ORA movement, the independence struggles of the 1950s, the short-lived Delta Republic in 1966, and the civil war all laid the foundations for the Ogoni movement that was to follow. But is was Saro-Wiwa's particular genius to manufacture a sort of Ogoni unity – in the face of local opposition and his own political weakness – by using international organizations such as the ILO Convention 169 on indigenous peoples and transnational environmental groups like Greenpeace to make MOSOP into a compelling mass movement.[91] Oil was key to this process because it provided an idiom in which claims-making and rights talk could be instigated; oil served as the ground on which claims could be made for corporate compensation and accountability, for resource control and self-determination, for human rights violations, and so on. The emergence of a national debate in Nigeria over resource control in the late 1990s is precisely a product of indigenous claims-making on the state, a process through which ethnic identifications must be discursively and politically produced. The Ogoni case shows that there is no pre-given ethnic identity, and that the space of indigeneity was fragile, heterogeneous and contested.[92] MOSOP contained all of the tensions of élite rule, and traditional clan power, attached to a popular civic mobilization. Ogoni nationalism with its anthem and flag appeared full-blown in 1993 but within a decade MOSOP was to all intents and purposes moribund. The fortunes of Ogoni governable space, in other words, rose and fell quite dramatically.

MOSOP under Saro-Wiwa's leadership had helped create an indigenous subject and an indigenous space. MOSOP's claims were territorial as a basis for an Ogoni state, and as a way of securing 'their oil'. But these property rights and the boundaries of the territory proved to be hotly contested since they were necessarily exclusivist (Ogoni oil was by definition not Andoni oil). The Ogoni movement, and those that followed, made the politics of territory and property of central concern and it was inevitable that conflicts between differing ethnic groups (each with long histories of conflict and accommodation with other local indigenous groups) would run afoul of the juridical and legal ambiguities surrounding the history of land and land rights. One of the legacies of MOSOP then has been the bitter and often violent inter-ethnic struggles over territory made in the name of custom or tradition or long-term occupancy. There is no doubt that the state and the oil companies exacerbated these conflicts – sometimes deliberately so.[93] But the incontestable fact is that land – and the customary institutions such as chieftainship that have regulated it – has become an object of intense conflict. Questions of boundaries and mapping are necessarily central to this territorial struggle. It is for this reason that of some of the inter-ethnic violence takes the form of urban struggles (rather than rural disputes over property or boundaries) over the delineation of electoral wards and the territorial basis for the creation of new Local Government Areas, all of which are in the service of providing dispersed ethnic groups with a political basis for claiming centrally controlled oil revenues, even if there is not literally oil within their immediate territorial jurisdiction. This is precisely what is at stake in the long-standing conflicts in Warri among the Ijaw, Itsekiri and Urhobo communities. At the heart of all of these governable spaces is a profound tension between rule in the name of indigenous institutions or governance practices (decentralized despotism) and the democratic impulses of a civic nationalism.[94]

Indigenous space was powerfully achieved through an imbrication of things and people – oil and ethnicity – and it has been generative of a profusion of indigenous movements. Indigeneity has in this sense unleashed the enormous political energies of ethnic minorities who recapitulate in some respects the post-colonial history of spoils politics in Nigeria. The effect of this multi-ethnic mobilization was the production of political and civic organizations and new forms of governable space; in short a veritable jigsaw of militant particularisms. The Kaiama Declaration in 1999 indicates that there is in the making a pan-ethnic solidarity movement, but its contours are at present limited[95] and often compromised by the explosion of communal violence. As the Ogoni case shows, much of this visibility and identification turned on the invention and reinvention of tradition and local knowledge, with an eye to the Nigerian constitution and international politics.[96] This is a case of the multiplication of governable spaces which stand in some tension or even contradiction with each other – they account in part for the explosion of inter-ethnic tensions in the delta – and within the national space of Nigeria, to which I now turn.

Space of Nationalism

One of the striking aspects of the governable spaces of indigeneity as they emerged in the delta is that they become vehicles for political claims, typically articulated as the need for a local government or in some cases a state. Indigeneity necessarily raises the question of a third governable space, that of the nation-state, an entity that pre-existed oil and came to fruition in 1960 at Independence. Oil in this sense became part of the nation-building process – the creation of an 'oil nation'. Nature and nationalism become inextricably linked. But how did petro-capitalism as a state-led, and thoroughly globalized, development strategy stand in relation to the creation of the governable space called modern Nigeria? Much has been written on the political history of the Nigerian federation and on Nigerian nation-building.[97] My purpose here is to provide a gloss on a larger argument[98] that links oil development to nationalism, emphasizing the contradictory role of centralized oil revenues inserted into an already deeply ethnic policy. On the one hand oil did keep Nigerians together (it purchased a sort of consent among the ethnic majorities). But on the other it has fragmented and destabilized the institutional and political practice of building an oil nation.

Here I want to start with the work of Mamood Mamdani and his observations on post-colonial African politics.[99] Colonial rule and decentralized despotism were synonymous says Mamdani. The Native Authorities consolidated local class power in the name of tradition (ethnicity) and sustained a racialized view of civic rights. The Nationalist movement had two wings, a radical and a mainstream. Both wished to deracialize civic rights but the latter won out and reproduced the dual legacy of colonialism. They provided civic rights for all Nigerians but a bonus 'customary rights' for indigenous people. The country had to decide which ethnic groups were indigenous and which were not a basis for political representation, a process that became constitutionally mandated in Nigeria. Federal institutions are quota driven for each state but only those indigenous to the state may apply for a quota. As Mamdani puts it:

> The effective elements of the federation are neither territorial units called states not ethnic groups but ethnic groups with their own states … Given this federal character every ethnic group compelled to seek its own home its NA, its own state. With each new political entity the non-indigenes continues to grow.[100]

Once law enshrines cultural identity as the basis for political identity, it necessarily converts ethnicity into a political force. As a consequence in Nigeria clashes in the post-colonial period came to be not racial but ethnic, and such ethnic clashes, which have dominated the political landscape in the last three decades, are always at root about customary rights to land, and derivatively to a local government or to a state that can empower those on the ground as ethnically indigenous.

Into this mix – that Mamdani brilliantly outlines – enters oil, that is to say a valuable, centralized (state-owned) resource. It is a national resource on which citizenship claims can be constructed. As much as the state uses oil to build a nation and to develop, so communities use oil wealth to activate community claims on what is seen popularly as unimaginable wealth – black gold. The governable space of Nigeria is as a consequence reterritorialized through ethnic claims making. The result is that access to oil revenues amplifies what I call sub-national political institution making; politics becomes then a *massive state making machine*. The centralization of oil revenues – so-called fiscal centralism – permitted by the decline of derivation and the rise of the Distribution Pool Account meant that state creation was a precondition to gain federal revenues (the DPA accounted for 66 per cent of all federally collected revenue).[101] Only in this way can one understand how, between 1966 and the present, the number of local governments have grown from 50 to over 700, and the number of states from 3 to 36! Nigeria as a modern nation-state has become a machine for the production of ever more local political institutions, and this process is endless.[102] The logic is ineluctable and of course terrifying.

What sort of national governable space emerges from such multiplication, in which incidentally the political entities called states or LGAs (local government areas) become vehicles for massive corruption and fraud – that is to say the disposal of oil revenues? The answer is that it works precisely *against* the creation of a national imagined community of the sort that Ben Anderson saw as synonymous with nationalism.[103] Nation building, whatever its imaginary properties, whatever its style of imaging, rests in its modern form on a sort of calculation, integration, and state and bureaucratic rationality which the logic of rent seeking, petro-corruption, ethnic spoils politics, and state multiplication works to undermine systematically. Lauren Berlant has said in her study of Nathaniel Hawthorne that every nation – and hence every governable national space – requires a 'National Symbolic'; a national fantasy which 'designates how national culture becomes local through images, narratives and movements which circulate in the personal and collective unconsciousness'.[104] My point is that the Nigerian National Symbolic grew weaker and more attenuated as a result of the political economy of oil. There was no sense of the national fantasy at the local level; it was simply a big lie (or a big pocket of oil monies to be raided in the name of indigeneity). At Independence, Obafemi Awolowo, the great western Nigerian politician, said that Nigeria was not a Nation but a 'mere geographical expression'; 40 years later this remains true but more so.

What we have then is not nation building – understood in the sense of governmentality – or a particular style of imagining but perhaps its reverse; the 'unimagining' or deconstruction of a particular sense of national community. Nicos Poulantzas noted that the national or modern unity requires a historicity of a territory and a territorialization of a history.[105] Oil capitalism and its attendant governmentality in Nigeria has achieved neither of these requirements. The governable space called Nigeria was always something of a public secret; 40 years of post-colonial rule has made this secret more public as ethnic segregation has continued unabated and undermined the very idea of the production of governable subjects. The double movement of petro-capitalism within the frame of a modern nation-state has eviscerated the governable space of the nation, it has compromised it and worked against a sense of governable subject. The same incidentally might be said of the impact of oil on the Muslim communities of Nigeria.[106] Oil and identity – people and things – have produced an unimaginable community on which the question of Nigeria's future hangs.

Reflections

The entire history of the petroleum history is, as Daniel Yergin details in his encyclopedic Whig account of the industry *The Prize*, replete with criminality, violence and the worst of frontier capitalism.[107] Graft, autocratic thuggery, and the most grotesque exercise of imperial power are its hallmarks. And it is to be expected in an age of unprecedented denationalization and market liberalization – to say nothing of the horrific rise of the gas-guzzling sports utility vehicle in the United States – the mad scramble to locate the next petrolic El Dorado continues unabated. Eastern Russia looks ever more like a slice of Mafiosi sovereignty. Petro-violence is in any case rarely off the front pages of the press. The Caspian basin reaching from the borders of Afghanistan to the Russian Caucuses is a repository of enormous petro-wealth; Turkmenistan, Kazakstan, Azerbaijan, Georgia and the southern Russian provinces (Ossetia, Dagestan, Chechnya) have however become, in the wake of the collapse of the Soviet Union, a 'zone of civil conflict and war', as the *San Francisco Chronicle* puts it.[108] The oil companies jockey for position in an atmosphere of frontier vigilantism and what the Azerbaijani President calls 'armed conflict, aggressive separatism and nationalism'.

My account questions some of the scholarship – particularly emerging from political science and economics – on the links between conflict and oil. Many of the dynamics noted by Collier and Ross emerge not from oil *per se* but from centralized resource revenues typical of many extractive industries. Both authors tend to steadfastly ignore how oil's contribution to war or authoritarianism builds upon pre-existing (pre-oil) political dynamics. And while oil can and does generate rents, and can and does enhance the military and security budget, and may generate limited employment and linkage effects, the sorts of conflicts and politics that emerge from what I have called the oil complex are spatially heterogeneous and not readily encompassed by the idea of predation, looting or rebellion. My entry point into these economies of violence has been through the governable spaces that emerge from, and are associated with, the oil complex and petro-capitalism – from the coupling of state, company, community and profit. Each governable space is marked by differing sorts of rule in which the oil complex has contributed directly to a restructuring of pre-existing forms of governance. Oil has been a sort of idiom in which new social forces are unleashed, overturning traditional power structures and in some cases generating violent conflict, albeit along a series of rather different vectors (age, class, ethnicity, and so on). A striking aspect of contemporary development in Nigeria is the simultaneous production of differing forms of rule and governable space, each the product of similar forces, which work against, and often stand in direct contradiction to, one another. Oil may indeed be a curse but its violent history – and its ability to generate conflict – can only be decoded if we are attentive to the unique qualities of oil itself, to the powerful corporate and state institutions for which it becomes a bearer, and not least to the ways in which oil becomes an idiom for doing politics as it is inserted into an already existing political landscape of forces, identities, and forms of power.

ACKNOWLEDGEMENTS

I am grateful to comments provided by Philippe Le Billon, and to the assistance in various ways of Oronto Douglas, Ike Okonta and Dimieari Von Kemedi. One anonymous reviewer did not like the article and posed a series of observations that seemed to me irrelevant but they provided (and prompted) an opportunity to clarify my arguments. Philippe Le Billon provided much useful commentary.

NOTES

1. P. Collier, *The Economic Causes Of Civil Conflict and their Implications for Policy* (Washington DC: The World Bank 2000).
2. M. Ross, 'Does Oil Hinder Democracy?', *World Politics*, Vol.53 (2001), pp.325–61.
3. <http://www.state.gov/s/ct/rls/pgtrpt/2000>.
4. Central Intelligence Agency, *Nigeria: Environmental Stresses and Their Impacts Over the Next Decade* (Langley, MD: Central Intelligence Agency, DCI Environmental Center, 2000).
5. US Department of Energy. See <http://www.eia.doe.gov/emeu/cabs/nigeria.html>.
6. J.-C. Servant, *Le Monde diplomatique*, 13 January 2003.
7. <http://www.iasps.org>.
8. J. Anderson, 'Blood and Oil', *The New Yorker*, 14 Aug. 2000, pp.46–59.
9. J. Anderson, *New York Times*, 14 Oct. 2001: III, p.1.
10. R. Kapucinksi, *Shah of Shahs* (New York: Vintage 1982), p35.
11. R. Vitalis, 'Black Gold, White Crude', *Diplomatic History*, Vol.26, No.2 (2002), p.186.
12. In a long running battle over onshore/offshore oil, the Obasanjo government asked the Supreme Court to intervene to support its position that all resources in territorial waters are derived from the federation. In a compromise the Dichotomy Bill has been sent back to the legislature with new language in which all offshore oil refers a 200 metre isobar limit (most producing fields are located within water depths of 200 metres or less).
13. Economists typically distinguish direct (so-called Dutch Disease) effects in which resource booms lead to recession, and indirect effects through rent seeking and institution building.
14. J. Sachs and A. Warner, *Natural Resource Abundance and Economic Growth*, NBER Working Paper 5398 (Cambridge, MA: National Bureau of Economic Research 1995).
15. C. Leite and J. Weidmann, *Does Mother Nature Corrupt?*, IMF Working Paper (Washington DC: IMF 1999) p.29.
16. M. Klare, *Resource wars* (Boston: Beacon Press 2001); T. Homer-Dixon, *Environment, Scarcity, and Violence* (Princeton, NJ: Princeton University Press 1999). P. Le Billon, 'The Political Ecology of War', *Political Geography*, Vol.20 (2001) pp.561–84; idem, 'Angola's Political Economy of War', *African Affairs* Vol.100 (2001), pp.55–80, provided a compelling critique of the resource abundance and scarcity arguments, and belatedly of much of what passes as environmental security, and explores the vulnerabilities resulting from resource dependence in the case of Angola. For an elaborate critique of Homer-Dixon's position, see N.L. Peluso and M. Watts (eds), *Violent Environments* (Ithaca, NY: Cornell University Press, 2001).
17. Ross, 'Does Oil Hinder Democracy?' (note 2) p.357. See also M. Ross, 'The Political Economy of the Resource Curse', *World Politics*, Vol.51 (1999), pp.297–322.

18. F. Coronil, *The Magic of the State* (Chicago, IL: University of Chicago Press 1997) p.49.
19. D. Leonard and S. Strauss, *Africa's Failed Development* (Boulder, CO: Reinner 2003).
20. Collier's work is an important contribution to the economics of civil war. But it is not clear that oil-dependent economies are any more prone to violence and rebellion than others – see B. Smith, 'Rethinking the Politics of the Resource Curse', paper presented to the annual meeting of the American Political Science Association, San Francisco, 2001. Furthermore, there are a number of ways apart from rebellion in which oil politics can appear (and this is part of my concern). Collier tends to forget that the states into which oil revenues are inserted are already weak. What makes oil different is that it generates unearned income that is highly centralizable through institutional alliances between states and corporations.
21. Le Billon (note 16).
22. M. Dean, *Governmentality* (London: Sage 1999).
23. N. Rose, *Powers of Freedom* (London: Cambridge University Press 1999).
24. See A. Mbembe, 'At the Edge of the World', *Public Culture*, Vol.12, No.1 (2000), pp.259–84.
25. M. Moore, 'Political Underdevelopment', paper presented at the Conference of the Development Studies Institute, LSE, London, 7–8 Sept. 2000.
26. I cannot in this article cover all of these forms (this is the subject of a forthcoming book). I do seek to emphasize however that I am focusing on three sorts of territorial oil politics, recognizing that there are other important sites in which petro-coercion (and petro-consent) may emerge. On the latter, I am involved in a research project with Ike Okonta and Von Kemedi comparing the differing dynamics, for example, of six different local oil-producing communities across the Niger Delta.
27. N. Smith, 'Geography, Difference and the Politics of scale', in J. Doherty, E. Graham and M. Malek (eds), *Postmodernism and the Social Sciences* (London: MacMillan, 1992), pp.57–9; Mbembe (note 24).
28. Mbembe (note 24) p.280.
29. Rose (note 23) pp.34–6.
30. See M. Foucault, *Power* (New York: The New Press 1978/2000); M. Foucault and C. Gordon, *Power/knowledge: Selected Iinterviews and Other Writings, 1972–1977* (New York: Pantheon Books 1980).
31. Foucault (note 30) p.211.
32. Dean (note 22) p.16.
33. See R.D. Putnam, *Bowling Alone. The Collapse and Revival of American Community* (New York: Simon & Schuster, New York 2000).
34. Rose (note 23) p.21.
35. 'Accordingly, we need to see things not in terms of the replacement of a society of sovereignty by a disciplinary society and the subsequent replacement of a disciplinary society by a society of government; in reality one has a triangle, sovereignty-discipline-government, which has as its primary target the population, and as its essential mechanism the apparatuses of security ... *I want to demonstrate the deep historical link between movement that overturns the constants of sovereignty on consequence of the problem of choices of government; the movement that brings about the emergence of population as a datum, a field of intervention ... the process that isolates the economy as a specific sector of reality; and political economy as the science and the technique of intervention of the government in that reality.* Three movements – government, population, political economy – that constitute from the eighteenth century onward a solid series, one that even today has assuredly not been dissolved.' Foucault (note 30) p.219, emphasis added.
36. Rose (note 23) p.21; Dean (note 23).
37. Some of these Foucaldian ideas have already been productively deployed in the understanding of nature and resource management – what one might call green governmentality – and the relations between nature and nationalism. See B. Braun, 'Producing Vertical Territory', *Ecumene* (July 2000), pp.7–46.
38. Foucault (note 30), pp. 208–209, emphasis added.
39. Rose (note 23), p.32.
40. Ibid., p.37.
41. Ibid.
42. Rhein quoted in P. Rabinow, *French Modern: Norms and Forms of the Social Environment*

(Cambridge: MIT Press 1989) p.142.
43. Rose (note 23), p.39.
44. I. Okonta, 'The Struggle of the Ogoni for Self-Determination', D.Phil., Oxford University, 2002.
45. T. Turner, 'Women's Uprising Against the Nigerian Oil Industry in the 1980s', *Canadian Journal of Development Studies*, Vol.14, No.3 (1993), pp.329–57.
46. *New York Times*, 13 Aug. 2002.
47. See O. Ibeanu, '(Sp)oils of Politics', paper delivered to a Conference on Oil and Human Rights, University of California, Berkeley, 24–26 Jan. 2003.
48. See M. Watts, *Struggles over Geography*, Hettner lectures (Heidelberg: University of Heidelberg 2000); T. Forrest, *The Advance of African Capital: The Growth of Nigerian Private Enterprise* (Edinburgh: Edinburgh University Press for the International African Institute 1994); T. Forrest, *Politics and Economic Development in Nigeria* (Boulder, CO: Westview Press 1995); S.A. Khan, *Nigeria: the Political Economy of Oil* (Oxford: Oxford University Press for Oxford Institute for Energy Studies 1994); C. Obi, *The Changing Forms of Identity Politics in Nigeria* (Uppsala: Africa Institute 2001).
49. M. Mamdani, *Citizen and Subject* (Princeton, NJ: Princeton University Press 1996).
50. R. Haussman, 'State Landed Property, Oil Rent and Accumulation in Venezuela', PhD dissertation, Cornell University, 1981.
51. The current constitutional debate over the onshore-offshore distinction is precisely about the maintenance of the state's ability to 'federally derive' all oil revenues.
52. Since the mid 1980s the Nigerian oil industry has been under pressure to privatize and in 1988 NNPC created 11 subsidiaries. In 1991 new memoranda of understanding were offered to the oil companies but calls to sell off NNPC have not transpired.
53. The derivation principle was first mooted by the Philipson Commission of 1946 which saw it as the principle through which a region would benefit from its non-declared revenue according to its proportional contribution to central revenue. In 1957 the scope of derivation was narrowed by setting up a Distribution Pool Account (DPA) for other taxes not declared regional or federal. From the 1960s onwards there was a progressive enlargement of DPA at the expense of derivation. As oil revenues increased as a proportion of national wealth so the share of derivation to the states has plummeted (from 50 per cent in 1960 to 3 per cent in the 1980s). See A. Adebayo, *Embattled Federalism* (New York: Peter Lang 1993).
54. In addition there are a number of special revenue accounts created by the state for specific development purposes for the Niger Delta deploying oil revenues; the Petroleum Fund (set up in the Abacha years), OMPADEC (Oil Mineral Producing Areas Development Commission) and now the Niger Delta Development Commission (NDDC) established by Obasanjo. All have been the source of spectacular corruption and waste, deployed to buy consent among increasingly angry Delta constituencies.
55. See Khan (note 48); G. Frynas, 'Legal Change in Africa: Evidence from Oil Related Litigation in Nigeria', *Journal of African Law*, Vol.43, No.2, 1999, pp.121–50.
56. See M. Watts, 'Oil as Money', in S. Corbridge, R. Martin and N. Thrift (eds), *Money, Power and Space* (London: Blackwell, 1994), pp.406–46.
57. Coronil (note 18), p.49.
58. Ibid.
59. Dean (note 22) p.209.
60. Nembe in its macro-usage refers to six towns (Bassimbiri, Ogbolomabiri, Okpoama, Odioma and Akassa) that are part of sixteen towns that comprise Nembe Kingdom. For the purposes of this article however Nembe town refers to Ogbolomabiri only.
61. See V. Kemedi, 'Oil on Troubled Waters', *Berkeley Environmental Politics Working Papers*, 2002; Human Rights Watch, 'The Bakassi Boys: The Legitimization of Murder and Torture', *HRW/CLEEN*, Vol.14, No.5(A) (May 2002), pp.1–45. See also Human Rights Watch, 'Testing Democracy', *Human Rights Watch*, Vol.15, No.9 (April 2003). The data for the case study was collected during a visit to the Niger delta in January and February 2001. I also rely on the assistance on Von Kemedi and his work (this note) and the Nembe Peace Commission, see M. Alagoa, *The Report of the Nembe Peace and Reconciliation Committee* (Port Harcourt 2001).
62. The war canoe houses were the units of the kingdom's defence forces. A war canoe house consisted of the head of the house and a formidable number of able-bodied men who were

responsible for defending the house and the King.

63. There is a long running dispute over kingly authority that has spilled over into the establishment of local government areas (LGAs). In this essay I do not address the conflicts between Bassambiri and Ogbolamabiri (two contiguous towns) over the authority of their respective paramount chiefs, and disputes over LGA territory (and hence access to oil rents). This has also been generative of conflict and violence and contributes to the ethos of violence that I describe here.

64. Alagoa (note 61); Human Rights Watch (note 61).

65. Human Rights Watch (note 61).

66. Alagoa (note 61); NDWC, *Mediation and Conflict Resolution of the Crisis in Nembe* (Port Harcourt: Niger Delta Wetlands Commission 2000).

67. A. Blok, *The Mafia in a Sicilian Village* (Waveland: Prospect Heights 1974).

68. See Putnam (note 33).

69. Foucault (note 30) pp.208–209.

70. See A. Brysk, A. *From Tribal Village to Global Village* (Palo Alto, CA: Stanford University Press 2000); D. Nelson, *Finger in the Wound* (Berkeley, CA: University of California Press 1999).

71. B. Naanen, 'Oil Producing Minorities and the Restructuring of Nigerian Federalism', *Journal of Commonwealth and Comparative Politics*, Vol.33, No.1 (1995), pp.46–58.

72. As constitutional preparations were made for the transition to home rule, non-Igbo minorities throughout the Eastern Region appealed to the colonial government for a separate rivers state. Ogoni representatives lobbied the Willink Commission in 1958 to avert the threat of exclusion within an Ibo-dominated regional government which had assumed self-governing status in 1957 but minority claims were ignored, see U. Okpu, *Ethnic Minority Problems in Nigerian Politics* (Stockholm: Wiksell 1977); M. Okilo, *Derivation: A Criterion of Revenue Allocation* (Port Harcourt: Rivers State Newspaper Corporation 1980).

73. The Ogoni and other minorities petitioned in 1974 for the creation of a new Port Harcourt State within the Rivers State boundary (Naanen (note 71), p.63).

74. According to the Nigerian Government estimates, Ogoniland currently (1995) produces about 2 per cent of Nigerian oil output and is the fifth largest oil-producing community in Rivers State. Shell maintains that total Ogoni oil output is valued at $5.2bn before costs.

75. Cited in T. Furro, 'Federalism and the Politics of Revenue Allocation in Nigeria', PhD Dissertation, Clark Atlanta University, 1992, p.282; see also O. Douglas and I. Okonta, *Where Vultures Feast* (San Francisco, CA: Sierra Club 2001).

76. *Village Voice*, 21 Nov. 1995, p.21.

77. J. Hammer, 'Nigerian Crude', *Harpers Magazine* (June 1996), p.61.

78. A. Ikein, *The Impact of Oil on a Developing Country* (New York: Praeger 1990).

79. The oil companies claim that sabotage accounts for a large proportion (60 per cent) of the spills, since communities gain from corporate compensation. Shell claims that 77 of 111 spills in Ogoniland between 1985 and 1994 were due to sabotage (Hammer (note 77)). According to the government commission, however, sabotage accounts for 30 per cent of the incidents but only 3 per cent of the quantity spilled. Furthermore, all oil-producing communities claim that compensation from the companies for spills has been almost non-existent.

80. Rainforest Action Network, *Human Rights and Environmental Operations Information on the Royal Dutch/Shell Group of Companies* (London: RAI 1997); Human Rights Watch, *The Price of Oil* (Washington DC: Human Rights Watch 1999).

81. Cited in Naanen (note 71), p.66.

82. K. Saro-Wiwa, *Genocide in Nigeria* (Port Harcourt: Saros International Publishers 1992).

83. K. Saro-Wiwa, *On A Darkling Plain* (Port Harcourt: Saros Publishers 1989) p.11.

84. Human Rights Watch (note 80); Okonta (note 44).

85. I. Okonta, 'When Citizens Revolt, unpublished manuscript, University of California, Berkeley, 2003.

86. E. Osaghae, 'The Ogoni Uprising', *African Affairs*, Vol.94 (1995), p.334.

87. *Ogoni Crisis?* (Lagos, Ministry of Information, Nigerian Federal Government, 1996). Saro-Wiwa was often chastised by Gokana (he himself was Bane) since most of the Ogoni oil was in fact located below Gokana soil. In other words on occasion the key territorial

unit became the clan or clan territory rather than a sense of pan-Ogoni territory.

88. Ibid., p.14.

89. Obi (note 48).

90. The US State Department, for example, refers to the minority and anti-oil movements as 'terrorist' and to the youth movements as undemocratic; a recent CIA report sees the problems as a result of 'environmental stresses'. Even those who champion the role of civic associations have seen the events of the last decade in the Delta as 'negative' and 'perverse' (Augustine Ikelegbe, 'The Perverse Manifestation of Civil Society: Evidence from Nigeria', *Journal of Modern African Studies*, Vol.39, No.1 (2001), pp.1–24). Such assessments misconstrue the history and dynamics of the relations between extraction, the environment and identity politics. But such judgements certainly do grasp the gravity of the crisis in the Delta.

91. C. Bob, 'Merchants of Morality', *Foreign Policy* (2002), pp.36–45.

92. See T. Li, 'Images of Community', *Development and Change* 27 (1996), pp.501–27.

93. See Human Rights Watch (note 80).

94. I have focused here on the making of community and the intra-communal (ethnic) conflicts that so often attended indigenous mobilization. But this is no sense exhausts the violence that has occurred in relation to ethnic mobilization around oil. Here the appalling record of the state security forces, the federal military and the private security forces of the oil companies have much to do with the brutality suffered by oil-producing communities and ethnic youth movements. This conflict has also contributed to the making of community, to the hardening of particular solidarities (however awful has been the record of the security forces in Ogoniland or the federal troops who slaughtered over 2000 in Odi in Baylesa State in 1999). I have focused here more on forms of governable space engendered by the intersection of oil and ethnicity – indigeneity examined from within so to say – and less on the state and company responses. See Human Rights Watch (note 80).

95. See Douglas and Okonta (note 75); Environmental Rights Action, *The Emperor has No Clothes* (Benin: Environmental Rights Action 2000).

96. Nelson (note 70).

97. See R. Suberu, *Federalism and Ethnic Conflict in Nigeria* (Washington DC: USIP 2001).

98. See M. Watts, 'Economies of Violence', *Politique Africaine*, forthcoming.

99. Mamdani, *Citizen and Subject* (note 49); M. Mamdani, *When Victims becomes Killers* (Princeton: Princeton University Press 2000).

100. M. Mamdani, 'When does a Settler become a Native?', Inaugural Lecture, University of Cape Town, manuscript, 1998, p.7.

101. E. Anugwom, 'Federalism, Fiscal Centralism and the Realities of Democratization in Nigeria', paper delivered to the Conference on Africa at the Crossroads, UNESCO, 2001, <www.ethnonet-africa.org/pubs/crossroads1.htm>.

102. At least three different states have been proposed for the broadly construed Ogoni area, for example.

103. B. Anderson, 'Nationalism, Identity and the World-in-Motion', in P. Cheah and B. Robbins (eds), *Cosmopolitics* (Minneapolis, MN: University of Minnesota Press, 1998).

104. L. Berlant, *The Anatomy of National Fantasy* (Chicago, IL: University of Chicago Press 1991) p.61.

105. N. Poulantzas, *State, Power, Socialism* (London: New Left Books 1978).

106. M. Watts, 'Islamic Modernities?', in J. Holston (ed.), *Cities and Citizenship* (Durham, NC: Duke University Press 1998), pp.67–102; Watts (note 48).

107. D. Yergin, *The Prize* (New York: Random House 1991).

108. *San Francisco Chronicle*, 11 August 1998, p.A8.

Oil and the Political Economy of Conflict in Colombia and Beyond: A Linkages Approach

THAD DUNNING and LESLIE WIRPSA

Introduction

Recent empirical studies in international political economy have contributed substantially to understanding and explaining the conditions through which natural resource endowments may incite, prolong or intensify violent conflict. The majority of these studies find a strong positive association between fiscal dependence on oil exports, in particular, and the incidence and duration of civil war.[1] Much of this literature has stressed the importance of bringing in economically motivated actors and actions, and the relationship of these to a positive political economy of conflict, to challenge explanations of internal warfare as almost exclusively the result of an irrational 'collapse of order' within the nation state or a failing of the state itself.[2] In this sense, resource wars are considered a variable, contributing to the emergence of an alternate political economy and political geography, one in which insurgents have access to rents, territorial control and mechanisms of legitimacy they could not obtain under conditions of peace. In this growing body of literature, the primary axis of conflict remains that between national states and their official armed police and militaries, and internal insurgents or other extralegal armed actors. These frameworks, which posit that resource revenues derived from lootable commodities like oil provide the 'fuel' that incites and/or sustains conflict between these parties, are generally conceptually bounded within the 'national' level of analysis.

We share the growing analytical conviction that it is essential to understand the economic factors driving the simultaneous and often deliberate 'emergence of another order' through conflict.[3] However, precisely because our analysis focuses on oil, a transnational commodity *par excellence*, we also take as fundamental the assertion that conflict must be considered in part explainable in terms of 'economic motivations that are specifically related to the intensification of transnational commerce in recent decades and to the political economy of violence inside a particular category of states'.[4] More specifically, by the end of the 1970s, virtually every major oil-producing country had at least partially nationalized oil production, but this nationalist trend has progressively reversed in recent decades.[5] Consequently, foreign direct investment by multinational corporations and by the state oil concerns of foreign countries has again attained a dominant role in the energy sectors of many developing countries, recalling in part the era of the late nineteenth and early twentieth centuries.[6] This re-intensification of foreign direct investment in local extractive activities coincided with not only a burgeoning global demand for oil and gas, but also with an increased willingness on the part of the United States to structure policy around the military protection of strategic energy sources. Consequently, today, in resource-rich regions like the Caspian Sea basin, the Persian Gulf, sub-Saharan Africa and parts of South America, the interactions and linkages among subnational, national, transnational, national and multinational actors with varied but abiding interests in promoting or restricting the flow of commodities like oil have a crucial impact on the incidence and character of localized conflict. These interactions both shape actors' goals in undertaking armed violence or in responding to belligerents with force, and they also delineate the range of possible strategies that these actors may use to articulate interests and to legitimate various forms of the use of force.

In this context, we contend that because of the particular characteristics of oil, contemporary examinations of the relationship of this commodity to conflict will benefit from prioritizing a landscape of analysis that includes political communities and dynamics beyond the national level of analysis and a multiplicity of actors at various levels of interaction. In this article, we argue that oil increasingly shapes the character of local conflict precisely because of the relationship of oil to actors and processes of the global political economy which become embedded within the local context.

Using Colombia as a case study within the geopolitical context of the broader Andean region, we attempt to demonstrate the utility of a framework that takes account of these interactions and linkages. This framework entails significant analytic complexity, which we believe is essential given the specific properties of a globally strategic resource like oil. First, oil is vehemently and simultaneously local, regional, national, and global. It is characteristically 'fixed'; therefore, extraction must occur at the specific, focal point of its location. This means the exploitation of oil has particular consequences for the security of the communities and territories in which it is embedded. Control of oil, however, requires the infrastructure, security and technology to convert it into an asset transportable over and through broad and complex regional, national, and transnational-national geographic space, usually across national borders.

Second, oil exploitation is simultaneously national and multinational. State oil companies and some of the world's most powerful private, transnational-national corporations, attempt to influence the domestic and global governance structures which manage the extraction, production and distribution of oil. Oil is also highly 'national,' discursively linked to notions of state identity and the 'national interest'.[7] At the same time, because of its global significance, trans- and multinational actors play a prominent role in the 'practices shaping [its] political economy'[8] and the social, cultural and institutional arrangements symbolically defining and pragmatically regulating it. Thus, where oil is concerned, 'the persistence of conflict and, in particular, the crystallization of war economies within 'weak' states can only be understood within a broader global context.'[9]

To this panorama we must add the centrality that oil and other natural resources have once again acquired in the military and security doctrines of the advanced industrialized countries, particularly the United States. In the wake of the end of the Cold War, the military protection of vital sea lanes and resource-rich areas overseas regained a pre-eminence it had in the nineteenth and early twentieth centuries, as a governing principle underlying US military deployments. These deployments increasingly reflect the geographic distribution of global natural resources as well as a range of operational dimensions – for example, the protection of fixed energy installations, control over territory through which pipelines traverse – associated with resource security. In this vein, an explicit policy link in advanced industrialized countries, particularly the United States, between economic security and military strategy, has led to the doctrine that military intervention may increasingly be used to protect the international flow of strategic resources like oil.[10]

In Colombia, these various tendencies have pushed oil into a central place in the political economy of violence of a pre-existing, internal war whose most recent phase has lasted nearly 40 years. A range of historical and political factors, including persistent structural inequalities and systemic political exclusion, point to the roots of Colombia's conflict, while analyses of 'war commodities' in the Colombian context have appropriately focused on the international drug trade and conflict over land tenure to explain and understand the country's complex trajectories of violence. Oil has steadily become more important to the Colombian economy over the past 20 years, and establishing control over oil installations, pipelines and the political and economic spoils of production has become a strategic priority for all of Colombia's armed groups, including the military, as well as for external actors.

In this essay we argue that contemporary analyses of oil and its role in conflict will benefit by starting with these linkages and interactions between local, national and transnational-national spaces. These interactions shape both the material objectives of competing local actors and also the discursive strategies upon which they draw to legitimate conflict and militarization. Conflict is driven by local dynamics, but it is essential to see the way in which these dynamics relate to the goals and actions of a range of national and transnational actors. This involves moving beyond state-centric conceptualisations of security. The state is just one actor which may or may not exercise dominion over the territorial space in which resource-related violence appears. Other actors – armed insurgents or paramilitaries, state officials from oil-importing countries, private military or security contractors and multinational corporations – are also central to an understanding of local-global interactions and conflicts propelled by the extraction and flow of materials considered 'vital' for the world economy.

In the Colombian case, we thus analyse two international/transnational dimensions relating to the link between oil and conflict. The first is the re-intensification of multinational direct investment in the oil sector, beginning in the mid-1980s. Multinational investment helped spark the re-emergence of Colombia as a net oil exporter; due to the development of Caño Limón in Arauca department and then Cusiana-Cupiagua in Casanare, by Occidental Petroleum and British Petroleum respectively. Within this context, oil soon surpassed coffee as Colombia's leading export. Yet control of oil production and transport facilities, or at least the ability to threaten the functioning of such facilities, has also become a strategic military objective for guerrilla groups, while repelling such attacks has involved the military, illegal paramilitary groups and public and private international security and military agents. As the oil and conflict literature would suggest, in Colombia the presence of oil has helped to finance in various ways all of these contending parties. For example, the revival of the National Liberation Army (ELN), Colombia's second largest guerrilla group, has been linked to payments received from foreign energy contractors. Oil rents therefore provide a credible mechanism linking petroleum exploitation to the persistence of conflict.

Yet attacks on oil installations, and struggles among Colombia's government forces and armed actors for control of resource-rich and strategic territory, motivate a discussion of a second international dimension linking oil and conflict. State officials from oil-importing countries, specifically the United States, and private sector representatives posit that attacks on energy infrastructure in Colombia, and especially the implications of Colombian instability for the broader energy-rich Andean region, pose a threat to a key source of oil supplies. This has coincided with the renewal of a US military doctrine focused on protecting strategic foreign sources of natural resources and strategies to diversify oil imports away from heavy dependence on the Middle East. Thus, violent attacks on Colombian energy installations, prior to and within the context of the post-11 September global anti-terrorism campaigns, have provided US lawmakers and members of the executive branch with legitimating arguments for increasing military aid to Colombia and expanding, significantly and without precedent, the US mission there beyond counter-narcotics to include counter-insurgency and counter-terrorism. Most prominently, in February 2002, the Bush administration announced the first attempt to direct military aid, equipment and 70 US military advisers to train a Colombian army brigade to protect the strategic Caño Limón-Coveñas oil pipeline. The pipeline is partly owned and operated by the US multinational, Occidental Petroleum; 44 per cent of the crude it pumps belongs to Occidental.[11]

Finally, the linkage between these two transnational dimensions of the oil/conflict nexus becomes apparent in the use of *foreign* (US) public funds and training resources to protect a *multinational*, privately operated infrastructure project. This linkage contributes to reshaping the local dynamics of conflict in a number of ways. First, for the US government, for which Colombia ranks the third-largest recipient of military aid in the world, the threat to an important source of petroleum supply located in the even more oil-rich and strategically important Andean region has reshaped the debate about military interventionism. For the Colombian government, the 'national interest' in protecting a major source of state revenue has provided new forms of discursive legitimacy for counter-insurgency actions, and more importantly has reshaped forms of military deployment with an increasing number of troops and resources deployed to protect energy infrastructure. Multinational corporations, meanwhile, have become more directly enmeshed in domestic security provisioning, bringing new actors – like private security agencies, some of which also serve as US government contractors – into the complex relationships linking oil and violence.

This article is structured as follows. In the first section, we analyse the relationship of the intensification of multinational direct investment in energy and the subsequent growth of Colombia as an oil exporter to the political economy of Colombia's internal conflict. This conflict appeared to threaten a growing source of revenue to the Colombian state and an alternative source of oil supply to the United States – a fact which provides the logical link to our second section, focused on the geopolitical dimension of the nexus between oil and conflict. Here, we outline the perceived importance to some US lawmakers and successive US administrations of 'stabilizing' a country located in the oil-rich Andean region, and we trace the process leading to the adoption of the pipeline protection programme. In the third section, we consider how these two transnational dimensions (multinational direct investment and energy geopolitics) intersect to reconfigure the terms of conflict on the ground, using the case of a massacre of civilians as an illustration of the broader linkages between the local, national and geostrategic dimensions of oil and conflict, and the ways in which 'local security patterns may be subordinated to the security imperatives of external actors'.[12] In the fourth section, we discuss the relationship between arguments about 'national security' to the incidence of petro-violence and the legitimation of local conflict, placing this relationship within our broader analytic framework. Finally, we conclude with a brief discussion of the potential utility of this conceptual framework for building a more general understanding of resource conflicts.

Oil and the Political Economy of Conflict in Colombia

Colombia became a net oil exporter in the mid-1980s, after Occidental's Caño Limón discovery of major deposits of approximately 500 million barrels of recoverable crude.[13] British Petroleum's Cusiana-Cupiagua field also helped production grow from around 100,000 barrels per day (bpd) in the early 1980s to top 800,000 bpd in 1999. Pipeline attacks, coupled with a downswing at Cusiana-Cupiagua and the depletion of Caño Limón, lowered output to an average 604,000 bpd in 2001. In conjunction with slower-than-anticipated results on new finds, output projections dropped to around 536,000 for 2003, prompting warnings that without new finds Colombia would again become a net oil importer. However, petroleum analysts simultaneously stress Colombia's untapped potential, and a combination of factors suggests that future, significant increases of production and reserves are plausible.[14] Between mid-2001 and March 2002, foreign investors tapped three new significant fields.[15] In late February 2002, Ecopetrol's president Alberto Calderon Zuleta announced that the next presidential administration would enjoy a petroleum 'harvest'.[16] Colombia vacillates between number five and number ten of the top foreign oil suppliers to the United States. Approximately half of Colombian oil, which provided the country with its largest source of foreign exchange and accounted for 35 per cent of export revenues in 2000, is exported to the United States (Figure 1).[17]

The growth of oil production and exports, and the role of foreign direct investment in this process, has given rise to new links between Colombia's internal conflict and oil exploitation. Oil monies obtained through official or illegal channels have paid all sides in the conflict, providing not only the state and its armies but also armed insurgents and in some cases, paramilitary groups with increased material capacity to wage war. Though

FIGURE 1

COLOMBIAN OIL PRODUCTION AND CONSUMPTION, 1980–2000

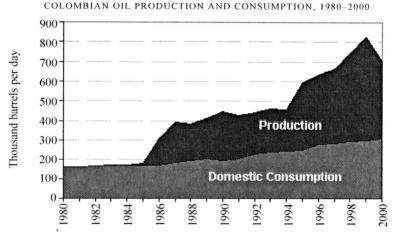

Source: EIA

a set of pre-existing grievances powerfully contribute to the origins and maintenance of internal warfare in Colombia, oil resources provide economic opportunities that both help perpetuate this conflict and also reshape the logic of violence on the ground. Struggles for control over strategic oil-rent producing areas adds a new territorial dimension to the conflict. Oil thus plays a significant role in sustaining violence, providing additional evidence to support recent arguments about the importance of resource predation in civil wars.[18] A brief outline of the actors enmeshed in Colombia's internal conflict, and their relationship to the oil/predation nexus, is helpful.

Guerrillas

In the late 1990s, Colombian guerrillas were estimated to be reaping around $140m per year from oil-related extortion and kidnaps,[19] compared to an estimated $200m to $500m from the cocaine and heroin trades.[20] Analysts and journalists have linked the revival in the mid-1980s of the ELN, the country's second largest guerrilla group, to $4m in extortion payments reportedly received from a German contractor involved in the construction of the Caño Limón-Coveñas pipeline. The group was allegedly reduced at the time to less than 40 members.[21] According to the US State Department, the ELN today numbers between 3,000 and 6,000.[22]

   Both the ELN and the FARC, Colombia's largest guerrilla group, have extracted so-called 'war taxes' from oil companies and local contractors using kidnaps, extortion and bombings of oil pipelines as leverage. In his testimony before a sub-committee of the United States House of Representatives in February 2000, Occidental Petroleum's Vice-President for Executive Services and Public Affairs, Lawrence P. Meriage, said: that the company's contractors paid a 'war tax' to rebels and that local workers 'in our installations find themselves obliged to pay for their 'protection' or put at risk the security of themselves and their families'.[23] When Occidental developed the Caño Limón field, the company's founder and former CEO told the *Wall Street Journal* in 1985, referencing Colombia: 'We are giving jobs to the guerrillas ... we take care of the local population. It has worked out so far, and they in turn protect us from other guerrillas.'[24]

Rebels in Arauca also divert money paid to municipalities from oil royalties by forcing contractors of public works projects to pay them a percentage.[25] At times, contractors may be doubly charged – paying off both the FARC and the ELN so work can proceed unimpeded. Situations have been reported where guerrilla informants working inside municipal offices influence who receives public works contracts: those businesses favoured are ones willing to provide rebels with a cut.[26] In January 2003, a probe by the National Royalties Commission and the Prosecutor General's Office of these types of irregularities and oil money corruption in general, led to federal intervention in the management of royalty payments in Arauca. Royalties were allegedly one element motivating FARC rebels in the late 1990s to expand their presence in Arauca – and to increase pipeline bombings in an attempt to wrest rents channelled to the ELN.[27] A violent struggle over control of royalties ensued.

Finally, rebels have openly declared war on both foreign oil firms and Ecopetrol, turning civilian personnel and workers as well as installations into rebel military targets. Half of the kidnappings committed in the world and an estimated one-third of terrorist attacks take place in Colombia, a large portion of them by guerrillas, and many against oil installations and company employees.[28] In one mass kidnap in April 2001, the ELN abducted, and later released, 100 Occidental workers who were leaving Caño Limón.

According to National Planning Department (DNP) statistics, guerrillas have dynamited Colombia's pipelines more that 1,000 times in the past 13 years, spilling 2.9 billion barrels of crude, damaging fragile ecosystems and water sources, causing environmental destruction and economic losses. In the case of the Caño Limon-Coveñas pipeline alone, nearly $1bn in losses were sustained from 1990 to 1995 – equivalent to around 7 per cent of Colombia's total export revenues of $13bn, according to DNP statistics. Attacks totalled 152 in 2000 and 170 in 2001 – setting new records each year.[29]

FIGURE 2

COLOMBIAN OIL PIPELINES

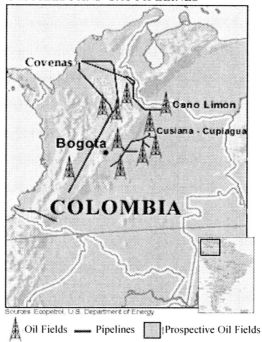

OIL FIELDS AND GAS PIPELINES

Covenas

Cano Limon

Cusiana - Cupiagua

Bogota

COLOMBIA

Sources: Ecopetrol, U.S. Department of Energy

Oil Fields ▬▬ Pipelines ☐ Prospective Oil Fields

Source: Ecopetrol.

Extralegal Mercenaries: Paramilitaries

Right-wing paramilitaries, to whom the majority of massacres and extra-judicial killings in Colombia are attributed, have moved into oil-rich provinces like Casanare, Arauca and Northern Santander to the east, Putumayo to the south, and the central Magdalena Valley. As Nazih Richani asserts, paramilitaries 'control an important sector through which the pipelines pass'. In the late 1990s, 'the prime objectives' of the forces of two major paramilitary leaders, Victor Carranza and Carlos Castaño, included 'establishing and consolidating a buffer zone that could diminish the guerrillas' influence in the surroundings of the pipelines'. The goal of this strategy is not only to 'push the guerrillas from villages located in the pipeline areas' but also to 'deny the guerrillas the extraction of protection rents that they obtained from the oil companies'.[30]

In the city of Barrancabermeja, in the Magdalena Valley, home to Colombia's largest oil refinery, paramilitaries intensified a campaign of murdering civilians in January 2001. Barrancabermeja is also home to the powerful state oil workers union, the *Union Sindical Obrera* (USO), which has drawn attention from international human rights organizations, given the assassinations of 85 USO members and the disappearances of two more since 1998. Lt.-Col. Hernán Moreno, head of the city's Nueva Granada Battalion, said of Barrancabermeja: 'Here, we pump out all the energy we need. The takeover of power is thus of prime importance to these armed groups.'[31] One human rights report on oil and security in Colombia claims paramilitaries in one region gleaned $2m from offering pipeline protection.[32] The Bogotá daily *El Espectador*, the London *Guardian* and the BBC reported an alleged link during the time of the construction of the Ocensa pipeline between British Petroleum, local military officials, foreign private security contractors, and paramilitaries, which the company denied. Paramilitary chief Carlos Castaño told a Bogotá newspaper that the paramilitaries 'tax the multinationals as the guerrillas do'.[33]

Paramilitaries have also built a cottage industry stealing gasoline by drilling holes in pipelines and transporting fuel, costing state oil company Ecopetrol $5m per month.[34] Reports indicate that in the Middle Magdalena valley, paramilitary groups routinely perforate pipelines with valves up to a dozen times a night and sell the gasoline on the sly to service stations or at reduced gallon prices along major departmental thoroughfares.[35] Paramilitaries, similar to the guerrillas, also allegedly benefit by capturing rents from construction contracts in oil zones, which in turn allows them to strengthen their presence in these strategic areas.[36] This presence and the control it implies in strategic areas rich in resources is believed to undercut guerrillas' territorial and political autonomy, as well as their material ability to wage war.[37]

Legal Mercenaries: Security Contractors and Multinational Corporations

An investigative report published in March 2002 in the *Los Angeles Times*, outlines the relationship between multinational oil corporations operating in Colombia and legal, private security firms, commonly based in the United States. According to the report, beginning in 1997, Occidental's operators in Colombia contracted the services of AirScan, 'a private U.S. company owned by former Air Force commandos'. For at least six months, the firm was to provide Occidental with high-tech surveillance of the pipeline and tracking of guerrilla movements. However, after the military requested more leeway for AirScan personnel to assist with operations far from the pipeline, Occidental officials received advice from the US embassy that AirScan should stick to protecting the pipeline. Soon thereafter the company transferred its contract with AirScan to the Colombian air force, an arrangement paid for by Ecopetrol.[38] In December 1998, a Colombian air force helicopter crew, accompanied by AirScan pilots, allegedly dropped a cluster bomb that massacred 17 civilians, including seven children, in the village of Santo Domingo, located just 30 miles south of Caño Limón's installations in the Arauca department.[39] The *Los Angeles Times* reports that Occidental 'provided crucial assistance to the operation ... directly or through contractors', including, 'troop transportation, planning facilities and fuel to the Colombian military aircraft, including the helicopter crew accused of dropping the bomb'.[40]

Richani cites a similar security relationship between British Petroleum, the British security company Defence Systems Limited and its Israeli counterpart, Silver Shadow, for pipeline protection in the Antioquia department during a period of heightened paramilitary massacres. These security contractors allegedly designed military and psychological strategies 'against the social base of the guerrillas'.[41] In sum, Richani asserts:

> Multinational corporations provide an opportunity for the extraction of protection rent exacerbating a competition between multi-national security companies and the local actors of the war system. Such a condition consolidates the war system as a modality for the distribution of protection rent among the contending forces.[42]

Military

The Colombian army receives significant income from the protection of oil. Beginning in 1992, a 'war tax' of roughly $1 per barrel on foreign oil corporations helped the army to dramatically increase troop presence in oil-producing regions.[43] In 1996, General Harold Bedoya, the army commander at the time, estimated that half of Colombia's troops were engaged full-time in protecting oil and mining installations.[44] Five years later, Brigadier General Carlos Lemus, the commander of the XVIII Brigade in Arauca, told a reporter that two-thirds of Colombian troops were protecting and monitoring oil facilities.[45] In 1997, the Office of the People's Ombudsman, said public funds destined to the security of oil installations were 'enormous.'[46]

Occidental alone estimated in 1997 that roughly 10 per cent of its in-country operating budget was destined to security, most of it through payments to the Colombian army.[47] According to another estimate by Occidental officials, the company has provided $750,000 a year in cash and in-kind payments to the Colombian military for logistics.[48] Ecopetrol, meanwhile, pumped $12m into the armed forces, $2.5m to a single battalion in the department of Casanare.[49]

The situation outlined above suggests that diverse degrees of territorial control by different actors in strategic territories, and competition for that control, creates a complicated panorama of resource-related conflict. According to a Colombian economist who studies the energy sector – in the past, when a particular armed group has supplanted the state as the monopolist of violence in a certain zone, companies or contractors will often 'comply with the existing authority' which is supplying services the state cannot. In zones where one or another group has fairly homogenous control, then, relationships are simplified: 'extortion is already factored in, monthly payments are made, there is no problem,' he said. But when no one group dominates, 'when a company must begin to pay off several groups – be they guerrillas, paramilitaries, or common criminals – that's when they prefer to pay off their own group to finish off the others'.[50] This 'push' can shift toward militarization to attempt official resumption of control, as in the request for army protection of pipelines and installations; or control may be further privatized through independent security contractors.

Thus far, we have described the processes by which the intensification of oil production and export has made control of resource-rich territory and/or rents a strategic objective for all of the parties involved in Colombia's internal conflict. The state's military apparatus has been deployed to protect an increasingly important source of fiscal revenue, which guerrilla groups have attacked and from which illegal paramilitary groups have also benefited. Multinational companies and their local security contractors have emerged as central to this story, both as a source of rents for legal and illegal armed groups and as a private entity for whom security arrangements, and militarization, have also played a key role.

Crucially, it is the threat to the supply of oil generated by this 'on the ground' conflict that provides the logical link to the subject of the following section – the global geopolitical dimension of the oil/conflict nexus. The global strategic nature of oil and energy security and the importance of protecting foreign sources of oil supply have been invoked by private companies and government representatives to convince US policymakers not only to increase military aid and the scope of US intervention, but to re-direct it to broader causes, including more direct counter-insurgency roles *vis-à-vis* protection of vital energy sources. In the next section, we place Colombian oil production in the broader context of the Andean supply of crude, where its strategic importance becomes more obvious, and we link the response of US policy to a military doctrine that increasingly privileges the protection of global sources of natural resource imports.

The Geopolitics of '300 Strategic Points'

Colombia's growing role as a supplier of crude oil to the United States and the presence of US and other multinational investors in the country's energy sector, played an important role in the build up of US military assistance to Colombia. This was the case even prior to a February 2002 aid request, in which funding extended beyond counter-narcotics efforts to include the protection of an oil pipeline partially owned and operated by Occidental Petroleum. As far back as 1998, General Charles Wilhelm, then head of the US Southern Command, told Congress that oil discoveries had increased Colombia's 'strategic importance'.[51] In April 2000, Senator Bob Graham and former National Security Adviser Brent Scowcroft, warned that Colombia's reserves, amounting to 'only slightly less than OPEC members Qatar, Indonesia and Algeria', would 'remain untapped unless stability is restored'.[52] As Senator Paul Coverdell commented when he introduced legislation for Plan Colombia, the original $1.3bn anti-narcotics military aid package approved by Congress in 2000:

> A decade ago the United States went to war with a powerful enemy partly to stabilize a major oil-producing region ... The oil picture in Latin America is strikingly similar to that of the Middle East, except that Colombia provides us more oil today than Kuwait did then.[53]

The centrality of energy issues in this policy debate reflected not only Colombia's but, especially, the Andean region's importance as an oil hub. For example, in 2000, Scrowcroft and Graham warned:

> Our nation's interests in the Andean region extend beyond helping to target the source of this drug flow. The struggle between insurgents and the Colombian government has bled into neighbouring nations ... Particularly troubling is the fact that one of those nations – Venezuela – is our largest petroleum supplier.[54]

Coverdell echoed the argument: 'The destabilization of Colombia directly affects bordering Venezuela, now generally regarded as our largest oil supplier.'[55] Recent political instability in Venezuela, including the attempted *coup d'état* against President Hugo Chávez on 11 April 2002, and the December 2002–February 2003 general strike which sought unsuccessfully to force him from power, disabled that country's oil sector, and in combination with uncertainty about Iraq in world oil markets, helped drive the price of oil above $36 a barrel. These events have helped to demonstrate further the US interest both in stabilizing the Andean region as a whole and in diversifying its import sources within the region, a strategic objective noted by Colombian analysts. Suggesting that the defiantly anti-

FIGURE 3

US OIL IMPORTS BY SOURCE

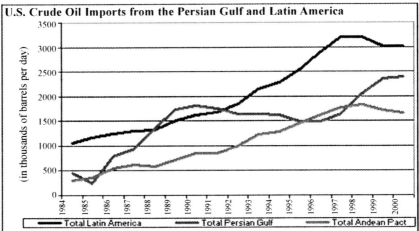

U.S. Crude Oil Imports from the Persian Gulf and Latin America

U.S. imports from the Persian Gulf are from Iran, Iraq, Kuwiat, Qatar, Saudi Arabia and United Arab Emirates. Imports from Latin America are from Brazil, Colombia, Ecuador, Mexico, Trinidad and Tobago and Venezuela.

(Data from U.S. Department of Energy, graph by the Center for Public integrity)

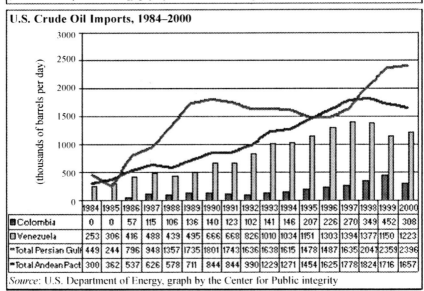

U.S. Crude Oil Imports, 1984–2000

	1984	1985	1986	1987	1988	1989	1990	1991	1992	1993	1994	1995	1996	1997	1998	1999	2000
Colombia	0	0	57	115	106	136	140	123	102	141	146	207	226	270	349	452	308
Venezuela	253	306	416	488	439	495	666	668	826	1010	1034	1151	1303	1394	1377	1150	1223
Total Persian Gulf	449	244	796	948	1357	1735	1801	1743	1636	1638	1615	1478	1487	1635	2047	2359	2396
Total Andean Pact	300	362	537	626	578	711	844	844	990	1229	1271	1454	1625	1778	1824	1716	1657

Source: U.S. Department of Energy, graph by the Center for Public integrity

US attitude of Chávez 'keeps U.S. strategists awake at night,' the former Colombian ambassador to the United States, Gabriel Silva, commented in the Colombian newspaper *El Tiempo*:

> This combination of a sensitive increase in risk to extra-regional supplies of petroleum, coupled with a progressively more and more hostile and messianic regime in the main supplier in the Americas, has forced the U.S. government to secure alternative sources of oil. This is the crossroads in which Colombia appears as a new strategic priority. The geopolitical re-evaluation of our country is something we should not misuse.[56]

On 5 February 2002, US officials announced an important shift in the reach and rhetoric of US policy in Colombia, one that reflected Silva's predictions. The Bush administration would ask the US Congress to funnel an additional $98m in fiscal year 2003 for military aid (22.3 per cent of the yearly military request for Colombia) to train an élite Colombian army brigade 'to protect the country's economic lifeline, an oil pipeline' from attacks by the FARC.[57] Trained by US Green Berets or contract employees, the XVIII Brigade of the Colombian army would incorporate approximately 2,000 troops and a mobile infantry unit skilled in surveillance and rapid deployment tactics, moving beyond anti-narcotics missions to protect the 480-mile Caño Limón-Coveñas pipeline.[58] A contingent of 70 US Special Forces troops was deployed to Arauca to begin the protection programme between December 2002 and January 2003.[59]

Prior to the announcement of the pipeline protection plan, in January 2002, Colombian officials visiting Washington lobbied to convince US authorities to extend the scope of US military assistance beyond the limits of anti-narcotics.[60] In the aftermath of a serious spate of FARC bombings of crucial infrastructure – electrical pylons, bridges, the edges of reservoirs, and pipelines[61] – Colombian President Andrés Pastrana appealed to the pervasive anti-terrorist climate in the United States, placing resources at the centre of both US and Colombian security affairs: 'Today the world is ready to unite against those who are attacking the interests of nations – and in this case the interest is energy.'[62] US Ambassador to Colombia, Ann Patterson, cited US strategic and corporate interests as well. Although she said protecting the pipeline, just one of 300 existing 'infrastructure points' in Colombia she defined as strategic to US interests, was outside the legal anti-narcotics boundary previously set for US military aid, 'it is something we have to do ... It is important for the future of the country (Colombia), for our petroleum supplies and for the confidence of our investors.'[63]

This strategic shift in aid and training provides evidence for Michael Klare's assertion that US military strategy has refocused on the protection of strategic natural resource supplies and economic security:

As the American economy grows and U.S. industries come to rely more on imported supplies of critical materials, the protection of global resource flows is becoming an increasingly prominent feature of American security policy. This is evident not only in the *geographic* dimensions of strategy – the growing emphasis on military operations in the Persian Gulf, the Caspian and other energy producing areas – but also in its *operational* aspects. Whereas weapons technology and alliance politics once dominated the discourse on military affairs, American strategy now focuses on oil-field protection, the defense of maritime trade routes, and other aspects of resource security.[64]

The Colombian pipeline programme, therefore, must be understood in the context of what Klare has termed the 'emergence of a new geography of conflict ... in which competition over vital resources is becoming the governing principle behind the disposition and use of military power'.[65] Thus the global geopolitics of petroleum, and in particular its link to the US energy security doctrine, constitutes a second distinct transnational dimension in the nexus between oil and internal conflict.

To be sure, the decision to provide US military funding to protect an oil pipeline owned and operated by a subsidiary of a US company suggests the extent to which this global geopolitical dimension can be linked to the first dimension of foreign direct investment. Energy companies operating in Colombia have become increasingly enmeshed in the debate over US government military policy regarding Colombia, spending millions on lobbying efforts and donating hundreds of thousands of dollars to campaign funds.[66] Occidental's Meriage, testifying to a House subcommittee hearing on Plan Colombia in 2000, urged the expansion of Plan Colombia's geographic scope to include the region housing Occidental's assets in the Northeast.[67] According to retired US Special Forces intelligence sergeant Stan Goff, who trained Colombian anti-narcotics troops, the aim of Plan Colombia was 'defending the operations of Occidental, British Petroleum and Texas Petroleum and securing control of future Colombian fields ... The main interest of the United States is oil.'[68]

In short, the strategic nature of oil and the economization of international security affairs contributed to a reconstruction and expansion of the US military role in Colombia, moving it closer to counter-insurgency.[69] The protection of energy infrastructure became an increasing preoccupation of international actors, while military intervention to secure oil production was invoked as a legitimate response to 'on the ground' conflict by both the Colombian state and the United States. Local conflict around oil generated a perceived threat to supply that was met by a geopolitical response, the strategic objectives of which were formulated with respect to a global frame of reference. But if the causal arrow logically runs upwards from the growth of local oil production and processes of local conflict to the global geopolitical dimension, there is also a feedback effect in which this dimension contributes to reshaping the incidence and character of local conflict. In the following section, we bring these reciprocal effects together in an analysis of the way in which local processes of conflict are subsequently transformed by this transnational dimension.

Local Conflict and Transnational Linkages

In this section, we discuss an example that illustrates some of the local consequences of the embeddedness of the relationship between oil and conflict in a variety of regional, national and transnational spaces. This is the alleged aerial bombing, mentioned earlier in this article, by the Colombian armed forces in 1998 of civilians in the village of Santo Domingo in Arauca province, which has become a controversial human rights case in Colombia. The case illustrates the mix of local, national and transnational-national actors and the intersection of a wide nexus of local and global fields of action and actors that we have argued is key to understanding the relationship of oil and violence in Colombia. It also adds to this complex picture the reduced accountability that ensues when public security functions are increasingly assumed by private actors.

In this case, two pilots employed by a company that had previously been under contract with Occidental Petroleum, allegedly helped direct Colombian air force pilots who dropped a cluster bomb from a Huey helicopter, killing 18 civilians, including seven children, in the town of Santo Domingo in Colombia's Arauca department. According to an investigative report published in the *Los Angeles Times* and based on court records and interviews, on 13 December 1998, a day after an engagement between the armed forces and FARC guerrillas near Santo Domingo, military officials from the air force and from the army's 18th Brigade gathered at Occidental Petroleum's Caño Limón headquarters, located 30 miles north of the town. The purpose of the meeting, according to the *Los Angeles Times*, was to plan the rescue of an army company that had been trapped by the FARC during fighting the day before. According to the *Times*, during a briefing with military officials, two pilots employed by AirScan, a private Florida-based company that had been hired on previous occasions by Occidental to provide surveillance of the Caño Limón pipeline, showed aerial videotape of the village and 'pointed out guerrillas who they said could be seen in the town, mingling with civilians'. Colombian air force pilots later told the *Times* that AirScan employees routinely supported Colombian military operations all over Arauca, providing surveillance of guerrilla movements. According to one armed forces crew member involved in the Santo Domingo operations, 'If there were confrontations between the army and guerrillas (AirScan operatives) were always there. They were our eyes.' Another said that AirScan employees 'frequently strayed from their missions to help us in operations against the guerrillas'.[70]

Although military officials initially claimed that the cluster bomb was dropped far from the town and that the deaths of the civilians were the result of a car bomb set by the guerrillas, government prosecutors and subsequent videotaped evidence revealed that the bomb was dropped from a helicopter directly on the villagers. Two Air Scan pilots, flying in a separate plane with a Colombian air force officer, helped direct the operation.[71] Colombian federal prosecutors sent metal fragments taken from the bodies of two deceased villagers to the FBI, which identified the shrapnel as 'consistent' with a US-made AN-M41 cluster bomb.[72] There is dispute as to whether the targeting of the civilians was intentional or an accident. Videotape conversation also 'makes clear that the pilots were in constant contact with a commanding officer at Caño Limón, the name of [Occidental's] oil complex.'[73]

During an initial stage, the *Times* reported that as part of the investigations of the killings it was difficult to trace the actions and whereabouts of the AirScan employees precisely because their status in the country was unclear. Although AirScan, a foreign-based private security company, was originally contracted by a US oil company, its employees became increasingly enmeshed in providing counter-insurgency assistance to the Colombian armed forces in a strategic oil-rich zone where US multinational oil interests were under attack. At the time of the Santo Domingo incident, AirScan was apparently in the pay of the Colombian state oil concern, Ecopetrol. In January 2003, the US State Department banned military assistance to the air force unit involved in the case.[74]

This case reveals the ways in which the agendas of local, national and transnational actors related to conflict over oil overlap and the ways in which conflict is reshaped by these intersections on the ground. It illustrates the complex interactions that occur when the security priorities of external economic actors – in this case two private American companies, in league with Colombian government actors – are embedded in a local context of conflict, and it highlights the consequence of this for local communities. It thus underscores the importance of a linkages approach.

The reality that various entities and groups create mechanisms and employ different actors to protect oil-derived revenues, provides only a partial illustration of the role of transnational linkages in fostering the relationship between oil and conflict. Petroleum production is accompanied by arguments that aim to legitimate particular uses of security forces or rebel violence. For example, the Colombian state claims by destining resources to protect oil installations, it is defending the 'national interest' – its pillar of export revenues and development monies. Government officials cite the increasing role of petroleum exports in the national budget to defend the legitimacy of devoting troops and resources, including augmented US counter-insurgency aid, to the protection of pipelines. Insurgents, meanwhile, attempt to legitimate attacks on oil installations, kidnappings and charging of extortion/protection rents by claiming foreign operations are illegitimate and imperialist. These important discursive aspects of the relationship between oil and conflict are embedded in transnational processes and the context of the broader global economy, as we argue in the fourth and final section below.

Legitimization, Petro-Violence and National Security

To understand the ways in which national states and multinational companies legitimate private or official militarization of oil infrastructure, on the one hand, and belligerents, on the other, justify attacks on oil infrastructure, it is important to consider claims made about the broader social and economic effects of petroleum development. In Colombia, proponents of US military assistance to petroleum-producing regions suggest that economic development through oil extraction, in the end, will allow the Colombian state to fight and win the war, and thus provide for the common good. For example, Occidental Petroleum Vice-President Meriage highlighted to the US Congress that the failure to develop new petroleum fields could have a 'devastating impact on [Colombia's] balance of payments and impede the government's efforts to stage a recovery from what is currently among the worst economic recessions in the country's history'.[75] Extending military assistance to oil development regions, Meriage argued, would strengthen the local presence of the Colombian state and thereby promote stability and overall economic recovery. By creating employment alternatives, improving infrastructure, supplying social investment, and providing resources for enhanced government presence in areas occupied by guerrillas and drug traffickers, Meriage's logic was that oil development operations would moderate the impact of narcotics wars. Another statement in this vein was the full-page advertisement in 1996 in major North American newspapers, sponsored by multinational oil companies, Ecopetrol and the Colombian Chamber of Petroleum Services, which touted 'a powerful new weapon … in the war against drugs'. The ad displayed the nozzle of a gas pump.[76]

Despite linkages of oil to the persistence of conflict, Colombian officials commonly stress that the failure to find and develop new oil resources would spell economic disaster for Colombia if the country reverts to net imports of oil. The extensive 'resource curse' literature in economics and political science has raised a set of important questions about the validity of the claim that oil exports foster economic and political progress, an empirical issue that lies beyond the scope of this article.[77] For purposes of understanding the relationship of oil to the legitimation of conflict, the important point is that the development of new oil production zones becomes deeply entwined with discourses of the 'national interest' and the 'common good'. As Michael Watts succinctly described,

> State landed property necessarily converts oil into a theatre of struggle in which its *national* qualities are paramount – an 'oil nation', 'our oil,' and so on ... Oil is unavoidably an engagement with some of the largest and most powerful forces of transnational capital (who show up on the local doorstep) and with all the contradictions of a pact (hardly a social contract) – a Faustian bargain – in which a national project (modernity, development, La Gran Venezuela) – exchanged for sovereignty, autonomy, independence, tradition and so on ...[78]

Claims to defend the 'national interest' take place in the context of Colombia's perceived relationship to the international economy and to transnational and multinational actors. This perceived relationship defines the ways in which notions of 'national interest' and 'common good' are deployed, not just by transnational investors and the Colombian government but also by rebel groups. Rebels, especially the ELN, have legitimated their attacks on multi-national investments with arguments that echo premises of the 1970s' dependency theory:

> Our country's energy and biodiversity riches have allowed it not to be positioned as a peripheral country within the capitalist circuit of accumulation. But this advantage keeps it subordinated to the North American strategic objective of national security and the present day and future biodiversity and energy needs of the United States, as well as to the usurious behaviour these resources create among the governing *criolla* class that turns them over and profits from them as if they were their patrimony – socially and politically marginalizing our people who are fragmented regionally ... The sacrifice of consumption of our population has run parallel to the satisfaction of the consumption of the countries of the capitalist world that are considered the 'centre.'[79]

In April 2002, the ELN expanded its justification for attacks on oil installations to include 'defence and conservation of natural resources for Colombians' in the face of 'the wars against terrorism which serve as masks for the appetite of the imperial countries and multinationals for the world's oil'.[80] The larger FARC consistently echo these arguments. Despite their own 'taxing' of companies with more than $1m in assets through self-declared Law 002, the FARC criticized Ecopetrol's supplying millions of dollars in 'war taxes' to the Colombian Armed Forces and emphasized external attacks on the solidity of the state oil concern.

Guerrilla groups have also attempted to obtain social and political capital, and to legitimate their pressure on multinationals, by negotiating with companies to provide funding for schools and public works projects in rebel controlled zones.[81] In April 2002, addressing the Second National Petroleum Conference, the ELN proposed a cease-fire of attacks on petroleum infrastructure if income saved from a decrease in security costs and repairs were invested in regional economic and social development.[82] Companies, in turn, have adopted strategic policies of 'good neighbour' relations and community development, providing everything from chess tournaments and fish ponds, to housing projects and university scholarships, and stressing the 'human face' of the petroleum industry, sustainable development alternatives and respect for culture and the environment.[83]

Such local initiatives notwithstanding, discourses of 'national interest' are commonly used to confront what are described as particularistic claims opposing oil development. Colombia's U'wa Indians, whose ancestral territory includes parts of the departments of Arauca, Boyacá, Norte de Santander and Santander, in which Occidental and more recently Ecopetrol have drilled for oil, waged a transnational campaign aimed at halting Occidental's Gibraltar well project. Occidental's Meriage claimed the U'wa Indians, by opposing oil development affecting their territory, were following their own 'narrow self-interests with total disregard for the harmful impact their actions have on the lives of 40 million Colombians'.[84] Yet indigenous peoples also frame their resistance in terms of the common good, critiquing the skewed results of national development models, and positing a different concept of national interests, human rights and global environmental protection. The U'wa, for example, claim their struggle to keep oil, 'the blood of mother earth,' in the ground will maintain spiritual and environmental equilibrium for their community and for the entire world.

Finally, it is important to note that the mobilization of the notion of the 'common good' or the 'national interest' by a range of political and social movements is often specifically related to the way oil production is embedded in transnational contexts. The *Union Sindical Obrera,* the powerful union of Colombia's oil sector whose struggle to nationalize oil created Ecopetrol, claims it is waging a 'patriotic fight' and 'democratic struggle' to 'establish clear rules that safeguard national interest', in order to protect Colombia's oil sovereignty, to counteract a neo-liberal/

multinational drive to privatize the state oil concern and reduce royalties in favour of transnational interests, and to prioritize the internal energy needs of all Colombians.[85]

Conclusion

The emerging literature on oil and conflict has done much to establish the empirical connection between variables, but much of it adheres to a national level of analysis. In this article, we have argued for the utility of a conceptual framework which takes account of the interactions between local and transnational actors as well. In Colombia, the re-intensification of foreign direct investment in local extractive activities, embedded within a pre-existing context of violence, has generated particular processes of conflict related to oil exploitation, concretely and discursively. These processes of conflict have posed a threat to the local operations of multinational companies as well as to global sources of supply. Coinciding with an increased willingness on the part of the United States to structure policy around the military protection of strategic energy sources, these interactions have generated a geopolitical response that has reconfigured both the material and rhetorical bases of conflict at the local level.

In recent decades, other resource-rich areas like the Caspian Sea basin, the Persian Gulf, sub-Saharan Africa, and elsewhere in South America, have variously witnessed the importance of both transnational dimensions we have identified in the Colombian case – i.e., the re-intensification of foreign direct investment in the energy sector and the global geopolitics of oil to which the first dimension often becomes linked. The question of the extent to which this conceptual framework will 'travel' beyond Colombia is therefore natural. Might closer attention to the relationship of the two transnational dimensions to local security arrangements in other contexts contribute to the construction of generalizations about the contemporary processes linking oil to local conflict?

A systematic answer to this question is beyond the scope of this article. But a brief examination of the dynamics of oil and conflict in Colombia's neighbour, Ecuador, supports our assertion of the significance of a local/transnational linkages approach in identifying security arrangements as important variables in shaping local conflict. The historical, social, economic and political relationships between oil development and conflict in Ecuador differ markedly from Colombia. Thus, we do not intend to provide a thorough comparison of the Ecuadorian case. We simply intend to illustrate the potential utility of conducting future research within the framework outlined through careful consideration of the Colombian case.

Conflict over resources, particularly oil, has different meanings in Ecuador. There are no national pre-existing guerrilla or paramilitary armies vying for territorial control or extracting rents through violence. Foreign direct investment, historically by the US multinational, Texaco, and more recently by a variety of companies, has long been a mainstay of Ecuador's oil industry. However, an intensification in recent years of new phases of foreign direct investment in the Ecuadorian oil sector, and an expansion of the 'oil frontier' deeper into the Amazonian region,[86] has begun to reshape the nature of conflict on the ground and has begun to introduce new security arrangements between domestic and transnational actors.

For example, private oil companies operating in Ecuador, along with the state oil concern Petroecuador, have recently reached an agreement whereby companies will allegedly pay the Ecuadorian army directly for oil-related security.[87] This arrangement comes at a time when social protests related to a substantial expansion of foreign direct investment in oil exploration and transport services has not only intensified, but has become acutely transnational in scope; on several occasions, these protests have been met with militarization.[88]

Geopolitically of concern to international investors, the Colombian conflict has spread across the country's southern border, complicating security in Ecuador's oil-rich northern Sucumbios province. Colombian insurgents have targeted energy infrastructure there, such as the existing Transandino pipeline, which pumps oil between Colombia and Ecuador, and which was bombed by the FARC 31 times in September 2000 alone.[89] More than 500,000 barrels in exports were held up by the bombing of this pipeline. The Ecuadorian military devotes some energy to protecting the TransEcuadorian tube, which links oil reserves in Ecuador's Oriente region to the Pacific Coast.[90]

This situation has not gone unnoticed by oil industry analysts. A 10 August 2001 report from the *Energy Compass*, an important US-based oil industry publication, highlighted the geopolitical concerns underlying this trend and their relationship to foreign direct investment. The publication noted that the bulk of Ecuador's oil production comes from those northern fields which are:

> close enough to the border that guerrilla groups – thought to originate in Colombia or to be influenced by Colombian rebels – have become a threat to operations. The groups have attacked Ecuador's main oil pipeline at least three times and have kidnapped 10 oil workers. And with the construction starting on a new heavy crude oil pipeline, companies are even more concerned about protecting their investment.[91]

Thus, as in Colombia, the dimension of security concerns related to foreign direct investment emerges in Ecuador. Moreover, the geostrategic concerns of transnational actors and US policymakers have begun to surface as potentially important variables shaping emerging local security arrangements there too. The intensification of multinational petroleum production and a spillover of Colombia's conflict into northern Ecuador comes at a time when US military aid and training, as well as direct US military presence, is increasing substantially in that country. In particular, approaching the relinquishment by the United States of control of the Panama Canal in 1999, the US Southern Command (South Com) reorganized, in part to increase the capacity of the US to respond to a litany of perceived threats that are specifically trans-border in nature. In addition to US operating posts inside Colombia, South Com added to its long-term strategy the opening of several new Forward Operating Locations (FOLs), the most notable of which is the 'Manta' air base on Ecuador's Pacific coast. Other new US Forward Operating Locations include Aruba, Curacao and El Salvador.

Thus the transnational linkages, broadly writ, that we have argued shape the relationship between oil and conflict in Colombia appear increasingly relevant, although of a different character, in the Ecuadorian case. These processes recall Le Billon's description of the

> restructuring of polities and commercial networks as countries become (selectively) incorporated into the global economy ... in a mutually dependent relationship which encourages and sustains armed conflicts, as the source of power becomes not political legitimacy but violent control over key nodes of the commodity chain.[92]

In short, in the establishment of control over nodes increasingly incorporated into the global economy, transnational actors and their local security arrangements become vitally important to understanding the incidence and character of local conflict. The development of oil production and export creates a new landscape of conflict, one in which struggles to control resource-rich territory become paramount for a variety of local/national/transnational actors. Yet these processes are embedded in a particular international political and geopolitical economy of resources. Thus, especially in the case of oil, the range of fundamental actors involved in these interactions has expanded well beyond the state and those opposed to it. To deepen our understanding of this nexus, we must find new ways to consider linkages and interactions among local, national and transnational actors and their relationship with the global economy.

ACKNOWLEDGEMENTS

We express our deepest gratitude to Terry Lynn Karl, who helped to launch us on this project. For their readings of earlier versions of this manuscript, we would also like to thank Hayward Alker, Jennifer Bussell, Marc Chernick, Catherine LeGrand, Arne Jacobson, Michael Ross, Suzana Sawyer, J. Ann Tickner, Michael Watts, members of the 'petro-group' at the University of California, Berkeley's Institute of International Studies, panellists at the International Studies Association's annual meeting in 2002, participants in conferences at the Center for Latin American Studies at Stanford University, the Hemispheric Institute on the Americas at the University of California at Davis, and the Universidad de los Andes, Bogotá, Colombia, and the two anonymous referees. Leslie Wirpsa gratefully acknowledges the Program on Global Security and Cooperation of the Social Science Research Council for support of fieldwork in Colombia. Any remaining errors are our own.

NOTES

1. See P Collier and A Hoeffler, 'On Economic Causes of Civil War', *Oxford Economic Papers* 50 (1998), pp.563–73; idem, *Greed and Grievance in Civil War*, World Bank Policy Research Working Paper 2355 (Washington DC, World Bank 2000). See also I de Soysa, 'The Resource Curse: Are Civil Wars Driven by Rapacity or Paucity?', in M. Berdal and D.M. Malone (eds), *Greed and Grievance: Economic Agendas in Civil Wars* (Boulder, CO: Lynne Rienner Publishers, 2000); M Ross, 'How Does Natural Resource Wealth Influence Civil War?', unpublished manuscript, Department of Political Science, University of California, Los Angeles, 2001.

2. Berdal and Malone (note 1), pp.4–5.

3. Ibid.

4. W Reno, 'Shadow States and the Political Economy of Civil Wars', in M. Berdal and D.M. Malone (eds), *Greed and Grievance: Economic Agendas in Civil Wars* (Boulder, CO: Lynne Rienner Publishers, 2000), p.44.

5. M Ross, 'Does Oil Hinder Democracy?', *World Politics*, Vol.53 (April 2001), pp.325–61.

6. For a history of the early period, see D. Yergin, *The Prize* (New York: Touchstone Books 1991).

7. See M. J. Watts, 'Petro-Violence: Some Thoughts on Community, Extraction, and Political Ecology,' Berkeley Workshop on Environmental Politics, Working Paper 99–1.

8. P Le Billon, 'The Political Ecology of War: Natural Resources and Armed Conflicts,' *Political Geography*, Vol.20 (2001), pp.561–84.

9. Berdal and Malone (note 1) p.2.

10. M.T. Klare, *Resource Wars: The New Landscape of Global Conflict* (New York: Metropolitan Books, Henry Holt and Company LLC 2001). See especially p.214, pp.28–9.

11. Colombia received $6m in FY 2002 Emergency Supplemental aid and $88m Foreign Military Financing (FMF) from the FY 2002 Foreign Operations Appropriations Bill. The administration's initial estimated request for FY 2004 for Colombia pipeline protection was $110m.

12. A.B. Tickner and A.C. Mason, 'Mapping Transregional Security Structures in the Andean Region', draft concept paper for a research project titled 'The Andean Security Complex', financed by the Grants for Research Collaboration in Conflict Zones Program, Social Science Research Council (SSRC), New York, Feb. 2002.

13. E. Pachón and L. Rodríguez, 'Revela el presidente de Ecopetrol: Viene otra 'cosecha' petrolera,' *El Espectador*, 24 Feb. 2002, pp.5–6 C.

14. In 2001 Ecopetrol set a goal of 1.3 million bpd production by 2010. A record 32 exploration contracts were signed with multinationals in 2000, with 28 more in 2001. While proven reserves are estimated at 2.6 billion barrels, projections of potential reserves range between 25 billion and 37 billion barrels. Oil company and government analysts persistently stress that only seven of 18 sedimentary basins with geological hydrocarbon potential have commercial production.

15. The finds included the Guando field, in Tolima department, discovered in June 2000 by

Canadian Occidental and Braspetro of Brazil, with an estimated 200 million barrels of recoverable crude; the Capachos field near Tame, Arauca, with 100 million barrels and a third field in the Upper Magdalena region. See 'Colombia' country profile, Energy Information Administration, <http://www.eia.doe.gov/emeu/cabs/colombia2.html>.

16. Pachón and Rodriguez (note 13).

17. Energy Information Administration, <http://www.eia.doe.gov/emeu/cabs/colombia2.html>.

18. See note 1.

19. 'Oil Boom Benefits Rebels', *Pittsburgh Post-Gazette*, 22 July 1996, citing a report in *El Tiempo*, 21 July 1996.

20. The Working Group on Colombia of the Council on Foreign Relations estimated that the FARC reap $300m annually from cocaine 'taxes'. See Working Group on Colombia, 'U.S. Interests and Objectives in Colombia: A Commentary,' Report of the Working Group on Colombia Sponsored by the Council on Foreign Relations (New York: CFR 2000). News reports commonly use the figure $500m. Colombian military sources claim guerrillas draw as much as $1bn from kidnapping, extortion and the drug trade.

21. 'Violence, Crime Continue to Cast Shadow Over Future Oil Investment in Colombia', *Oil and Gas Journal*, Vol.98, No.3 (17 Jan. 2000), p.32; 'Colombian Pipeline Hit by Sabotage Blitz,' *The Houston Chronicle*, 17 Sept. 2000.

22. US Department of State, Office of the Coordinator for Counter-terrorism, 'Appendix B: Background Information on Terrorist Groups', from the State Department's 'Patterns of Global Terrorism 2000' report, 30 April 2001, <http://www.state.gov/s/ct/rls/pgtrpt/2000/2450.htm> (accessed on 3 December 2002.

23. L.P. Meriage, 'Testimony of Lawrence P. Meriage, Vice President of Executive Services and Public Affairs, Occidental Oil and Gas Corporation, before the United States House of Representatives Government Reform Subcommittee on Criminal Justice, Drug Policy and Human Resources, Hearing on Colombia', 15 Feb. 2000.

24. Y Ibrahim, 'Black-Gold Mine: Discovery in Colombia Points Up Big Change in World Oil Picture', *The Wall Street Journal*, 13 May 1985.

25. Royalties are paid to municipalities and departments based on the volume of daily production per field or contract: up to 5,000 barrels a day (this includes approximately 85 per cent of fields) generate 5–8 per cent royalties; production between 5,000 and 125,000 bpd, the percentage rises steadily until it reaches 20 per cent (which is the flat percentage received by municipalities with fields that produce between 125,000 and 400,000 bpd). See <http://www.ecopetrol.com.co/paginas.asp?pub_id=713&cat_id=425&idCategoriaprincipal=8&8cat_tit=Responsabilidad%20Social%20y%20Ambiental>; and Gonzalo Castaño and Luisa Maria Nieves Camacho, *Empresas Petroleras Canadienses en Colombia* (Bogotá: Censat Agua Vida 2001).

26. 'Como intervienen las FARC en los presupuestos municipals de Arauca?', *El Tiempo*, 30 Jan. 2003.

27. T.C. Miller, 'Blood Spills to Keep Oil Wealth Flowing', *The Los Angeles Times*, 15 Sept. 2002.

28. See I Gómez *et al.*, 'Narcotics and Economics Drive U.S. Policy in Latin America', *The International Consortium of Investigative Journalists*, 12 July 2001, <http://www.public-i.org/story_02_071201.htm>.

29. Y. Ferrer, 'Rebel Attacks Hurt Exports While Prices Soar', *Interpress Service*, 19 Sept. 2000, p.6.

30. N. Richani, *Systems of Violence: The Political Economy of War and Peace in Colombia* (New York: State University of New York 2002) p.116.

31. J. Forero, 'Colombian Paramilitaries Adjust Attack Strategies', *New York Times*, 21 Jan. 2001.

32. *Drillbits and Tailings*, 21 Dec. 1997, citing 'Colombia: Human Rights Concerns Raised by the Security Arrangements of Trans-national Oil Companies,' *Human Rights Watch* (April 1998).

33. Quoted in Richani (note 30) p.125.

34. 'Paramilitares se financian con robo de combustible a ECOPETROL,' *El Tiempo*, 13 Nov. 2001.

35. F de Roux, speech presented at the Second National Petroleum Congress, Bogotá, 23–25 April 2002.

36. Comisión de Paz y Derechos Humanos de la Union Sindical Obrera (USO), 'Combustible

Para la Paz', paper presented at the Second National Petroleum Congress, Bogotá, 23–25 April 2002).
37. Richani (note 30) p.126.
38. However, reports indicate that the relationship between oil companies and private contractors remains an important part of the security protocol in Colombia.
39. T.C. Miller, 'A Colombian Village Caught in a Cross-Fire: The Bombing of Santo Domingo Shows How Messy U.S. Involvement in the Latin American Drug War Can Be', *Los Angeles Times*, 17 March 2002.
40. Ibid.
41. Richani (note 30) p.116.
42. Ibid.
43. J. Barret, 'Managing Energy Company Security Risks in Latin America', *Oil and Gas Journal*, Vol.95, No.23 (June 1997), pp.44–7.
44. J. Barret, 'Violence, Crime Continue to Cast Shadow Over Future Oil Investment in Colombia', *Oil and Gas Journal*, Vol.97, No.48 (29 Nov. 1999), p.21.
45. M. Hodgson, 'Oil Inflames Colombia's Civil War; Bush Seeks $98 Million To Help Bogotá Battle Guerrilla Pipeline Saboteurs', *Christian Science Monitor*, 5 March 2002.
46. J.F. Castro Caycedo, Defensor del Pueblo, *En Defensa del Pueblo Acuso: informe sobre impactos ambientales, económicos y sociales de la voladura de oleoductos en Colombia* (Bogotá: Defensoría del Pueblo 1997).
47. L. Wirpsa, 'Indians Threaten Mass Suicide to Safeguard Oil Rich Land', *National Catholic Reporter*, 20 June 1997.
48. Miller, 'A Colombian Village' (note 39).
49. Comisión de Paz y Derechos Humanos de la Union Sindical Obrera (USO), 'Combustible Para la Paz', paper presented at the Second National Petroleum Congress, Bogotá, 23–25 April 2002, p.2.
50. Interview, Bogotá, April 2002, confidentiality requested.
51. Wilhelm also compared Venezuela strategically to the Middle East, reminding that the country 'provides the same amount of oil to the U.S. as do all the Persian Gulf states combined'. See C.E. Wilhelm, '1998 United States Congressional Hearings: 21st Century Security Threats: Statement of Gen. Charles E. Wilhelm USMC, Commander in Chief, United States Southern Command Before the 105th Congress Committee on Armed Services, U.S. Senate', 5 March 1998, <http://www.fas.org/irp/congress1998_hr980305 w.htm>.
52. Brent Scowcroft and Bob Graham, *Los Angeles Times*, 26 April 2000.
53. P.D. Coverdell, 'Starting With Colombia', *The Washington Post*, 10 April 2000.
54. Scowcroft and Graham (note 52).
55. Coverdell (note 53).
56. G. Silva, 'Petróleo por Seguridad', *El Tiempo*, 12 Feb. 2002.
57. R. Scarborough, 'FARC triggers concern in US', *The Washington Times*, 11 Feb. 2002.
58. L. Tayler, 'Oil a Key to U.S. Role in Colombia: Protecting Pipeline a Big Part of the Equation', *Newsday*, 4 March 2002. Scarborough (note 57).
59. N.E. Karsin, 'Series of Blasts Shatters Short-Lived Colombian Peace: Violence Linked to a Backlash Over Oil Pipeline', *San Francisco Chronicle*, 12 Feb. 2003. F Robles, 'U.S. Trains Colombians to Protect Oil Pipeline: Green Berets Have Arrived', *Miami Herald*, 13 Dec. 2002.
60. D. Adams and P. de la Garza, 'Post Sept. 11, U.S. shifts to broader military role', *St. Petersburg Times*, 11 Feb. 2002.
61. J.P. Toro, 'Colombia Renews Pressure for U.S. Assistance to Strengthen Oil Sector Security', *Oil Daily*, 25. Jan. 2002.
62. Ibid.
63. C.I. Rueda G., 'E.U. cuidará sus intereses en Colombia', *El Tiempo*, 10 Feb. 2002.
64. Klare (note 10) p.6.
65. Klare (note 10) p.214. In 1980, President Jimmy Carter insisted that any attempt by hostile powers to constrict the flow of oil in the Persian Gulf would be 'repelled by any means necessary, including military force'. Klare (note 10) pp.4–5.
66. Gómez *et al.*, 'Narcotics and Economics Drive U.S. Policy in Latin America', p.2.
67. Meriage (note 23).
68. I Gómez, 'El objetivo de los E.U. es petróleo', *El Espectador*, 8 Oct. 2000.

69. For over a decade, US military policy in Colombia has been limited legally to anti-narcotics assistance; however, human rights organizations and policy analysts have frequently linked US support to the Colombian military, and indirect support for paramilitary groups, not only to counter-insurgency, but also to gross violations of human rights.
70. Miller, 'A Colombian Village' (note 39).
71. T. Christian Miller, 'Colombia: Videotape Shows Americans' Role in Village Bombing', *Los Angeles Times*, 16 March 2003.
72. A more recent FBI report stated that 'the size (of the elements of the bomb) was so small that they could not be identified' and thus the analysis produced 'negative results'; 'Molestia en E.U. por intento en Colombia de desviar investigación de bombardeo a Santo Domingo', *El Tiempo*, 23 Jan. 2003.
73. T. Christian Miller, 'U.S. Pair's Role in Bombing Shown', *Los Angeles Times*, 16 March 2003.
74. '1998 Bombing Cited as U.S. Decertifies Unit in Colombia', *Reuters*, 14 Jan. 2003.
75. Meriage (note 23).
76. B. Williams, 'Drugs, Oil Don't Mix', *Oil and Gas Journal*, 30 Sept. 1996.
77. T.L. Karl, *The Paradox of Plenty: Oil Booms and Petro-States* (Berkeley, CA: University of California Press 1997) and T. Karl, 'The Perils of the Petro-State: Reflections on the Paradox of Plenty', *Journal of International Affairs*, Vol.53, No.1 (Fall 1999), pp.32–48; J. Sachs and A. Warner, *Natural Resource Abundance and Economic Growth*, Harvard Institute for International Development, Development Discussion paper No.517 (1995); and M. Ross, 'The Political Economy of the Resource Curse', *World Politics*, Vol.51 (1999), pp.297–322.
78. Watts (note 7) p.7.
79. Ejército de Liberación Nacional, 'Una propuesta energética del ELN,' in *Petróleo en las Conversaciones de Paz* (Bogotá: Agenda Ciudadana para la Paz – INDEPAZ, Feb. 1999), pp.185–8.
80. Ibid.
81. Richani (note 30) p.86.
82. Ejército de Liberación Nacional, Comando Central, 'La Tregua: Una Oportunidad para Colombia,' press release, 23 April 2002, Bogotá.
83. N Wray, *Pueblos Indígenas Amazónicos y Actividad Petrolera en el Ecuador: Conflictos, Estrategias e Impactos (*Quito: Oxfam America Julio 2000).
84. Meriage (note 23).
85. See, for example, Unión Sindical Obrera, 'La USO y su Lucha por una Política Nacionalista', paper presented at the Second National Petroleum Congress, Bogotá, 23–25 April 2002.
86. Ecuador aims to boost oil production from 390,000 bpd to 612,000 bpd over the next four years, and increase exports to 456,400 bpd, with new Amazonian developments and a doubling of transport capacity through the controversial $1.3bn Heavy Crude Pipeline project, with investment from a consortium of six foreign oil companies and one construction firm. 'Ecuador plans to bump up output', *Energy Compass*, 17 April 2003.
87. 'Ecuadorean Producers to Pay Military Protection', *Energy Compass*, 10 Aug. 2001.
88. In February 2002, for example, municipal authorities, indigenous movements and local peasants in the north paralysed crude production for two weeks in the bi-provincial oil hub of Sucumbios and Orellana provinces, near the Colombian border. This region produces 60 per cent of Ecuadorian crude and contributes more than 40 per cent to the government's central budget. These strikes demanded that the consortium building the Heavy Crude Pipeline invest $10m in infrastructure and social projects as compensation and that the government improve local electricity services and roads. The government declared a state of emergency there, deploying security forces. At least one protester was killed by troops.
89. Ferrer (note 29); Steven Dudley, 'Rebels Pull the Plug on Colombian Exports', *The Washington Post*, 23 Nov. 2000.
90. See <http://www/amnesty-usa.org/justearth/countries/ecuador2.htm>, (accessed 22 March 2002).
91. 'Ecuadorean Producers' (note 87).
92. Le Billon (note 8) p.573.

From Free Oil to 'Freedom Oil': Terrorism, War and US Geopolitics in the Persian Gulf

PHILIPPE LE BILLON and FOUAD EL KHATIB

Persian oil ... is yours. We share the oil of Iraq and Kuwait. As for Saudi Arabian oil, it's ours.

President Roosevelt to British Ambassador (1944)[1]

Storming the Arabian Peninsula ... plundering its riches ... here come the crusader armies ... to annihilate what is left of the Iraqi people and to humiliate their Muslim neighbors ... despite the huge number of those [already] killed ... as thought they come not content with the protracted blockade imposed after the ferocious [Gulf] war ...

Fatwa by Bin Laden (1998)[2]

The war in Iraq has nothing to do with oil, not for us, not for the U.K., not for the United States ... we don't touch it, and the U.S. don't touch it. We cannot say fairer than that.

Prime Minister Tony Blair to MTV audience (2003)[3]

Introduction

The vast oil wealth of the Persian Gulf is a key dimension of geopolitics in the Middle East and an emblematic prize of so-called 'resource wars'.[4] After 'black gold' was discovered in Persia in 1908, this resource drastically exacerbated the stakes in the struggle over the spoils of the Ottoman empire and the Western security imperative to prevent the (re)emergence of a powerful regional rival. Following their victory over the 'German-Ottoman Axis' in the First World War, France and Britain extended their colonial control, drawing borders and occasionally selecting rulers, before the Second World War enabled the United States to assert a predominant role in the region, notably through the oil for security swap defining its 'special relationship' with the Saudi ruling family.[5] Western diplomatic and military support of friendly local regimes in the Persian Gulf was closely linked to the protection of western oil interests. Domestic threats to western oil interests were faced by military interference and destabilization efforts by

British intelligence and the Central Intelligence Agency (CIA), notably in Iran to topple Mossadegh's government in 1953 and reinstate the Shah or in Iraq to avoid the communists from taking power after the 1958 *coup d'état* or to retaliate against Baghdad's nationalization of the oil industry in 1972.[6] Beyond domestic threats, the fear of losing Middle East oil to the Soviet bloc, through a local left-leaning regime or an outright invasion, sustained a pro-active western policy maintained successively through British military forces, a 'surrogate strategy' based on Saudi and Iranian alliance, and since the 1980s, a permanent and increasingly pro-active military presence of the United States (see Figure 1). The end of the Cold War did not significantly shift this strategic stance, as government or opposition movements deemed hostile to western 'security interests' – such as Iran, Iraq, or Al Qaeda – continued to be perceived, or portrayed, as a threat justifying the continuation of such military doctrine. Yet beyond the threat to western and regional security that these may represent, what remains at stake is the access to the world's largest oil reserves.

Oil has not only motivated foreign interests in the region, but has also significantly affected the balance of power within and between regional states. The vast revenues available to states and the élites have drastically increased inequalities in wealth and power, which despite religious or nationalist ideologies and populist economic measures often exacerbated internal dissent and instability. If the existence and clout of states like Saudi Arabia did not initially emerge from oil wealth, but rather from the consolidation of local dynasties and Islamic legitimacy, oil wealth played a role in shifting the balance of economic and military power from the larger and agricultural countries in the region to the petro-states of the Persian Gulf through massive arms purchases, financial aid and remittances, as well as the clout of their powerful industrialized allies. Since at least the Iranian revolution in 1979, many western strategists have argued that the oil wealth exacerbates the 'inherently problematic' geopolitical structure of the Gulf, and calls for an active presence of outside (western) forces. On one hand, Iraq's strength was seen as unable to 'balance' Iran without threatening Saudi Arabia and the emirates of the Gulf, thereby justifying a US imperial posture in the Middle East and the controversial presence of troops on the 'holy soil' of the Arabian Peninsula.[7] On the other, the concentration of spare oil production capacity and 'reasonable price' policy of Saudi Arabia and some emirates have led Iran and Iraq to accuse them of privileging the economic interests of industrialized countries over those of the local populations.[8] Moreover, oil has enabled a military build up aggravating conflicts in the region, including that with Israel.

Oil has also lent greater importance to the territorialization of states and the definition of boundaries sometimes foreign to the political geography and lifestyles of the Arabian Peninsula.[9] As foreign companies have concentrated on gaining and sustaining their control of oil fields, local rulers have awarded concessions in border regions, hoping that the association of capitalist claims and backing of foreign troops would secure their share of the new-found wealth. Territorial disputes, such as the issue of the Iraqi access to the sea or the exploitation of cross-border oil fields, have been among the main reasons and justifications for armed conflicts in the region.[10] Protracted conflicts associated with oil, within and between competing regional states as well as foreign interests, have shaped a history of violent geopolitics in the region in which the terrorist attacks of '9/11' and the US-led military invasion and occupation of Iraq in March 2003 represent the most recent episodes.

This article reflects on the geopolitical implications of oil dependence and its violent dimensions for petro-states in the Persian Gulf in light of the US occupation of Iraq. The first section of the study briefly examines the links between oil dependence, governance, and armed conflicts in producing countries, as well as discursive constructions about oil and the power of associated narratives. The second reviews the 'mutual dependence' of oil producers and consumers in relation to the Persian Gulf. The third engages with the debate about the connections between oil, terrorism, and US policy in the region, focusing on the possible 'oil agenda' of the US 'war on terror' in Afghanistan and Iraq. Before concluding, the article discusses potential US policy moves from 'free oil' – securing militarily and politically free access to oil – to 'freedom oil', through which a better governance of oil in producing countries would provide freedom rather than authoritarianism to local populations and help resolve dilemmas between US energy and security agendas.

The 'Curse' of Petro-States

Interpreted as a key instrument of modernization and political emancipation for Arab nationalists, or a long-term financial rent by Muslim traditionalists – not to mention a 'weapon' against Israel – oil has turned out to be a curse for many of the people who succumbed to authoritarian regimes and devastating wars financed or motivated by what Juan Pablo Pérez Alfonzo, the co-founder of the Organization of Petroleum Exporting Countries (OPEC), called the 'devil's excrement'.[11]

Nationalization policies and the oil boom of the 1970s and early 1980s provided unprecedented wealth to the élites of most Persian Gulf countries, and in many of them oil revenues were widely distributed through welfare state policies.[12] Yet after more than a decade of rising oil prices, the collapse from \$52 to \$15 per barrel in the mid-1980s debilitated many oil-producing economies which had failed to diversify, and jeopardized their political systems. In Saudi Arabia, economic growth did not keep pace with rising population size and aspirations, resulting in a halving of per capita income over the next 15 years and growing inequalities between the extended royal family and most of the population. In Iraq, oil gave Iraqi leaders – most notably Saddam Hussein – the means to pursue (historically and personality-based) ambitions of leadership both in relation to Arab nationalism and towards military ventures in the region. Confronting a huge debt resulting from its military build up and its war with Iran, Iraq justified its invasion of Kuwait in 1990 by accusing it of tapping into cross-border oil fields and maintaining a low price policy which undermined Iraqi oil revenues, ultimately resulting in a devastating combination of war, economic sanctions, domestic rebellion and internal repression.[13]

Many other countries economically reliant on resource wealth have been characterized by poorer economic growth and lower standards of living, higher levels of income inequality and corruption, as well as political authoritarianism.[14] Although these problems characterize many developing countries unsurprisingly relying on raw material exports, some economists and political scientists assert that resource wealth can be more of a 'curse' than a 'blessing' given the trajectory of underdevelopment followed by many resource-rich countries.[15]

Resource dependence can have a number of adverse effects on governance and societies. Through a 'rentier' effect, governments can rely on fiscal transfers from resource rents, rather than statecraft, to sustain their regime.[16] Large resource rents independent of public taxation can result in a 'coercive' effect as rulers finance higher internal security expenditures, warding off democratic pressure domestically and inciting aggressive posturing and policies towards their neighbours and international norms. At a societal level, a 'non-modernisation effect' associated with the enclave economic nature of many extractive resource sectors, such as oil, can fail to bring about socio-professional and cultural changes that tend to promote democracy and a thriving civil society. Political scientist Michael Ross finds tentative support for all three of these effects in the case of oil exporters.[17] Corruption on a grand scale is facilitated by the secrecy and discretionary power of decision-makers as well as international competition over lucrative resource projects. If compounded by a lack of welfare-oriented fiscal policies, such governance generally results in high levels of inequality. Even without corruption, clientelist politics weaken state capacities, as benevolent governments come under pressure to relinquish resource rents and have to trade coherent economic policies, maximizing long-term welfare for short-term management of the demands of political constituencies and mitigation of social tension.[18]

The economy and politics of oil-dependent states are also affected by their propensity to spend more on defence.[19] The priority of military expenditures over civilian ones reflects the rulers' fears of domestic or regional opposition, corruption opportunities, as well as foreign incentives to trade resources for arms for the sake of mutually profitable political and resource flow stability. Since the 1970s, the arms build up in the Persian Gulf region has been the largest among developing countries.[20] Not only is the overall economic productivity of the country affected by such military overspending, but wealth and power become increasingly dependent upon controlling rents from the resource sector and transfers to the military apparatus, raising the stakes of military control and potentially pitting military against civilian officials.

Resource-dependent countries appear to figure amongst the most conflict-ridden countries – the highest risk is for those countries where primary commodity exports represent about a third of Gross Domestic Product (GDP).[21] Countries with a low level of resource-dependence tend to be industrialized democracies, a group largely insulated from civil wars. Highly resource-dependent countries essentially include oil producers in a position to 'buy out' social peace from relatively small populations, and benefit from the support of powerful foreign allies. In this regard, however, sanctions – imposed notably by the US on Iran, Libya, or Sudan – also reflect the fact that energy policy and business interests are not the only factors in determining foreign policy towards oil-producing states, at least when world supplies are plentiful. Nor is a policy of support towards friendly regimes without its own potentially violent consequences, as demonstrated by the anti-US stance that characterized the overthrow of the Shah of Iran in 1979 and the rise of the Islamic terrorist group Al Qaeda during the 1990s.

If many empirical studies support the concept of a 'resource curse' affecting petro-states, the discursive associations of oil with 'corruption', 'dictatorship', and 'evil' have also proved in themselves powerful social constructions. Most sides in the political conflicts surrounding terrorism and the 'war on terror' have used the symbolism of oil in their discursive construction of 'reality', whether it is to denounce the corruption and authoritarianism of local regimes or the greed of corporations and politicians. More than just a source of money and energy, oil has been socially instrumentalized as a source of power at the discursive level. In this respect, the world-wide movement against the US-led war on Iraq benefited from the dark side of the mystique of 'black gold' to build a mobilizing 'no blood for oil' argument. Similarly, by using the 'prosperity' side of the oil mystique, the US administration has been able to evade its role in the sufferings of Iraqis associated with the UN sanction regime and illegal invasion of Iraq, through a discourse of 'liberation', incorporating a vision in which better-managed oil will bring 'freedom' to the Iraqi people.

Gulf Oil and Mutual Petro-Dependence

Oil has gained a global predominance among energy sources in industrialized economies due to its relative versatility, low cost, and transportability. Relationships of mutual dependence along the oil commodity chain have been consolidated in recent years. A 'new political economy of oil' – contrasting in particular with that of the 1970s and characterized by a more 'reasonable' approach to pricing by key producers and to a reduction of conflicts between producers, consumers, and intermediaries – has resulted from the greater influence of markets over governments, the relative failure of the use of the 'oil weapon' by both producing and importing countries, and the diversification of sources of oil supply made possible by technological advances.[22]

Despite the diversification of oil supply, which responded in part to price hikes imposed by OPEC, the Persian Gulf remains *the* core region within the global political economy of oil, with currently 65 per cent of the world's oil reserves and 28 per cent of the world's production. This region also maintains – mostly through Saudi Arabia – around 70 per cent of the global current excess oil production capacity, leaving the world with limited options in case of supply disruption. Reciprocally, the current levels of economic dependence on oil revenues in the region are high – ranging from 22 per cent to 53 per cent of GDP – and in the absence of economic diversification, governments will most likely continue to rely heavily on oil rents.

This mutual dependence is expected to grow with regard to the Persian Gulf. Oil from this region as a share of world consumption is expected to increase from 27 per cent of world trade in 2001 to 34 per cent by 2025 (or 42 per cent in a scenario of low oil price).[23] In terms of market share, the region has a wide range of consumers including Japan, the EU, US, and China (see Table 1). Japan is the most oil-dependent on the region, and although it supported the latest US-led war in Iraq it may distance itself from US policies, while also searching for better relations with Russia to both reduce its dependence and to balance China. Already the second largest energy consumer after the US, China is also facing growing oil import dependence that could reach almost 45 per cent in 2010.[24] Oil accounts for about 30 per cent of India's total energy consumption, and some 57 per cent of this oil is currently imported. Future oil consumption in India is expected to almost double by 2010.[25] Overall Asian dependence on Persian Gulf oil will rise significantly and the Asian demand in oil is to overtake the

European and North American respective demands by 2010.[26] European reliance on oil imports could grow from 70 per cent at the moment to almost 90 per cent in 2030, with significant imports from the region even if its energy security policy favours Russian supplies.[27] US net world-wide oil imports are expected to continue their steady growth, from about half to two-thirds of its consumption by 2020, but its reliance on the region may remain relatively low.[28] The US market has been by far the most problematic because of its political dimensions, in terms of maintaining a security umbrella for allies such as Saudi Arabia, and economic sanctions for 'enemies' such as Iran. In short, the Middle East is becoming increasingly dependent on economic growth in Asia, while Asia will become even more dependent on a favourable political-military stability in the Persian Gulf region.[29]

As far as oil flow is concerned, nearly 88 per cent of oil exported from the Persian Gulf currently transits by tanker, through the Straits of Hormuz, which is by far the world's most important oil 'chokepoint', accounting for the transit of around two-fifths of the world's traded oil. Oil destined mainly for Europe and the United States heads westwards, by tanker, from the Persian Gulf towards the Suez Canal or the Sumed pipeline and must pass through the Bab al-Mandab, located between Djibouti and Eritrea in Africa, and Yemen on the Arabian Peninsula. The relative vulnerability of this route was demonstrated by the terrorist attack on a French supertanker near the coast of Yemen in October 2002.[30] Before the US-led military campaign in Iraq, around 12 per cent of oil from the Persian Gulf was exported via routes apart from the Straits of Hormuz. This oil was exported by several means: via the Saudi East-West pipeline to the port of Yanbu on the Red Sea; via the pipeline from Kirkuk (Iraq) to the Turkish port of Ceyhan; by truck to Jordan; and through various means (smuggling by truck and small boat,

TABLE 1

DEPENDENCE ON OIL IMPORTS FROM THE PERSIAN GULF

Importers	Regional imports (m bbl/d)	Regional share of world-wide imports (%)	Saudi Arabia	Iran	Iraq	UAE	Kuwait	Oman	Qatar	Yemen
Japan	4.1	74	31	12	–	32	13	–	11	–
China	0.7	57	24	32	–	–	–	24	–	19
EU	3.1	45	42	25	25	–	7	–	–	–
US	2.5	22	63	–	25	–	11	–	–	–

Source: Energy Information Administration 2001, World Bank Development Indicators 2001.

mainly) to a variety of destinations, including Kurdish areas of northern Iraq, Turkey, Jordan, Iran, India, and Pakistan, among others. The (re)opening of pipelines out of Iraq will significantly reduce vulnerability to a blockage of the Straits of Hormuz.

Besides oil, the Persian Gulf region also has huge reserves of natural gas accounting for 34 per cent of the total proven world gas reserves.[31] The importance of these reserves is likely to grow in coming years, as both domestic gas consumption in the region and gas exports to East and Southeast Asia (by pipeline and also by liquefied natural gas tanker) increase, while gas exploitation by oil companies and transportation costs are becoming increasingly competitive. Western Europe is also slowly switching from oil to cleaner fuels such as gas, due to greater environmental sensitivity. The switch to natural gas and the anticipated growth in the use of this source of energy raises a new series of geopolitical issues, leading to new political alignments.[32] Political relations in the gas sector matter even more than in the oil sector, since gas networks are much more vulnerable to political and economic disruptions than oil.[33] Since gas networks increase the interdependence of the societies they connect, they create a pressure on all the countries along the transmission route to minimize their political differences and cement their economies together. Once the network is paid for, the benefits of stable gas supplies provide strong incentives for countries to co-operate – with the risk of being counter-productive in terms of improving human rights abuses by domestic governments (as for example, with the Burma-Thailand gas pipelines).

Oil and US Security in the Persian Gulf

On 11 September 2001, 19 (mostly Saudi) terrorists targeted the key symbols of US power. Osama Bin Laden, presumed leader of the Islamic terrorist network Al Qaeda, supported and congratulated the 'martyrs' who had rammed Boeing planes into New York's Twin Towers and the Pentagon, having previously justified this *jihad* by the oil-related presence of US troops on the 'Holy Soil' of the Arabian Peninsula and the moral corruption of the oil-rich Saudi regime.[34] Although other political and ideological agendas were clearly involved, the events of '9/11' demonstrated the conflicting relations between identities, territories, and resource control – in this case, Islam, the Arabian Peninsula, and US access to oil.

There have been frequent tensions and dilemmas between US energy and security objectives in the Persian Gulf, both within and between US administration and corporate interests.[35] Since the fall or weakening of its regional allies (principally Iran under the Shah and Saudi Arabia), US state policy entailed the support of *each* of its allies – in part because of tensions

FIGURE 1

PETROLEUM AND US MILITARY STRATEGY IN THE PERSIAN GULF REGION

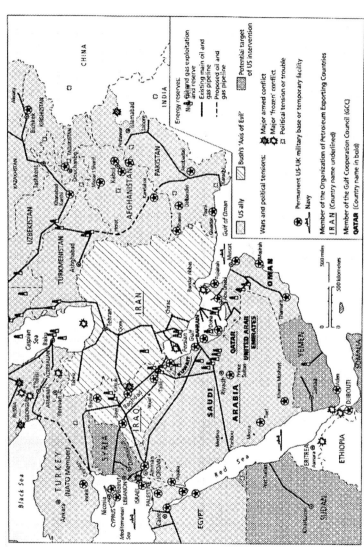

Adapted from Philippe Rekacewicz (Le Monde) with kind permission. Sources: Energy Map of the Middle East and Caspian Sea, Petroleum Economist and Arthur Andersen, London, 2002; Comité professionnel du pétrole (CPDP), Central Intelligence United States Energy Information Administration (US EIA); Organisation du traité de l'Atlantique nord (OTAN); www.Globalsecurity.org; United States Department of Defense (US DOS).

TABLE 2

OIL PRODUCTION AND RESERVES IN THE PERSIAN GULF

	Total	Saudi Arabia	Iran	Iraq	UAE	Kuwait	Oman	Qatar	Yemen
Production (m bbl/d)	21.2	8.6	3.5	2.6	2.5	2	0.9	0.7	0.4
Proven reserves (bn bbl)	672	263	90	112	98	96	5	4	4
Economic oil dependence (% GDP)		44[a]	25[a]	n.a.	n.a.	32[b]	25[c]	53[b]	22[c]

[a] 2000.
[b] 1999.
[c] 1998.

Note: Bahrain has insignificant oil production (75,000 bbl/d) and proven reserves (125 mn bbl), but relies for 50 per cent of its GDP on (refined) oil exports.

Source: *Energy Information Administration 2001, World Bank Development Indicators 2001.*

within and between them – and the 'dual containment' and weakening of regional challengers, mostly Iran and Iraq (which included supporting both sides during the Iran-Iraq war, and since redefined as 'rogue' states).[36] Such policy has been contradictory both in terms of stability and energy goals. In terms of stability, this policy has prolonged regional tensions by preventing the emergence at the regional level of a hegemon or effective co-operative partnership.[37] At a domestic level, the support of (corrupt) local élites – or blanket sanctions against a country – has also aggravated domestic tensions associated with the frustrations and grievances of dissatisfied groups. In terms of energy goals, sanction policies have entailed significant losses for US corporations and an economically harming reduction of oil flows. Some of these contradictions can be linked to the '9/11' terrorist attack and subsequent 'war on terror' including the US-led occupation of Iraq in March 2003.

Oil, Saudi Arabia, and Al Qaeda

Although the ire of the US initially focused on Afghanistan, where affiliated terrorists had their base, and then in a controversial and curious twist to Iraq, some of the roots of the attack against US targets on 9/11 are to be found in the governance and conflicts affecting Saudi Arabia. Returning from Afghanistan to their home countries after the Soviet withdrawal in 1989, many Arab fighters, emboldened by their victory but alienated by their home governments, initiated (or continued, as in the case of Egypt) a fight against domestic rulers and their foreign supporters with the goal of establishing Islamic states.[38] In both Algeria and the Gulf monarchies, petroleum interests provided a powerful discursive theme for criticism and mobilization around the themes of corruption and western exploitation. A 'golden boy' of the Saudi society thanks to the fortune of his father (but not a member of the royal family), Osama Bin Laden's discourse of resistance echoed dissent voiced as early as the 1940s about the corruption of the House of Al Saud and its collusion with Americans. As argued by political scientist Robert Vitalis, while the US government's and oil firms' activities in Saudi Arabia wrapped their racism and ordinary imperialism in the cloak of a 'special relationship' and 'development' discourse, 'a multivocal record of resistance to the Americans' project ... can be found in the oil camps and towns in the 1940s and 1950s, in the new ministries and prisons, and in the palaces that the Bechtel brothers outfitted for the Al Sau'd'.[39] This discourse was itself amplified by growing grievances among the Saudi population bearing the uncertainties of the economic downturn faced by the country – not to mention marginalized Shia, Yemeni and migrant populations.

If the oil wealth has immensely benefited tiny élite groups such as the privileged members of the Al Saud royal family, the rising living standards experienced by most of the population of petro-states within the region as a result of the oil boom of the 1970s and early 1980s have since been declining. Saudi Arabia's economy remains, despite attempts at diversification, heavily dependent on oil. Oil revenues make up around 90–95 per cent of total Saudi export earnings, 70 per cent of state revenues, and around 35–40 per cent of the country's gross domestic product (GDP). Meanwhile, Saudi Arabia's desire to join the World Trade Organization is behind some of the push towards economic liberalization in the country. Saudi Arabia is also promoting a policy of 'Saudization' to increase employment of its own citizens by replacing a large number of foreign workers in the country, including low-skilled jobs. Beyond the discourse of opposition to Israel and western oil interests, the motives and mobilization of Saudi terrorists may thus be linked to domestic and international relationships between oil wealth, authoritarian governance, economic resentment, and a religion providing both much of the basis of the current domestic order and one of the few channels for criticizing the state.[40] The oil wealth of Saudi Arabia is also suspected of having contributed to the funding of Al Qaeda, through the personal fortune of Bin Laden and donations by rich supporters.[41] Played out in the mass media as a call to boycott Middle Eastern oil and search for 'terrorist-proof energy source', this possible financial connection became caricatured through ads portraying Americans 'financing al Qaeda' by driving gas-guzzling Sports Utility Vehicles.[42]

The 9/11 attacks illustrated the complexity of US interests in the Persian Gulf and the dilemma of oil dependence for the West, whereby preserving energy interests could undermine 'homeland security' by fostering anti-Americanism in the region. Ironically, the 'war on terror' led by the US aggravated this situation through the controversy over the 'oil undercurrents' of the US-led strikes on Afghanistan and Iraq.

Afghanistan and Iraq: Oily 'Wars on Terror'?

The post 9/11 US policies were not particularly novel in their general security objectives, such as punishing states supporting anti-US terrorism, the preclusion of a new Iraqi drive on the Kuwaiti or Saudi oil fields, the deterrence of Iran from threatening oil flow in the Straits of Hormuz, and the prevention of unfavourable political change within allied states, particularly Saudi Arabia.[43] What seems novel is a possible drive for a resource grab in countries where divergent US foreign policy objectives had so far undermined US corporate oil interests, namely Iraq and Iran (and, to a much lower degree, Afghanistan). Along with the connections of prominent members of the Bush administration to the oil sector, the 'war for oil' argument became one of the rallying calls within the public discourse opposing the US-led wars, and the focus of allegations about the timing and motivation of the US administration.[44]

Allegations of US oil interests in the war in Afghanistan have been limited, because of the demonstrated presence of Al Qaeda and the limited petroleum stakes in the country. Allegations have focused on the interests of UNOCAL, a California-based company, in a pipeline linking Turkmenistan gas fields to Pakistan via Afghanistan (see Figure 1). The US energy company was engaged in negotiations with the Taliban in Afghanistan despite major protests from human rights groups, until its project was terminated in late 1998 as the US militarily retaliated against Al Qaeda's terrorist attack on the US embassy in Nairobi.[45] Following the US military toppling of the Taliban regime in 2001, Pakistan, Afghanistan and Turkmenistan signed a pipeline agreement and the Afghan minister for mines and industries declared that UNOCAL was the 'lead company' for the project, although UNOCAL declares having 'no plans or interest in such a pipeline today'.[46] Controversially, President Bush's special envoy to Afghanistan and Iraq, Zalmay Khalilzad, worked with Cambridge Energy Research Associates on UNOCAL's pipeline project in Taliban-ruled Afghanistan.[47] Beyond potential US corporate interests in the region, Turkmenistan was eager to see a pipeline route independent of Russia while the US opposed an alternative route through Iran; the Afghan route would thus consolidate both US strategic and Turkmen economic interests while further marginalizing those of Iran and Russia in the region.[48]

Allegations of oil interests in the US-led war in Iraq have proved much more pervasive. Iraq contains the second largest proven oil reserves in the world after Saudi Arabia, but its true resource potential may be understated. Iraq also potentially contains the world's second or third largest gas reserves.[49] The economic stakes are thus undoubtedly high. Furthermore, Iraq has also the human, agricultural, mineral resources, and geostrategic position to re-establish itself as a major economic and security player in the region (even if its quasi land-locked position makes its relatively vulnerable). Yet after its wars with Iran and Kuwait, Iraq has been subjected to more than a decade of drastic sanctions that have left the country politically isolated and economically crippled. Although drastically weakened, deprived from overt access to arms imports and technology, and ideologically at odds with Al Qaeda, the US and some regional countries continued to perceive Iraq's leadership as a potential threat.

The Bush administration stated eight objectives for its war, the first of which being to remove Saddam Hussein from power and to ascertain that all weapons of mass destruction (WMD) and means to produce them have been eliminated from the country.[50] The fact that the US-led war was 'pre-emptive' and unauthorized by the UN Security Council, that the suspected ties between the government of Saddam Hussein and Al Qaeda were extremely tenuous, and that so far no weapons of mass destruction have been found cast further doubts about the stated goals of the US administration and UK government. At the heart of the policy change on the 'Iraqi issue' were two strategic decisions. First, the Iraq 'problem' had to be solved, not simply managed as it was during the previous two US administrations. The 9/11 attacks provided the justifying context of the US strike, while allegations of imminent WMD threat helped to construct the justifying motive.[51] Second, Washington was prepared to push beyond the limitations imposed by international (including Arab) public opinion and the UN Security Council.

The idea that the US-led forces were invading Iraq to 'liberate' its oil sector – and secure oil interests – have been repeatedly denied by the US administration and British government, although they rarely elaborated on the reasons why such a factor was discounted – simply asserting that Iraq's oil reserves would not be 'exploited for the United States' own purpose [but] be held in trust for the Iraqi people, to benefit the Iraqi people'.[52] While some analysts simply stress that the United States have 'a *legitimate* and critical interest in seeing that Persian Gulf oil continues to flow copiously and relatively cheaply' to prevent the oil-based global economy from 'collapsing',[53] several more specific arguments have been presented *against* the 'war for oil' perspective.[54]

The first argument is that oil is available on the international market and there is no reason why the US as a country would seek to invest heavily in a military venture to obtain what can be easily purchased commercially. In this respect, the US was already among the largest buyers of Iraqi oil on the international market within the UN's 'oil for food' programme. Yet, following a US energy policy focusing on the provision of cheap and abundant oil to the world economy, what matters is the level of investment in oil-producing countries and their willingness to provide large volumes of oil at low prices. In this respect, Saddam Hussein's government was prone to embargo all oil exports for political reasons (for example, because of the Israeli military campaign in Palestinian areas in April 2002).[55] Moreover, Iraq was heavily underinvested because of the sanction regime and had one of the lowest production/reserve ratio among major oil producers. While sanctions could have been lifted to ensure this energy objective, it created a dilemma with the US policy goals of regime change and disarmament in Iraq; removing Saddam Hussein by force, rather than removing sanctions at the UN, allowed the Bush administration to solve this dilemma. As a result, more oil should flow as sanctions are finally lifted and major oil investments can take place if Iraq becomes 'stable and safe'. Finally, Iraq long participated in sustaining 'above market' prices as a member of OPEC; even if the US is unlikely to force it to leave the organization, the US may yield greater influence on it while the Iraqi reconstruction imperative will make it hard to justify limited production quotas once an Iraqi government is internationally recognized and allowed to participate again in the organisation.[56] Although cheaper oil would have a positive effect on the US and world economy, while hawks in the Bush administration may hope that lower prices could undermine OPEC and devastate the economies of rogue states (i.e., Iran, Syria and Libya), too low prices would undermine a cost-recovery reconstruction of Iraq as well as the stability of key US allies and oil interests (including among the independent Texan oil industry with which Bush family businesses were associated).[57] It is thus in the US interest to see more oil flow out of Iraq at 'reasonable prices' as a result of this war.

A second argument against the oil-driven war perspective is that Iraq will remain a relatively marginal oil producer for years to come: it currently produces only 2 per cent of the world's oil production, and it may take 5 to 10 years for it to reach a 6–7 per cent share.[58] Yet such levels are significant and given the importance of Iraqi reserves and the low cost of their exploitation, this share in the oil market is likely to grow. Furthermore, this relatively long time frame is compatible with that of major oil companies and long-term US strategic interests, such as maintaining its world predominance unchallenged. The life cycle of oil development projects, from negotiation and exploration to exploitation and exhaustion, frequently takes place over several decades. The US–Saudi Arabia 'special relationship' served US interests for more than five decades; the same is true for US relations with Germany or Japan. Although a similar outcome is not guaranteed in the Iraqi case, it would greatly benefit the US.[59] Furthermore, although it may take several years for Iraqi oil production to significantly affect the global supply of oil, it will lessen US dependence on Saudi spare oil production capacity. Along with the withdrawal of US troops from Saudi Arabia allowed by the occupation of Iraq, the Iraqi production increase should allow for greater 'room for manoeuvre' by the US administration in its relationship with the Kingdom.

A third argument against the oil connection of the US-led war on Iraq is that markets were 'unnerved' by the prospect of war, as demonstrated by declining indices on major stock exchanges.[60] The previous Gulf Oil had indeed had a negative impact on the US economy. However, some business reports also voiced the hope that a quick US victory would 'kill the bear market' and help boost the US economy, which had been facing a downturn since 2000.[61] From a corporate point of view, major US and UK energy and engineering companies will benefit from greater opportunities and leverage to access the Iraqi market. As with the politics of UN sanction lifting on Iraq – which would have allowed for investments – oil interests are likely to play a significant role. In this respect, the French threat of UN veto against the US-led war has been linked to the fact that the French oil company Total had the highest stake in Iraq, and although it had no contract with the government of Saddam Hussein, the two oil fields under negotiation could double its reserves.[62] Access to Iraqi oil fields is also of major importance to Russian and Chinese companies. Although no major US oil company was openly active in Iraq, companies from several countries supporting the US-led war had stakes in Iraq.[63] Several key tests will help determine the place of oil interests in the outcome of the war, including the preferential awarding of Iraqi-paid reconstruction and oil infrastructure rehabilitation contracts to US firms close to the administration; the cancellation or significant modification of current oil development contracts of (non-US) companies; non-competitive awarding of contracts to US/UK oil companies; and the privatization of the Iraqi National Oil Company in a manner preferential to US/UK interests. Indeed, within weeks of the US appointment of an Iraqi oil minister, several Russian and Chinese companies lost or had their 'Saddam era' oil deals suspended.[64] Yet, given the huge investments required in the Iraqi oil sector, the risks involved, and potential image problems, it is unlikely that US corporate interests will come to monopolize these sectors.

Peripheral Perspectives?

A US-friendly regime in Baghdad would not only better suit US corporate and strategic oil interests, but it could also provide a source of leverage for its foreign policy. As analyst Michael Renner has pointed out, by opening the flow of investment into the Iraqi oil sector, the US is reinforcing the reliance and preference of the world economy on oil and its own standing as the guarantor of this energy system (through its close relationship with key producers, military bases, sea lane protection, US currency trading).[65] Moreover, as US Vice-President (then secretary of defense) Dick Cheney testified to the Senate Armed Services Committee, a single power controlling the flow of Persian Gulf oil would have a 'stranglehold' on the economy of most of the nations of the world.[66] Having sought to prevent such a risk since the Iranian revolution in 1979 through a doctrine justifying 'any means necessary, including military force', the US is now fast becoming that single power.[67]

Russia is probably the country with the most immediate stakes in the reshaping of the Persian Gulf. Energy is a key factor influencing Russia's security perceptions, and President Putin's foreign diplomacy.[68] From the perspective of a strategic security planner in Moscow, the vulnerabilities of Russia's energy-export corridors are a source of significant concern, while international prices and Russian market share are key to both state finances and the economy. As far as the Middle East is concerned, Russia has three economic considerations. First, like for most other arms exporters, arms sales provide substantial income to its military-industrial complex. Second, Russia benefits from tensions in the region when they produce rising oil prices. As an oil exporter, it also benefited from the constraints placed on Iraqi oil sales between 1991 and 2002 by United Nations Security Council resolutions and by US sanctions on Iran, that to some extent have limited the development of major competitors on the energy resources market. In such circumstances, Russia appeared as an attractive alternative to Middle East oil producers and was eager to maintain a situation in which it can increase its production and benefit from high prices at the expense of OPEC, and Saudi Arabia in particular. Third, Russian oil companies, and in particular Lukoil, have significant contracts in Iraq that they do not wish to lose. Part of the pre-war diplomatic negotiations between Moscow and Washington hinged on this issue, to the point that Iraq scrapped an oilfield deal with Lukoil in December 2002 after the company had reportedly received assurances from the Russian government and President Bush that the contract would not lapse if Saddam Hussein was ousted.

Despite their economic importance and dependence on Gulf oil, the European states played a limited role in recent decision-making processes within the region. Incapacity to forge a common foreign policy towards the Middle East was most clearly demonstrated by the divergence of views on the US-led war in Iraq, with the UK actively participating while France threatened to use its UN veto against the use of force as long as all diplomatic options (including weapons inspections) were not fully explored. Lacking diversification, the European energy market is very sensitive to geopolitical factors and to the decisions made by the cartels of oil and gas exporting countries. Such a situation threatens the still vulnerable and integrating European economy. Unlike the US, the main objectives of a future European energy strategy are to reduce the energetic dependence of the EU by managing energy demand, and to improve in the long term the security of its oil and gas imports while preserving the environment.[69] Direct access to Middle East oil resources should nevertheless remain a priority for the European Union, in addition to the traditional imports coming from Russia. Europe is also likely to pursue diplomatic efforts to lift US sanctions against Iran and Libya, even if the present *status quo* favours European oil companies.

The US move is also of particular significance to two major Asian oil importers, China and India. Chinese officials strongly disapprove of the presence of US military forces in the Gulf, characterizing this as interference. Given the limited capability of the Chinese navy and economic obstacles to viable pipeline transportation of oil from Central Asia (for example, Kazakhstan), China perceives US strategic domination over the broader region of South West Asia as the primary source of vulnerability to its energy supply.[70] Given the US occupation of Iraq, Iran may become even more important to Beijing officials, with arms sales viewed as a critical element of China's regional policy.[71] India was also opposed to military action in Iraq, as the Hussein regime was favourable to India in both business terms – Iraq was the largest bilateral trading partner of India before 1991 – and geopolitical terms, as Iraq was the only Arab country supporting India's stand on Jammu and Kashmir.[72] If access to oil is likely to take priority among the regional foreign policy objectives of these two major Asian countries, from a defence perspective, however, none of them has the capacity to significantly influence their relationship. With the US playing an even greater role in regional stability, these objectives will thus have to match that of the US, especially in terms of weapons transfer. In this regard, the US will be particularly attentive to the relationship between China and Iran, but also Saudi Arabia.[73]

Regionally, there was no effective stand against the war; in fact, support from several countries (many among the 'anonymous' of the US 'Coalition') emphasized both the isolation of Iraq in the region, and the dominance of the US. Unsurprisingly, Kuwait was the Gulf State at the forefront of the Arab support to the US-led war in Iraq (direct support included allowing two US air bases and positioning of 115,000 US soldiers on its soil). Kuwait's geography, small size, and limited population has made it one of the most vulnerable Gulf States; a position that the government counterbalanced through the longest British protectorate in the region and then continued backing by 'powerful friends'. Its location on Iraq's border has also been the source of continuing Iraqi threats, and military confrontation notably over the Kuwaiti field of Ratqa (Iraq's Rumaila), and it remains to be seen if it will gain from a new Iraqi regime. Bahrain, Qatar, and Oman, which are not major oil producers, all directly supported the US. Saudi Arabia and Turkey limited their involvement, but *de facto* also sided with the US. Only two countries – and potential US targets – Iran and Syria opposed the military invasion of Iraq, but both carefully refrained from intervening even indirectly in a military manner.

The slow build up of a new US policy on Iraq also clearly revealed that no country in the region contested the need to maintain Iraq's unity and territorial integrity.[74] The Sunni-ruled Gulf monarchies are wary of Iraq's Shiite majority seizing political power or creating in southern Iraq a Shiite state that could be allied with Shiite Iran, thereby aggravating dissent in the sensitive Shiite areas of the oil-rich Al Hasa province of Saudi Arabia or among the majority Shiite population of Bahrain. Turkey also vigorously opposed the independence of Iraq's self-ruled Kurdish areas out of fear of irredentist claims on ethnically Kurdish areas of Turkey itself and has also opposed the attribution of the Iraqi oil fields of Kirkuk and Mosul to Kurdish control.[75]

If the settlement of arguments over the 'oil undercurrents' of the invasion of Iraq will take time, the US use of force *within* Iraq marked a watershed in its recent regional involvement (but arguably not in the historical pattern of British imperial engagement with the region). Most importantly, the perception of an 'imperial America' extending its reach further within the Middle East is now stronger.[76] Given that this perception is expected to foster further terrorism and slow down reforms throughout the region, the US may engage in a policy direction focusing on oil and governance.

Future US Policy: From 'Free Oil' to 'Freedom Oil'?

In addition to neighbouring sources – Canada, Mexico, and Venezuela – US international oil policy has essentially relied on 'free access' to oil from the Middle East, for both domestic needs and international markets.[77] This policy of 'free oil', however, has frequently conflicted with other US foreign policy interests. The greater need for oil in the future is at odds with some of the US-driven policies towards 'rogue' petro-states. Sanctions against Iraq, Iran, and Libya have reduced the flow of oil to the world economy and complicated cost-effective development and transportation of Caspian and Central Asian oil resources; they also partially excluded major

American oil and gas companies from such endeavours while having no result in terms of preventing terrorism and effecting US-desired 'regime change' in these countries. The US National Energy Policy presented by Vice-President Dick Cheney in 2001 exposed some of these problems through its embedded assumption that Middle East oil suppliers (such as Saudi Arabia and Kuwait) were unreliable; its call for greater access to Persian Gulf oil (i.e., Iraq and Iran); its claim that the concentration of oil production supply in any one region (i.e., the Gulf) was contributing to market instability and above-market prices; and its recommendation of diversification of supply for the US.[78] Beyond its 'free oil' policy, the US administration may try to move towards a 'freedom oil' policy targeting essentially 'rogue states' and countries 'breeding terrorism'.

'Freedom Oil' for the Iraqi?

From an energy strategy perspective, the contradiction between energy and security agendas has certainly been a strong incentive for the Bush administration to remain in Iraq after toppling *manu* military the regime of Saddam Hussein. A consensus-based and long-lasting 'solution' to Iraq is fundamental to avoid harming the credibility of some prominent actors on the domestic front, while the avoidance of 'blowback' such as the Iranian revolution in 1979 is essential to the administration at the regional and international level. Iraq will remain an oil-rich and oil-dependent country in the foreseeable future, and a risk to be considered by the international community is that of future domestic or regional conflicts to be tackled by the next generation of politicians. The need for redefining a new Middle East energy and defence equilibrium seems obvious. From a long-range point of view, the greatest opportunity of the current crisis is to offer an opportunity to act in order to return Iraq (and one may argue in reference to the sanction regime, the so-called 'international community') to a responsible political and economic role for the Iraqi population and the region.

The control of the Iraqi oil sector is giving the Bush administration the opportunity of testing a 'freedom oil' policy. Narratives around 'freedom' versus 'evil' have been extensively used by the Bush administration in its discursive construction of terrorism and the justification of the 'war on terror'. The same need to contrast the 'Saddam era' from the (US) 'liberation era' entails that oil come to play a different role for the population than is associated in the 'oil curse' narrative commonly used to portray the previous Iraqi regime (and most of those in the region). In other word, oil needs to bring 'freedom' rather than 'evil' in Iraq and the broader region. Such discursive construction entails a number of policies, whereby the US would take an active role in creating and sustaining a political and institutional environment, as well as investments and infrastructure, in which oil and oil revenues consolidate a stable democratic regime and lessen regional tension – thereby also resolving some of these conflicts and dilemmas between energy and broader foreign policy goals.[79] At a domestic level, new political and economic institutions could ensure that oil is allocated in a transparent and accountable manner for the interest of the population, and not the payment of 'oil for arms' debts inherited from the 'Saddam era' or lucrative reconstruction contracts for western companies. The UN Security Council decided, for example, that the proceeds of all export sales of petroleum shall be deposited into a Development Fund for Iraq, to be used 'in a transparent manner ... for purposes benefiting the people of Iraq' and to be internationally audited, until an internationally recognized, representative government of Iraq is properly constituted.[80] At an infrastructure level, the option of giving Iraq multiple accesses to oil and gas markets (and its associated corporate interests) could connect regional societies and pressure all the countries along the transmission routes to minimize their political differences and cement their economies together, becoming thus more interdependent and less inclined to engage in ruinous wars. Most controversially, the 'Haifa' pipeline linking Iraq to Israel and a possible new Palestinian state via Jordan already exists, but has been closed since the end of the British mandate in 1948 and needs reconstruction.[81]

Such 'freedom oil' policy could play a key role in President Bush's 'vision for the Middle-East', which includes a democratic and stable post-Saddam government in Iraq, providing an example for the region, and the resolution of the Israeli–Palestinian conflict.[82] In this perspective, an Iraqi success would suggest drastic domestic changes in regional political regimes and political economies. However, as discussed above, the very oil wealth of these regimes prevent much of the popular or foreign-driven reform agenda. Arguably, UN sanctions have led (so far) to more Iraqi victims than the US-led war. Seeking direct management of oil revenues, the Bush administration may (worryingly) see in an Iraqi success an invitation to remove regimes, rather than sanctions. How much muscle flexing, destabilization, and nation-building efforts the US will deploy to bring about 'freedom' in petro-states, and with what consequences for local populations remains highly speculative. In the perspective of the White House, however, the targets of such 'freedom oil' policy can already be clearly identified. Within the region, these would include Iran, Syria, and possibly Saudi Arabia. Beyond, priority targets would include Libya and Sudan.

Freedom Oil and Regime Change

After Afghanistan and Iraq, the US administration is now in the process of singling out Iran as being the major troublemaker in the region. Still in the process of revolutionary change, Iran is currently divided between 'reformers' who have public support, and 'conservatives' who control the military, security system, and judiciary institutions. Although defeated in recent local elections, the 'reformers' now seem to be the strongest faction, and change may take a peaceful and positive course. Iran's regime has become steadily more pragmatic under Presidents Rafsanjani and Khatami, and more concerned with Iran's national interests and economic development in the Gulf than the export of revolution.

Besides its major oil reserves, the world's second largest gas reserves, and its strategic position on the Straits of Hormuz, Iran also influences the development of energy resources in the Caspian and Central Asia and sees itself as a natural transit route for oil and gas exports from the landlocked Central Asian countries to world markets. Iran has thus undoubtedly a vast strategic importance in the near future. As such, Iran is very conscious that American military presence in Iraq and Central Asia are part of a strategy to encircle it. Tehran is currently facing the wrath of the United States over alleged sponsorship of terrorism, support of warlords in Afghanistan, and development of weapons of mass destruction (not to mention media reports on the suspicion of harbouring Bin Laden). Meanwhile Iran is focusing its limited defence resources on improving its conventional capability and pursuing its production of ballistic missiles capable of targeting the Gulf countries.

Despite the relative failure of US occupation, the results of US military campaigns in Afghanistan and Iraq may encourage the Administration's hawks to set their sights on a next 'domino' in the region. Iran was recently identified as being in breach of the International Atomic Energy Agency guarantees that it was committed to – the third 'Axis of Evil' state may be further down the nuclear weapons path than had previously been expected. No doubt the Iranian government, like the North Korean one, sees the acquisition of nuclear weapons as a deterrent against potential US aggression, but this does not lessen Washington's concern. But even if the US sees Iran as a potential target, going to war to bring the regime down would be difficult and senior administration staff have publicly rejected the option.[83] Its geographic position in the Persian Gulf also makes Iran a real threat to oil shipments and the Gulf States, given its navy and missiles arsenal. Iran is as well a more difficult diplomatic target. Unlike Afghanistan and Iraq, Iran is not in breach of any UN Security Council resolution. At the international court of justice, Iran is the plaintiff, not the defendant, with regard to military hostilities (i.e., US destruction of Iranian oil platforms during the last stages of the Iraq-Iran war). At this stage of the development of a crawling crisis between Tehran and Washington, an attack on Iran by the US is therefore even more unlikely to receive the support of the international community.

For Michael Leeden, of the conservative think-tank American Enterprise Institute, the US should not be considering an invasion of Iran, but 'the kind of support for freedom fighters that the United States has traditionally delivered even in countries that were not involved in a terrorist war against us'.[84] Thomas Friedman, foreign affairs columnist at the *New York Times*, echoes this strategy of brutal regime change by arguing that what the US needs to trigger 'is not a war with Islam, but it is a war within Islam'.[85] Referring to growing dissent in Iran, Friedman is not advocating direct US support to 'freedom fighters', but US pressure for elections across the region – with Saudi Arabia as the main target. Certain that fundamentalists will win the race, Friedman augurs that such a result would trigger civil wars ultimately delivering stable democracies in the region and sees a very positive sign in what he perceives as a growing dissent within Iran.

However, in the domino theory advocated by some decision-making circles in Washington, Damascus might very well be the next target on the list, squeezed between US forces in Iraq and Israeli defence forces. With proven oil reserves expected to last only about 10 to 20 more years and a population growing at 2.5 per cent per year, Syria may become a net importer of oil within the next decade. The exploration for oil and natural gas is thus a top priority in Syria, but exploration activity has been slow in recent years due to unattractive contract terms and poor exploration results; only a few international companies remain in the country at present. Syria's relations with Iraq have improved significantly over recent years, including a reopening of the border and possibly of the Kirkuk-Banias pipeline, thereby allowing Iraqi oil exports.[86] This development, followed by various security-related US accusations, has not helped the Syrian government in its relations with the US.[87] From an energy point of view, a US-friendly regime in Damascus would facilitate unlocking Iraqi oil with pipelines running through Syria to the Mediterranean Sea, avoiding a Persian Gulf route or a 'Palestinian' route (i.e., the Haifa pipeline) that could be threatened or even closed. A US-friendly regime in Damascus may also facilitate, in Washington's perspective, a resolution of the Palestinian–Israeli conflict and terrorist bases in Lebanon. It should be noted that, although desirable, the Arab–Israeli peace process might not be perceived in Washington as vital to the US national security. On the other hand Iraq and Iran have repeatedly being singled out as immediate threats to American interests in the Gulf. The Bush administration might be tempted to decouple those two issues.

The world's largest price 'swing' producer – and with one-quarter of the world's proven oil reserves, the religious centre of Islam, and 15 out of 19 of the 9/11 hijackers – Saudi Arabia is a major cause of concern for the US. Despite Friedman's argument of transition through revolution, the predominant concern on the part of the US administration is to prevent an

Iranian-style 'anti-American' revolution from taking place in Saudi Arabia.[88] Likewise, the House of Saud is eager to subsidize US oil imports – up to a $1 a barrel – to maintain the US security umbrella for its country, and for itself.[89] Although Saudi Arabia does not face any imminent risk of instability, it has entered the twenty-first century in the midst of major political, social, economic, and military transitions, all this in an environment of continuing uncertainties in the world energy market, a factor that drives virtually every aspect of the Saudi economy.[90] Besides a domestic revolution, conservative analysts in the US were also wary that its failure to contain Saddam Hussein would further motivate a Saudi-Iranian rapprochement; the US-led war served to 'restore its credibility in the Persian Gulf by demonstrating that it [was] serious about overthrowing Saddam Hussein, not just containing him'.[91] Following this argument, the US is more likely to assist in the stabilization of Saudi Arabia, than to attempt to reform it, or to foment a revolution.

Freedom and its Limits

Besides contemplating a 'freedom oil' policy, the US is likely to follow a more usual approach. In the short term, and from a defence perspective, the necessity to protect maritime energy-shipment routes combined with the political-military need to rely less on host nations when deploying forces, lends support to the strategy of maintaining a strong US Navy presence in the Persian Gulf region, and may plead for a stronger US Pacific Fleet. In terms of broader US strategy, and apart from opening lucrative reconstruction contracts and oil reserves to US corporate interests, the occupation of Iraq and the installation of a friendly regime will more likely secure larger oil flows to the US and its industrial partners. Greater influence in the region, and through its influence on OPEC and the oil market – not to mention the show of force – may also consolidate the US in its position as the sole world superpower, although it is unlikely to put an end to terrorism.

In the event of an oil supply disruption in the Persian Gulf, the world would be left with relatively limited options for making up the lost oil production, as the Persian Gulf countries maintain around 70 per cent of the world's excess oil production capacity. The oil coming from Caucasus and Central Asia might help to smooth any disruption in the Persian Gulf, although projected reserves have been much revised down. Despite the main stage of the war in Iraq being over, the potential for other armed conflicts in unstable energy-producing areas of the region remains high as does a small risk that terrorism will disrupt supplies. A weakening of US alliance relationships in Europe, the Persian Gulf, or Asia could have major impacts on US energy security.

In the broader region, Washington might consider that a union around Moscow of the Caucasus and Central Asian oil exporters and a domination of the energy routes by Russia may become a major security concern. In this perspective, one can reasonably expect that Washington will continue to strongly support Turkey, a cornerstone of its military and strategic interests in the region, disregarding the position Ankara took during the Iraqi crisis.[92] In the middle term and from a military perspective, although US officials are denying such a policy they will discreetly keep US troops for a few years in the region. The cover of military assistance and support for the war against terrorism is a convenient way for Washington to keep an influence on the pipeline grids of the Middle East and Central Asia (see Figure 1). Along with increased US military presence and influence in Central Asia, this is likely to weaken Russia's regional influence and crucial oil revenues. In the medium to long-term, such a position offers the possibility of economic and geopolitical pressure on China, a key future contender to US supremacy.

Conclusions

The debate on the links between oil and US security has significantly shifted as a result of the '9/11' terrorist attacks. If on one side, those opposing US military interventionism have argued that the 'war on terror' provided one more convenient cover for a renewed imperialist 'oil grab'; on the other, the links between oil dependence and terrorism pointed at the importance of governance in oil producing countries. As such, 9/11 both highlighted the multidimensionality of the link between oil, terrorism and a 'war on terror' that also became justified as a 'war of liberation' against oil funded dictators. In an ironic twist, some conservative analysts came to actually share some of the arguments of Bin Laden – even if they did not share the opinion that western interests had much to do with the problem of governance in oil-rich countries in the first place.

In this regard, the contradictions and limitations of the US foreign policy demonstrated that the unconditional support of regional allies, such as Saudi Arabia, can foster domestic opposition, while the sanction regimes imposed against 'rogue states' such as Afghanistan or Iraq did not satisfy the White House's security agenda. Beyond money and energy, the power of oil also resides in its discursive construction. Contrasting its own policies with the 'dark side' of oil – the funding of dictatorships and terrorism – the US administration is moving towards associating oil with its version of 'freedom' through better management practices and constructive mutual dependence within the region. By doing so, it moves beyond the dilemma of the sanction regime (through which not enough oil revenue was flowing to the population, but enough was to sustain Saddam Hussein's regime) and absolves its own past responsibilities as both buyer of Iraqi oil and main supporter of the sanctions. The focus provided by the 'freedom oil' agenda on the relationship between oil dependence, domestic governance, and the behaviour of foreign governments and oil companies could nevertheless serve to reshape the social contribution of a resource sector that negatively affected the lives of millions. Beyond the case of Iraq, however, many of the scenarios of regime change in the region, from supporting 'freedom fighters' to fomenting civil war are reminiscent of the worst period of the Cold War when the fight between the US and a 'threatening' Soviet Union justified the sacrifice of millions of people in the South.

To demonstrate that the US war on Iraq was not an oil grab, the Bush administration (and its successors) will have to make 'freedom oil' a reality, and prove that indeed oil benefits first and foremost ordinary Iraqis. To address the contradiction of its energy and security agendas in the region, the US will have to promote a stronger governance agenda with regard to oil management – something that will require a broad set of initiatives, from diplomatic efforts and institutional building to more stringent regulation of oil corporations and banking institutions in matters of transparency, corrupt practices, and accountability. In this regard, the Bush administration may find allies in a nascent coalition of international agencies, non-governmental organizations (NGOs), governments, and businesses attempting to bring about a better governance of the oil sector at a global level. Among the many initiatives, the World Bank has taken an indirect oversight role over the development of the oil sector in Chad; NGOs and the UK government have launched transparency initiatives for oil companies to 'publish what they pay' to host governments; some businesses have implemented stricter codes of conduct on security, environment, and labour; and judicial processes have allowed the repatriation of funds embezzled by 'oil dictators'.[93] So far, however, the Bush administration has proved reluctant to engage into a *mandatory* governance agreement for the oil industry. Given the number of war victims and potential vested interests in Iraq, there is yet little evidence that a US policy shift from 'free oil' to 'freedom oil' is genuine and viable.

NOTES

1. Reported in D. Yergin, *The Prize: The Epic Quest for Oil, Money and Power* (New York: Simon and Schuster 1991) p.401.
2. World Islamic Front, 'Statement Urging Jihad Against Jews and Crusaders', *al-Quds al-Arabi*, 28 Feb. 1998.
3. Cited in J. Wardell, 'Blair Says Britain, U.S. Won't Touch Iraqi Oil', *Associated Press*, 6 March 2003.

4. Defined as armed conflicts revolving 'to a significant degree, over the pursuit or possession of critical materials', see M.T. Klare, *Resource Wars: The Changing Landscape of Global Conflict* (New York: Henry Holt 2001) p.23.

5. J. Calabrese, 'The United States, Great Britain, and the Middle East: How Special the Relationship?', *Mediterranean Quarterly*, Vol.12, No.3 (2001), pp.57–84.

6. See S.K. Aburish, *A Brutal Friendship. The West and the Arab Elite* (London: Indigo 1997).

7. Significant tensions between Iran and Iraq dated at least back to the 1969–1971 Shatt El Arab dispute and Iranian occupation of Iraqi islands in the Gulf. A. Garfinkle, 'The US Imperial Postulate in the Middle East', *Orbis*, Vol.41, No.1 (Winter 1997), pp.15–29.

8. E.L. Morse and A. Myers Jaffe, *Strategic Energy Policy: Challenges for the 21st Century*. (New York: Council on Foreign Relations 2001) p.24.

9. Richard Schofield, *Territorial Foundations of the Gulf States* (London: University College London 1994); Aymeric Chauprade, *Géopolitique. Constantes et Changements dans l'Histoire* (Paris: Ellipses 2001). For a discussion of oil and other resources in relation to the geography and political economy of war, see P. Le Billon, 'The Political Ecology of War: Natural Resources and Armed Conflicts', *Political Geography*, Vol.20, No.5 (2001), pp.561–84.

10. Iraq's posture towards its neighbours is geographically rooted in its British inherited borders, resulting in a very limited and lockable access to the sea and territorial claims over Kuwait.

11. Cited in T.L. Karl, *The Paradox of Plenty: Oil Booms, Venezuela, and other Petro-states* (Berkeley, CA: University of California Press 1997) p.4.

12. R. Said Zahalan with R. Owen, *The Making of the Modern Gulf States* (London: Ithaca Press 1998).

13. A. Alnasrawi, *Iraq's Burdens: Oil, Sanctions, and Underdevelopment* (Westport, CT: Greenwood Press 2002); A. Arnove, *Iraq Under Siege: The Deadly Impact of Sanctions and War* (Cambridge MA: South End Press 2002).

14. C. Leite and J. Weidmann, *Does Mother Nature Corrupt? Natural Resources, Corruption, and Economic Growth*, IMF Working Paper WP/99/85 (Washington DC: IMF, 1999); M.L. Ross, *Extractive Sectors and the Poor*, Oxfam America Report (New York: Oxfam, 2001); J.D. Sachs and A.M. Warner, 'Natural Resources and Economic Development. The Curse of Natural Resources', *European Economic Review*, Vol.45 (2001), pp.827–38.

15. R.M. Auty, *Sustaining Development in Mineral Economies: The Resource Curse Thesis* (London: Routledge 1993); M.L. Ross, 'The Political Economy of the Resource Curse', *World Politics*, Vol.51, No.2 (Jan. 1999), pp.297–322. For a counter-argument, see G.A. Davis, 'Learning to Love the Dutch Disease: Evidence from the Mineral Economies', *World Development*, Vol.23, No.10 (1995), pp.1765–79.

16. M.D. Shafer, *Winners and Losers: How Sectors Shape the Development Prospects of States* (Ithaca, NY: Cornell University Press 1994); Karl (note 11).

17. M.L. Ross, 'Does Oil Hinder Democracy', *World Politics*, Vol.52 (April 2001), pp.356–7.

18. R.M. Auty (ed.), *Resource Abundance and Economic Development* (Oxford: Oxford University Press 2001).

19. Ross, *Extractive Sectors* (note 14), p.15.

20. *SIPRI Yearbook* (Oxford: Oxford University Press, various).

21. With a maximum risk of war of 22 per cent for a country whose exports account for 32 per cent of GDP compared to a risk of 1 per cent for a similar country with no primary commodity exports. See P. Collier and A. Hoeffler, *Greed and Grievance in Civil War* (Washington DC: World Bank, 2001).

22. See E.L. Morse, 'A New Political Economy of Oil?', *Journal of International Affairs*, Vol.53, No.1 (Fall 1999) pp.1–29.

23. Persian Gulf oil production capacity is expected to reach about 45 million bbl/d by 2025, see *International Energy Outlook 2003*, tables D4 and D6.

24. China's demand in oil should double by 2025 (ibid.).

25. Evolving from 1.9 million bbl/d in 2001 to 3.4 million bbl/d by 2010 (ibid.).

26. R.E. Ebel and J.R. Schlesinger (eds), *The Geopolitics of Energy into the 21st Century* (Washington DC: Center for Strategic and International Studies 2000).

27. See S. Peters, 'Courting Future Resource Conflict: The Shortcomings of Western Response

Strategies to New Energy Vulnerabilities', *Energy Exploration and Exploitation* (forthcoming).

28. 'National Energy Policy 2001', Report of the National Energy Policy Development Group, Washington DC, p.X.

29. Oil import dependence from the region could reach 90 per cent by 2010. See F. Fesharaki, 'Energy and Asian Security Nexus', *Journal of International Affairs*, Vol.53, No.1(1999). pp. 85–99.

30. 'Al-Qaeda Terrorists Pose Biggest Threat to Persian Gulf Oil Transportation', *Oil and Gas Journal*, 19 March 2003.

31. Iran and Qatar hold the world's second and third-largest reserves (behind Russia). *Energy Information Administration*, Feb. 2001.

32. Asian demand for natural gas is expected to reach perhaps 25 trillion cubic feet by 2020. See F. Mohamedi and Y. Sadowski, 'The Decline (But Not Fall) of US Hegemony in the Middle East', *Middle East Report* (Fall 2001). pp.12–24.

33. K. Morita, *Gas for Oil Markets* (London: Royal Institute of International Affairs, 2000).

34. M. Dobbs, 'Inside the Mind of Osama Bin Laden. Strategy Mixes Long Preparation, Powerful Message Aimed at Dispossessed', *The Washington Post*, 20 Sept. 2001, p.A01; World Islamic Front, 'Statement Urging Jihad Against Jews and Crusaders' (note 2).

35. G. Bahgat, 'Oil Security in the New Millenium: Geo-economy vs. Geo-strategy', *Strategic Review*, Vol.26 (Fall 1998), pp.22–30; M. Monshipouri, 'The Paradoxes of U.S. Policy in the Middle East', *Middle East Policy*, Vol.9, No.3 (2002). pp.65–84. For a history of US involvement, see M.A. Palmer, *Guardians of the Gulf: A History of America's Expanding Role in the Persian Gulf, 1833–1992* (New York: Macmillan 1992).

36. P. Bennis, 'And They Called It Peace', *Middle East Report* (Summer 2000), pp.4–7.

37. The Gulf Cooperation Council is only a limited club in this regard. See Said Zahalan (note 12); A. Saikal, 'The United States and Persian Gulf Security', *World Policy Journal*, Vol.9, No.3 (1992), pp.515–31.

38. A.M. Lesch, 'Ossama Bin Laden: Embedded in The Middle East Crises', *Middle East Policy*, Vol.9, No.2 (June 2002), pp.82–91.

39. R. Vitalis, 'Black Gold, White Crude: An Essay on American Exceptionalism, Hierarchy, and Hegemony in the Gulf', *Diplomatic History*, Vol.26, No.2 (2002), p.187. Bechtel is a US engineering and construction company.

40. M. Donovan, *Islam and Stability in Saudi Arabia* (Washington DC: Center for Defense Information 2001); M. Yamani, *Changed Identities: The Challenge of the New Generation in Saudi Arabia* (London: Royal Institute of International Affairs 2002).

41. M. Huband, 'Bankrolling Bin Laden', *Financial Times*, 28 Nov. 2001.

42. 'TV Ads Say S.U.V. Owners Support Terrorists', *New York Times*, 8 Jan. 2003.

43. Klare (note 4).

44. Bush Sr and Jr both founded oil companies in Texas, his Vice-President Dick Cheney was CEO of Halliburton, while commerce secretary Donald Evans was CEO of the independent oil company, Tom Brown Inc. Army secretary Thomas White was executive at Enron, and undersecretary of commerce Kathleen Cooper was chief economist at Exxon. National security advisor Condoleezza Rice sat on the board of Chevron, which named a tanker after her in 1993. Collectively, the top 100 appointees of the Bush administration had most of their holdings in the energy sector, see D. Wetherell, *Bush Top 100* (Washington DC: Center for Public Integrity 2002). Oil and energy companies, including Exxon, Enron, and BP Amoco, were among the biggest donors to Bush's presidential campaign, and corporate energy gave 75 per cent of its 1999–2000 campaign contributions to Republicans, see *The Nation*, 4 Feb. 2002.

45. A. Rashid, *Taliban: Islam, Oil and the New Great Game in Central Asia* (New York: Tauris 2001).

46. 'Afghanistan Plans Gas Pipeline', *BBC News Online*, 13 May 2002; 'Central Asian Pipeline Deal Signed', *BBC News Online*, 27 December 2002; pers. com., June 2003.

47. Khalilzad was a US political appointee in the Reagan and Bush Sr administrations and supporter of Mujahideen groups in Afghanistan during the Cold War. See K. Sengupta and A. Gumbel, 'New U.S. Envoy to Kabul for Taliban Oil Rights', *Independent*, 10 Jan. 2002.

48. S. Winter, 'Turkmenistan: US Questions Gas Pipeline via Iran', *RFE/RL*, 16 Oct. 1997. On US oil interests in Turkmenistan, see S. O'Hara in this volume.

49. Iraq contains 112 billion barrels of proven oil reserves, along with roughly 215 billion barrels of probable and possible resources, as well as 110 trillion cubic feet (Tcf) of proven natural gas reserves and roughly 150 Tcf in probable reserves. *Energy Information Administration*, Feb. 2003; *Gulf News Online*, 9 November 2001. However, Canada's proven oil sand reserves (255 billion barrels) could place it in second place.

50. The objectives included: ending Saddam Hussein's regime; eliminating weapons of mass destruction; searching for, capturing and driving out terrorists who have found safe haven in Iraq; locating intelligence on terror activities being planned from Iraq; locating intelligence on the global terrorist network that has been formed; delivering humanitarian relief; securing Iraq's oil fields; and helping the Iraqi people's quick transition to self-government while ensuring the nation's territorial integrity. See US Defense Department's daily press briefing, 21 March 2003.

51. See President Bush's speech at the United Nations General Assembly on the first anniversary of 9/11 (12 September 2002); US Deputy Secretary of Defense, Paul Wolfowitz, admitted that invading Iraq would strategically allow a removal of US troops from Saudi Arabia, but 'for reasons that have a lot to do with the US government bureaucracy, we settled on the one issue that everyone could agree on: weapons of mass destruction', see 'Wolfowitz Interview with Sam Tannenhaus, Vanity Fair', United States Department of Defense, 9 May 2003.

52. Cited in W. Vieth, 'Powell: U.S. Won't Claim Iraq's Oil', *Los Angeles Times*, 23 Jan. 2003.

53. K.M. Pollack, 'Securing the Gulf', *Foreign Affairs*, July/August 2003, p.3.

54. This section builds on a review of English and French language public media on this issue.

55. BBC News, 'Iraqi Cuts Off Oil Exports', 8 April 2002.

56. 'OPEC Grappling with Postwar Iraq Questions', *Oil and Gas Journal*, 19 May 2003.

57. Y. Sadowski, 'Vérités et Mensonges sur l'Enjeu Pétrolier', *Le Monde Diplomatique*, April 2003, pp.18–19.

58. V. Marcel, *The Future of Oil in Iraq: Scenarios and Implications*, Briefing Paper No.5 (London: Royal Institute of International Affairs 2002).

59. L. Sieg, 'Post-war Japan Occupation No Road Map for Iraq', *Reuters*, 17 April 2003.

60. T. Jackson, 'The Delusion That It Is All About Oil', *Financial Times*, 14 Feb. 2003.

61. D. Roche, 'The Bear Market, Iraq and the Dollar', *Forbes*, 9 Dec. 2002.

62. Marcel (note 58).

63. Australian BHP, UK/Dutch Shell, and Italian ENI; see Marcel (note 58).

64. BBC News, 'Iraq halts Russian and Chinese oil deals', 26 May 2003.

65. M. Renner, 'Post-Saddam Iraq: Linchpin of a New Oil Order', *Foreign Policy in Focus*, Jan. 2003.

66. Cited in M.T. Klare, 'The Coming War With Iraq: Deciphering the Bush Administration's Motives', *Foreign Policy Focus*, Jan. 2003.

67. See Klare (note 4) ch.3.

68. Energy exports represent more than 20 per cent of Russia's gross domestic product and roughly 50 to 60 per cent of its total hard currencies earnings. See Troika Dialog Bank report, Oct. 2001.

69. European Commission, 'Towards a European Strategy for the Security of Energy Supply', Green Paper, 2000; Report from the Science and Technology Commission of the European Council, Parliamentary Assembly, 'Basis for an Energy Strategy for Europe', Doc. 8653, 21 Feb. 2000.

70. E. Strecker Downs, *China's Quest for Energy Security* (Santa Monica CA: RAND 2000). China's own main oil province, Xinjiang, has become a scene of unrest in recent years by Turkic-speaking Uighurs, seeking to create an independent Muslim state called East Turkestan. The separatist militants are based mainly in neighbouring Kazakhstan and Kyrgyzstan.

71. S. Troush, *China's Changing Oil Strategy and Its Foreign Policy Implications* (Washington, DC: Brookings Institution 1999).

72. P. Jayaram, 'US Plans War to Control Iraq's Oil Wealth: Experts', *Indo-Asia News Service*, 23 September 2002.

73. 'US Sanctions Firms in China, Iran, and Moldova', *Arms Control Today*, June 2003.
74. For a US perspective on the break-up of Iraq, see Daniel Byman, 'Let Iraq Collapse', *National Interest* (Fall 1996), pp.48–60.
75. It is unlikely, however, to claim this region for the State of Iraq by reasserting the invalidity of agreements allocating the area to the Kingdom of Iraq; see D. Pipes, 'Hot Spots: Turkey, Iraq, Mosul', *Middle East Quarterly* (Sept.1995).
76. For example, the Rumsfeld mission as a Middle East peace envoy to Baghdad in 1983 – in the midst of the Iran–Iraq war – entailed discussions with Saddam Hussein of a pipeline deal that Bechtel was negotiating, see R. Oppel, 'Bechtel Has Ties in Washington, and to Iraq', *New York Times*, 18 April 2003.
77. Morse and Myers Jaffe (note 8) p.16.
78. Report of the National Energy Policy Development Group, May 2001, p.8–6; National Security Strategy, Sept. 2002, p.20. Although some analysts expected the Bush administration to do as little as Clinton officials in applying the 1995 Iran–Libya Sanctions Act (ILSA), the US administration had toughened its position towards Iran, and notably about its nuclear programme, see *Reuters*, 5 July 2001; *AFP*, 28 May 2003.
79. US policy promoting the use of oil wealth to fund 'politically stabilizing development projects' is not new, see W. Taylor Fain, 'John F. Kennedy and Harold Macmillan: Managing the "Special Relationship" in the Persian Gulf Region, 1961–63', *Middle Eastern Studies*, Vol.38, No.4 (2002), pp.95–122.
80. UN Security Resolution 1483 (2003).
81. E. Vuillamy, 'Israel Seeks Pipeline for Iraqi Oil', *The Observer*, 20 April 2003.
82. G.W. Bush, 'Freedom and the Future', speech at the American Enterprise Institute, 26 Feb. 2003.
83. Condoleeza Rice, cited in P. Renolds, 'Analysis: Dealing with the "Axis"', *BBC News Online*, 21 Oct. 2002.
84. M.A. Ledeen, 'The Real War', *National Review Online*, 11 Dec. 2002.
85. T.L. Friedman, 'Anti-Terror Fight Has to Be a Marathon Run on Wilsonian Principle, Not Cheap Oil', *YaleGlobal*, 7 Feb. 2003.
86. On 14 July 1998, Syria and Iraq signed a memorandum of understanding on reopening the IPC pipeline, which links the Kirkuk oil fields in northern Iraq with Syria's port of Banias. *Energy Information Administration 2001*.
87. So far the US 'charges' include: suspected of harbouring and supporting terrorist groups, allegedly possessing a large stockpile of chemical weapons, and having openly chosen to be on the side of the Iraqi regime and harbouring former Iraqi leaders. D. Milbank, 'White House Escalates Diplomatic Pressure on Syria', *The Washington Post*, 14 April 2003.
88. E. Sciolino, 'US Pondering Saudis' Vulnerability', *New York Times*, 4 Nov. 2001.
89. E.L. Morse and J. Richard, 'The Battle for Oil Dominance', *Foreign Affairs*, March/April 2002.
90. A.H. Cordesman, *Geopolitics and Energy in the Middle East* (Washington DC: CSIS 1999).
91. J.A. Phillips, 'The Real Reason for OPEC's Newfound Muscle', *Press Room Commentary*, 3 April 2000.
92. See, for example, the speeches of US Deputy Secretary Of Defense Paul Wolfowitz, on 2 Feb. 2002 at the 38th Munich Conference on Security Policy, and Colin Powell during his visit in Ankara on 2 April 2003.
93. See P. Le Billon, *Fuelling War: Natural Resources and Armed Conflicts* (London: International Institute for Strategic Studies 2003).

Great Game or Grubby Game?
The Struggle for Control of the Caspian

SARAH L. O'HARA

Introduction

The sudden collapse of the Soviet Union at the end of 1991 precipitated a struggle for the control of the Caspian Sea Basin (CSB). Representing one of the last major unclaimed hydrocarbon territories in the world,[1] the development of the CSB's largely untapped energy resources became a main attraction for international energy companies and a significant number of regional and extra-regional governments. At present, proven oil reserves in the region are slightly less than those of the North Sea, with proven gas reserves being comparable to the USA.[2] However, it is expected that continued exploration will reveal larger reserves of both oil and gas.[3] The region therefore has the potential to offer a strategic counter-weight to the growing importance of the Organization of Petroleum Exporting Countries (OPEC) as global oil demand increases and output from non-OPEC countries declines.[4]

The region, however, is far from stable and a number of observers have noted that the Caspian displays many of the attributes that characterize conflict-ridden parts of the world.[5] Indeed, Klare[6] has argued that the combination of 'contested boundaries and border disputes, the prevalence of authoritarian regimes, severe economic disparities, long-standing regional rivalries, and a cauldron of ethnic and religious strife' is a recipe for violent conflict and, consequently that the 'Caspian could prove the setting of a major regional conflagration'. While such statements may appear alarmist the strategic importance of natural resources, such as oil, 'have played a conspicuous role in the history of armed conflict'[7] with countries that are heavily reliant on the export of primary commodities being particularly vulnerable.[8] This is especially true of petroleum-dependent states with many such countries being ravaged by conflict[9] with oil not only been the target of military intervention by external powers, but also being a factor fuelling civil conflicts.

The Caspian, however, is no stranger to conflict and the oil fields of the Caucasus have been fought over on numerous occasions in the past. Significantly, major events in the struggle for control of the Caspian have been of geopolitical significance and in this paper I examine the way in which resource competition and conflict in the region have become entwined in the development of geopolitical thought and ideas since the late nineteenth century. I do this by focusing on a number of important stages in the history of hydrocarbon exploitation in the Caspian Basin. First, I examine the period at the end of the 1800s when Baku, located on the western shore of the Caspian, rose to become the most important oil-producing centre in the world. I then move on to consider the strategic importance of the Caucasian oil fields during the First World War and the Second World War and the significance placed on the control of these resources by the various warring factions. In doing so I argue that the struggle for control of the Caspian was an important factor in the development of Mackinder's 'heartland' thesis which, although deeply flawed,[10] was highly influential to the evolution of US ideas on containment.[11] In the final part of the article I focus on the events in the Caspian since independence and argue that the underlying desire to control the 'heartland', that has been a central tenet to geopolitical thoughts and practice since the turn of the twentieth century, is been played out again via the control of the region's energy resources.

Baku: The Commercial Prize of the Late 1800s

In January 1904 Sir Halford Mackinder delivered his seminal lecture 'The Geographical Pivot of History' to the Royal Geographical Society in London.[12] Considered to be a defining moment in the history of geopolitics,[13] Mackinder argued that the development and expansion of railway networks had fundamentally shifted the balance of power away from seafaring nations, such as Britain, to those nations that controlled continental interiors. Such regions, he argued, were inaccessible by ship and as such were not vulnerable to attack by sea-powers. He further argued that whoever controlled the world's landmasses would have access to their vast resource wealth and that global dominance in the future would depend on the control and exploitation of such resources. In his view, Central Asia represented the 'pivot' and strategic control of the region would belong to either Tsarist Russia or a Russo-German combination – but, should China and Japan join forces, they too had the potential to be an important world force.[14]

The inclusion of the Caspian within Mackinder's 'pivot' is not surprising. He wrote at a time of great change; a period marked by a shift from an older industrial capitalism based on steam, coal and iron to one based on gas, electricity and, more significantly, oil.[15] As oil emerged as a key commodity in the latter part of the 1800s, Baku located on the western shore of the Caspian Sea, rose to prominence and control of both the production and export of its apparently limitless oil wealth became a major objective of the rapidly expanding oil business.[16] As the competition for Baku increased, so did output and by the turn of the twentieth century, it had emerged as the world's premier oil-producing region, accounting for more than 50 per cent of global production.[17] To Mackinder, the importance of Baku, and indeed other important oil-producing regions in the Caucasus,[18] would not have gone unnoticed. Although he had not visited the area,[19] the region Mackinder identified as his 'pivot' had throughout the mid to late 1800s been the focus of a campaign of espionage and counter-espionage with British interests pitted against those of the Russian Empire in an attempt to gain influence in Central Asia, Afghanistan and Persia. The Royal Geographical Society, which Mackinder joined in 1886, played a central role in this 'Cold War' of the Imperial age, sponsoring various expeditions to the region, hosting lectures and seminars and in effect acting as a repository for intelligence on the geography, politics, economics, mineral wealth and military capabilities of the region. A number of Mackinder's associates, notably Lord Curzon, had also travelled through the region and wrote extensively on the subject. Curzon, for example, visited the Caucasus and Central Asia in 1888, travelling on the recently constructed Trans-Caspian railway.[20] On his return to Britain he both wrote and lectured about his travels, commenting on the region's vast petroleum resources, noting that Baku's petroleum industry had reached 'the most gigantic proportions'.[21]

In 1904 and again in 1905, Baku experienced a series of strikes and periods of ethnic unrest.[22] These events not only had a significant impact on Baku, but sent shock-waves through global oil markets as the industry came to terms with the fact that conflict could disrupt oil supplies and render massive investments worthless. Despite these events, Baku was still considered to be of considerable commercial importance with James Henry, the British editor of *Petroleum World* commenting that, 'The Caucasus is endowed by nature with practically an inexhaustible mineral wealth. We are near the time when this vast region will be thrown open to Foreign financiers.' Moreover, he implores Britain to further strengthen its links with the region, stating that 'What we have in Russia we must hold, and now that Germans and Americans are bidding more vigorously for Russian favours and options, British financiers should give serious thought to the question of how they can best secure a fair share of those fields of industry.'[23] Such sentiments clearly had an impact and of the estimated $214m invested in the Russian oil industry by 1914, over $130m came from foreign investors, with investments from Britain accounting for over 60 per cent of this figure.[24]

Baku: The Strategic Prize of the First World War

By 1914, the commercial importance of Baku had declined and the region accounted for only 15 per cent of world production.[25] It was, however, still the most significant source of oil on Europe's immediate periphery and with the outbreak of the First World War, the oil fields of the Caucasus assumed considerable strategic importance. Until 1917, the region remained firmly under Russian domination, but the situation changed dramatically after the Bolshevik revolution and subsequent collapse of the Tsarist regime, which precipitated a frantic struggle for control of the region.[26] Initially the oil fields of Baku came under the control of the newly established Baku Soviet,[27] who were instructed by Lenin to continue and indeed increase output.[28] Germany's leaders, in desperate need of fuel, saw events in Russia as their opportunity to gain access to Baku's oil and immediately opened negotiations with revolutionary Russia.[29] Turkey, Germany's ally, also took advantage of these events to secure a foothold in the region and immediately following Azerbaijan's May 1918 declaration of independence,[30] the Turkish authorities signed an agreement with the new leadership giving them access to Baku's oil.[31] The implications of either Germany or Turkey gaining access to Baku were immense with an editorial published in the *New York Times* in June 1918 arguing that 'The primary task of the allies is to invade the important oil regions of the Caucasus.' By this stage, however, British forces had already been deployed to the region and on 4 August 1918, 1400 troops under the command of Major-General Dunsterville entered Baku.[32] Although they only managed to hold the city for a few weeks, it was long enough to deny the Germans access to much-needed crude oil at a critical moment in the war and, within weeks of Dunsterville's withdrawal, the war was at an end.

The British, however, were keen to ensure that their interests in Baku were protected and, under the terms of the Murdos Agreement which brought to an end hostilities between Britain and Turkey, the British were given the right to re-enter Baku. In a statement delivered shortly before his troops re-took the city, General Thomson announced that 'Baku with its oil fields would be occupied.'[33] This move was applauded in Britain with one of the leading British industrialists of the time, Herbert Allen, declaring that: 'The Russian oil industry liberally financed and properly organised under British auspices would in itself be a valuable asset to the Empire ... a golden opportunity offers itself to the British government to exercise a powerful influence upon the immense production of Grosni, Baku and Transcaspia fields.'[34]

Once in control of the city, Thomson established the British Oil Administration to run the oil industry and began an assessment of the state of the industry, commenting that 'Owing to its oil wealth', Baku has 'an influence far out of proportion to its size.'[35] In a series of reports to the Foreign Office, General Thomson detailed some of the problems facing the Baku oil industry and the barriers that the British needed to overcome if they were to control it. In his reports he notes, amongst other things, the problems of oil shipments because rivalries between Azerbaijan and Georgia were causing problems with rail shipments, and that transportation via the pipeline had ceased because 'of a tariff war' between the two countries. Yet, despite these apparent difficulties, the British managed to export 850,000 tonnes of oil from the region between December 1918 and August 1919 when international pressure forced them to quit Baku.[36]

The struggle for the Caucasus continued long after the November 1918 Armistice, but even in the midst of the ongoing chaos, Baku continued to attract investors. Standard Oil (of New Jersey), who had tried unsuccessfully to break into the Baku oil industry some 30 years before,[37] saw the situation as an opportunity to get a foothold in the region and in June 1919 signed an agreement with the fledgling Azerbaijani government to buy 100,000 tonnes of oil at $33 per tonne, with a commitment for another 100,000 tonnes in the following year.[38] But British investors in the region, notably Royal Dutch/Shell, were concerned by the deal, seeing it as a move by the Americans to penetrate the Baku oil industry. Considering such a move would undermine British interests in the region, the Azerbaijani government was put under considerable pressure by the British administration to renege on the deal; which it did. In April 1920 the Soviet Red Army determined to capture Baku Oil, as the source of energy to fuel the socialist revolution, re-took Baku and immediately re-nationalized the oil sector. Standard Oil were not to be deterred from gaining a foothold in the Baku oil industry and, despite the risk that the Bolshevik revolution would succeed, in July 1920 purchased a substantial amount of stock in the Nobel's concern. This investment proved a huge miscalculation on their part as the much-hoped for failure of the Bolshevik regime did not materialize, and international concerns were excluded from the region for the next 70 years.[39]

The First World War had put oil firmly on the map and at a meeting of the Inter-Allied Petroleum Conference held in London days after the Armistice, the chairman Lord Curzon, proclaimed that the allies had 'floated to victory on a wave of oil'.[40] The fact that the Caucasus had been so bitterly fought over, with control of its oil fields being seen as vital to all sides in the conflict, can only have served to bolster Mackinder's belief that resource control was essential to world power and it was against this background that he published a revised and expanded version of his 1904 analysis in early 1919.[41] Clearly written at speed, *Democratic Ideals and*

Reality was an attempt on Mackinder's part to influence the outcome of Versailles Peace negotiations. In it he argued that control of the 'pivot', which he now termed the 'heartland', remained important, but Eastern Europe should be considered a gateway to the 'heartland', proclaiming that 'Who rules Eastern Europe commands the Heartland; Who rules the Heartland commands the World-Island: Who rules the World-Island commands the World.'[42] The underlying tenet of Mackinder's thesis was the need to contain Germany and to prevent the Germans from forming an alliance with Russia, which would then undermine Britain's position in the world.

Initially, Mackinder's thesis had relatively little impact, with his ideas being roundly criticized in some quarters.[43] In Germany, however, his work attracted the attention of the former German General, Karl Haushofer, who considered Mackinder's thesis to be a geopolitical masterpiece.[44] Drawing on Mackinder's theories and concepts, Haushofer suggested that Germany should form an alliance with Russia and Japan, creating a 'Eurasiatic great continental bloc' which could challenge and eventually overwhelm the British Empire.[45] While Mackinder's ideas attracted attention in Germany, they provoked little reaction or comment from the Russians – somewhat surprising given the implication of his ideas for them. Hauner notes that following the publication of Mackinder's 1904 article, it was as if 'a silent conspiracy took place among the Russians to ignore completely the unintentional but provocative challenge made by the British Geographer'.[46] Likewise there is little mention of his work by the Soviets, although there is some suggestion that the Soviet leadership did take note of Mackinder's ideas and, during Stalin's reign, there was a radical spatial shift towards the east with the development of new resources and industries in the traditional heartland region. Moreover, strategic industries were relocated from the European frontier zone to this region which now benefited from improvements in rail infrastructure. Significantly, during the first five-year plan, Stalin created a formidable military industrial base in the Eurasian heartland roughly at the centre of his Soviet Empire.[47]

Out of the Blue: Hitler's Caucasian Dream

The Soviet administration, aware of the economic importance of the Caucasian oil fields, made enormous efforts to reverse the massive decline in output, precipitated by both internal and external unrest. By the late 1920s, production had returned to the levels achieved at the turn of the century and increased further during the first five–year plan (1928–32).[48] Production reached a high in the late 1930s, at which point the region accounted for 80 per cent of Soviet oil output.[49] By this stage war in Europe was considered inevitable and attention was once again focused on Baku and the Caucasus, which still remained the most important oil resource on Europe's periphery. As in the First World War, concerns centred on the possibility of the Germans gaining access to Baku's oil. Fears that Stalin would provide Hitler with oil were heightened following the signing of the German-Soviet Non-Aggression Pact, prompting France and Britain to discuss the possibility of bombing Baku,[50] with the British Royal Air Force (RAF) going as far as drawing up bombing maps outlining which facilities in the city should be destroyed.[51] Hitler's plan, however, was not to form an alliance with the Soviet Union but to invade it and, in June 1941, over 3 million German troops poured over the Soviet border. Unsurprisingly the capture of the Caucasian oilfields was central to Hitler's Russian campaign, with the aim of depriving the Soviets of fuel[52] and, more importantly, ensuring Germany's own supplies. Indeed Hitler is quoted as saying that, if he failed to take the oil fields of the Caucasus, he might as well end the war.[53] So confident was he of success that he assembled a 15,000-strong Technical Oil Brigade who would be responsible for rehabilitating and running the Russian oil industry.[54] Initially Hitler's plans appeared to be going well and, in August 1942, German troops captured Maikop, an important oil-producing centre in the western Caucasus, with the date for the attack and seizure of Baku being set for 25 September 1942. A few days prior to this, Hitler's generals presented him with a large decorated cake depicting the Caspian Sea and Baku. Hitler, apparently amused by the gesture, is shown in film footage of the event as taking the most desirable piece – Baku – for himself.[55] Within weeks, however, Hitler's army had become embroiled in the Battle for Stalingrad and Baku was never taken.

From Heartland to Rimland: The Development of the US Containment Policy

Haushofer's links with the Nazi leadership – he was a close friend of Rudolph Hess and met Hitler on a number of occasions – provoked considerable speculation in both the US and British media, that his ideas formed the basis for Hitler's master plan.[56] The attention afforded to Haushofer's work during the Second World War also rekindled an interest in Mackinder's ideas,[57] and he was invited by the editor of *Foreign Affairs* to provide an update of his 'heartland' concept, which was published in mid-1943. At the time of writing the third and final modification of his theory, Germany's push into the Eurasian heartland had apparently vindicated his earlier concerns, leading Mackinder to comment that his heartland concept was even more 'valid and useful today than it was either twenty or forty years ago'.[58] At roughly the same time, however, Mackinder's basic hypothesis was challenged by the American geopolitician, Nicolas Spykman. Like Mackinder, Spykman highlighted the importance of the arrangement of the continents to matters of global power.[59] But, whereas Mackinder viewed the control of the heartland to be crucial, Spykman viewed control of the 'inner crescent',[60] surrounding the heartland to be the key factor. Renaming this area the 'rimland', he argued that 'Who controls the rimland rules Eurasia; who rules Eurasia controls the destinies of the World'.[61] This revised heartland theory gained prominence in American thinking after the Second World War, although by now the term heartland had become synonymous with the USSR.[62] From the late 1940s onwards, key documents and government statements make reference to Eurasia, highlighting the need to contain this area.

The idea of containment was first introduced into public debate by George Kennan in his anonymous X-article, published in *Foreign Affairs* in 1947.[63] Kennan believed that a 'long-term, patient but firm and vigilant containment of Russian expansive tendencies' was required and, according to Dalby,[64] US foreign policy drew directly on this theme 'to formulate its strategies for the conduct of the (geopolitical) rivalry with the Soviet Union'. In this framework, the US created a network of multilateral or bilateral alliances, including NATO, SEATO, CENTO and ANZUS, that successfully lined up against the Soviet coalition. The US policy of containing the USSR, which dominated global geopolitics between the Second World War and the end of the 1980s, was summed up in the 1988 National Security Strategy of the United States published by the Reagan administration, which states that

> It is the conviction that the United States' most basic national interests would be endangered if a hostile state or group of states were to dominate the Eurasian landmass- that part of the globe often referred to as the world's heartland.....since 1945, we have sought to prevent the Soviet Union from capitalising on its geostrategic advantage to dominate its neighbors in western Europe, Asia and the Middle East and thereby fundamentally alter the global balance of power to our disadvantage.[65]

As the US put in place strategies to counter threats to its own security and its interests elsewhere, the USSR, having pushed back the German invaders, made a parallel move to increase the safety of its own national interests. The Soviets did this by bringing the countries of Eastern and Central Europe under their control to form a buffer zone against the West, and then, like the US, building up a huge military industrial complex.[66] One of the most important sites was the massive Polygon Military Complex located at Semipalatinsk in Kazakhstan, where far from the prying eyes of the West,

Stalin established his nuclear testing programme.[67] The siting of one of the Soviets' most strategically important military complexes in the Central Asian heartland stimulated further US interest in the region, and ensured its continued prominence in US geopolitical thinking throughout the Cold War.

Centre-Stage Once Again: The Caspian after 1991

The disintegration of the Soviet Empire heralded a new phase in the competition for the Caspian, which has been both multifaceted and multilayered.[68] The possibility that the Caspian Sea Basin contains vast hydrocarbon reserves triggered a flurry of interest in the region, placing at it the heart of global energy politics.[69] For the newly independent countries of the region, particularly energy-rich Azerbaijan, Kazakhstan and Turkmenistan, Caspian energy promised a path to rapid economic development. Eager to distance themselves from Moscow, the governments of these countries actively courted the businessmen and diplomats, who in the wake of the collapse of the Soviet Union, descended on their capitals in droves. For their part, international energy companies, lured by the prospect of enormous hydrocarbon reserves, were happy to sign potentially lucrative deals in order to ensure their 'piece' of the Caspian.[70]

In the initial euphoria of the post-independence period much was made of the fact that the region could hold as much as 200 billion barrels of oil, prompting the former US Secretary of State, James Baker, to state that 'Caspian oil may eventually be as important to the industrialized world as Middle East oil is today'.[71] But political strategists have never made a distinction between possible, probable, and recoverable oil reserves, and while a 2002 US Department of Energy estimate states that the Caspian could hold up to 233 billion barrels (BBL) of possible reserves, only 10 BBL are actually proven.[72] Although it is expected that continued exploration will reveal larger reserves of oil,[73] the most likely 'yet-to-find' projection for Caspian oil is 50–70 BBL.[74] Likewise while possible reserves of natural gas stand at 475 trillion cubic feet (tcf), proven reserves are significantly less, being between 177 and 182 tcf. Analysts now estimate that by 2015–2020 oil output from the Caspian will be between 2[75] and 6 MBD[76] and at most will account for c.3–4 per cent of total global demand. Gas output will meet a slightly higher percentage of demand and, based on existing discoveries, the Caspian has the potential to produce c.6.2 tcf per annum by 2010, with output by 2020 expected to meet c.5–6 per cent of global requirements. These rather modest forecasts of the Caspian's production potential, particularly given the considerable hype that surrounded early estimates, beg the question: why has the region attracted so much contemporary international attention? The answers to this question are quite simple: firstly, Caspian energy resources could be important to energy supply security;[77] secondly, despite the numerous risks, energy companies involved in developing Caspian hydrocarbons will undoubtedly benefit financially; and thirdly, and possibly most importantly, whoever controls the Caspian's energy resources will wield considerable influence in what can be considered the heart of the heartland.

The Scramble for the 'Heartland'

The US were quick to take advantage of the power vacuum that followed the collapse of the Soviet Union, establishing diplomatic missions throughout Central Asia and the Caucasus and forging its own links with the newly independent states. The chief stated goals of US policy is to encourage the countries of the Caucasus and Central Asia to evolve into strong, independent states based on democracy, market economics, the rule of law, and integration into the international community,[78] with the former Deputy Secretary of State, Strobe Talbot commenting that:

> The emergence of such a community represents a profound break with the past for all the peoples involved, but for none more than those of the Caucasus and Central Asia, who have, for so much of their history been subjected to foreign domination. Today, they have the chance to put behind them forever, the experience of being pawns on a chess board, as big powers vie for wealth and influence at their expense.[79]

Despite the turmoil within its own borders, Russia was keen to ensure that it remained a forceful presence in its former southern tier and in July 1994, President Yeltsin signed a secret directive on 'Protecting the Interests of the Russian Federation in the Caspian Sea,' in which it was argued that Russia should maintain its sphere of influence in the region.[80] Russia's activities throughout the 1990s, however, have been seen as being both obstructive and confrontational and it is widely believed that Russia was both directly and indirectly involved in a number of regional conflicts, which flared up in the immediate post-independent period.[81] Specifically, Russia is thought to have been instrumental in the 1993 coup which ousted the pro-Turkish, anti-Russian Azerbaijani President Elchibey from power, and the 1995 and 1998 attempted assassinations of the Georgian President, Edvarde Shevardnadze.[82] Russia also supported Armenia in its war with Azerbaijan by providing the Armenians with over $1bn of arms between 1993 and 1995.[83]

A number of other countries also viewed the collapse of the Soviet Union as an opportunity to gain a foothold in Central Asia and the Caucasus. Turkey, for example, was quick to rekindle its once strong links with the region, especially with the Turkic republics of Azerbaijan, Kazakhstan, Kyrgyzstan, Turkmenistan and Uzbekistan. This policy was supported by western governments, particularly the United States, as a means of countering Iran's growing influence in the region and was welcomed by the fledgling governments of the newly independent states, who were desperate for international recognition and economic support.[84] But after an initial period of enthusiasm Turkey's influence waned somewhat and, according to Aydin,[85] Turkey's 'excessive emphasis on commonalties' between the two regions became a source of resentment rather than co-operation. Notwithstanding this fact, Turkey remains an important player in the region and has become increasingly involved in Caspian energy issues and pipeline politics. Significantly Turkey has been an aggressive promoter of an East–West export corridor and has been keen to ensure that both gas and oil pipelines cross Turkish territory.

While attention has been focused on the antics of Russia and America and, to a lesser extent Turkey, China has been quietly strengthening its links in the region. In 1996, for example, China (as the main sponsor), Russia, Kazakhstan, Kyrgyzstan and Tajikistan, came together to form the Shanghai Five. Initially a forum to resolve old Soviet–Chinese border disputes, its remit changed somewhat in 2001 when Uzbekistan joined the group, which now renamed itself the Shanghai Cooperation Organisation (SCO). A year later the six nations signed a charter, transforming the SCO security bloc into a fully-fledged international organization with a permanent secretariat based in Beijing.[86] China's sponsorship of the organization is considered a significant move, particularly given that China has traditionally been considered isolationist and wary of multilateral alliances. China, however, clearly sees the SCO as a means of countering the growing US influence in the region,[87] and at its inaugural meeting, China's deputy foreign minister with responsibility for SCO affairs, stated that Beijing intended to use the organization to promote trade and investment in its search for influence over Central Asia.[88]

Who Controls The Export Routes, Controls The Oil And Gas; Who Controls The Oil and Gas, Controls the Heartland

Gaining control over the routes by which oil and gas will be exported has been a crucial part of the struggle for control of the Caspian. Russia argues that the northern route represents the most economical and technically feasible option for exporting both oil and gas from the region. A number of pipelines already exist including the Baku-Novorossiysk Pipeline, which links Azerbaijan to the Russian Black Sea port of Novorossiysk and the Atyrau-Samara pipeline, which takes Kazakh oil to the Russian oil hub at

Samara and from there to Europe via the Druszhba system. A third pipeline, backed by the Caspian Pipeline Consortium, was completed in March 2001 and exports oil from Kazakhstan's massive Tengiz field via Russia to Novorossiysk. Taken together, the three pipelines provide Russia with a virtual monopoly over exports from the region: a situation considered undesirable by other Caspian littoral states as well as a number of western governments and energy companies, who have accused Russia of using its pipeline monopoly to put pressure on the littoral states to sign agreements that are beneficial to Russia.

In an effort to break Russia's pipeline monopoly, various other export routes that bypass Russia have been proposed.[89] The project receiving the most attention has been the Baku-Ceyhan pipeline, which will take oil from Azerbaijan to the Turkish Mediterranean port of Ceyhan via Georgia. The idea for this pipeline was initially promoted by the governments of Azerbaijan, Georgia and Turkey, who viewed it as a desirable alternative to the existing Baku-Novorossiysk pipeline. Azerbaijan, for example, considers this route as central to its efforts to keep Russia's influence in the region at bay, while Georgia and Turkey stand to gain substantially from transit fees for any oil which crosses their territory. Initially, the project looked unlikely to come to fruition as western oil companies questioned its economic viability, highlighting the benefits of other routes, particularly those to the south. Moreover, they expressed concern over pipeline security as it would pass through or close to some of the most unstable areas of the southern Caucasus, as well as the Kurdish region of north-eastern Turkey. The situation changed in late 1997 when the US government, who had had previously supported the idea of multiple pipelines, adopted a new stance giving its full and unreserved support for the project. In the intervening period the US government has vested considerable political capital in the project, arguing that it is politically and environmentally desirable as well as being economically viable.[90] It has been argued that US involvement in the region is more about ensuring American interests are catered for and preventing other external powers, namely Russia and Iran, from gaining power. According to Rem Vyakhirev,[91] the US sponsorship of the East-West export corridor has overt political objectives to pull the countries of the Caucasus and the Caspian Sea into the western orbit and world economy, while at the same time isolating Iran and diversifying the West's energy sources away from the Middle East.[92]

Iran has long maintained that routes through its territory to the Persian Gulf are the shortest and most economical for the transport of oil from the Caspian Region, either by direct transportation along pipelines or by oil swaps. America, however, is opposed to the transit of Caspian energy through Iran and, since 1995, US companies have been prohibited from conducting business with Iran. Furthermore, the US Iran and Libya Sanctions Act (ILSA)[93] of 1996 imposed sanctions on non-US companies that made large investments in the Iranian oil and gas sector. The US has not only tried to prevent investment in Iran itself, but it has put considerable pressure on the Caspian states not to do business with Iran. Iran's $20bn gas sales agreement with Turkey signed in 1996, for example, was stalled because of American pressure on Turkey not to go ahead with the deal.[94]

According to Hunter,[95] Pakistan saw the US policy of preventing exports via Iran as an opportunity to strengthen its own links with the region and importantly to establish itself as a major transit route for Caspian energy.[96] However, with no direct borders with Central Asia, pipelines would have to cross Afghanistan and herein lay a problem. Since the withdrawal of Soviet troops in 1989, Afghanistan had been racked by civil war with various groups vying to take control of the country. Despite the chaos, a number of energy companies were exploring the possibility of exporting Caspian energy via Afghanistan and Pakistan, though this would require the region to be stable. The emergence of the Taliban brought, what was viewed by some, as stability to the region with the US energy company, Unocal, quickly establishing a dialogue with the Taliban's leadership.[97] Unocal's involvement in Afghan pipeline projects fuelled speculation of US support for the Taliban and US officials did little to dispel such ideas. In November 1996, for example, US Assistant Secretary of State, Robin Raphel, speaking at the UN conference on Afghan peace, commented that 'The Taliban control more than two-thirds of the country; they are Afghan, they are indigenous and, they have demonstrated staying power. It is not in the interests of Afghanistan or any of us here that the Taliban be isolated.'[98] Ahmed Rashid has gone as far as stating that the Clinton administration was clearly sympathetic to the Taliban, as they were in line with Washington's anti-Iran policy and were important for the success of any southern pipeline from Central Asia that would avoid Iran.[99] Although the US position on the Taliban changed dramatically in the late 1990s,[100] prompting Unocal to withdraw from the Afghan pipeline project, the US administration continue to view Afghanistan as a potential export route. Significantly, only a week before the events of '9/11', the US Energy Information Administration posted an updated brief on Afghanistan, which stated that:

> Afghanistan's significance from an energy point of view is its geographic position as a potential transit route for oil and natural gas exports from Central Asia to the Arabian Sea. This potential includes the possible construction of oil and natural gas export pipelines through Afghanistan, which was under serious consideration in the mid 1990s.[101]

While debates have tended to focus on whether Caspian energy will be exported north, south or westwards, China has been looking at the possibility of building pipelines to the east. Underlying these plans is the fact that China's energy demands are rapidly increasing while domestic supplies are declining.[102] The country now faces a significant gap between indigenous supply and demand and will become increasingly dependent on energy imports. China now considers the diversification and expansion of its oil supplies as a high security priority and in recent years it has acquired the rights to develop several prospective oil fields in Iraq, Venezuela and Kazakhstan, with many considering China's involvement in Kazakhstan to be the most promising given its geographical proximity and political stability.[103] In 1997 the China National Petroleum Corporation surprised many industry analysts when it outbid Russian, American and other foreign competitors for the rights to develop jointly the Aktyubinsk and Uzen fields in western Kazakhstan.[104] As part of this deal China pledged to build two oil pipelines, one 2,800 kms in length linking Atyrau on the Caspian Sea to Urumchi, the capital of Xinjiang, and a second shorter pipeline from Kazakhstan to the Iranian border via Turkmenistan. China's investment in the project was set at US$9bn.[105] Although developments subsequently stalled,[106] the Chinese have continued to court Central Asia's leaders and have increased their commitments in Caspian energy developments.[107]

The Caspian Region post-9/11

Events in the CSB since independence have been compared by political and business analysts alike, with the 'Great Game' of the late nineteenth century[108] and the 'Cold War'.[109] By the end of the 1990s the situation looked firmly established; the US and Turkey on one side, and Russia and Iran forming an uneasy alliance on the other. On the margins were the EU and China both with growing interests in the region but relatively little influence. In many respects a situation reminiscent of both the Great game and the Cold War. '9/11', however, had significant implications for the Caspian region and saw the US further strengthening its position in the area. Within days of the attack US officials were visiting the region's capitals soliciting support for the US-led coalition against terrorism. Their effort received a largely positive response with a number of countries, notably Uzbekistan, Kyrgyzstan and Tajikistan, granting the US access to military bases on their territories with other key states allowing the US the use of their airspace.[110] Within weeks, US personnel began arriving in the area and today US troops are stationed in former Soviet bases at Khanabad (Uzbekistan), Manas (Kyrgyzstan) and Dushanbe (Tajikistan). The US has also used the threat that Al-Qaeda terrorists could be hiding out in Georgia's

Pankisi Gorge as a reason for sending special military advisers to the country.[111] Although US officials have continually reiterated that they do not intend to establish permanent bases in the region, some observers have commented that the scale of the military build up suggests that they are intending to establish a long-term presence in the area.[112] Indeed in a February 2002 statement, Assistant Secretary of State, Elizabeth Jones, commented that '*we do not want US bases in Central Asia*', but what the US government does want is for the governments in Central Asia to continue granting us access to their bases '*for as long as we need them.*'[113]

Russia's reaction not only to the growing US presence in their former territory, but to the fact that their old enemy are camping out in their former bases has been mixed. While President Putin granted the US access to Russian airspace and gave tacit approval for the US to set up bases in Central Asia, there has been growing concern in other quarters that he has allowed the United States to gain too much influence in the region, and that such influence could jeopardize Russia's future security. The reaction from military circles has been particularly vocal with the Russian armed forces newspaper, *Krasnaya Zvezda*, complaining about the inexorable growth of the US military presence in Central Asia.[114] There was an even greater outcry over the deployment of US advisors in Georgia, sparking a strong reaction from the Russian authorities with the Foreign Minister, Igor Ivanov, stating that such a development could destabilize the area;[115] although the Russian parliament later passed a resolution approving the deployment. Despite such concerns, the increased US interest in the region, and with it increased US spending, has been welcomed by many of the region's governments, some of whom see US support as essential to keeping Russia at bay.

The Spectre of Mackinder?

The demise of the superpower that had controlled the much-coveted heartland for over 70 years has inevitably rekindled an interest in Mackinder's ideas.[116] To some the Eurasian heartland is still of considerable strategic importance with the former US National Security Advisor, Zbigniew Brzezinski, stating that:

> Eurasia is the world's axial supercontinent. A power that dominated Eurasia would exercise decisive influence over two of the world's three most economically productive regions, Western Europe and East Asia. A glance at the map also suggests that a country dominant in Eurasia would almost automatically control the Middle East and Africa. With Eurasia now serving as the decisive geopolitical chessboard, it no longer suffices to fashion one policy for Europe and

another for Asia. What happens with the distribution of power on the Eurasian landmass will be of decisive importance to America's global primacy and historical legacy.[117]

It is not just in the US where Mackinder's ideas are receiving attention, but in the heartland itself, with growing interest in his ideas amongst Russian intellectuals and politicians.[118] The emergence of 'Eurasianism', which has gained support from both the far right and the far left, is viewed by some as the means by which Russia will regain some of its former glory and Eurasian extremists, such as Alexandr Dugin, argue that the 'heartland' forms the geographic launch pad for a global anti-western movement which has the ultimate aim of eliminating American influence from the region. Thus 100 years after he first published his study, Mackinder's ideas continue to have their supporters aı d continue to influence policy. What remains to be seen is how China's growing influence in the heartland, something Mackinder warned against in 1904, is interpreted both within and beyond the heartland.

In this article I have explored the ways in which the commercial and military competition for the oil fields of the Caspian between the late 1800s and the 1940s became intertwined with the development of geopolitical ideas and the practices of the twentieth century. Mackinder's inclusion of the Caspian within his 'pivot' was important and the fact that it was fought over in both the First World War and the Second World War, served to reinforce his 'heartland' theory. Thus despite the fact that his concept was flawed, his beliefs on global power were influential in shaping the post-Second World War political landscape and ensured that the 'heartland' became embedded in 'Cold War' geopolitics. The continued prominence of the 'heartland' in post-Cold War thinking is more to do with this legacy than reality. Moreover, while the struggle for control of the Caspian was important in the creation of the 'heartland', it is the very existence of the 'heartland' that has fuelled much of the recent interest in the region. Borrowing from Thomson's 1919 assessment, it could be argued that the Caspian has had and will continue to have an influence far out of proportion to its size.

NOTES

1. A. Mateeva, 'Brave Explores Required', *Accountancy*, Vol.125, No.1279 (2000), pp.62–3.
2. US Energy Information Administration, 'Caspian Sea Country Analysis Brief', July 2002, available through <http://www.eia.doe.gov/emeu/cabs/caspian.pdf>.
3. L. Ruseckas, 'State of the Field Report: Energy and Politics in Central Asia and the Caucasus', *The National Bureau of Asian Research, AccessAsia Review*, Vol.1, No.2 (1998), <http://www.nbr.org/publications/review/vol1no2/essay2.html>; T. Adams, 'Not the New Middle East', *Petroleum Economist*, Vol.68, No.12 (Dec. 2001), p.32.

4. Global energy demands are forecast to increase from 77 million barrels/day (mbd) to 120 mbd by 2020, with much of this demand being met by increased output from OPEC countries, in particular Saudi Arabia. See, for example, US Energy Information Administration, 'International Energy Outlook 2002', <http://www.eia.doe.gov/oiaf /ieo/contents.html>; R. Forsythe, *The Politics of Oil in the Caucasus and Central Asia: Prospects for oil Exploitation and Exports in the Caspian Basin*, Adelphi Papers No.300 (Oxford: Oxford University Press1996); E.L. Morse and J. Richard, 'The Battle for Energy Dominance', *Foreign Affairs* Vol.81, No.2 (2002), pp.6–31.

5. R. Ebel and R. Menon (eds), *Energy and Conflict in Central Asia and the Caucasus* (Lanham, MD: Rowman and Littlefield 2000), p.267; M. Klare, *Resource Wars: The New Landscape of Global Conflict* (New York: Metropolitan Books 2001).

6. Klare (note 5) p.132.

7. P. Le Billon, 'The Political Ecology of War: Natural Resources and Armed Conflicts', *Political Geography* Vol.20, No.5 (2001), pp.561–84.

8. P. Collier and A. Hoeffler, 'On Economic Causes of Civil War', *Oxford Economic Papers* No.50 (1998), pp.563–73; P. Collier and A. Hoeffler, 'Greed and Grievance in Civil War,' *World Bank Project* (2001), <http://www.worldbank.org/research/conflict/papers/ greedandgrievance.htm>.

9. See, for example, T.L. Karl, *The Paradox of Plenty: Oil Booms and Petro States* (Berkeley, CA: University of California Press 1997) p.380.

10. It is not my aim in this essay to provide a critique of Mackinder – this has been done in detail elsewhere; see, for example, W.H. Parker, *Mackinder: Geography as an Aid to Statecraft* (Oxford: Clarendon Press 1982) p.295; G. Ó Tuathail, 'Putting Mackinder in his Place: Material Transformations and Myth', *Political Geography Quarterly*, Vol.11 (1992), pp.100–18.

11. See, for example, S. Dalby, 'American Security Discourse: The Persistence of Geopolitics' *Political Geography Quarterly*, Vol.9, No.2 (1990), pp.171–88.

12. H.J. Mackinder, 'The Geographical Pivot of History', *Geographical Journal*, Vol.23 (1904), pp.421–42.

13. M. Heffernan, 'Fin de Siècle, Fin du Monde? On the Origins of European Geopolitics, 1890–1920', in K. Dodds and D. Atkinson (eds), *Geopolitical Traditions: A Century of Geopolitical Thought* (London: Routledge, 2000), pp.27–51.

14. H.J. Mackinder, 'The Geographical Pivot of History', pp.421–42.

15. M. Heffernan (note 13) pp.27–51.

16. The competition for Baku was a long and bitter struggle involving most of the major oil companies of the time including, the Swedish Nobels, the French Rothschilds, Royal Dutch Shell, the US giant Standard Oil as well as numerous smaller concerns. See, for example, D. Yergin, *The Prize: The Epic Quest for Oil, Money, and Power* (New York: Simon & Schuster 1991) pp58–72; 121–33; R.W. Tolf, *The Russian Rockefellers: The Saga of the Nobel Family and the Russian Oil Industry* (Stanford, CA: Hoover Institution Press 1976) p.269.

17. H. Hassmann, *Oil in the Soviet Union: History, Geography, Problems* (Princeton, NJ: Princeton University Press 1953) p.173.

18. Grozny emerged as an important centre for oil production in the early 1890s and later finds were made at Maikop and Emba.

19. Mackinder only visited the part of the world he referred to as the pivot/heartland on one occasion, then only for a few weeks in late 1919–early 1920, during his brief tenure as British High Commissioner to Southern Russia. Even then he spent most of his time stationed on a British war ship anchored off the Black Sea port of Novorossiysk, only venturing in land on one occasion to interview General Denikin at his headquarters. See M. Hauner, *What is Asia to Us?: Russia's Asian Heartland Yesterday and Today* (London: Routledge 1992) p.x; B. Blouet, 'Sir Halford Mackinder 1861–1947: Some New Perspectives', *School of Geography Oxford, Research Paper* No.13 (1975), p.40. For an analysis of the likely influences on Mackinder's thinking about Central Asia in the years before his famous 1904 address see S. O'Hara, M. Heffernan and G. Endfield, 'Halford Mackinder, the "Geographical Pivot", and British Perceptions of Central Asia', in B.

Blouet (ed.), *Mackinder and the Defence of the West: The Geographical Pivot of History* (London: Frank Cass, forthcoming 2004).
20. G.N. Curzon, *Russia in Central Asia in 1889: and the Anglo-Russian Question* (London: Case 1967; original ed, 1889) p.477.
21. Ibid., p.30. Curzon goes on to comment that the reader should refer to the work of Charles Marvin, *The Region of the Eternal Fire: An Account of a Journey to the Petroleum Region of the Caspian in 1883* (London: W.H. Allen & Co.) p.422.
22. J.D. Henry, *Baku: An Eventful History* (London: Constable 1905; reprint, New York: Arno Press 1977).
23. Ibid., p.x.
24. H. Hassmann (note 17) p173. Hassmann also notes, on p.28, that Britain accounted for 60 per cent of foreign investment in Baku, 50 per cent in Grozny and 90 per cent in the smaller fields at Emba and Maikop. In total over 320 companies were involved in the region's oil industry.
25. Ibid., p.35.
26. For a detailed overview of events see F. Kazemzadeh, *The Struggle for the Transcaucasus (1917–1921)* (New York: The Philosophical Library of New York 1951) p.356.
27. On 1 June 1918, the Baku Soviet of National Commissars (Baksovnarkom) issued a decree on the nationalization of the oil industry followed by a second decree on 5 June 1918, which nationalized the Caspian Trade Fleet.
28. N. Maxwell, 'The Oil Issue In The Policy Of Azerbaijan's Government in 1918–1920', *Caspian Crossroads*, Vol.2, No.3 (Winter 1997), <http://ourworld.compuserve.com/homepages/usazerb/236.htm>.
29. F. Kazemzadeh (note 26) p.356.
30. In the immediate aftermath of the Bolshevik revolution, Georgia, Armenia and Azerbaijan came together to form the Transcaucasian Federation. Differences between the three groups, however, undermined the alliance which quickly floundered and in May 1918 all three states claimed independence.
31. J. Hassanov, 'The Struggle For Azerbaijani Oil At The End Of World War I', *Caspian Crossroads*, Vol.2, No.4 (1997), <http://ourworld.compuserve.com/homepages/usazerb/246.htm>.
32. L.C. Dunsterville, *Stalky's Reminiscences* (London: Jonathan Cape 1928). In his memoirs Dunsterville comments that he was informed that he was to be deployed 'overseas' in late December 1917 and he was soon made aware that his new posting covered North West Persia and the Caucasus. He goes on to comment that '*During June and July* (1918*) all our thoughts were concentrated on Baku towards which the Turks were pressing with all haste with a view of capturing the valuable oil wells.*' – see p.284.
33. Cited in F. Kazemzadeh, (note 26) p.164.
34. *Financial News*, 24 December 1918.
35. For a summary of Thomson's comments, see T.D. Adams, 'Back to the Future: Britain, Baku Oil and the Cycle of History', *Azerbaijan International*, Vol.6, No.3 (1998), <http://www.azer.com/aiweb/categories/magazine/63_folder/63_articles/63_adams.html>.
36. Maxwell (note 28).
37. Standard Oil was broken up into a series of smaller concerns in 1911 with the interested party being Standard Oil of New Jersey.
38. Hassanov (note 31).
39. Yergin (note 16) pp.237–43.
40. *The Times*, 22 November 1918, p.6.
41. H.J. Mackinder, *Democratic Ideals and Reality: A Study in the Politics of Reconstruction* (London: Constable and Co. Ltd. 1919) p.272.
42. Ibid.
43. G.G. Chisholm 'The Geographical Pre-requistes of a League of Nations: A Review', *Scottish Geographical Magazine*, Vol.35 (1919), pp.248–56; C.R. Dryer, 'Mackinder's World Island and its American Satellite', *Geographical Review*, Vol.9 (1920), pp.205–7.
44. W.H. Parker, *Mackinder: Geography as an Aid to Statecraft* (Oxford: Clarendon Press 1982) p.295.

45. H. Weigert, *Generals and Geographers: The Twilight of Geopolitics* (Oxford: Oxford University Press 1942) p.342.
46. M. Hauner, *What is Asia to Us? Russia's Asian Heartland Yesterday and Today* (London: Routledge 1992) p.147.
47. Ibid., p.52.
48. Hassmann (note 17) p.47.
49. T. Shabad, *Basic Industrial Resources of the USSR* (New York: Columbia University Press 1969) p.393.
50. V. Agayev *et al.*, 'World War II and Azerbaijan', *Azerbaijan International*, Vol.3, No.2 (1995), <http://www.azer.com/aiweb/categories/magazine/32_folder/32_articles/32_ww22.htm>; P.R. Osborn, *Operation Pike: Britain versus the Soviet Union, 1939–1941* (Westport, CT: Greenwood Press 2000) p.274. According to Osborn this was not the first time that the British authorities had considered bombing the oil fields of the Caucasus. In 1927, during a period when relations between Britain and the USSR were somewhat strained, the British government began drawing up plans to bomb Soviet petroleum centres in Grozny and Baku.
51. A copy of the RAF bombing map is held in the National Library of Scotland, Edinburgh. According to Osborn the RAF flew two covert missions in early 1940 in order to photograph the main oil-producing regions of the Caucasus. On 30 March, for example, a British aircraft devoid of RAF markings spent over an hour photographing Baku and its oil complexes. A second mission was undertaken a week later, this time over Batum on the Black Sea Coast, although on this occasion the plane was spotted and a Soviet fighter attempted to intercept. See Osborn (note 50) p.274.
52. In 1942, for example, about 70 per cent of all Soviet tanks, aeroplanes and armoured vehicles were operating with Baku oil. A. Abbaszade, 'War and its Legacy: Memories of World War II', *Azerbaijan International*, Vol.7, No.3. (1999), <http://www.azer.com/aiweb/categories/magazine/73_folder/73_articles/73_warandlegacy.htm>.
53. F. Paulus, *Ich Stehe Hier auf Befehl* (Frankfurt am Main 1960), p.157, cited in A. Beevor, *Stalingrad* (London: Viking 1999) p.69.
54. Yergin (note 16) p.336.
55. Agayev *et al.* (note 50).
56. The extent of his influence on Nazi thinking is questionable and while the signing of the German–Japanese Anticomintern Pact in 1936 and the Nazi–Soviet Non-Aggression Pact of 1939 would be in accordance with Haushofer's ideas – the invasion of the USSR was not. See for example H. Heske, 'Karl Haushofer: His role in German Geopolitics and in Nazi Politics', *Political Geography Quarterly*, Vol.6 (1987), pp. 135–44; G. O'Tuathail, *Critical Geopolitics: The Political Writings of Global Space* (London: Routledge 1996) p.314.
57. In addition to a number of articles about his work several pieces including *Democratic Ideals and Realities* were also republished.
58. H.J. Mackinder, 'The Round World and the Winning of the Peace', *Foreign Affairs* (July 1943), pp.595–605.
59. N.J. Spykman, *The Geography of Peace* (New York: Harcourt and Brace 1944).
60. Mackinder considered the 'pivot' to be surrounded by an 'inner crescent' consisting of mainland Europe and Asia and an 'outer crescent' comprising the islands and continents beyond Eurasia.
61. Spykman (note 59) p.43.
62. P.J. Taylor, *Political Geography: World-Economy, Nation-State and Locality* (Longman Scientific and Technical 1985) p.238.
63. "X" (G. Kennan), 'The Source of Soviet Conduct', *Foreign Affairs*, Vol.25, No.4 (1947), pp.566–82.
64. S. Dalby, 'American Security Discourse: The Persistence of Geopolitics', *Political Geography Quarterly*, Vol.9, No.2 (1990), pp.171–88.
65. Cited in ibid., p.X.
66. G. O'Tuathail '"Introduction" to Imperialists Geopolitics', in G. O'Tuathail, S. Dalby and P. Routledge (eds), *The Geopolitics Reader* (London: Routledge, 1998), pp.15–25.

67. The Soviet Union tested its first simple fusion bomb, Joe 4, at the Semipalatinsk test site in Kazakhstan in August 1953. It was here that over 65 per cent of Soviet nuclear tests were undertaken and it represented one of the most secret military facilities in the world.

68. M.P. Amineh, *Towards the Control of Oil Resources in the Caspian Region* (New York: St Martin's Press 1999) p.x; W. Ascher and N. Mirovitskaya (eds), *The Caspian Sea: A Quest for Environmental Security* (Dordrecht: Kluwer 2000); M.P. Croissant and B. Aras (eds), *Oil and Geopolitics in the Caspian Sea Region* (Westport, CT: Praeger 2000); R.Ebel and R. Menon (eds), *Energy and Conflict in Central Asia and the Caucasus* (Lanham, MD: Rowman and Littlefield 2000) p.267; Klare (note 5) p.289.

69. Ruseckas (note 3).

70. The Tengizchevroil joint venture between the US company Chevron and the Kazakhstani Tengiz oil field went in to operation in April 1993. The deal worth $20 billion was one of the first major deals to be signed in the former Soviet Union. A second major deal was announced by the Azerbaijan International Operating Company (AIOC) in September 1994 in what has been described as 'the deal of the century' –they signed a 30-year, $8bn contract to develop the region.

71. J.A. Baker, 'America's Vital Interest in the "New Silk Road"', *New York Times*, 21 July 1997.

72. Proven reserves are defined as oil and natural gas deposits that are considered 90 per cent probable, while possible reserves are defined as oil and natural gas deposits that are considered 50 per cent probable.

73. See, for example, Ruseckas (note 3); T. Adams, 'Not the New Middle East', *Petroleum Economist*, Vol.68, No.12 (Dec. 2001), p.32; H. McCutcheon and R. Osbon, 'Discoveries Alter Caspian Region Energy Potential', *Oil & Gas Journal* (17 Dec. 2001) pp.20–25. In July 2000 the Kazakh authorities announced a major off shore find in the northern Caspian stating that it represented the 'largest oil and gas discovery in the world in over 30 years', see 'Foreign Consortium Has Large Oil Find At Kashagan Field', *Wall Street Journal*, 15 March 2001; US Energy Information Administration, *Kazakhstan Country Analysis Brief* (July 2002), available through <http://www.eia.doe.gov/emeu/cabs/kazak.pdf>.

74. Ruseckas (note 3); T. Adams, 'Not the New Middle East', *Petroleum Economist*, Vol.68, No.12 (Dec. 2001), p.32.

75. McCutcheon and Osbon (note 73).

76. US Energy Information Administration, *Caspian Sea Country Analysis Brief* (July 2002), available through <http://www.eia.doe.gov/emeu/cabs/caspian.pdf>.

77. It has been suggested that the addition of even small amounts of Caspian oil 'at the margin' could have a major impact on world oil prices and erode some of the political control of the OPEC states. As well as limiting the market power of the major producers, Caspian oil will also broaden the supply base and could potentially reduce the impact of supply disruptions. Consequently Caspian oil could have greater importance that its rather modest reserves would otherwise suggest. See, for example, L. Pugliaresi, *Energy Security: How Valuable is Caspian Oil?*, Belfer Center for Science and International Affairs, Caspian Studies Program, Policy Brief No.3, Harvard University (2001), <http://ksgnotes1.harvard.edu/bcsia/library.nsf/pubs/Pugliaresi>.

78. This stance has been reiterated in a number of interviews conducted by the author with the present and former US special presidential advisors on the Caspian. Interview with Elizabeth Jones held on 29 January 2001. Interview with Steve Mann held on 21 March 2002.

79. S. Talbot, 'A Farewell to Flashman: American Policy in the Caucasus and Central Asia', address given at the Central Asian Institute School of Advanced International Studies, The Johns Hopkins University, 27 July 1997. A copy of the speech can be found at <http://www.sais-jhu.edu/pubs/speeches/talbott.html>.

80. R.V. Barylski, 'Russia, the West, and the Caspian Energy Hub', *Middle East Journal*, Vol.49, No.2 (1995), pp.217–32.

81. In 1988 there were violent clashes between ethnic Armenians and Azeris when the former called for the largely Armenian autonomous oblast of Nogarno-Karakakh in Azerbaijan to be united with Armenia. Azeris vehemently opposed this plan arguing that the Karabakh

region was part of Azerbaijan's territory. The collapse of the Soviet Union turned the conflict into a full-scale war and in 1992 Armenian-backed Karabakh militiamen effectively took control of the Karabakh region as well as surrounding territories, eventually controlling nearly 20 per cent of Azerbaijan. Although a cease-fire was brokered in 1994, periodic outbreaks of violence continue and a final peace settlement has yet to be agreed. Similar ethnic-related conflicts have flared up elsewhere in the Caucasus and since 1988 the region has suffered widespread civil unrest with outbreaks of violence between Georgia and South Ossetia, Georgia and Abkhazia, Russia and Chechnya, Russia and Dagestan and between North Ossetia and Ingushetia. The current status of these conflicts varies but as yet there has not been a single peace agreement between any of the warring factions and the situation throughout large parts of the Caucasus remains extremely tense. See, for example, S. Heslin, *Key Constraints to Caspian Pipeline Development: Status, Significance and Outlook* (James A. Baker Institute for Public Policy 1998); E. Herzig, *The New Caucasus: Armenia, Azerbaijan and Georgia* (London: The Royal Institute of International Affairs 1999), p.165; A. Zverev, 'Ethnic Conflicts in the Caucasus 1988–1994', in B. Coppieters (ed.), *Contested Borders in the Caucasus* (1996), <http:// poli.vub.ac.be/publi/ContBorders/eng/ch0101.htm>.

82. BBC News online, 'Eduard Shevardnadze – the great survivor', 10 March 1998, <http://news.bbc.co.uk/hi/english/despatches/newsid_64000/64267.stm>.

83. US Energy Information Administration, 'Caspian Sea Region: Regional Conflicts', July 2002, <http://www.eia.doe.gov/emeu/cabs/caspconf.html>.

84. G. Winrow, 'Turkey and the Newly Independent states of Central Asia and the Transcauscasus', *The Middle East Review of International Affairs* (1997), <http:// meria.idc.ac.il/journal/1997/issue2/jv1n2a5.html>.

85. M. Aydin, 'Turkey and Central Asia', *Central Asian Survey*, Vol.15, No.2 (1996), pp.165–6.

86. A. Blau, 'Central Asia: "Shanghai Six" Form Charter As International Organisation', *RFE/RL*, 7 June 2002, <http://www.rferl.org/nca/features/2002/06/07062002164836.asp>.

87. B. Gill, 'Shanghai Five: An Attempt to Counter U.S. Influence in Asia?', *Newsweek Korea*, 4 May 2001 <http://www.brook.edu/views/op-ed/gill/20010504.htm>.

88. R. Cutler, 'U.S. Intervention in Afghanistan: Implications for Central Asia', *Foreign Policy in Focus*, Nov. 2001, available through <http://www.foreignpolicy-infocus.org/pdf/gac/0111afghanint.pdf>.

89. To date only one oil pipeline has been built, the relatively small Baku-Supsa pipeline, which connects Azerbaijan to the Georgian Black Sea port of Supsa.

90. J. Wolf, US special presidential advisor on the Caspian, personal communication, Oct. 2000.

91. Rem Vyakhirev was the chairman of Gazprom, the Russian gas monopoly until 2001.

92. S. Fidler and L. Boulton, 'Pipeline Dispute Fuels West's Fiery Relations', *Financial Times*, 18 November 1999, p.18.

93. The Iran and Libya Sanctions Act was enacted in 1996. It sanctions foreign companies that provide new investments of over $40m for the development of petroleum resources in Iran or Libya, or that violate existing UN prohibitions against trade with Libya in certain goods and services such as arms, certain oil equipment, and civil aviation services. The law allows the president to waive sanctions against a foreign company if doing so is deemed to be in the US national interest. US companies are prohibited by US law from engaging in any commercial or financial transactions with Iran or Libya. The election of George W. Bush to the US Presidency further fuelled speculation that an improvement in relations between the two countries was imminent. In August 2001, however, Bush signed into law H.R. 1954, the ILSA Extension Act of 2001 – a 5-year extension of the Iran and Libya Sanctions Act (ILSA). Iran's support of the anti-terrorism coalition established in the wake of 11 September increased the expectations of improving relations between the US and Iran. But following Iran's explicit inclusion in Bush's 'Axis of Evil' statement, any talk of a thaw in relations has ceased.

94. J.H. Noyes, 'Fallacies, Smoke and Pipe Dreams: Forcing Change in Iran and Iraq', *Middle East Policy*, Vol.7, No.3 (2000), pp.28–50.

95. S. Hunter, 'The Afgan Civil War', in R. Ebel and R. Menon (eds), *Energy and Conflict in Central Asia and the Caucasus* (Lanham, MD: Rowman and Littlefield 2000), pp.189–208.
96. Historically Central Asia's main trade access to the sea was through modern Pakistan, but after its incorporation into the USSR the region became linked into the Soviet economy.
97. See, for example, BBC Online, 'Taleban in Texas for Talks on Gas Pipeline', 4 December 1997, <http://news.bbc.co.uk/1/hi/world/west_asia/37021.stm>.
98. Statement by US Assistant Secretary of State, Robin Raphel, at the UN conference on Afghanistan, 25 November 1996. A complete text of the statement can be found at <http://www.usembassy-israel.org.il/publish/press/state/archive/november/sd2l126.htm>.
99. A. Rashid, *Taliban: Militant Islam, Oil and Fundamentalism in Central Asia* (New Haven, CT: Yale University Press 2000) p.288. For a different view see M. Rubin, 'Who is responsible for the Taliban', *Middle East Review of International Affairs*, Vol.6, No.1 (March 2002), <http://meria.idc.ac.il/journal/2002/issue1/jv6n1a1.html>.
100. Following the 1998 bombings of the US embassies in Kenya and Tanzania. The Saudi dissident, Osama Bin Laden, a major supporter of the Taliban and whose activities were orchestrated from Afghanistan, was implicated in these events. The Taliban's failure to hand him over to the US authorities resulted in the US launching a bombing raid on suspected Al-Queda strongholds in Afghanistan.
101. US Energy Information Agency, 'Afghanistan Country Brief', Sept. 2001, <http://www. eia.doe.gov/emeu/cabs/afghan.html>.
102. E.S. Downs, *China's Quest for Energy Security* (Santa Monica, CA: Rand Publications 2000) p.68.
103. S. Troush, *China's Changing Oil Strategy and its Foreign Policy Implications*, Brookings Institution Center for Northeast Asian Policy Studies Working Paper, Fall 1999, <http://www.brook.edu/fp/cnaps/papers/1999_troush.htm>.
104. G. Christoffersen, 'China's Intentions for Russian and Central Asian Oil and Gas', *NRB Analysis*, Vol.9, No.2 (1997), available through <http://www.nbr.org/publications/analysis/vol9no2/v9n2.pdf>.
105. Troush (note 103); J. DeLay, 'The Caspian Oil Pipeline Tangle: A Steel Web of Confusion', in Croissant and Aras (note 69), pp.43–81.
106. Following the sharp drop in oil prices in 1999 these plans were put on hold and some analysts believe it is unlikely that they will ever be built as a CNPC's feasibility study has indicated that there will be insufficient oil to make the project economically viable. Significantly, the CNPC now argues that the agreement it signed in 1997 represented a Memorandum of Understanding and not a binding contract.
107. The former Chinese President, Jiang Zemen, met four of the five Central Asian presidents at the Shangai Forum in Tajikistan in July 2000, before travelling to Turkmenistan where he signed an agreement with the Turkmen government to develop oil – see, for example B. Pannier, 'Central Asia: U.S. Interests Suffer Setbacks', *RFE/RL*, 18 July 2000, <http://www.rferl.org/nca/features/2000/07/F.RU.000718150038.html>. In March 2003 British Gas agreed to sell its 16.67 per cent interest in the Northern Caspian in two equal parts to Sinopec, China's number two oil producer and CNOOC, the region's third biggest. P. Wonacott, 'China's CNOOC Targets Gas Deal In Caspian Sea', *Wall Street Journal*, 10 March 2003).
108. See, for example, P. Hopkirk, *The Great Game: On Secret Service in High Asia* (Oxford: Oxford University Press 1991) p.576; K.E. Meyer and S.B.Brysac, *Tournament of Shadows: The Great Game and the Race for empire in Central Asia* (Counterpoint Press 1999) p.688. A. Rashid, 'The New Great Game: The Battle for Central Asia's Oil', *World Press Review* Vol.44, No.6 (1997), pp.32–3; A. Cohen, 'The "New Great Game": Pipeline Politics in Eurasia', *Caspian Crossroads Magazine* Vol.2, No.1 (1996), <http://ourworld. compuserve.com/homepages/usazerb/213.htm>; J. Stadelbauer, *A New 'Great Game' in the Caspian Region?*, Russian Regional Research Group Working Paper, No.20, School of Geography and Environmental Sciences, Centre for Russian and East European Studies, University of Birmingham and Department of Geography, University of Leicester, 2000.
109. A.M. Jaffe, and R.A. Manning, 'The Myth of the Caspian "Great Game": The Real

Geopolitics of Energy', *Survival* Vol.40 (1998), pp.112–29; J.R. West and J. Nanay, 'Caspian Sea Infrastructure Projects', *Middle East Policy*, Vol.7, No.3 (2000), pp.111–21; Klare (note 5) p289.

110. J.-C. Peuch, 'Central Asia: U.S. Military Buildup Shifts Spheres Of Influence', *RFE/RL*, 11 Jan. 2002, <http://www.rferl.org/nca/features/2002/01/11012002091651.asp>.

111. Shortly afterwards Washington also announced it would be providing the Georgian Army with light weapons, vehicles, and communications equipment worth *c.* $64m, as part of its effort to enhance its ongoing military co-operation with Tbilisi.

112. V. Loeb, 'Footprints in Steppe of Central Asia', *The Washington Post*, 9 Feb. 2002, p.9.

113. E. Jones, 'US wants engagement, not bases, in Central Asia', Transcript of US Assistant Secretary of State Elizabeth Jones's briefing, issued on 11 February 2002, <http://www.usinfo.state.gov/topical/pol/terror/02021110.htm>. Significantly, in October 2003 Russia opened in Kyrgyzstan its first new foreign airbase since the collapse of the Soviet Union. The base, located at Kant, some 20 miles from the US base at Manas, will house a new rapid reaction force aimed at strengthening security in the region and is viewed by some as a counter to the growing influence of the United States; see for example, 'Russia opens Kyrgyzstan base', BBC Online, 23 October 2003, <http://news.bbc.co.uk/1/hi/world/asia-pacific/3206385.stm>.

114. See <http://www.guardian.co.uk/russia/article/0,2763,630205,00.html>.

115. J.-C. Peuch, 'Caucasus: Russia To Reluctantly Agree To U.S. Military In Georgia', *RFE/RL*, 28 Feb. 2002. <http://www.rferl.org/nca/features/2002/02/28022002084915.asp>.

116. C.J. Fettweis, 'Sir Halford Mackinder, Geopolitics and Policymaking in the 21st Century', *Parameters* (Summer 2000), pp.58–71. In 1996 the US National Defence University reprinted Mackinder's *Democratic Ideals and Realities*.

117. Z. Brzezinski, 'A Geostrategy for Eurasia', *Foreign Affairs*, Vol.76, No.5 (1997) pp.50–65; idem., *The Grand Chessboard: American Primacy and its Geostrategic Importance* (New York: Basic Books 1998) p.233.

118. C. Clover, 'Dreams of the Eurasian Heartland: The Reemergence of Geopolitics', *Foreign Affairs*, Vol.78, No.2 (1999), pp.9–13; I. Berman, 'Slouching towards Eurasia?', *Perspectives*, Vol.12 (2001).

Resources and Conflict in the Caspian Sea

SHANNON O'LEAR

On 23 July 2001, Iranian navy and air force units approached an unarmed, geologic research vessel in a section of the Caspian Sea claimed by Iran's neighbour, Azerbaijan. Since the five littoral states of the Caspian Sea had not agreed upon the legal status and division of the Caspian Sea waters and oil-rich seabed, there remained doubt about which oil fields belonged to which state. Emphasising this action, Iranian jets violated Azerbaijan's airspace several times within a week of the incident. As if to respond, Turkey, a close ally of Azerbaijan, sent military jets on a demonstrative flight over Baku. Additionally, the US State Department expressed displeasure at Iran's aggressive actions.[1] Although the encounter, later referred to as the 'Alov event' after the oil field in question, concluded without an outright military clash, it illustrates how the Caspian region is in a state of flux where geoeconomic soft power has not fully overcome geopolitical power. The Caspian is a case where traditional control of territory is meeting with a newer, commercial-based means of allocating resource benefits. In the absence of clear boundaries or resource distribution agreements among all littoral states, international corporate contracts and military forces appear poised to vie for who gets what in the Caspian.

The Caspian Sea is an interesting example of shifting modes of resource control and implications for conflict. On one hand, littoral states maintain a degree of realpolitik approach to controlling resources by controlling territory, but on the other hand, states are pursuing commercial involvement in the exploitation of Caspian resources. Each approach to securing resource benefits involves a division of resources, one by traditional border demarcation and military enforcement of resource claims, and the other by diplomatic or commercial agreement upon the division of resources in the Caspian Sea. This article considers implications for resource-related conflict in the Caspian Sea where neither approach – territorial control nor diplomatic and commercial agreement – has fully surpassed the other.

The following section gives a brief review of literature on resource and conflict. That section frames the Caspian resource situation and provides a basis from which to examine more specifically the context of the Caspian. The third section of this paper provides an overview to geographic aspects of Caspian Sea resources. The geography of resources, in some cases, influences how resources may be controlled, but the location and distribution of resources alone are not sufficient for understanding complexities of resource conflict in the Caspian. The fourth section highlights a few other cases of inland water bodies to illustrate that the context of any inland water body is critical to understanding the possibility and parameters of conflict or collaboration there. That section also includes a discussion of the United Nations Convention on the Law of the Sea and the legal status of the Caspian Sea. The fifth section reviews the recent regional negotiations to determine boundaries in the Caspian, and the sixth section discusses militarization trends in the Caspian region. Negotiations have, in several cases, led to diplomatic agreements on the division of resources in the Caspian, but such business-friendly arrangements do not necessarily preclude more traditional form of geopolitical power demonstrated by military might.

Resources and Conflict

The literature on resources and conflict is vast and varied.[2] It has been pointed out that: 'Resources have been used in the past, and will be used in the future, as tools or targets of war and as strategic goals to be fought for.'[3] Yet causal links between resources and conflict are not always clear. One perspective is that resource scarcity underlies conflict. This perspective views scarcity in the form of depleted freshwater supplies, overexploitation of fisheries or of arable land and forests as a trigger to conflict.[4] One research group has argued that supply-induced scarcity, demand-induced scarcity and structural scarcity are all forms of environmental or resource scarcity that have triggered or hastened social, economic and political instability and conflict.[5] Other work contends that a new geography of conflict will emerge at flashpoints determined by the uneven distribution of highly demanded resources such as water, minerals, gems, oil, gas, and timber.[6]

A different perspective on resources and conflict argues that resource abundance, rather than resource scarcity, leads to conditions more likely to motivate conflict. Dependence on resource export can shape how states develop their capacity or incapacity to guide development.[7] Although the type and abundance of resources do not necessarily determine successful state-building, resource-rich states, which can range from 'predator states' to 'development states',[8] may stumble into failure unless development policies are actively pursued to avoid perverse economic and political dependence on resource export. Oil-rich Kazakhstan and agriculture-rich Uzbekistan are cases wherein governments of resource-abundant states engage in rent-seeking behaviour and corruption rather than institutional capacity-building,[9] thus increasing the risk for conflict.

Scholars have also contended that specific resource characteristics are important factors to consider. For example, point-source resources such as mining, or diffuse resources such as land used for peasant farming, will each contribute to different patterns of capital ownership and distribution of resource benefits throughout society.[10] The 'lootability' of a resource, whether or not a resource is linked to extractive or to productive industries, and the proximity of a resource to centres of control are other factors adding an important dimension to our understanding of the nature of conflicts in which natural resources play a key role.[11] Oil, like foci of other extractive industries, is an example of a point resource as opposed to diffuse resources from which generate productive industries. Point resources are usually easier to monopolize but more vulnerable to disputes over control.[12] Furthermore, environmental or resource factors alone are not sole indicators of conflict. Economic and political factors are just as significant as environmental factors as predictors of conflict.[13] In addition to these differing views on how resources may be related to conflict, there are other challenges to conducting research on connections between natural resources or environmental degradation and conflict. Methodologically, clear linkages between the environment and conflict have yet to be made conclusively in terms of time frame and data samples to substantiate a general theory about how resources are related to conflict.[14] Also, conflict does not necessarily result from environmental or resource degradation, nor do environmental issues always translate into security issues.[15] Sociopolitical factors, such as a lack of regulatory mechanisms, historical effects, and opportunities for actors to mobilize, appear to be more important as indicators of conflict than environmental change in and of itself.[16] Social and institutional adaptation may take place in response to environmental change or degradation in a variety of ways[17] and preclude the escalation of tension into conflict. Finally, how resources are integrated into local political economies is an important aspect underlying the emergence of conflict related to resources.[18]

Boundaries are key in resource conflict scenarios. The field of political geography has traditionally considered many aspects of boundaries including the delimitation of offshore boundaries and cases of boundaries and resource disputes[19], recognizing, to quote the poet Robert Frost, that 'good fences make good neighbors'. Another challenge to understanding how natural resources are related to conflict is determining where to begin the 'story' of environmental degradation and conflict in any particular context. Since most conflicts involve multiple scales, time frames, actors, social, economic and political dimensions, the approach adopted by the researcher will shape the analysis of any given conflict. As for the possibility of an environmental dimension to conflict, it has been argued that 'it is not whether the environment matters that is interesting, but how it matters and what specific contributions it imparts on a given violent conflict or war'.[20] Assessing potential conflict in the Caspian includes an understanding of the types of resources that might be at the centre of a conflict and how the benefits of those resources are negotiated among the littoral states.

Although oil is indeed a key resource of the Caspian Sea, it should also be noted that Caspian resources are multifaceted. That is, more than merely drawing lines on a map, determining who benefits from Caspian resources also involves negotiations over the division of the seabed versus division of the waters and surface uses of the Caspian. Just as previous political geographic work has considered ocean spaces and other water bodies as more complex systems than mere two-dimensional territory,[21] this article considers the Caspian Sea a case of overlapping historical, economic, political, and physical dimensions.

Resources of the Caspian Sea

In the Caspian Sea region, estimates of proven oil reserves, defined as deposits of oil and natural gas considered to be 90 per cent probable, range between 17–33 billion barrels. This figure may be compared to proven oil reserves in the United States at 22 billion barrels and the North Sea at 17 billion barrels.[22] Figure 1 illustrates the approximate location of major oil fields in the Caspian. Of secondary economic importance are the caviar-producing sturgeon that migrate through the waters of the Caspian. In addition to the type of resource, previous work on resource conflicts indicates that the location and concentration of resources can play a significant role in the degree of concentration of ownership and control and can shape networks that emerge to channel benefits from these resources.

Resource location is either proximate or distant from the seat of power, yet the relative location of resources may have little to do with how states exert control over them. In the case of the littoral states of the Caspian, only Azerbaijan's capital, Baku, is located on the Caspian, and Iran's capital, Tehran, is within 150 kilometres of the coast. Capitals of the other states, Moscow (Russia), Astana (Kazakhstan), and Ashgabat (Turkmenistan), are deep in the interior of the countries and far from Caspian Sea resources. However, the main resource of concern in the Caspian Sea, offshore oil, may be monopolized through contracts with international companies and may be protected by naval units. Indeed, each of the littoral states is involved in a complex array of agreements with international actors to develop and exploit oil reserves[23] and in so doing, each state exerts control over oil reserves. As for the naval protection of offshore resources, flotillas of each state will be addressed later in this article.

FIGURE 1
APPROXIMATE LOCATIONS OF MAJOR OILFIELDS IN THE CASPIAN SEA

Sources: Map of Caspian Sea Region North and South, produced by the U.S. Central Intelligence Agency; Perry-Castaneda Library Map Collection at the University of Texas. Available online at <http://www.lib.utexas.edu/maps/>. Energy Map of the Middle East & The Caspian, Third Edition. Produced by the Petroleum Economist, Ltd., London. 2003.

Key:

1 Kashagan
2 Kurmangazy
3 Khvalynskaya
4 Tsentralnoye (approximate location)
5 Apsheron Island
6 Apsheron Bank
7 Darvina Bank
8 Artem Island/ Pirallakhi
9 Gyurgyang-Deniz
10 Zhiloy Island
11 Gryazevaya Sopka/Palchyg Pilpilas/Neft Dashlary/Neftian ye Kamni
12 Azi-Aslanova
13 27th May/ Guneshli
14 Chirag/ Kaverochkin/Do stlug
15 Azeri/26th Baku Commissars
16 Pricheleken
17 Zhdanov
18 Lam Bank
19 Gubkin Bank (Shafag)
20 Livanov
21 Kapaz/ Promezhutoch/ October Revolution
22 Yuzhnaya 1 and 2
23 Shah-Deniz
24 Bakhar
25 Kurdashi
26 Khamandag
27 Araz (Alov-Sharg-Araz; Alborz)
28 Lerik
29 Garasu
30 Shirvan
(Serdar)
31 Bulla-Deniz
32 Alyaty-Deniz
33 Bulla Island/ Duvanny-Deniz/ Sangachaly-Deniz
34 7th March
35 Lokbatan-More
36 Gum-Deniz/ Peschanyy More

Perhaps more important than location of resources in relation to the location of seats of power is the location of Caspian resources in terms of concentration. Resources are either diffuse or concentrated as point-source resources. Previous work done on resource-abundant, transitional economies suggests that these economies will benefit differently depending on whether their predominant resources are point source or diffuse.[24] Since mining or oil exploitation, both examples of point-source resource activity, are capital-intensive and generate economic networks usually controlled by the government, the benefits from them tend to be concentrated as well and do not generally foster diversification in the overall economy. The oil and natural gas in the Caspian Sea basin are point resources since they issue from particular oil fields and gas fields. In the cases of Azerbaijan, Kazakhstan and Turkmenistan, the oil wealth each has gained – or stands to gain – as newly independent states appears to have hindered the restructuring of their economies in contrast to resource-poor, newly independent states of the region which have progressed further through the reform process.[25] In each case, lack of reform and corruption are not, however, dictated so much by resource wealth as by governance structures. Therefore, the concentration of point-source resources in the Caspian suggests that littoral states stand, potentially, to benefit from these resources depending on how each state negotiates its benefits from these resources.

The distribution of resources, specifically the distribution of oil fields throughout the Caspian and the access that each state has to these oil fields, is a particularly important element in understanding possible tensions in the region. During the Soviet era, the Caspian Sea was bordered by only two states: the Soviet Union and Iran. Now, there are five states bordering the Caspian, and each of them is eager to maximize their benefits, however defined, from the oil-rich Caspian. Although these five states have not established a Caspian-wide agreement on how to divide the Caspian amongst themselves, most of them are proceeding with exploration, drilling and extraction of Caspian Sea oil. The value of this oil depends greatly on the availability of reliable pipelines and on sufficient export volume to render existing (or planned) pipelines economically viable. The complex issue of export pipelines for Caspian Sea oil is beyond the scope of this article. Lacking a Caspian-wide, formal demarcation or delimitation of boundaries and the clarification of legal ownership that such an arrangement would provide, these states have resorted, in varying degrees, to bilateral border and resource use agreements. Such bilateral agreements provide a more secure environment for investment and commercial contracts for oil field exploration and extraction and preclude militaristic enforcement of their state's view on the division of the Caspian.

Just as the length of state borders along the Caspian varies greatly, the value, both economic and geopolitical, of Caspian oil to each of the five littoral states is not uniform. For example, in February 2002, Russia was well positioned to surpass Saudi Arabia as the world's largest oil producer[26] and was looking to expand into 'downstream' assets such as refineries and pipelines.[27] The majority of Russia's oil wealth, however, extends well beyond the Caspian Sea basin with major output centres in West Siberia with potential for expanded oil projects in East Siberia, the Arctic region and Sakhalin Island. Oil resources in the Caspian Sea, then, are probably not as economically significant to Russia as is the issue of geopolitical leverage and foreign influence in its own backyard.

Likewise, since Iran's oil wealth is concentrated in the Persian Gulf region of the state, Caspian oil may carry less of an economic significance for Iran and more of a geopolitical significance. Although the collapse of the Soviet Union might seem to have left Russia and Iran rivals at either end of the Caspian Sea, the two countries have instead converged along shared apprehension of increased US and Turkish influence in the region.[28] Yet both countries have exhibited a stance of conflict towards the Caspian in their initial (and Iran's continued) promotion of a collective model of division of the Caspian, simultaneous to their interest in partaking in international agreements based on sectoral division of the sea. Initially following the Soviet collapse, Russia, together with Kazakhstan and Azerbaijan, wanted to divide the Caspian into national sectors based on shoreline length. This plan would leave Iran with an approximately 13 per cent share of the Caspian. Turkmenistan's leadership, although inconsistent in its approach to the division of Caspian resources, has supported Iran's demand for an equal, five-way division of the Caspian. Part of Iran's motivation for taking this stance on the division of the Caspian is the Alborz oil field which Iran has claimed. This oil field, known as Alov-Sharg-Araz by Azerbaijan, had begun to be explored by British Petroleum (BP) under contract to the Azerbaijani government.[29] It was at this oil field that the incident between the Iranian military and geologic researchers, described at the beginning of this article, took place.

Despite the fact that Caspian oil is of interest to both Russia and Iran, it is probably not as economically important to them as it is to the other three littoral states still developing their post-Soviet economies. Azerbaijan, Kazakhstan and Turkmenistan have greater economic stakes in Caspian resources. Not only are these states potentially more vulnerable economically through resource dependence, but they are also likely to be more vulnerable to external pressure given their strategic situation in a historically turbulent region.

Baku, located on the Apsheron Peninsula that curls into the Caspian Sea, has long been known for its oil. Home to ancient Zoroastrians who worshipped the fires igniting from flammable gas (an indicator of oil deposits), Baku later attracted the Nobels and other oil barons in the late 1800s.[30] Once incorporated into Soviet territory, Baku's oil industry infrastructure was enhanced to focus on the centralized economy with the main pipelines for exporting oil passing through Russia. Now an independent country again, Azerbaijan exhibits regional disparity in its oil wealth and power. As noted earlier, oil is a proximate resource controlled by a government through commercial contracts. In Azerbaijan's case, the geography of oil coincides with the geography of power. Not only is the heart of the oil industry located in and around the capital, thus making government control easier, but the fact that there are no other major resources elsewhere in the country to counterbalance the power of Baku further centralizes power in Baku.[31] Azerbaijan's current leadership benefits from this concentration of power, and it remains to be seen if the increased influence of western businesses and non-governmental organisations will, in the long run, benefit the quality of life for most of the people living in Azerbaijan.[32]

Caspian oil is the lifeblood of the state of Azerbaijan as it has shaped itself since independence in 1991. In 1994, Azerbaijan's President Aliyev signed the 'Contract of the Century' to secure investment and to designate oil production sharing agreements for offshore oil fields with oil companies from the US, the UK, Turkey, Norway, Saudi Arabia and Russia.[33] Russia did not officially endorse Azerbaijan's sectoral claims in the Caspian, but the Russian oil company, LUKoil, participated in the 'Contract of the Century'. Furthermore, in late 1994, Russia distributed a paper to the United Nations which included the statement that Moscow 'reserved the right to take appropriate measures' against other littoral states that explored the Caspian seabed unilaterally.[34] Despite the contradiction of Russia's early stance on the Caspian, Azerbaijan has proceeded with several Production Sharing Agreements with international oil companies to research, extract and export Caspian oil off the Azerbaijani coast.

Turkmenistan has been somewhat more vulnerable to Russian influence. Turkmenistan is home to the world's fifth largest reserves of natural gas and also has substantial oil reserves.[35] Due to the inland location of Turkmenistan's gas fields, there is ample opportunity to expand this industry, particularly eastwards toward China. However, Caspian oil remains important to Turkmenistan, in particular oil fields claimed by both Turkmenistan and Azerbaijan: the Kapaz oil field (known as the Serdar oil field in Turkmenistan) and the Azeri-Chirag-Guneshli areas. At an earlier time when Russia still avidly promoted the joint management of the Caspian resources rather than national sectors, Russia used military clout in an attempt to secure support for its position:

In order to demonstrate to Turkmenistan that signing on to the Azerbaijani model [of national sectors] would prove costly and risky, Russia threatened at one point to withdraw Russian officers (vital for the Turkmen military that is under joint Russian-Turkmen command) from the Turkmen armed forces and Russian border guards who patrol Turkmenistan's borders with Iran. This was reinforced by a reminder that Russia could block the access of Turkmen shipping to the Volga River. Turkmenistan's backtracking from the Azeri model and its confusing approach to the Caspian dispute indicates that the message was received.[36]

Due to its long border with Russia and the fact that 38 per cent of its population is ethnic Russian, Kazakhstan is also vulnerable to Russian influence.[37] Although Kazakhstan has greater potential for economic independence from Russia given Kazakhstan's Caspian and inland oil and gas reserves, many of the critical export pipelines travel through Russian territory.

Although the location of oil fields relative to seats of power is rendered less important by way of control through commercial contracts, there remains an uneven geography of Caspian oil in terms of the distribution of oil fields and each state's access to benefits of this oil through jointly recognized access to oil field exploitation and oil export. The uneven geography extends to the varying value – both economic and geopolitical – that Caspian resources have for each littoral state.

Inland Water Bodies and International Law

Similar to any other kind of resource area, inland water bodies do not necessarily determine conflict or stability. Yet historically, bodies of water in border regions have been militarized when the borders were less than mutually accepted. For example, in the 1700s and 1800s, the Great Lakes, forming a strategic border between the US and British-controlled Canada, were armed by multiple gunboats to ward off territorial expansion from the opposing side. Negotiation to disarm the Great Lakes was fraught with suspicion on both sides, but was finally successful with the signing of the Rush-Bagot Agreement in 1817.[38] Eastern Africa's Lake Tanganyika was militarized during the time of European colonization in Africa. The German naval flotilla was viewed as a threat to Belgian and British territories in the area, and a collaborative attack on the German fleet was successfully carried out between 1915 and 1916.[39]

The Black Sea, too, has a particularly rich history of militarization and demilitarization. In 1909, before the dawn of the Soviet era, several regional states signed an agreement of neutralization. This agreement permitted only merchant vessels on the Black Sea and omitted the necessity for Turkey and Russia to maintain military arsenals on the Black Sea.[40] The Soviets, however, viewed the Black Sea, as the Caspian Sea, as a closed sea that would ideally be controlled by littoral states, that might be influenced by the international community, but that would not be under the control of a single, foreign power.[41] In the 1990s, a challenge of the post-Soviet Black Sea was the negotiation process between Russia and Ukraine over the division of the Black Sea fleet. Underlying this dispute were attempts by both sides to define the role of the Black Sea and the port city of Sevastopol in the national identities of both Russia and Ukraine.[42] Also, a few years prior to the Soviet collapse, the Black Sea was the site of an ecological disaster. An exotic species of jellyfish, *Mnemiopsis leidyi*, diffused suddenly and voraciously through the Black Sea devastating fish populations and causing explosive phytoplankton blooms.[43] This disaster motivated the six littoral states of the Black Sea, in 1992, to adopt the Convention on the Protection of the Black Sea against Pollution that established regional rules of protection for the marine environment.[44] Another example of an inland water body that has recently been the site of post-Soviet collaboration rather than conflict is the Peipsi-Chudskoye Lake that forms part of the border between Estonia and Russia.[45] Clearly, the historical and contemporary contexts of each case are important factors in the state of militarization, conflict, or collaboration on inland water bodies. Militarization has often been the means of managing international, inland bodies of water, but collaboration has also emerged in some cases. Militarization is not necessarily the only way to manage shared inland water bodies.

One of the central questions dominating discussions of Caspian Sea resources since the collapse of the Soviet Union is usually summarized as, whether or not the Caspian Sea is, in fact, a sea. In essence, this is a debate about legal protocol for the division of resources among littoral states. One side of the debate argues that the Caspian is a sea and is therefore subject to the United Nations Convention on the Law of the Sea (UNCLOS). 'Sea' status would give precedent for establishing national zones along the coast but joint management in the centre (see Figure 2). This 'condominium' arrangement would allow all littoral states to share the resources of the joint area. In the early 1990s, both Russia and Iran promoted the view of the Caspian as sea. Part of the reason for this position was that a division of the Caspian into national sectors would put Russia and Iran at a disadvantage in terms of access to major, known oil fields. One argument that Russia and Iran utilized to support their stance was that, as an ecosystem, the Caspian should be managed jointly.[46] However, if determined to be a lake, the Caspian could be divided into national sectors or zones that would meet at an equidistant median line (see Figure 3). The national sector arrangement favours Azerbaijan, Turkmenistan and Kazakhstan by allocating to them some of the best areas for oil exploitation.

The UNCLOS is applicable not only to the high seas, but also to enclosed or semi-enclosed seas that it defines as:

> ... A gulf, basin or sea surrounded by two or more States and connected to another sea or the ocean by a narrow outlet or consisting entirely or primarily of the territorial seas and exclusive economic zones of two or more coastal States.[47]

FIGURE 2

APPROXIMATE DIVISION OF THE CASPIAN AS A SEA WITH NATIONAL ZONES AND A COMMONLY MANAGED AREA

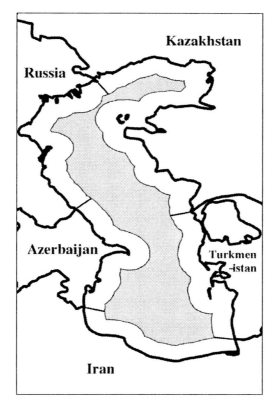

Sources: 'Caspian Sea Region: Legal Issues', from the US Energy Information Administration website <http://www.eia.doe.gov/cabs/casplaw.html#CASP>; 'Put Your House in Order', *The Economist*, 5 February 1998.

FIGURE 3

APPROXIMATE DIVISION OF THE CASPIAN AS A LAKE WITH THE
ESTABLISHMENT OF NATIONAL SECTORS

Sources: 'Caspian Sea Region: Legal Issues', from the US Energy Information Administration
website <http://www.eia.doe.gov/cabs/casplaw.html#CASP>; 'Put Your House in
Order', *The Economist*, 5 February 1998.

The Caspian Sea does not meet these criteria. Perhaps this makes even more difficult the task of translating geographic description and classification into normative, legal practice. As one legal scholar has argued,

> The real issue is not whether the Caspian Sea is a sea or a lake as such, but whether, in light of its natural, political, and historic characteristics, its regime is, or should be, analogous to the regime we normally associate with lakes, or with historic bays, or with marine, semi-enclosed seas, in each case bordered by more than one state.[48]

Indeed, the status of the Caspian has historically been the centre of palaeogeographical, geopolitical and legal conversations.[49]

Variants of the 'lake or sea' debate emerged throughout the decade following the Soviet collapse. For example, it was argued that the Law of the Sea should be applied selectively to the resources of the seabed and the subsoil of the Caspian but that previous bilateral treaties and historical practice in the Caspian should also be recognized.[50] Previously, Russia argued that historic treaties both with Iran and, prior to that, with Persia, implied that the Caspian Sea could not be divided at all. A close inspection of the historical agreements on the Caspian reveals that in 1723, Iran, known as West Persia at the time, 'ceded in perpetuity to Russia the length of the Caspian Sea'.[51] Since then, Iran has been trying to regain territory in the Caspian Sea. One of the challenges to identifying a physical or legal baseline for Soviet–Iranian division of the Caspian is that a maritime boundary was not specifically established. Instead, points on the eastern and western sides of the coastline marked the territorial division between Soviet and Iranian territory, and these coastal points were simply connected across the water as an implied boundary known as the Astara-Hassanqoli line. Furthermore, when the Soviets began in earnest to exploit oil reserves offshore from Baku, there was no official communication between the Soviet Union and Iran as to opposing or collaborative claims to the mineral resources of the Caspian Sea.

Following the Soviet collapse, newly independent states in the Caspian basin took different views. For example, in 1995 Azerbaijan promoted a 'lake theory', proposing that the sea be divided into national sectors that would extend from the subsoil of the sea bed to the air space above the water and including water, mineral and fish resources in between. This view was quite different from the stance taken by Kazakhstan at the time, which held that beyond exclusive coastal zones there should be a communal area open for fishing, navigation, over flight and the laying of cables and pipelines.

Securing access to or control of oil and gas resources, oil being preferable since proximate markets are not as critical, is not the only value of the Caspian. Navigation is important for the conduct of economic activity in the region:

> Kazakhstan does not abut Iran and Azerbaijan. Turkmenistan does not abut Russia and Azerbaijan. Iran and Russia do not abut each other on the Caspian, either. If the surface of the Caspian were to be divided into sovereign national sectors, then all shipping between Iran and Russia would be subject to the consent of Azerbaijan or Turkmenistan, through whose waters the ships must pass before attaining the other side. The Caspian is the only highway that physically connects all five

countries. The principles of freedom of navigation and over flight are therefore essential to the preservation of this basin's historical trade, naval, and transportation links. That is the reason why the Iranian, Russian, and Kazakh positions have insisted on freedom of navigation. Azerbaijan, on the other hand, had sought to define its sector in the Caspian in such a manner so as to close its waters to navigation by others.[52]

Establishing borders in the Caspian, then, is a matter not just of dividing the resource benefits, but also of maintaining stable transportation systems to enhance interstate and commercial relations.

Recent Negotiations

There has been a warming trend between Russia and its two littoral neighbours, Azerbaijan and Kazakhstan. One point of tension between Azerbaijan and Russia has been the Qabala radar station that was originally built in the Azerbaijani Soviet Socialist Republic for the Soviet military. During a meeting of Presidents Putin and Aliyev in January 2002, Russia formally recognized the radar station as the property of Azerbaijan and agreed to lease the Qabala radar station for US$7m annually over the next ten years.[53] At the same meeting, the countries confirmed that they share a view to divide the Caspian seabed along a modified median line, and Azerbaijan renewed an agreement to export 2.5 million tons of oil annually through the Baku-Novorossiisk pipeline that terminates in Russia. Kazakhstan and Russia have also agreed to delimit a modified median line dividing the Caspian seabed – and its mineral wealth – between those two countries.[54] This agreement involves determining the development rights to oil fields where the median line is to pass. Russia's LUKoil is already developing the Tsentralnoye and Khvalynskoye oil fields in the area. A Kazakhstan official recently announced that Kazakhstan would agree to acknowledge Russia's rights to both of those fields, since the approximate reserves of hydrocarbon in Kazakhstan's Kurmangazy oil field 'balances the reserves' of the other two.[55] The agreement signed by Russia and Kazakhstan in 1998 was the first international legal agreement on the post-Soviet Caspian Sea. Since then, Azerbaijan and Russia have agreed on their Caspian borders which partition the seabed along a modified median line and allow joint use of the waters. Since this demarcation is based on shoreline length, if it were extended to the remainder of the Caspian which remains disputed, Iran would be left with access to approximately 13 per cent of the Caspian. Turkmenistan has been inconsistent in its stance in the debate, and Iran continues to demand at least 20 per cent of the Caspian.[56]

Hence, a settlement of borders and resource allocation in the southern portion of the Caspian remains to be seen.

Overall, there has been uneven progress towards agreement on boundaries among the littoral states. Russia, Kazakhstan and Azerbaijan have agreed that the Caspian seabed should be divided into national sectors along a modified median line, Iran insists on either joint control of the Caspian or at least 20 per cent of the sea to itself (although a division into national sectors based on shoreline length would give Iran a 13 per cent share of the sea), and Turkmenistan has not taken a stance on either side.[57] Russia, Azerbaijan and Kazakhstan all agree on the principle and method of dividing seabed rights along a modified median line, Turkmenistan only agrees on the principle of dividing the Caspian, and Iran approves of neither the principle nor method of dividing the Caspian. Instead, Iran prefers that the littoral states would adopt a 'condominium' approach wherein the states use the sea jointly and by consensus. Barring that option, Iran would prefer that all work on the Caspian should be halted until the legal status of the Caspian is determined and agreed to by all five littoral states. Iran points to treaties it signed with the Soviet Union in 1921 and 1940, which call for sharing Caspian resources between the two countries, as the legal baseline for determining a new legal regime in the Caspian.[58]

Iran has asserted that it will not wait for maritime borders to be determined before it exploits what it views as its own portion of the Caspian. Adding to that tension, Victor Kalyuzhny, Russian President Putin's advisor for the Caspian Sea, recently stated that:

> There are no Russian or Iranian or Azeri zones on the Caspian because there [is] not fixed status of the Caspian Sea ... Let me repeat again that today there are no zones belonging to this or that Caspian country. I believe that the Caspian Sea rightfully belongs to the Russian market.[59]

With this statement, the Russian official reverted to 1994 policy and seemed to question the recent agreements on seabed division with Kazakhstan and Azerbaijan.

In late April 2002, leaders of the five littoral states met in Ashgabat, Turkmenistan to discuss, for the first time, the division of the Caspian Sea. In the previous month, the UN lifted an eight-month ban on harvesting caviar-producing sturgeon by the four former Soviet states in recognition of their accomplishment in implementing joint management of this resource.[60] Although the presidential summit on Caspian border delimitation began on this positive note, no agreements were signed on the major issues of concern: the division of the seabed, fishing and ecological degradation.

Russia's President Putin was optimistic at a press conference following the meeting, touting the summit's atmosphere as 'very constructive' and noting an agreement among the leaders to 'pursue talks on all areas of cooperation'.[61] Even Iran's President Khatami said, 'I consider the summit has been successful', and added, 'What prevailed in our talks was understanding, and that we should solve our problems through understanding. Naturally no one expects the problems to be solved overnight.'[62] Kazakhstan's President Nazarbayev stated, 'The problem was larger than we expected.[63] Additionally, Kazakhstan and Iran signed a declaration on bilateral co-operation based on non-interference into internal affairs, mutual respect, and a shared interest in peace and stability in the Caspian region.[64] The two countries also signed intergovernmental agreements on trade and multifaceted co-operation. Azerbaijan's President Aliyev raised his concerns about the ecology of the Caspian Sea identifying pollution and the decline of valuable, caviar-producing fish stocks as concerns that need to be addressed by the Caspian states.[65] He also commented positively on the meeting, stating that it would provide an important foundation for future meetings.

Although this first-ever presidential summit resulted in positive impressions by most participants, statements from Turkmenistan's leader, Saparmurat Niyazov, were more aggressive:

> There was no concrete decision on determining the border zones of each state. When we started talking about this, we disagreed. In determining a median line, we also disagreed, [Niyazov told a post-summit press conference.] Nobody dared to take responsibility and sign a resolution [Niyazov said, adding:] we will need to work on the Caspian for a long time yet.[66]

Twice during the summit, Niyazov said that 'the Caspian smells of blood',[67] and warned that the hydrocarbons of the Caspian would bring bloodshed.[68] However, Niyazov also stated, at the end of the meeting, that all five of the Caspian littoral states had 'agreed to prevent conflicts and behind-the-scenes games'.[69]

These apparent steps of progress backtracking, and unilateral statements in determining who gets what in the Caspian Sea, indicate a degree of confusion or disagreement over Caspian borders as well as a potential for instability related to Caspian resources. Differing perspectives of the Caspian states' leaders are particularly intriguing, given the recent rush of media coverage on military activity in the Caspian. It is precisely in the midst of this confusion that it is evident that commercial agreements have not fully replaced a *realpolitik*, military approach to the division of resources in the Caspian. The next section addresses this issue.

Flotillas and Military Influence in the Caspian

Writing about global 'hot spots' for resource wars, Michael Klare devotes an entire chapter to potential energy conflicts in the Caspian Sea region.[70] He argues that Russia, which has inherited the Soviet infrastructure in the region, and the US, which has an interest in promoting the export of Caspian region oil, are 'preparing the battlefield' by strengthening their own military positions there. He asserts that neither Russia nor the US has put into place the military means to conduct a major conflict, but the more likely scenario is that smaller scale proxy wars, supported by either side, may erupt. Nagorno-Karabakh, Abkhazia, and Chechnya are a few sites where proxy wars may escalate. Disputes over resources, he argues, may not be the sole motivating factor in these potential conflicts, but they may heighten tensions related to ethnic hostility and economic disparity. Indeed, defence spending throughout the Caucasus and Central Asian regions generally increased between 1995 and 2000 (except for Georgia and Kazakhstan). Most countries in the area are importing an increasing number of weapons as well as developing infrastructure for the production of weapons, and US and NATO aid to the region are increasing as well.[71] The Caspian littoral states are building their own military capacity either through the expansion of military forces or through the development of alliances, and these activities are likely to shape patterns of conflict (or a lack of conflict) in the region.

Figure 4 summarizes current data on naval fleets in the Caspian. At the time this data was collected, only four of the ships listed in Azerbaijan's fleet were operational. Azerbaijan's coast guard was formed in July 1992 with a transfer of ships from the Russian flotilla and border guard. However, by 1995, Russia had resumed control of Azerbaijan's coast guard in order to provide adequate maintenance and support until Azerbaijan can meet these needs independently.[72] Kazakhstan only inaugurated its own flotilla in August 1996, and of the six patrol craft, only five were operational at the time this data was reported.[73] Even Russia has had a shortage of funds to pay for dockyard repairs, spare parts and fuel since 1991. A result of this is that several of its major surface warships have rarely been to sea or operated at a distance from their local exercise areas. It is important to note that numbers of ships do not necessarily equate with independent naval capacity, and nor can military might or the likelihood of conflict be measured by flotilla size. Without consistent access to maintenance (which requires a steady influx of funds) and spare parts (a challenge throughout much former Soviet space), naval fleets lose their fighting value. Maintenance is key. When Russian President Putin visited Baku, Azerbaijan in January 2001, the Russian Caspian flotilla, coincidentally or not, staged an impressive demonstration off the coast of Baku. Unexpectedly, at least one of the vehicles experienced mechanical difficulties and was towed in to be repaired by a crew of mechanics from Baku.[74]

Another reason that flotilla size may not be an indicator of conflict is that conflict between states is more complex than mere military leverage. One of the specific areas of the Caspian that is generating tension is the area between Azerbaijan and Iran. Two recent events, in addition to Iran's gunboat diplomacy of July 2001, are likely to influence the degree and pattern of militarization of the Caspian between these two countries. The first event is the recent defence agreement between Iran and Armenia.[75] On

FIGURE 4

CASPIAN NAVAL FLOTILLAS

Country	Personnel strength	Fleet strength	Base location
Azerbaijan	2,200	Patrol Forces: 2 Stenka (205p), 1 Svetlyak (1140), 1 Osa II (without SSM), 1 Zhuk	Baku
Kazakhstan	200	Patrol Forces: 4 KW 15 (Type 369) Class (PC), 2 Zhuk (Type 1400) Class (PB), 1 Dauntless Class (PB), 2 Saygak (Type 1408) Class (PB)	Aktau (Caspian HQ), Aralsk (Aral Sea)
Iran	18,000	Submarines:3, Midget Submarines 3, Frigates 3, Corvettes 2, Fast Attack Craft-Missile 20, Large Patrol Craft 8, Coastal Patrol Craft 123.	Bandar-e Anzali (Caspian), Also has bases on Persian Gulf, Indian Ocean and Pasdaran.
Russia	8,000 in Caspian	Frigates: 2, Patrol Boats: 12, Other small craft: approximately 50*	Astrakhan
Turkmenistan	125	Patrol Boat Squadron being established. Currently, Patrol forces consists of 1 Point Class (WPB) transferred from United States on 30 May 2000.	Turkmenbashi

Source: R. Sharpe (ed.), Jane's Fighting Ships: 2000–2001 (Alexandria: Jane's Information Group, 2000).
*Russian Caspian Flotilla data from the Federation of American Scientists website. Available online at <http://www.fas.org/nuke/guide/russia/agency/mf-caspian.htm>, visited 14 April 2003.

5 March, leaders of the two countries signed a communication of understanding intended as a foundational agreement for bilateral military co-operation. Given the ongoing dispute between Azerbaijan and Armenia over the Nagorno-Karabakh region, an area that is Armenian-populated but that lies within Azerbaijan's territory, enhanced co-operation between Armenia and Iran is not likely to be well-received by Azerbaijan. The second event which is likely to influence patterns of militarization near Azerbaijan and Iran in the near future are recent remarks made by Iran's Oil Minister, Bijan Zanganeh, that Iran intends to proceed with Caspian oil and gas projects before all five littoral states agree on demarcation of the Caspian.[76] Additionally, and more to the point of potential conflict, Zanganeh also stated that, 'Our position is clear; we are not going to wait till the clarification of the Caspian Sea's legal regime ... We start our activities based on our own understanding of the sea's legal regime and will prevent the activities of others in the parts we consider to be ours'). Both of these processes may motivate a more aggressive stance by both Iran and Azerbaijan in the southern Caspian Sea.

Following 11 September, Azerbaijan provided support to the US military effort in Afghanistan and continued to express a pro-western stance. In January 2002, President George Bush temporarily repealed US sanctions on Azerbaijan which had been in place since 1992, and by April he made Azerbaijan, Armenia and Tajikistan eligible for US defence aid under the Foreign Assistance Act and the Arms Export Control Act.[77] This change in policy is thought by some to 'fill a dangerous vacuum in Azerbaijan and to provide Russian-armed Armenia with an alternative in terms of assistance'.[78] Azerbaijan's former foreign policy adviser, Vafa Guluzade, also observed that the change in US policy on military assistance to Azerbaijan and Armenia could 'accelerate the entry of the United States in the region [and] help Armenia along the difficult road [of] renouncing the strategic partnership with Russia'.[79] Although the focus of this article is not the ongoing territorial dispute between Armenia and Azerbaijan over Karabakh and the surrounding regions, it is important to note that any gain or loss in military strength by Azerbaijan in relation to the Karabakh issue could carry over to border issues on the Caspian. Indeed, one aspect of US military assistance to Azerbaijan includes the enhancement of Azerbaijan's naval capabilities to enable that state to secure its maritime borders, economic zone and territorial waters.[80]

Part of the US argument for its support of Azerbaijan is that this policy fits into a larger scale plan to ensure that terrorism cannot gain a foothold in the Caucasus and Central Asian regions and to lay the groundwork for a lasting US presence there. However, another effect of US military support of Azerbaijan could be a stronger US stand against Iran.[81] Several countries reacted to the 'Alov' episode described at the beginning of this article – the incident between the Iranian navy and petroleum workers operating in an Azerbaijani-claimed sector of the Caspian. Russian President Vladimir Putin called Iran's use of force 'impermissible', and the US condemned Iran's act as 'proactive'.[82] US officials clarified, however, that the US would not be sending troops or other forces to support Azerbaijan's position on the Caspian Sea. At any rate, Azerbaijani officials have made it clear that to have foreign security forces on Azerbaijani soil would defeat the purpose of being an independent state.[83]

Following the recent presidential summit of the Caspian states, Iran's President Khatami called for the demilitarization of the Caspian Sea. This approach may seem to counter the often-cited aggression by Iran in the southern portion of the Caspian Sea. Iran's military activity may, in fact, be aimed at stalling the development of Caspian resources until a settlement more suitable to Iran is achieved. As previously noted in this article, Iran has declared that it plans to move ahead with its own exploration projects in disputed areas of the Caspian, yet clearly Iran's access to the Persian Gulf assures it ample access to petroleum resources which are more easily exploitable and exportable than petroleum resources of the Caspian Sea. True, oil from the Caspian would provide a more accessible supply to Iran's northern population. On a regional scale, it would be in Iran's interest to act before Russia, Kazakhstan and Azerbaijan are successful in persuading Turkmenistan to join them in favouring a modified median line as the basis for seabed division. The 'Alov' incident in July 2001 may also have been intended for two audiences.[84] The first audience includes the other littoral states and the international companies involved in extracting and exporting Caspian petroleum. The message to them was that Iran will take military action as necessary to defend its interest in securing a 20 per cent share of the Caspian seabed. The other audience may well have been the citizens of Iran. The likely objective there was to demonstrate that the leadership of Iran is, indeed, acting in their national interest. As reformists in Iran gain support, conservatives currently in power are motivated to act. As for a strategy to buy time and put off investors until a border settlement more favourable to Iran is reached, the 'Alov' incident has had repercussions. Not only has British Petroleum had to halt work on the Alov-Sharg-Araz area (which would technically become Iranian territory if equal sectors were created), but the state of Azerbaijan is also having difficulty attracting an investor for a 20 per cent stake in the Lerik field.[85] As one western oil executive remarked, 'If you are sitting in Houston or London and you hear about gunboats then you assume the whole region is unstable so your corporate management view might be more negative than it should be.'

Far from seeking demilitarization of the Caspian, Russia appears to be building up its naval forces and has called for combined-arms exercises involving Russia's Caspian Flotilla, border guard cutters, Russian marines, and land-based combat aviation in the northern and central parts of the Caspian. President Putin is calling for improved readiness against terrorism and drug trafficking, and he has expressed concern that the Russian fleet has not been tested in over a decade, since it lost 18 warships and 62 auxiliary vessels to the division among Caspian states in the early 1990s.[86] Following the summit in Ashgabat, he appeared on Russian television saying, 'We must strengthen our [military] presence as an essential factor in promoting our political and economic interests in the Caspian Sea. Our Flotilla constitutes a unique instrument in promoting the interests I just mentioned'.[87] However, Russia's recognition of Iran's efforts in the current struggle against terrorism suggests that Russia is flexing its military muscle, perhaps not so much to intimidate Iran as to intimidate the oil-rich, pro-western Caspian littoral states. Maintenance issues aside, Russian naval power in the Caspian remains uncontested, and Russia's military exercises which took place following the April 2002 summit demonstrated Russia's interest in guaranteeing security in the region.[88]

Concluding Comments

Iran's recent military manoeuvres in the southern Caspian region may indeed have only been intended to buy time until the Caspian states reach a deal more favourable to Iran. Such militaristic manoeuvres are likely to reinforce Iran's isolation from western investment and western-supported export pipeline expansion. Iran's threats toward its immediate Caspian neighbours strategically influences western perceptions of current Caspian security, but a Caspian-wide clash is not in Iran's or any other state's interest. Additionally, growing international attention to terrorism and drug trafficking may fuel militarization in the region, but western aid will likely be involved (such as in the case of Azerbaijan). Therefore, the US and other western states may view a military build up in the Caspian Sea region as securing, rather than threatening, their interests in the region.

Economic concerns are important to all the Caspian states. International investment is vital to gaining resource benefits from the exploitation of point-source oil fields. It is not, therefore, in the interest of any state to halt all exploitation or to scare away investors uniformly through militaristic confrontation over borders in the sea. Despite the uneven distribution and concentration of oil fields in the Caspian, littoral states are not relying completely on military prowess to defend their claims to Caspian resources. Russia, Kazakhstan and Azerbaijan have established bilateral agreements in the northern part of the Caspian, thus clearing the way for economic activity to thrive there. Borders in the southern portion of the Caspian, however, remain disputed as Azerbaijan, Turkmenistan and Iran have yet to agree on the division of resources and water usage. The Caspian has not yet been demilitarized, and Russia's military power in the region outweighs the other states, particularly the post-Soviet states. Yet the establishment of bilateral agreements in the northern part of the Caspian suggests that although Russia may have significantly more military power in the Caspian Sea region, it is also pursuing agreements that make that use of that power less likely.

Other aspects of Caspian Sea petroleum and, to a lesser but locally significant degree, sturgeon resources that deserve careful attention, are the local impacts and resulting disparities created by current regimes and their courtship of western investment in the petroleum industry. How people's livelihoods or how their perceptions of their governments have changed since the internationalization of Caspian oil and gas development may be a most telling factor in whether and how resource abundance in this region and a scarcity of equally distributed benefits may or may not ignite into conflict.

ACKNOWLEDGEMENTS

I wish to thank Bill Walters for his insights in the formative stages of this article, Ray Hrinko for his assistance in compiling material from which this article draws, John Rafferty for his work on the maps, Philippe Le Billon for organizing this special issue and three anonymous reviewers for their valuable and helpful comments on a previous draft.

NOTES

1. N. Nassibli,' Iran's Caspian Policy: Time to Make a Decision?', *Central Asia-Caucasus Institute Analyst*, Johns Hopkins University, 10 February 2003, <http://www.cacianalyst. org>.
2. For more in-depth perspectives on resources, conflict and stability, see A. Westing (ed), *Global Resources and International Conflict: Environmental Factors in Strategic Policy and Action* (New York: Oxford University Press 1986); N. Myers, *Ultimate Security: The Environmental Basis for Political Stability* (New York: W.W. Norton and Company 1993); D.H. Deudney and R.A. Matthew (eds), *Contested Grounds: Security and Conflict in the New Environmental Politics* (Albany, NY: State University of New York Press 1999); M. Suliman (ed.), *Ecology, Politics and Violent Conflict* (New York: Zed Books 1999); J. Barnett, *The Meaning of Environmental Security* (New York: Zed Books 2001); P.F. Diehl and N.P. Gleditsch (eds), *Environmental Conflict* (Boulder, CO: Westview Press 2001).
3. P.H. Gleick, 'Environment and Security: The Clear Connections', *Bulletin of the Atomic Scientists*, Vol.47, No.3 (1991), pp.18–22.
4. M. Renner, *Ending Violent Conflict*, Worldwatch Paper No.146 (Washington: Worldwatch 1999).
5. T. Homer-Dixon, 'On the Threshold: Environmental Changes as Causes of Acute Conflict', *International Security*, Vol.16, No.2 (1991), pp.76–117; T. Homer-Dixon, 'Environmental Scarcities and Violent Conflict: Evidence From Cases', *International Security*, Vol.19, No.1 (1994), pp.5–40; T. Homer-Dixon, *Environment, Security and Violence* (Princeton, NJ:

Princeton University Press 1999); T. Homer-Dixon and J. Blitt, *Ecoviolence: Links Among Environment, Population, and Security* (Lanham, MD: Rowman & Littleman Publishers, Inc. 1998).

6. M.T. Klare, 'The New Geography of Conflict', *Foreign Affairs*, Vol.80, No.3 (2001), pp. 40–61; M.T. Klare, *Resource Wars: The New Landscape of Conflict* (New York: Metropolitan Books 2000).

7. T.L. Karl, *The Paradox of Plenty: Oil Booms and Petro-States* (Berkeley, CA: University of California Press 1997).

8. P. Evans, *Embedded Autonomy: States and Industrial Transformation* (Princeton, NJ: Princeton University Press 1995).

9. R.M. Auty, 'Reforming Resource-Abundant Transition Economies: Kazakhstan and Uzbekistsan', in R.M. Auty (ed.), *Resource Abundance and Economic Development* (New York: Oxford University Press, 2001).

10. R.M. Auty, 'Natural Resources, the State and Development Strategy', *Journal of International Development*, Vol.9 (1997), pp.651–3; Auty, 'Reforming Resource-Abundant Transition Economies' (note 9).

11. P. Le Billon, 'The Political Ecology of War: Natural Resources and Armed Conflict', *Political Geography* Vol.20, No.5 (2001), pp.561–84.

12. Ibid.

13. W. Hauge and T. Ellingsen, 'Causal Pathways to Conflict', in P.H. Diehl and N.P. Gleditsch (eds), *Environmental Conflict* (Boulder, CO: Westview Press, 2001).

14. N.P. Gleditsch, 'Armed Conflict and the Environment', in P.H. Diehl and N.P. Gleditsch (eds), *Environmental Conflict* (Boulder, CO: Westview Press, 2001).

15. B.R. Shaw, 'When are Environmental Issues Security Issues?', *The Woodrow Wilson Center Environmental Change and Security Project Report*, Issue 2 (1996), pp.39–44; D. Deudney, 'Environment and Security: Muddled Thinking', *Bulletin of the Atomic Scientists*, Vol.47, No.3 (1991), pp.23–8.

16. G. Baechler, 'Why Environmental Transformation Causes Violence: A Synthesis', *The Woodrow Wilson Center Environmental Change and Security Project Report*, Issue 4 (1998), pp.24–44.

17. S.C. Lonergan (ed.), *Environmental Change, Adaptation and Security* (Boston, MA: Kluwer Academic Press, 1999).

18. N.L. Peluso and M. Watts (eds), *Violent Environments* (Ithaca: Cornell University Press 2001).

19. J.V. Minghi, 'Boundary Studies in Political Geography', in R.E. Kasperson and J.V. Minghi (eds), *The Structure of Political Geography* (Chicago, IL: Aldine Publishing Company, 1969).

20. G. Baechler, 'Environmental Degradation and Violent Conflict: Hypotheses, Research Agenda and Theory-Building', in M. Suliman (ed.) *Ecology, Politics and Violent Conflict* (New York: Zed Books, 1999).

21. See, for example, J. House, 'War, Peace and Conflict Resolution: Towards an Indian Ocean Model', *Transactions of the Institute of British Geographers*, Vol.9, No.1 (1984), pp.3–21; P. Steinberg, *The Social Construction of the Ocean* (Cambridge: Cambridge University Press, 2001).

22. The U.S. Energy Information Administration website on the Caspian Sea Region is at <http://www.eia.doe.gov/emeu/cabs/caspian.html> (accessed 5 April 2002).

23. See the U.S. Energy Information Administration's website on the Caspian Sea region for detailed information on each littoral state, <http://www.eia.doe.gov/emeu/cabs/caspian.html> (accessed 5 April 2002).

24. Auty, 'Reforming Resource-Abundant Transition Economies' (note 9).

25. R.M. Auty, 'Natural Resources, Governance and the Transition in Energy-Rich Azerbaijan, Kazakstan and Turkmenistan' (Background Paper 3 prepared for the NBR Planning Meeting on Energy Resources, Governance and Welfare in the Caspian Region, Washington, DC, 15 June 2001).

26. M. Lavelle, 'Russian Rigs to the Rescue', *U.S. News & World Report*, 11 February, 2002.

27. 'Oil Concerns in Russia Branch Out', *The New York Times*, 2 April 2002, p.W1.

184 THE GEOPOLITICS OF RESOURCE WARS

28. R. Menon, 'Treacherous Terrain: The Political and Security Dimensions of Energy Development in the Caspian Sea Zone', *NBR Analysis*, Vol.9, No.1 (1998), pp.7–37.
29. D. Albrighton, 'No Deal as Caspian Summit Ends in Failure', *Agence France Presse*, 24 April 2002.
30. D. Yergin, *The Prize: The Epic Quest for Oil, Money & Power* (New York: Simon & Schuster 1992).
31. D.I. Hoffman, 'Azerbaijan: The Politicization of Oil', in R. Ebel and R. Menon (eds), *Energy and Conflict in Central Asia and the Caucasus* (Lanham, MD: Rowman & Littlefield Publishers, Inc., 2000).
32. S. O'Lear, 'Azerbaijan: Territorial Issues and Internal Challenges in Mid-2001', *Post-Soviet Geography and Economics*, Vol.42, No.4 (2001), pp.305–12.
33. Russian policy in the Caspian fluctuated in the mid-1990s. In late 1993, Russia signed an agreement with Azerbaijan in which Russia recognized an Azerbaijani sector in the Caspian Sea, but in 1994, Russia called for a condominium division of the Caspian with no sectoral divisions beyond a 10-mile nautical zone from the shoreline. See E.M. Fersht, 'Oil and the Demarcation of the Caspian Sea', in M.H. Nordquist and J.N. Moore (eds), *Security Flashpoints: Oil, Islands, Sea Access and Military Confrontation* (The Hague: Marinus Nijhoff Publishers, 1998).
34. Ibid., p.288.
35. See the U.S. Energy Information Administration Country Analysis Brief on Turkmenistan at <http://www.eia.doe.gov/emeu/cabs/turkmen.html>, (accessed 5 April 2002).
36. Menon, 'Treacherous Terrain', p.16.
37. R. Menon, 'In the Shadow of the Bear: Security in Post-Soviet Central Asia', *International Security*, Vol.20, No.1 (1995), pp.149–81.
38. E. Battenfield, '150 Years of Peace Under a Six Month Pact: The Great Lakes Armament Arrangement', *Inland Seas*, Vol.23, No.2 (1967), pp.137–48.
39. J. Hussey, 'Reflections From a Lake: Memories of Lake Tanganyika', *Army Quarterly and Defense Journal*, Vol.123, No.3 (1993), pp.334–8.
40. 'Provisions Concerning the Neutralization of the Black Sea and Danube River Contained in the General Treaty between Great Britain, Austria, France, Prussia, Russia, Sardinia, and Turkey', *American Journal of International Law*, Vol.3, No.2 (April 1909), pp.114–16.
41. K. Grzybowski, 'The Soviet Doctrine of Mare Clausum and Policies in Black and Baltic Seas', *Journal of Central European Affairs*, Vol.14, No.4 (1955), pp.339–53.
42. K. Covert, 'Overlapping Imagined Communities: The Black Sea Fleet Negotiations Between Russia and Ukraine, 1992–1996', *Canadian Review of Studies in Nationalism*, Vol.24, No.1–2 (1997), pp.21–31.
43. See N. Ascherson, *Black Sea* (New York: Hill and Wang 1995).
44. P. Sands, *Principles of International Environmental Law 1: Frameworks, Standards, Implementation* (New York: Manchester University Press 1995).
45. S. O'Lear, 'E-mail Communication and Transboundary Environmental Policy: A Case of Successful Cooperation in the former Soviet Republics', *Geographical Review*, Vol.87, No.2 (1997), pp.275–90.
46. C.M. Croissant and M.P. Croissant, 'The Legal Status of the Caspian Sea: Conflict and Compromise', in M.P. Croissant and B. Aras (eds), *Oil and Geopolitics in the Caspian Sea Region* (Westport: Praeger, 1999).
47. United Nations Convention on the Law of the Sea Part IX Enclosed or Semi-Enclosed Seas, Article 122, <http://www.un.org/Depts/los/convention_agreements/texts/unclos/closindx.htm> (accessed 9 April 2002).
48. B.H. Oxman, 'Caspian Sea or Lake: What Difference Does it Make?', *Caspian Crossroads Magazine*, Vol.1, No.4 (Winter 1996), <http://ourworld.compuserve.com/homepages/usazerb/141.htm> (accessed 9 April 2002).
49. W. Raczka, 'A Sea or a Lake? The Caspian's Long Odyssey', *Central Asian Survey*, Vol.19, No.2 (2000), pp.189–221.
50. B.M. Clagett, 'Ownership of Seabed and Subsoil Resources in the Caspian Sea Under the Rules of International Law', *Caspian Crossroads Magazine*, Vol.1, No.3 (Fall 1995), <http://ourworld.compuserve.com/homepages/usazerb/131.htm>, (accessed 9 April 2002).

51. G. Mirfendereski, *A Diplomatic History of the Caspian Sea: Treaties, Diaries and Other Stories* (New York: Palgrave 2001).
52. Ibid.
53. 'Giving Away the Store?', *Radio Free Europe/Radio Liberty Caucasus Report*, Vol.5, No.5, 31 January 2002, <http://www.rferl.org/caucasus-report/archives.html>.
54. 'Kazakh President, Russian Deputy Premier Discuss Economic Cooperation', *Radio Free Europe/Radio Liberty Newsline*, 10 April 2002, available through < http://www.rferl.org/ newsline>; 'Russia, Kazakhstan to Sign Agreement on Delimitation of Caspian Seabed', *Russian Economic News* (Ria-Novosti), 9 April 2002.
55. 'Kazakhs to Give Caspian Tsentralnoye Oilfield to Russia', *BBC Monitoring International Reports*, 9 April 2002.
56. M. Lelyveld, 'Caspian: Impasse On Setting Sea Borders Continues', *Radio Free Europe/ Radio Liberty (RFE/RL)*, 9 April 2002; <http://www.rferl.org/nca/features/2002/04/0904200 2083316.asp>.
57. Lelyveld, 'Caspian: Impasse' (note 56).
58. 'Caspian Sea Region: Legal Issues', U.S. Energy Information Administration; <http:// www.eia.doe.gov/emeu/cabs/casplaw.html#CONSENSUS> (accessed 11 April 2002).
59. M. Lanskoy, 'Kalyuzhny Muddies the Water', *The NIS Observed: An Analytical Review*, Vol.7, No.5 (13 March 2002), available online at <http://www.bu.edu/iscip/digest/vol7/ ed0705.html> (accessed 11 April 2002).
60. 'Caspian Sea Caviar Ban Lifted after Countries Join on Sturgeon Quotas', *Agence France Presse*, 6 March 2002.
61. Albrighton (note 29).
62. Ibid.
63. D. Seward, 'Leaders of Caspian Sea Fail to Reach Agreement on Dividing Caspian Sea', *Associated Press* (AP Worldstream), 24 April 2002.
64. I. Cherepanov, 'Kazakhstan, Iran Sign Declaration on Friendly Relations', *ITAR-TASS News Agency*, 24 April 2002.
65. 'Azeri President Insists on Ecology in Caspian Status Deal', *Financial Times Information, Global News Wire – Asia Africa Intelligence Wire*, 25 April 2002.
66. Albrighton (note 29).
67. Seward (note 63).
68. I. Traynor, 'Warning of Bloodshed as Shoreline States Argue Over Carve-Up of Oil and Gas Reserves', *The Guardian*, 25 April 2002, p.16.
69. Seward (note 63).
70. M.T. Klare, *Resource Wars* (note 6).
71. M. Eaton, 'Major Trends in Military Expenditure and Arms Acquisitions by the States of the Caspian Region', in G. Chuffrin (ed.), *The Security of the Caspian Sea Region* (Oxford: SIPRI/Oxford University Press, 2001).
72. R. Sharpe (ed.), *Jane's Fighting Ships: 2000–2001* (Alexandria: Jane's Information Group 2000), p.35.
73. Ibid., pp. 397–8.
74. Personal communication with Elin Suleymanov of the Embassy of the Republic of Azerbaijan, Shepherdstown, West Virginia, 15 March 2002.
75. 'Armenia, Iran Sign Defense Cooperation Agreement', *Radio Free Europe/Radio Liberty Newsline*, 6 March 2002, <http://www.rferl.org/newsline/2002/03/060302.asp>.
76. 'Iran to Move on Own Area', *Hart's European Offshore Petroleum Newsletter*, No.27, February 2002.
77. 'Memorandum for the Secretary of State', Presidential Determination No.2002–15, 19 April 2002, distributed by the Office of International Information Programs, U.S. Department of State, <http://usinfo.state.gov>.
78. V. Socor, 'America, Azerbaijan and Armenia', *Jamestown Foundation's The Fortnight in Review*, Vol.8, No.8 (19 April 2002).
79. Ibid.
80. 'US Formally Drops Arms Sales Restrictions on Armenia, Azerbaijan', *Agence France Presse*, 29 March 2002.

81. S. Blank, 'U.S. Military in Azerbaijan, to Counter Iranian Threat', *Central Asia-Caucasus Analyst*, 10 April 2002; available through <http://www.cacianalyst.org/ archives.php>.
82. M. Lelyveld, 'Iran/Azerbaijan: U.S. Rejects Military Involvement In Caspian Dispute', *Radio Free Europe/Radio Liberty*, 9 April 2002, available through < http://www.rferl.org/ newsline/2002/04/090402.asp >.
83. 'Iran: Envoy Says No Foreign Forces will be Stationed in Azerbaijan', *Financial Times Information, Global News Wire – Asia Africa Intelligence Wire*, 24 April 2002.
84. B. Aghai Diba, 'Iran and Caspian Region: Political and Legal Issues', presentation and comments given at the IREX and Woodrow Wilson International Center for Scholars 2002 Caspian Sea Regional Policy Symposium, Shepherdstown, WV, 14–17 March 2002.
85. C. Lowe, 'Caspian Sea Border Row Chills Investment for Oil Companies', *Agence France Presse*, 3 May 2002.
86. V. Sokolova, 'Caspian Fleet to Hold Military Exercise this Summer – Putin', *ITAR-TASS News Agency*, 26 April 2002.
87. V. Socor, 'Caspian Basin to See Greater Displays of Russian Military Muscle', *Jamestown Foundation's The Monitor: A Daily Briefing of the Former Soviet States*, Vol.8, No.84, 30 April 2002.
88. P. Baev, 'Gunboats in the Great Anti-Terrorist Game', *Central Asia-Caucasus Analyst*, 28 August 2002, available through <http://www.cacianalyst.org/archives.php>.

Coercive Western Energy Security Strategies: 'Resource Wars' as a New Threat to Global Security

SUSANNE PETERS

Introduction

Following the end of the Cold War, there was a short period of time when it looked as if the world was entering an era of political stability, enduring peace, and the absence of conflicts. It was at this time that Francis Fukuyama wrote his famous book *The End of History and the Last Man*, which announced that the global spread of capitalism and liberal democracy would bring global prosperity and peace, even to the Third World. It did not take long for this dream to be shattered: a new wave of ethnic conflicts with unprecedented dimension and geographical spread brought home the message that domestic conflict would proliferate rather than decline in the post-Cold War era. Moreover, the 1991 Gulf War, in which Western powers were directly involved, and the 2003 western coalition's war against Iraq made it more than evident that interstate war is not a relic of the pre-globalization age. In several of these wars of the 1990s, natural resources 'could even appear as the *main* motive',[1] thus compelling the realization that the notion of resource wars as a threat to global security again must be given attention.

In the following, I argue that in the future we will be confronted with new resource wars in the international system, which will be precipitated by two developments: first, an anticipated oil supply crisis as a first consequence of the decline of global oil reserves and second, the uneven distribution of these declining resources along the North–South axis. It is further argued that in response to these developments, the coercive character of traditional US strategies for securing energy will intensify, thus bearing the potential to escalate into further armed conflicts. It follows from this discussion that there are only two sustainable strategies for conflict prevention: first, the reduction of the dependency on fossil fuels by developing alternative and renewable energy, and second, the pursuit of a global policy based on more equitable and controlled energy distribution.

In the beginning it is demonstrated that there are limits in international relations theory to explain interstate resource wars. These limitations are apparent in the field of international relations as well as subfields that deal explicitly with environmental conflicts. Two further exacerbating factors for resource conflicts are discussed: first, shortages in oil production anticipated to set in after 2010, and second, the North–South dimension of these conflicts in view of the concentration of the remaining resources in developing countries and the high energy consumption of the developed countries. The last section of the article compares EU and US strategies of energy supply security.

Explaining 'Resource Wars': Theoretical Limitations of International Relations and its Subfields

The phenomenon of 'resource wars' and the connection between resource scarcity and violent conflict has been long acknowledged and researched in international relations. In 1986, Arthur Westing presented a list of 12 'wars and skirmishes' of the twentieth century, ranging from world wars to secession, decolonization and civil wars. All were triggered by a dispute over access to renewable and non-renewable sources, real or even imaginary (as, for example, in the Falklands/Malvinas case, in which the existence of offshore oil was assumed rather than proven[2]). Accordingly, Westing concluded:

> Global deficiencies and degradation of natural resources, both renewable and non-renewable, coupled with the uneven distribution of these raw materials, can lead to unlikely – and thus unstable – alliances, to national rivalries, and, of course, to war.[3]

In particular, the two oil crises of the 1970s triggered concern and research on the prospects of conflicts caused by resource scarcity and oil supply crisis. Several studies appeared at that time which put the oil crisis in the context of the North–South conflict and the South's demands for a New International Economic Order. It was argued that the western states had to acknowledge the reality of their new dependency on the developing world's commodities and resources, and prospects were discussed for armed encounters between North and South in terms of the 'necessity of resource management' and 'the oil weapon'.[4] Since then, western foreign affairs offices also began to treat disruptions of energy supplies as a national security issue to be counteracted by military strategy.[5] In the early 1980s after the Soviet invasion of Afghanistan, the term 'resource wars' emerged in the US to indicate the perceived threat that the Soviet Union was denying the US access to Middle Eastern oil and African minerals.[6]

But interest in North–South studies as well as research on the prospect of interstate resource wars faded in the course of the 1980s,[7] for three reasons: first, after the shock of the two oil crises of the 1970s, the western states successfully reduced their dependency on the Middle Eastern states by diversifying their suppliers; second, globalization has taken the bite out of the North–South conflict by smoothing the deep division between some developing and developed states; therefore, conflicts along the North–South axis seemed less likely; and third, with the advance of neo-liberal ideas and the globalization debate, an optimistic world view of economics prevailed with its belief that the limitless power of technology could compensate for any kind of resource scarcity that western societies might confront, including fossil fuel scarcity. As a result of these developments, it has not yet been sufficiently understood that the first major interstate war of the post-Cold War era, the 1991 Gulf War, which was fought for the control of the region's oil, does not represent an aberration to the international system as being caused by a very specific constellation, but instead hints at the evolution of a new pattern of war.[8] It has yet to be seen to what extent the 2003 western coalition's occupation of Iraq will be interpreted as a further example of this new threat to global security. However, there are limits in international relations' subfields on the environment as well as in international relations *theories* to explain *interstate resource wars*, because first, the theories are concerned with 'resources of economic value'[9] and thus fail to consider the aspect of resource scarcity; second, the theories do not offer concepts of 'interstate conflict' or do not focus on conflict at all; and third, they are incapable of explaining how to avoid conflicts of this sort.

The international relations subfield of 'environmental conflict and security'[10] reflects the developments in the international system that led to a decline in interest in interstate wars over non-renewable resources. Since oil, the most salient of the non-renewable resources, seemed (according to its low price) to exist in abundance, *interstate* conflicts over oil seemed very unlikely. The research of two of the subfield's exponents reflects this: Homer Dixon's claim that renewables are crucially different from non-renewables[11] is based on the assumption that there exists an oversupply of non-renewables. He agrees with Repetto's view that '(i)n economic terms, exhaustible resources have not become significantly more scarce over the past century and, by some measures, most have become less scarce'.[12] Deudney's optimistic view, that the prospect of resource wars is very slim, is based on his unchallenged confidence in the achievements of technology for substituting non-renewable resources.[13] His optimism reflects the ideas of neo-liberal institutionalism and globalization when he argues that the prevalence of global capitalism and the intensification of international trade will enhance the efficiency of resource use, make violent conflicts more costly, and reduce incentives for territorial conquest.

In international relations theories, the classical domain for 'interstate wars' has been realism and its reinterpretation in the form of 'structural' or 'neo-realism'. With its assumption that conflict and insecurity are constant features of the international system, one would expect it to be the most adequate theory to explain 'resource wars'. However, realism as well as neo-realism fail to offer a powerful analytical framework for conflict prevention because, though the theories expect and explain conflict, their 'determinism for structure' renders them incapable of accounting for change.[14] Moreover, with its tenet derived from realism that states have to pursue their national interest – if necessary at the expense of morality – neo-realism can be used to justify military interventions for the sake of energy security in lieu of proposing how to avoid them. Also, at the end of the 1980s, theories with a focus on the role of economics in international relations seemed more apt to explain the new reality of an intensified globalization process, which boosted theories that belong to the school of neo-liberalism, such as neo-liberal institutionalism. Neo-liberalism assumes that its global spread yields greater interdependency among states and makes their borders more permeable, thus fostering international co-operation and world peace. In this view, co-operation replaces conflict as the dominant feature of the international system.[15]

Post-structuralist and postmodern theories,[16] which have gained increasing recognition in international relations over the last decade, are also not capable of explaining resource wars. First of all, since in the postmodern view conflicts are ubiquitous, postmodern theories have not generated a clear and explicit concept of conflict.[17] Moreover, with their 'uncompromisingly anti-empirical'[18] stance, post-structuralists strive to overcome structuralism and emphasize that reality is socially constructed and that 'social structures are constructed by humans rather than themselves being natural'.[19]

At first glance, theories belonging to the discipline of International Political Economy seem to offer a feasible analytical framework for today's interstate resource wars. The variations of theories of world systems, imperialism, and dependency – all of which imply a 'Marxist perspective'[20] – are able to explain the dynamics of a world system in which northern core states exploit southern peripheral states by extracting their cheap raw materials and by exploiting their workforce in low-cost production sites. But some more recent studies, which use these theories to explain the connection between armed conflicts and natural resources,[21] suffer from being 'sub-complex' in response to their economic determinism.[22]

As a challenge to the prevalence of neo-liberal ideas, Neo-Marxist theories gained new attention and acknowledgement in the 1990s. While these theories – like realism – 'direct attention to conflict',[23] Neo-Gramscian theory's central element of transnational historical materialism is more apt to explain conflict between state and civil society than conflict among states. Moreover, while Robert Cox includes 'ecological dangers' and other conflicts of non-economic character in his analysis, the theory's economic focus makes it again difficult to explain a conflict of ecological nature.

The subfield of 'political ecology' developed over the last two decades as a radical critique of 'rigid, structural Marxist'[24] and neo-Malthusian explanations of environmental clashes and conflicts. Combining Marxian political economy, the 'new ecology' and cultural studies, 'political ecology' offers a promising approach to analyse conflicts originated by 'the forms of access to and control over resources.'[25] Researchers using this approach seriously consider 'the causal powers inherent in Nature itself' and start from the assumption that there exists '"a dialectic of Nature-Society" relations'.[26] But as Le Billon has pointed out, 'political ecology' so far has focused on 'social conflicts' such as rebellions and riots, and neglected research on 'large-scale violent conflicts'.[27] The downside of the field's constriction is obvious: since 'social conflicts' are considered a feature of the underdeveloped third world, conflicts with Western involvement are ignored. Thus, Jon Barnett's criticism of 'environmental security' is also valid for the field of 'political ecology', though his statement is limited to the domestic level:

> The environment-conflict literature is almost entirely premised on the ethnocentric assumption that people in the South will resort to violence in times of resource scarcity. Rarely, if ever, is the same argument applied to people in the industrialized North.[28]

In order to serve as a powerful analytical tool for interstate resource wars, 'political ecology' will have to be expanded to overcome these shortcomings.

The most recent occupation of Iraq, which occurred 12 years after the first Gulf War, brought home the message that 'resource wars' do not constitute a deviation within the international system. By the end of the 1990s, new ecological trends emerged that will oblige us to look again at the interstate level and non-renewable energy as a potential cause for violent conflicts: ever more experts warn of a future oil supply crisis and an increasing energy vulnerability of western states.

Prospects and Causes of Oil Supply Crisis

Among non-renewable resources, oil is the most important in the economies of the industrialized countries. It is an extensively used raw material and an important factor for transport and the agricultural sector. The petrochemical sector would collapse without oil supply and, so far, no replacement is in sight. In particular, the agricultural sector has become energy-intensive in every respect: farm machinery depends on diesel fuel or gasoline; fertilizer production requires natural gas; pesticides and herbicides are synthesized from oil; and transportation and processing of agricultural products also depend on oil.[29] But with oil prices plunging to record lows during most of the 1990s, there seemed to be no reason to think about the West's heavy dependence on its supply. However, after the dramatic increase of oil prices during the last three years – at one point, by as much as 300 per cent – it now appears that new problems and crises are on the horizon with respect to energy supply, and not only with oil, but also with gas – though in a more long-term perspective. Thus, the question of how long the oil reserves will last gains new urgency. For an evaluation of this question, one needs to look both at the demand and the supply side.

While there is much debate with regard to supply, i.e., to what extent and with what speed the pie is getting smaller, there does not seem to be any disagreement that demand will increase significantly in the coming decades. According to the World Energy Outlook of the International Energy Agency, the most authoritative source for providing forecasts on the outlook of world energy, demand for oil is expected to rise between 1997 and 2020 at a growth rate of 1.9 per cent per year. Most of the demand will come from the transport sector, where chances for a significant substitution are not yet visible.[30] But it is on the demand side where hopes are high to reverse the threatening prospects of an energy crisis, by implementing efficient energy-saving programmes and by developing commercially profitable alternative energy.

The forecasts for the supply side are much more complex and controversial. Due to the geological condition of fossil fuels, located deep in the soil, offshore, and in polar regions, predictions and estimates of the remaining base of all oil and gas resources are naturally hard to make. Moreover, there is significant disagreement and confusion among the various forecasts on the definitions of 'reserves', which makes it even harder to compare them. The most important swing factor in the forecasts is the category of non-conventional oil. Non-conventional oil comes from oil shale, tar sands, enhanced recovery, hostile environments (such as deep or polar water), very small accumulations, heavy oil, and also comes in the form of Natural Gas Liquids (NGL). Non-conventional oil is difficult and expensive to extract, and the crucial question for the future will be to what extent technology will develop to facilitate access to this non-conventional oil. Some estimates therefore separate these two categories; others aggregate data of conventional and unconventional oil. There are different parameters by which the degree of depletion of fossil fuels is estimated.

R/P Ratio and Peak Production

Most analyses use the category of a global oil 'reserves-to-production ratio' (R/P ratio) to indicate the 'theoretical expected lifetime of reserves under constant production at the current level'.[31] The global R/P ratio is estimated as being enough to provide 40 years of supply at current rates,[32] thus, any risk for oil supply is dated well beyond the 40 years. But the R/P ratio is misleading as an instrument for indicating the years of affordable remaining oil, since it does not factor in fluctuations either in demand or in production capacities. In reality, there exists nothing close to a constant production level in a country, since the past has shown that the production ratios of the main producer countries have varied greatly over time, due to the level of investment in production infrastructure, the use of new technologies, etc. And even more importantly, as some scientists argue, depletion of oil does not follow the pattern of a constant production rate with a sharp decline when the last drops of oil are extracted. According to the model of the geologist M. King Hubbert, oil discoveries and oil production follow similar trajectories in the form of a bell curve with a midpoint of depletion which corresponds approximately to peak production. Peak production means that half of the world's finite supply of conventional oil will have been consumed. After peak production comes shortage because production is slowly going to decline, a process we are witnessing currently for US and North Sea oil production, both of which reserves have already 'peaked'.[33]

As Bentley spells out clearly, 'it is this *declining* production' after the midpoint of depletion, 'in other words unsatisfied demand, that is the key factor about future oil supply'.[34] Scientists following the Hubbert model of oil production therefore believe that the assessment of the 'midpoint of depletion' is a more valuable indicator for the time remaining to confront and compensate for the irreversible depletion of the finite resource oil. There is considerable disagreement about when this peak occurs, but according to Luciani, 'nevertheless, the reality of a global peak is not under discussion: production has been declining for many years now in the United States, and is expected to soon decline also in the North Sea.'[35] According to an international group of petroleum specialists (Association for the Study of Peak Oil, ASPO), the world supply of oil will peak as early as 2010, provoking soaring energy prices and economic upheaval.[36]

Remaining Reserves and Yet-To-Find

The forecast for the peak of production depends on the estimates of the remaining and yet-to-find reserves of conventional and non-conventional resources, which is another category that indicates the process of depletion. There is no disagreement that so far 1700 Gb (Giga barrels) of oil have been found in the world. Moreover, most of the more than 60 estimates that have been made in recent decades, indicate that the total ultimately recoverable quantity of *conventional* oil would be somewhere around 2000 Gb.[37] However, there are authoritative estimates that deviate grossly from this average. In a 2000 study, the US Geological Survey (USGS) estimated that following different models the world's remaining oil could add up to anywhere from 2100 to 2800 Gb with different probabilities. In a second analysis, the USGS included the factor of 'reserve growth', based on the US experience in which (by applying new technology and methods) more oil than expected could be pumped.[38] The USGS then assigned probabilities to these 'reserve growths' which raise the above figures to the range of 2300 to 4000 Gb.

A key factor responsible for the substantial variations in these studies is different expectations of how much oil is yet-to-find. Expectations of the remaining undiscovered reserves depend on interpretations of past discovery patterns, from which scientists extrapolate future discovery trends. But even past discovery trends are read differently by different geologists and oil experts. ASPO scientists argue that the big discoveries have all been made. According to their interpretation, the peak of discovery occurred in the 1960s and the discovery rate has fallen dramatically in the last 35 years, now averaging about 10 Gb/yr.[39] This finding has recently been confirmed by oil company executive, Harry Longwell, Director of Exxon Mobile.[40] On this basis, ASPO member Colin Campbell estimates a yet-to-find figure of 130 Gb. At the other extreme, the USGS forecasts three times more than ASPO, projecting an average of 30 Gb found oil per year. Their study suggests that, with a 50 per cent probability, another 732 Gb will be found between 1995 and 2020, assuming that US know-how is applied in the rest of the world.

One of the reasons for the surprising differences of interpretation in past discovery trends is distortion in the reporting of proven reserves, which are published unquestioned and unchanged year after year by the *BP Statistical Review*. While it is widely believed that BP provides its own estimates, it merely reports *Oil & Gas Journal* non-backdated reserves as reported by governments. Assessments of reserves are subject to diverse political motivations to understate or overstate the quantities involved. In the 1980s, several members of the Organization of Petroleum Exporting Countries (OPEC) reported considerable increases in reserves, which misled oil experts into believing that we 'are running into oil'.[41] But this sudden 'reserve growth' was not caused by changes in the OPEC countries' reservoirs, but rather by a 'quota war' among several OPEC members, because production quota depends on the quantity of the reserve base.[42] It started with Iraq, when it added an 11 billion barrel increase that, in fact, was a delayed report of a discovery in the late 1970s. Venezuela followed by doubling its reserves in 1987 by the admission of, at that point, large amounts of *heavy* oil it had found long before. Iran, Iraq, Abu Dhabi, Dubai and later Saudi Arabia felt compelled to counteract Venezuela's action by reporting huge increases of their own, practically overnight. The actual figures might be somewhere in the middle, because the old numbers (provided by the companies before being expropriated) could be understated. Moreover, it is implausible that a large and increasing number of countries report unchanged numbers year after year, although 'production eats into reserves'. According to Bentley, 'more than half of all countries with reserves reported by the *Oil & Gas Journal* (and hence also by the *BP Statistical Review of World Energy*) are not generally reporting reserves *changes*.[43]

In order not to lose orientation in this jungle of polarized figures, governments and institutions tend to rely on the energy estimate of the *International Energy Agency* (IEA) and its annual *World Energy Outlook*. In 1998, the *World Energy Outlook* for the first time launched a warning that soon there might be an oil supply problem. For the year 2020, the report estimated a total oil *demand* for 111.5 million barrels per day, which is juxtaposed to 92.3 million barrels a day of world oil *supply*. Thus, global demand would have a deficit of 19.1 million barrels a day in 2020. These missing barrels of oil were then miraculously matched by a category labelled 'Unidentified Unconventional Oil', declared at 19.1 million barrels a day and just compensating for the deficit between supply and demand. As a consequence of this analysis, the report estimated that the peak of conventional oil production might arrive before 2020.[44] These data have been understood as a message by some IEA agents to their client states that there might be soon a problem. But the IEA staff member in charge of this part of the report, J. M. Bourdaire, left the IEA shortly thereafter, and with the publication of the upbeat 2000 USGS report, subsequent annual IEA reports are again much more optimistic.[45] The IEA 2002 report starts from the assumption of 'ample' oil resources, though it also warns that 'more reserves will need to be identified in order to meet rising oil demand to 2030'.[46]

However, it is obviously not necessary to start from the assumption of a progressive decline of the oil resource base in order to foresee serious problems with future oil supply. An independent task force, set up in late 2000 by the Baker Institute and the Council on Foreign Relations on the 'Strategic Energy Challenges for the 21st Century', comes up with an alarming analysis:

As the 21st century opens, the energy sector is in critical condition. A crisis could erupt at any time from any number of factors and would inevitably affect every country in today's globalized world. While the origins of a crisis are hard to pinpoint, it is clear that energy disruptions could have a potentially enormous impact on the US and the world economy, and would affect US national security and foreign policy in dramatic ways.[47]

According to the authors of the report, this dramatic 'energy challenge' has nothing do with the global hydrocarbon resource base, which they believe is still 'enormous'. Rather, it is prompted by energy infrastructure constraints, combined with strong economic and oil-demand growth. First, too rapid economic growth during the past has surpassed the production capacity of the oil and gas producers, rendering them incapable to keep up with increasing global demand. Second, for the last two decades the most important energy producers refrained from investing in production infrastructure due to the falling real prices for oil. Furthermore, the report identifies as a cause for this looming supply crisis a lack of trained energy sector workers and – with an eye to the more special US situation – the consequences of energy market deregulation and market liberalization. While the report's authors are aware that 'American people continue to demand plentiful and cheap energy without sacrifice or inconvenience,'[48] they also point out the reality that neither emerging new technologies or the necessary surplus energy capacity is on the horizon to meet such demands. Many of the independent task force's recommendations have been incorporated in the 'National Energy Policy', a May 2001 governmental study on the state of affairs of US energy policy.

During the last few years, experts of the oil industry have joined the camp of those who warn of a supply crisis in the foreseeable future. This includes Franco Bernabé from ENI (the Italian energy company),[49] as well as the chief executive of ARCO, Michael Bowlin, who declared in February 1999: 'We've embarked on the beginning of the last days of the age of oil.'[50] Also BP's new corporate name 'Beyond Petroleum' acknowledges that there will be a problem of oil supply in the future.[51] And Exxon Mobile's Harry Longwell puts it as follows:

> The catch is that while demand increases, existing production declines. To put a number on it, we expect that by 2010 about half the daily volume needed to meet projected demand is not on production today – and that's the challenge facing producers.[52]

According to those who warn of a supply crisis but don't see it caused by a dwindling resource base, the challenge is to develop the technology to exploit existing fields more efficiently and to extract the reserves of unconventional oil in a commercially profitable fashion. This is the central point on which the debate will centre in the future. But here comes the downside: if oil companies are to replace the output lost from ageing fields and meet the world's ever rising demand for oil, the IEA reckons they must invest $1 trillion in non-OPEC countries over the next decade alone. But it is more than questionable whether technology can really succeed in increasing the discovery rate to the extent necessary to satisfy demand. The fact of the matter is that for every two barrels used, only one new one is found.[53]

The extent to which conservation strategies and the substitution of oil can compensate for the decline in oil production, and the time frame in which they may do so, is very hard to assess.[54] Some promising progress has been made, in particular with the replacement of oil with natural gas. The share of gas in generating electricity and heating is constantly increasing. But since gas is a finite resource, the replacement of oil with gas will not solve the problem but only 'buy time' for a switch to renewable sources. New energy extractions (for example, from wind turbines and solar power) have made considerable progress, but in view of the investment and technology needed to turn them into a profitable energy sector, it will still take decades before renewables constitute a considerable share of the energy mix. In any case, the biggest problem remains with transportation, where all hopes rest on the development of fuel cells produced from hydrogen. However, to turn fuel cells in a universal battery for transportation applications requires an entirely different energy infrastructure and a 'transition to a hydrogen economy'.[55] Moreover, it is a problem that the production of hydrogen currently relies mainly on natural gas. Thus, the production of the fuel cell will also eat into the dwindling gas reserves.

The ASPO scientists stress that there is no reason to panic and that there is time left to counter this looming supply crisis:

> The World is not about to run out of oil. At peak, there is as much left as we have used so far, but we do need the high supply, while it lasts, to achieve an orderly transition.[56]

But there are no signs of serious preparations for an orderly transition. With demand progressively surpassing production over the next decades, we can expect a fight over the distribution of the remaining resources, with the South no longer prepared to accept the existing North's disproportionate consumption of energy. Therefore, the assumption has to be questioned that the North–South conflict – or however we label the gap in wealth between rich and poor countries – is a relic of the pre-globalization age.

North–South Dimension of Resource Conflicts

There is no question that the process of globalization has blurred the distinction between the impoverished South and the rich North to the extent that the analytical concept of the North–South conflict seems to have lost its explanatory power.

While it is beyond the purpose of this article to analyse the benefits and disadvantages of globalization for the developing world, it is argued here that there still exists a wealth gap between groups of states which can be roughly assigned to the South and to the North of the globe. In conflicts caused by disputes over the distribution of oil as a consequence of the decline in oil production or by an increased western import dependency on certain countries, it matters that those states which consume most of the energy belong to the rich OECD states, and those who possess most of the remaining oil reserves belong to the non-OECD world, the Group of 77, or simply to the 'developing world'.

Notwithstanding globalization's positive effects for some East Asian countries (such as China), globalization has widened the gap *between* states, the *external* gap, as well as *within* states, the *internal* gap. In this context, only the external gap is of interest. According to the World Bank's Development Report, between 1970 and 1995, the average per capita income of the *poorest* and *middle thirds* of *all* countries decreased steadily compared to the average income of the richest third. Expressed in percentages, this means that the average per capita GDP of the middle third has declined from 12.5 per cent to 11.4 per cent of the richest third, and that of the poorest third from 3.1 per cent to 1.9 per cent of the richest third.[57] In view of the dimension of this increasing gap, it seems justified to assume that the relationship between two- thirds of all countries with a low and very low income and the remaining one-third of all countries with a high income bears the potential of tension and conflict.

In the following it is argued that this potentially conflictual relationship between these groups of countries can be further exacerbated due to the fact that 80 per cent of total oil reserves is held by countries that are labelled as 'developing countries'. Table 1 is meant to express this link.

1. The first column ranks the countries' oil wealth in terms of *percentage share* of global proven oil reserves.[58] In this context, data for *proven reserves* is considered more reliable than the data for *production*, since production is often subject to unforeseen fluctuation and because production in OECD countries is expected to decline soon.
2. The second column indicates the *Human Development Index* (HDI) ranking of 2000.[59]
3. The third is the 2000 Gross Domestic Product (GDP) per capita in dollars.[60]

4. The fourth and the fifth columns indicate *GDP per capita annual growth rate by percent (%)*. The fourth column indicates the time period between 1975–2000, the fifth for 1990–2000.[61]

Countries whose share of total proven oil reserves is *less than 0.5 per cent* are left out of this chart. Also, the OECD countries that together provide 8.1 per cent share of the total of global oil reserves are not listed.

Table 1 indicates that *88.6 per cent of total proven oil reserves* are held by the *19 non-OECD countries* listed above. Except for the Russian Federation, Kazakhstan and Azerbaijan, all the remaining 16 non-OECD countries are listed as 'developing countries' by the 2002 UN Human Development Report.[62] The six countries of the Gulf Cooperation Countries (GCC) – Saudi Arabia, Kuwait, the United Arab Emirates (UAE), Qatar, Oman and Bahrain – hold together a 45.5 per cent share of total proven oil reserves.[63] Although the data for GDP per capita and Human Development Index indicates that their status is, in some cases, not much worse than that of the low-ranking OECD countries such as Mexico and Poland, prospects are such that – unlike for Poland and Mexico – their economic status will not improve greatly and may likely worsen. This expectation of an

TABLE 1

OIL WEALTH OF DEVELOPING COUNTRIES

Country	Share of proven oil reserves (%)	HDI ranking	GDP per capita (PPP US$) 2000	GDP per capita annual growth rate (%)	
				1975–2000	1990–2000
Saudi Arabia	24.9	71	11,367	–2.2	–1.2
Iraq	10.7	no data	no data	no data	no data
Kuwait	9.2	45	15,799	–0.9	–1.4
UAE	9.3	46	17,935	–3.7	–1.6
Iran	8.5	98	5,884	–0.7	+1.9
Venezuela	7.4	69	5,794	–0.9	–0.6
Russia	4.6	60	8,377	–1.2	–4.6
Libya	2.8	64	7,570	–6.7	no data
Nigeria	2.3	148	896	–0.7	–0.4
China	2.3	96	3,976	+8.1	+9.2
Qatar	1.4	51	18,789	no data	no data
Algeria	0.9	106	5,308	–0.3	–0.1
Brazil	0.8	73	7,625	+0.5	+1.5
Kazakhstan	0.8	79	5,871	no data	–3.1
Azerbaijan	0.7	88	2,936	–9.6	–7.3
Oman	0.5	78	13,356	+2.8	+0.3
Angola	0.5	161	2,187	–1.9	–1.8
India	0.5	124	2,358	+3.2	+4.1
Indonesia	0.5	110	3,043	+4.4	+2.5
Total:	88.6				

unsatisfying economic performance is based on the well-established assumption that, among the developing countries, those countries with a 'high value of resource-based exports to GDP'[64] tend to have a lower growth rate than resource-poor countries. The chart above demonstrates this connection for the three major oil-producing Middle Eastern countries: Saudi Arabia, Kuwait, and UAE. For the period between 1975–2000, their GDP per capita annual growth rate was negative; for the UAE, it was even as low as 3.7 per cent. The reason for this negative growth is obvious: resource-rich countries do not have an incentive to develop competitive industrialization and instead prefer to maintain a dependence on their commodity exports.[65] Thus, without major restructuring of the economy, no dramatic reversals of these negative trends are to be expected. However, the surge in oil prices, as we have witnessed since 1999, will mitigate, possibly halt this process of economic deterioration.[66]

Independently of the major oil-producing countries' economic performance, what matters in any conflict between energy-producing and energy-consuming countries is to what extent they themselves self-identify as developing countries and, therefore, in opposition to the developed world. Sixteen of the 19 oil-producing countries listed above – with the exception of Russia, Kazakhstan and Azerbaijan – are members of the G-77, the 'largest third world coalition in the United Nations'.[67] While the group has kept its name, it has enlarged to 132 members. According to its own declaration, the G-77 'provides the means for the developing world to articulate and promote its collective economic interests and enhance its joint negotiating capacity on all major economic issues in the United Nations system, and promote economic and technical cooperation among developing countries'.[68] The G-77's group identity as being disenfranchised and disadvantaged by the developed world is expressed when the G-77 declares that their member states' common identity is that of 'nations who were subjected to colonialism ... and who needed development'.[69] The fact that identities can change is seen in the example of Mexico, which left G-77 to join the OECD in 1994.

The warning of the 1979 Council on Foreign Relations' study that a group of developing countries that 'perceives a global equity crisis' might attempt to use the resource issue as an 'opportunity and instrument for change'[70] seems to gain new actuality in view of the data expressing the bad economic situation of the oil-producing countries. Further contributing to a fuelling of the developing world's perception of a 'global equity crisis' might be the persistent and disproportional distribution of energy consumption between the population of the OECD and the non-OECD world. On a per capita basis, a person in the developed world uses *8.2 times* more *oil* than a person in the developing world; for full consumption of *energy,* the factor is 5.5.

Against this background two scenarios are possible. In the first, the wealth gap between the developing and developed world further deepens, and the North–South dimension of producer-consumer relations provokes the non-OECD producer states to copy OPEC's policy of the 1970s and thus to launch a new attempt to mitigate the global equity crisis by using the 'oil weapon'. This time, however, there is the potential for a broader consensus, possibly in the framework of the G-77, or OPEC, which covers 67.3 per cent of all proven oil reserves,[71] or the Arab League, which covers the interests of 8 of the 19 non-OECD oil-producing countries and almost 60 per cent of global oil reserves.

In the second scenario, globalization succeeds in accelerating the economic development of the oil-producing countries, which then narrows the gap between them and the OECD countries. This scenario implies that demand of the developing countries is growing. As of now, the demand for oil in the developing world is estimated *to rise three times as fast as in the developed world*, from today's 43 per cent of total world oil consumption to 55 per cent by 2020. Thus the pie (of oil) is getting smaller and more parties are going to consume it. When production of oil declines, conflict will build over the distribution among the almost exclusively energy-producing states of the South, whose demand will grow significantly, and the energy-consuming states of the North. Therefore, the assumption has to be questioned that conflicts in the context of the North–South dialogue – or however we label the gap in wealth between countries in the North and in the South – are a relic of the pre-globalization age.

The future oil supply crisis and the North–South dimension constitute the framing conditions precipitating future resource wars. However, wars are usually caused by a complex combination of motives, therefore a war exclusively fought for the control of and access to resources has not yet been fought. The use of the term 'resource war' implies that the concern for access to and control of resources is the most important motivation. With this in mind, it will be argued in the following that, as a consequence of the US coercive strategy to secure energy supplies, we have witnessed two post-Cold War wars which deserve the label 'resource wars'. Moreover, by using Michael Klare's analysis, it is argued that implementation of the imperatives of the US National Energy Policy will necessarily imply the use of coercive strategies, resulting in the risk for all energy-rich countries to be confronted in one form or another with the military power of the United States.

The Dynamics of US Coercive Strategies of Energy Security

In its search for energy security the western oil-dependent states have taken a 'diversity of initiatives'[72] over the last decades, including diplomatic efforts, stockpiling of strategic resources, and diversifying energy suppliers, as well as the pursuit of a 'geopolitics of energy'. A 'geopolitics of energy' encompasses a comprehensive approach of projecting power into energy-rich regions, ranging from military deployments with the consent of the host country to covert military interventions or the occupation of the energy-rich territory by means of full-scale war.

The first *coup d'état* related to western oil interests was the British and US forces' military coup to overthrow the Mossadeq regime in Iran and to install the pro-western Shah (1953) in response to Mossadeq's nationalization of the British oil corporations.[73] The second was the 1956 Suez crisis following Egypt's nationalization of the Suez canal, which was answered by Britain, France and Israel by a military attack on Egypt. It was the United States which settled the crisis and also compensated for the subsequent interruption of supply by exporting to its oil-consuming allies in western Europe and Japan.

Well into the 1960s, the United States still had enough excess capacity to act as a swing producer in case of crisis.[74] But US production peaked during the late 1960s and the subsequent decline in its production capacity became obvious during the first 'oil crisis' in 1973, when the US proved unable to supply the market with additional excess oil. The West's first encounter with this new phenomenon occurred when an oil embargo was imposed by the OAPEC[75] on the United States and the Netherlands for their support of Israel during the 1973 Arab–Israeli war.[76] As a response to the oil-producing countries' first use of the 'oil weapon', US senior officials launched threats to intervene militarily, but these threats did not materialize.[77]

Since the 1973 oil crisis, energy supply security has been treated as a top priority of US foreign policy. As an institutional effort to mitigate the effects of future supply interruptions caused by OPEC policies, the International Energy Agency (IEA) was established as part of the OECD in 1974 with the primary mission of providing a mechanism for energy security and emergency response. To that end the IEA designed an integrated set of *emergency response measures*, which include stockdraw, demand restraint, fuel-switching, surge of oil production, and sharing of available supplies. While the IEA still failed in the two oil crises of 1979 and 1980,[78] it managed successfully the 1990–91 Gulf War supply crisis and prevented supply interruptions and drastic price surges[79] as possible effects of the most recent war with Iraq.[80]

A further response of the US and other western countries to these crises of the 1970s was their corporations' *diversification strategies*, which involved finding promising new sources in Alaska, the North Sea, Mexico and elsewhere, often offshore. Also, nuclear energy was further developed, and coal achieved a massive comeback in the electricity sector. In addition, programmes for saving energy displayed some success.

But the US did not limit themselves to relying solely on strategies of crisis prevention and crisis managem :nt by the establishment of institutions and the pursuit of diversification strategies for guaranteeing energy supply. The United States developed doctrines and military strategies to deal successfully with any scenario of a supply disruption. Cold War dynamics helped to legitimize the threat of the United States to use force also for the pursuit of its national interest. Thus, the infamous 'Carter doctrine' of 1980, which declared the Persian Gulf as a region of 'vital interests' to the US, was justified only by the Soviet Union's invasion into Afghanistan, which had been interpreted as a Soviet move to encroach closer to the Gulf region.[81] But the 1991 Gulf War was evidence that the threat of the Soviet Union denying the West access to its lifelines had been used as a pretext and that, in addition, after the end of the Cold War the US would not accept any geopolitical changes in the western-dominated petroleum system. Still, by rallying the war alliance behind the US in the 1991 Gulf War, the argument for the necessity of a restoration of international law by liberating Kuwait played an important role. But it seems that with the distance of more than a decade, the decisive motivation for this war can now be spelt out more explicitly: it was for control of the region's oil. Had Iraq not been defeated and instead occupied the Kuwaiti oil fields, it would have controlled 20 per cent of the region's oil or some 6 mb/d of capacity, turning it into 'the head of OPEC' and therefore controlling pricing.[82] Edward Morse puts it boldly:

> The Gulf War of 1991 was the first war in modern history fought specifically over oil. It serves as a reminder that as long as hydrocarbon resources remain fundamental to economic growth – and as long as there are powerful governments that want to ensure access to hydrocarbon supplies – there will be a commitment to use force to prevent any single government from controlling the market.[83]

As Michael Klare also demonstrates, after the end of the Cold War the US never left a doubt that access to cheap oil was still a national security issue, which had to be, if necessary, secured by military means.[84] This self-confidence in the justification of US power projection for achieving US foreign policy goals is displayed even by hard-core liberals such as Francis Fukuyama, who predicts that oil will be one of three axes along which the North and the South will collide militarily in the future.

The Democratic Clinton administration with its emphasis on economics was no exception to this geopolitical approach to energy – in fact, even more so. With an 'economization of international security affairs'[85] and the blending of economics with national security,[86] the Clinton administration did not leave any doubt that 'the economic well-being of our society' constituted a national security interest which might have to be defended also by the use of force.[87] And security of energy supply is regarded as an essential constituent of economic well-being. One expression of Clinton's geopolitical approach to energy was, for example, to declare Venezuela and Colombia as zones of 'vital American interests' because of their oil resources,[88] as well as military co-operation with the states bordering the Caspian.[89]

The Republican Bush administration began with a strong focus on the Persian Gulf as an area of strategic interests,[90] and the Bush administration's May 2001 *National Energy Policy (NEP)* stipulated that the Gulf will 'remain vital to U.S. interests'.[91] As Michael Klare has pointed out, the NEP recognizes that the United States' dependence on foreign sources for securing energy supply is going to increase further.[92] Klare notes that implementation of this new energy supply strategy with its heavy emphasis on importing energy will shape future American foreign and security policy and warns:

> Not only will American officials have to negotiate access to these overseas supplies and arrange for the sorts of investments that will make increased production and export possible, but they must also take steps to make certain that foreign deliveries to the United States are not impeded by war, revolution, or civil disorder. These imperatives will govern U.S. policy toward all significant energy-supplying regions, especially the Persian Gulf area, the Caspian Sea basin, Africa, and Latin America.[93]

With this acknowledgement on the part of the US administration that the United States is dependent on energy supply from foreign sources, it is difficult to dissipate claims that the war against Iraq was mainly about US interests to gain access to cheap oil. While during the Cold War it was the antagonism towards the Soviet Union that would have justified a 'resource war' following the imperative of the 'Carter Doctrine', a resource war of the post-Cold War era, following the imperative of the NEP, is being legitimized by the fight against the proliferation of weapons of mass destruction and Islamic terrorism – a rationale that collapsed within the first weeks of Iraq's invasion by US and British forces.

With the regime change in Baghdad, international and, most of all, US oil companies gained access to invest in Iraq's vast oil fields, which have been left almost untapped over the last decade due to the UN sanction policy. It is estimated that Iraq possesses 112 billion barrels of oil, the largest reserve in the world outside Saudi Arabia and 11 per cent of global proven reserves. For years international oil companies have been trying to gain access to the oil-rich Gulf region, but so far with success only for downstream production and without any prospect for penetrating the attractive and profitable upstream production. One of the NEP's recommendations to the President is 'to support initiatives by Saudi Arabia, Kuwait, Algeria, Qatar, the UAE and other suppliers to open up areas of their energy sectors to foreign investment'.[94] However, the authors of the NEP must have been aware of the limits to implementing their recommendation, since Saudi Arabia and the Kuwait parliament have made it unmistakably clear that they are not going to repeat the mistake of the past by allowing the western oil companies too much control of their precious treasures. The most recent regime change in Baghdad mitigates this impasse in the international oil companies' strategy to return to the Middle East, by providing access to a country with abundant cheap conventional on-shore oil that does not exist anywhere else in the world. But it remains to be seen whether this scenario will unfold as planned and whether the Iraqi oil industry will be capable of living up to the expectation of acting as a future swing producer.[95]

As Klare also points out, most of the countries that are selected to supply the United States with energy foster strong anti-American sentiments or are haunted by violence and internal disorder, or both.[96] As a result, the pursuit of the new US energy security strategy is 'almost certain to encounter violent disorder and resistance in many key producing areas' thus provoking a 'spiral of confrontation and conflict.'[97] But also for the American people, it is foreseeable that the day will come when they have to understand that even a coercive strategy cannot guarantee any more the procurement of abundant and cheap energy without sacrifices on their part.

The EU and the Provision of Energy Security: A Patchwork of Ineffective and Non-Coercive Strategies[98]

In view of its high import dependency, the EU's energy supply strategies are also of vital importance for the economic well-being of its member states. Since North Sea crude oil production is projected to decline progressively after having reached peak production around 2000, Europe's *oil* import dependency is expected to increase drastically in the mid-term future. The EU currently imports 76 per cent of its oil energy requirements; by 2020, this is projected to increase to 90 per cent. While the EU imports roughly half of its oil from OPEC countries, in terms of individual countries the source of supplies is as follows: the number one oil supplier for the EU is Norway, and the number two is Russia. For *gas* imports, the prospects are not much better. Currently the EU imports 40 per cent of its gas consumption, with Russia and Algeria being the main external suppliers.[99]

The EU began only in the mid-1990s to advance its own analyses and strategies to deal with potential supply crisis. To that end, the EU Commission launched the widely acknowledged 2000 Green Paper, 'Towards a European strategy for the security of energy supply'. But the Green Paper is disappointing with respect to the dearth of feasible and effective strategies for securing the EU's energy supply. As the most important strategy, the Green Paper recommends diversification of suppliers, but without specifying recommendations for its implementation. For the strategy of replacement of fossil fuels energy with renewables, the Green Paper acknowledges that the goal that had been regularly set since 1985, which was to double the share of renewables in the production of electricity, had been missed. Renewables still account for only 6 per cent of Europe's supply, including 2 per cent for hydroelectricity.[100] A further strategy recommended by the EU Commission is the establishment of a strategic oil reserve in addition to the 90 days' existing reserves for finished products,[101] and the call for better Community mechanisms (such as centralized decision-making mechanisms) for the release of oil to the market. So far these are only recommendations that wait to be implemented.

Of utmost concern for the EU is to secure energy supplies from Russia – the EU's most important gas and second-most important oil supplier. This objective was supposed to be met by the long-term strategy of setting up the Energy Charter Treaty (ECT). The purpose of the ECT is to establish legal rights with respect to investment, trade, and the transit of energy. But the most important issue is security of transit, with all signatories obliged to allow the transit of energy from third parties, including in the event of a conflict with one of the parties. By now the Energy Charter Treaty totals 51 signatories, including all members of the European Union, several Eastern European countries, Russia and the CIS states, plus Australia and Japan. The Treaty entered into force in 1998 following the ratification of 30 signatories (ratification for other countries is still pending). Unfortunately, one of the countries whose ratification is still pending is Russia, and it does not appear that the Russian parliament intends to ratify the treaty in the foreseeable future.[102] In order to at least partially compensate for the collapse of the ETC as an instrument to secure Russian energy supplies, the EU succeeded in achieving an 'energy partnership' with Russia. This initiative has been launched as one policy outcome of the EU Green Paper, stipulating that Russia's share of current gas and oil supply for the EU is planned to double in the next 20 years. But, in sum, it has to be acknowledged that both policy initiatives, the Charter Treaty and the Energy Partnership, fall short of guaranteeing energy delivery from Europe's most important energy supplier.

However, the EU's pursuit of these non-coercive strategies for securing energy supply does not mean that individual European member states completely abstained from the use of force if need arose to restore the geopolitical structure that guaranteed accessible and affordable oil. The participation of European forces in the 1991 Gulf War, in which France and Great Britain joined US military forces, has been interpreted as proof 'that NATO states will not stand by idly if a South-South dispute jeopardizes oil supplies ...'.[103] British forces participated again in the 2003 Gulf War, and 5 of the 15 EU member states – Denmark, Italy, the Netherlands, Spain, and Portugal – supported the war politically or even militarily, though in a very limited fashion. But in view of the strong opposition of EU key members, France and Germany, against the war in Iraq, it seems highly unlikely that a joint and comprehensive EU geopolitical approach for access to and control of energy will materialize any time soon.

However, if the EU does not get its act together and begin without delay the set up and implementation of a kind of 'EU Marshall Plan for Renewable Energies', which would involve a 'dramatic, decisive and massive EU industrialization effort',[104] it will not succeed in the long run in preventing itself from being manoeuvred into joining the US in its aggressive policy to take care of its energy import needs.

Conclusion

While it has been acknowledged by now that both major interstate wars of the post-Cold War era were motivated to a considerable extent by concern to gain access to resources, these are still regarded as abnormalities caused by a particular constellation that will not repeat itself. But for an effective prevention of conflicts of this sort, it needs still to be recognized that resource wars constitute a new feature in the international arena and a threat to global security.[105] Two framing conditions have been identified for an increased probability of future resource wars: the first is an anticipated oil supply crisis as a first consequence of the decline of global oil reserves, and the second framing condition is the uneven distribution of oil along the North–South axis.

Contributing to this lack of understanding that resource wars have developed into a new feature of the international system, are international relations theories which are not well suited to explain the phenomenon of interstate resource conflicts, nor to engage in analysis for their prevention. This applies particularly to the mainstream theories of neo-liberal institutionalism and neo-realism: the former, because it believes that the positive effects of globalization will render the disappearance of 'conflict' as the dominant feature of the international system, and the latter, because with its focus on the *status quo* rather than change, neo-realism is more prone to provide subsequent justifications of resource wars rather than useful explanations of how to avoid them. Also, the strong belief in the power of technology and ideas – as promoted by neo-liberalism – that informs in part research in the subfield of 'environment and conflict', obscures the inevitable truth that fossil fuels are finite resources and that the production of oil is going to decline after 2010. Thus, given the growing energy import dependency of most western states and a future oil supply crisis emerging on the horizon, the future potential of interstate resource conflicts has to be taken seriously.

One important dimension of these future conflicts constitutes cases of armed conflict in which the US coercive strategy of securing energy supply is being implemented. The imperatives for US foreign and security policy to secure access and safe transport of imported oil – following the newly formulated US National Energy Policy – is a further manifestation of the anticipated global oil supply crisis and the incapacity of the United States to compensate for the decline of its domestic reserves by virtue of its own innovative and technological strength. Thus for all energy-rich countries the potential for armed conflicts involving US military forces will intensify.

For the EU it seems that any preliminary considerations to copy the US coercive energy security strategies, either by joining US military operations or by developing a distinctive EU strategy, have come to a full stop with the war against Iraq. After the shock of fully grasping the implications of a 'US geopolitics of energy', the EU might now be more willing to turn to alternative innovative strategies for avoiding conflict over resources. One such strategy is to conserve energy by means of taxation and legislation, as well as by dedicating resources to the research and development of alternative energy. Another strategy would be to search for new avenues within the framework of the UN by initiating a dialogue between producer and consumer countries, in order to arrive at a more equitable distribution of energy. A determined pursuit of these alternative approaches might still have a chance to delay or prevent the occurrence of the anticipated supply crisis. However, when the effects of global decline of oil production become visible after 2010, and when an increasing number of countries have to import an increasing amount of fossil fuels from a dwindling reserve base, it will be difficult to avoid conflicts over the distribution of this invaluable and indispensable resource. And the axis along which these conflicts will erupt will be that of consumers and producers of energy, with most producers of energy belonging to the South and with the consumers belonging to the North.

NOTES

1. Philippe Le Billon, 'The Geopolitical Economy of "Resource Wars"', this volume.
2. See Arthur H. Westing, *Global Resources and International Conflict. Environmental Factors in Strategic Policy and Action* (Oxford: Oxford University Press 1986), Appendix, pp.204–10.
3. Ibid., p.1.
4. See Ruth W. Arad *et al.*, *Sharing Global Resources*, 1980s Project/Council of Foreign Relations (New York: McGraw-Hill Book Company 1979). See also Philip Connelly and Robert Perlman, *The Politics of Scarcity. Resource Conflicts in International Relations* (London, New York, Toronto: Oxford University Press 1975).
5. For a historical analysis of the influence of resource vulnerability on US military strategy, see Ian O. Lesser, *Resources and Strategy* (Basingstoke: Macmillan 1989).
6. Le Billon, 'The Geopolitical Economy of "Resource Wars"' (note 1).
7. For confirmation of this observation, see Hanns W. Maull, 'Energy and Resources: The Strategic Dimension', *Survival*, Vol.31, No.6 (November/December 1989), pp.500–15; here, p.505. See also Jock A. Finlayson and David G. Haglund, 'Whatever Happened to the Resource War?' *Survival*, (September/October 1987) pp.403–15. This article covers the case of minerals in South Africa.
8. For a discussion of the analyses of the 1991 Gulf War, see the subsection on US geopolitics.
9. Jon Barnett, *The Meaning of Environmental Security. Ecological Politics and Policy in the New Security Era* (London and New York: Zed Books 2001) p.50.
10. For a good overview of the field's development, see Daniel H. Deudney, 'Environmental Security: A Critique', in Daniel H. Deudney and Richard A. Matthew, *Contested Grounds: Security and Conflict in the New Environmental Politics* (Albany, NY: State University of New York Press 1999) pp.187–219.
11. Thomas F. Homer Dixon, *Environment, Scarcity, and Violence* (Princeton University Press 1999) p.113.
12. Robert Repetto, quoted in ibid., p.33.
13. Deudney, 'Environmental Security: A Critique' (note 10) p.20.
14. In an interview, John Mearsheimer, one of the exponents of structural or neo-realism, explains: 'Realism has a very pessimistic view of international politics. It says there has always been conflict, there is conflict today, and there always will be conflict, and there's not much you can do about it.' But John Mearsheimer does not endorse the Bush administration's emphasis on the use of force in the fight against terrorism. See John Mearsheimer in 'Conversation with John Mearsheimer', <http://globetrotter.berkeley. edu/people2/>. For an interesting elaboration of structural realism, see Werner Link's structural conflict theory explained in Ralf Roloff, 'Die Konfliktheorie des Neorealismus', in Thorsten Bonacker (ed.), *Sozialwissenschaftliche Konflikttheorien. Eine Einführung* (Opladen: Leske und Budrich, 2002), pp.99–120.
15. If there exists a 'conflict theory' of neo-liberal institutionalism, it would be part of a comprehensive theory of the organization of international relations and therefore rather an 'implicit conflict theory'. See Manuela Spindler, 'Die Konflikttheorie des Neoinstitutionalismus', in Bonacker (note 14) pp.143–64.
16. For the purpose of this discussion, post-structuralism and postmodernism are regarded as synonymous. For this see Pauline Marie Rosenau, *Post-Modernism and the Social Sciences. Insights, Inroads, and Intrusions* (Princeton, NJ: Princeton University Press 1992) p.3.
17. Thomas Diez, 'Die Konflikttheorie postmoderner Theorien internationaler Beziehungen', in Bonacker (note 14) p.190.
18. Rosenau (note 16) p.3.
19. Daniel Deudney, 'Bringing Nature Back In: Geopolitical Theory from the Greeks to the Global Era', in Deudney and Matthew (note 10) p.50.
20. Hans-Jürgen Bieling, 'Die Konflikttheorie der Internationalen Politischen Ökonomie', in Bonacker (note 14) p.121.

21. See, in particular, Jyrki Käkönen, *Natural Resources and Conflicts in the Changing International System. Three Studies on Imperialism* (Aldershot: Avebury 1988). One of the shortcomings of this otherwise interesting study is that today the rivalry among capitalist countries would not lead to war like in Lenin's international system. For this line of argument see Bruse Russett, who assumes that 'the risks of international great power confrontation stemming from economic causes will be critical in coming years'. Bruce Russett, 'Security and the Resources Scramble: Will 1984 be like 1914?, *International Affairs* (Winter 1981–82) pp.42–58.
22. Bieling (note 20) p.122.
23. Robert W. Cox, 'Social Forces, States and World Orders: Beyond International Relations Theory', *Millennium*, Vol.10, No.2 (1981) p.131. For a discussion of the concept of conflict in Neo-Gramscian theory, see Bieling (note 20).
24. Classification given by Nancy Lee Peluso and Michael Watts (eds), *Violent Environments* (Ithaca, NY and London: Cornell University Press 2001) p.24.
25. Ibid., p.25.
26. Ibid.
27. Philippe Le Billon, 'The Political Ecology of War: Natural Resources and Armed Conflicts', *Political Geography*, Vol.20, No.5 (2001) pp.563.
28. Barnett, (note 9) p.53.
29. See the insightful chapter by Richard Heinberg, *The Party's Over. Oil, War and the Fate of Industrial Societies* (Gabriola Island: New Society Publishers 2003) pp.175–9.
30. International Energy Agency, *World Energy Outlook 2001*, p.35.
31. Giacomo Luciani, 'Emerging Challenges in the Field of Energy Policy for Europe, the US and Russia' background document, Conference organized by the Aspen Institute Italy, Grand Hotel, Florence, 9–10 July 2002, p.13.
32. See Roger Bentley, 'Global Oil & Gas Depletion: an Overview', *Energy Policy*, Vol.30 (2002) p.198, emphasis added.
33. For a good explanation of Hubbert's peak model, see Kenneth Deffeyes, *Hubbert's Peak: The Impending World Oil Shortage* (Princeton, NJ: Princeton University Press 2001) ch.7.
34. Bentley (note 32) p.198. For an extensive analysis of these arguments, see Global Challenges Network, *Das Ende des Erdölzeitalters und die Weichenstellung für die Zukunft* (Deutscher Taschenbuch Verlag 2002).
35. See Luciani (note 31) p.3.
36. See press release of the *Association for the Study of Peak Oil (ASPO)*, Uppsala 2002. BP has adopted ASPO's depletion model in the official Norwegian Petroleum Diary (No.3, 2002) to demonstrate its serious commitment to solar energy.
37. Campbell, communication among ASPO members.
38. See Colin Campbell in *Geotimes*, November 2002.
39. Bentley (note 32) p.200.
40. See Harry J. Longwell, 'The Future of the Oil and Gas Industry: Past Approaches, New Challenges', *World Energy*, Vol.5, No.3 (2002) pp.100–104; Figure 3, p.101.
41. Odell, quoted in Bentley (note 32) p.197.
42. For details, see Colin Campbell and John H. Laherrèrre, 'The End of Cheap Oil', *Scientific American* (March 1998) pp.80–86 and Colin Campbell, in BBC, 'The Money Programme', screened 8 January 2000.
43. Bentley (note 32) p.197, emphasis added.
44. International Energy Agency, *World Energy Outlook 1998*, p.101.
45. David LaGiesse, *US News & World Report*, 17 Sept. 2001.
46. International Energy Agency, *World Energy Outlook 2002*, p.29.
47. Edward Morse and Amy Myers Jaffe, 'Strategic Energy Policy, Challenges for the 21st Century', report of an Independent Task Force, Sponsored by the James A. Baker III Institute for Public Policy of Rice University and the Council on Foreign Relations, Washington, April 2001, p.9.
48. Ibid., p.5.
49. Franco Bernabé, paper given at the Oil and Money Conference, London, 17 Nov. 1998, p. 3.
50. Quoted in Christopher Flavin and Seth Dunn, 'A New Energy Paradigm for the 21st

Century', *Journal of International Affairs*, Vol.53, No.1 (Fall 1999) pp.168.
51. See *The Economist*, 6–12 Nov. 1999.
52. Longwell (note 40) p.101.
53. Bentley, personal communication.
54. See, for this, Heinberg (note 34) and Global Challenges Network (note 35).
55. Heinberg (note 29) p.148.
56. *ASPO Newsletter*, No.9, September 2001.
57. World Bank, *World Development Report 1999/2000, Entering the 21st Century*, p.14.
58. Data from *BP Statistical Review of World Energy*, June 2002, p.4.
59. Data from the United Nations Development Programme, *Human Development Report 2002*. The Human Development Index is a 'composite index measuring average achievement in three basic dimensions of human development – a long and healthy life, knowledge and a decent standard of living'. Ibid., p.265. The HDI, provided by the UNDP, ranges from 1 through the number of countries providing data, usually over 170.
60. Under Purchasing Power Parity (PPP) in dollars.
61. United Nations Development Programme, *Human Development Report 2002*, p.191.
62. Ibid., p.271.
63. Although also Gulf states, Iran and Iraq are usually not lumped together with the Gulf Cooperation Council (GCC) monarchies since they do not follow the classical model of the rentier state. For Iraq there is also no data available.
64. Jeffrey D. Sachs and Andrew M. Warner, *Natural Resource Abundance and Economic Growth*, Working Paper 5398, National Bureau of Economic Research, Dec. 1995, p.2. See also Richard Auty, 'Natural Resources and Civil Strife', this volume.
65. See Ibid.
66. For the positive relationship between high oil prices and growth, see Dipak Dasgupta, Jennifer Keller and Srinivasan T.G. Srinivasan, 'Reform and Elusive Growth in the Middle East – What has Happened in the 1990s?', Discussion paper of the World Bank, July 2002.
67. <http://g77.org/>.
68. 'What is the Group of 77?', <http://g77.org/main/main.htm>. The group was established at the conclusion of the first meeting of the United Nations Conference on Trade and Development (UNCTAD). It is wider in scope than the Non-Aligned Movement.
69. G-77 webpage (note 67).
70. Arad (note 4) p.99.
71. For the time being, Iraq is treated as a non-OPEC country.
72. For this list of initiatives, see Le Billon, 'The Geopolitical Economy of "Resource Wars" (note 1).
73. See the chapters dealing with the 1953 coup, in Peter J. Schraeder (ed.), *Intervention into the 1990s. US Foreign Policy in the Third World* (Boulder and London: Lynne Rienner Publisher 1992). For a detailed analysis see Stephen Pelletière, *Iraq and the International Oil System: Why America Went to War in the Gulf* (Westport and London: Praeger 2001) ch.3. See also Stephen Krasner, *Defending the National Interest. Raw Materials Investments and U.S. Foreign Policy* (Princeton, NJ: Princeton University Press 1978) pp.120–23.
74. See Daniel Yergin, *Der Preis. Die Jagd nach Öl, Geld und Macht* (Frankfurt am Main: Fischer Verlag 1993) pp.599–618.
75. Organization of Arab Petroleum Exporting Countries.
76. Yergin (note 74) p.746.
77. Arad (note 4) p.56. See also the Kissinger statement, quoted in Joseph Nevins, 'Resource Conflicts in a New World Order' (this volume).
78. Robert Keohane, *After Hegemony: Cooperation and Discord in the World Political Economy* (Princeton, NJ: Princeton University Press, 1984) p.204.
79. US prices increased by only 50 per cent, and only briefly. See *Wall Street Journal Europe*, 29 July 2000, p.A5.
80. The IEA obviously managed to reach a bargain with OPEC over the last two years, that in a crisis the IEA would release its stocks only as a last resort, while OPEC committed itself not to cut production. See ibid.

81. For an interesting recapitulation of the various steps in the US strategy to control the Persian Gulf, such as the set up of the Rapid Deployment Force and the Central Command, see Robert Dreyfuss, 'The Thirty-Year Itch', <http://motherjones/com/news/feature/2003/>.

82. Pelletière (note 73) p.x. But Pelletière, from the US Army War College, argues in this book that it is not the US government that is to blame for the 1991 Gulf War, which he himself finds 'inexcusable'. He instead blames the US media, the Israelis and British, as well as part of the Arab community for pushing Bush into the war. Moreover, these pro-war forces acted without hindrance because the international oil system had broken down in the aftermath of the events in the 1970s.

83. Edward Morse, 'A New Political Economy of Oil?', *Journal of International Affairs*, Vol.53, No.1 (Fall 1999), p.16.

84. See Michael Klare, *Resource Wars. The New Landscape of Global Conflict* (New York: Henry Holt and Company 2002).

85. Ibid., p.10.

86. Donald Losman, 'Economic Security. A National Security Folly?, *Policy Analysis*, No.409 (1 Aug. 2001).

87. Excerpts from the 'National Security Strategy', White House, Dec. 1999, quoted in ibid, p.2.

88. William Pfaff, 'In Colombia, Remember: Foreigners Cannot Win a Civil War', *International Herald Tribune*, 15 May 2000.

89. Michael Klare, 'The Bush/Cheney Energy Strategy: Implications for U.S. Foreign and Military Policy', paper presented at the Second Annual Meeting of the Association for the Study of Peak Oil, Paris, France 26–27 May 2003, p.10. See <http://www.peakoil.net>, p.11

90. See interview with Condoleezza Rice, 9 Aug. 2000, available through <http://www.policy.com/issues.htm>.

91. National Energy Policy, 'Report of the National Energy Policy Development Group', Washington, May 2001, ch.8, p.4.

92. Klare, 'The Bush/Cheney Energy Strategy' (note 89) p.4. The document itself encompasses eight chapters, of which only the last chapter deals with the imperative for 'Strengthening Global Alliances.' The other seven chapters deal with the necessity to increase America's use of renewable and alternative energy and to enhance 'energy conservation and efficiency.' But as Klare points out, aside from the proposal to drill in the Arctic National Wildlife Refuge (ANWR), 'there is *nothing* in the NEP that would contribute to a significant decline in U.S. dependence on imported petroleum' (p.3).

93. Ibid., p.4.

94. National Energy Policy (note 91) ch.8, p.5.

95. See *ASPO Newsletter* No.24, Dec. 2002.

96. Klare, 'The Bush/Cheney Energy Strategy' (note 89) p.5.

97. Ibid.

98. For an elaborated version of this section, see Susanne Peters, 'Building up the Potential for Future Resource Conflicts: the Shortcomings of Western Response Strategies to New Energy Vulnerabilities', RSCAS Working Paper, Sept. 2003, European University Institute, Florence.

99. European Commission, 'Towards a European Strategy for the Security of Energy Supply', Green Paper, 2000, p.46.

100. Ibid., p.47.

101. Ibid, p.86.

102. The explanation for the Soviet reluctance to commit to this treaty is due to the transit protocols.

103. Gareth Winrow, 'A Threat from the South? NATO and the Mediterranean', *Mediterranean Politics*, Vol.1, No.1 (Summer 1996), p.52.

104. J.N. von Glahn, Chairman, SHE Group Holdings, Solar Hydrogen Energy Group, communication among APSO members.

105. For an insightful case study to show the relevance of identifying 'resource scarcity' as a cause for intrastate conflict, see Francisco Magno, 'Environmental Security in the South China Sea', *Security Dialogue*, Vol.28, No.1 (1997) pp.97–112.

The Geopolitics of Conflict and Diamonds in Sierra Leone

MARILYN SILBERFEIN

Introduction

The long-term conflict that has consumed Sierra Leone for a decade is representative of a type of endemic warfare that has become more common in the post-Cold War world and is closely linked to the presence of readily captured resources. In effect, Sierra Leone became a site for a protracted conflict because it possessed sources of wealth that could be diverted into the hands of an organized rebellion.[1] Furthermore, the battle for access to the country's wealth could be sustained over time, given the ease with which resources could be exchanged for supplies of small arms.

Resource-based conflicts have expanded with the process of globalization. International trade has reached ever more widely into isolated pockets to find the raw materials needed to maintain high levels of industrial production as well as other sources of wealth.[2] As the demand for a range of resources continues to climb, transnational companies, eager to expand their inventories, do not necessarily pay close attention to the circumstances under which resources are acquired. Transnational exchanges are also less likely to be based on states as trading partners are more likely to be linked to alternative political entities that overlap with or replace states. These trading relationships illustrate the 'boundary-transgressing processes' that are an important part of the current geopolitical reality.[3]

The war in Sierra Leone also provides an example of the emergence of a non-state entity with a variable territorial structure – in this case, a war-lord insurgency. All that is required for such an insurgency to be sustained is control over three elements: a resource base, one or more routes over which resources can be moved out of the source area, and exchange points where resources can be traded for weapons and other needed goods or services.[4] Charles Taylor, the leader of the war-lord insurgency in Liberia, ran his own non-state entity known as greater Liberia. He received no official international recognition but he maintained many of the trappings of a state as he dominated access to Liberia's tropical hardwoods, gold and diamonds, controlled the port city of Buchanan, and established close ties to several trading partners.[5]

A typical insurgency bears a close resemblance to criminal activity. Such conflicts have, in fact, been referred to as 'crime disguised as war' and the perpetrators have been termed 'entrepreneurs or businessmen of war'.[6] It is also true that an insurgency may be battling a state that is also integrated into complex criminal networks and that the state itself may be privatized or criminalized.[7] It is not unusual for both war-lords and state functionaries to be dealing not just with the exploitation of natural resources but also with drugs, money laundering, and other illegal activity. Conflicts between war-lords and criminalized states tend to be particularly devastating for civilians who are caught between warring parties and considered dispensable except as captive workers or soldiers. The brutality and single-mindedness of these confrontations between fighters and civilians also creates a distinctive landscape. Large rural areas may be emptied of population, their roads rendered impassable, and the structures, that once provided human habitation, completely destroyed. Towns and cities, on the other hand, may swell with internally displaced persons (IDPs), often living in overcrowded camps on the outskirts of built up areas.

Another part of this landscape is the ubiquitous roadblock which appears along the few usable roads that lead to urban centres or mining areas. The roadblocks are typically manned by soldiers or rebels, and always present the traveller with the threat of a shakedown or worse. So widespread is this practice that children caught up in an insurgency frequently make a game of tying a rope across a road and demanding money from anyone who passes for filling (and refilling) pot-holes. These landscapes of conflict have not received much attention, but there have been some descriptions of 'warscapes' which show up on maps as areas full of landmines with few safe entry and exit points, or even areas that are 'forgotten to death' because their isolation has made it difficult to determine what horrors have gone on there.[8]

Conflicts that are resource-based can be intractable. Some of the participants in the war may actually benefit from the unsettled conditions that can facilitate access to resources, smuggling and certain kinds of trade. The beneficiaries are understandably reluctant to terminate the conflict, thus militating against a peace settlement. The end result may be a stand-off, a condition that is neither peace nor war but which continues to leave civilians vulnerable, services moribund, and the larger economy stagnant to declining. This phenomena has been termed 'negative peace', a condition in which the basic structural imbalances that caused the conflict in the first place remain in place.[9]

Although the conflict in Sierra Leone has closely followed the scenario described above, there are three factors in particular that are critical to an understanding of the confrontation that took place there. Each of these will be considered in turn:

1. The war was always closely connected to the competition for resources, particularly diamonds, and this association was strengthened through time,
2. the conflict can be linked to the collapse of the state, the emergence of pervasive criminality among state and non-state actors along with the proliferation of small arms, and,
3. the Sierra Leone war has never been restricted to a single state; rather, it has always been part of a regional process whereby boundaries have not impeded the flows of resources and weapons or the movement of people.

The Diamonds of Sierra Leone

Although the economy of Sierra Leone has been diversified during both the colonial and post-colonial period, diamonds have played a special role since their initial commercial exploitation in the 1930s. Diamonds are an unusual resource in that they are extremely valuable per unit of weight and thus small quantities can bring substantial returns; diamonds are, in other words, very lootable. The value associated with these gems reflects an almost century-long effort by the De Beers company, originally of South Africa, to create an artificial demand by successfully associating diamonds with love and marriage, while at the same time controlling the supply through a world-wide cartel.

Diamonds appear in Africa in two forms: in kimberlite dikes which are usually mined by centralized organizations using heavy machinery and in alluvial deposits which are much more accessible. Most West and Central African diamonds are alluvial, and thus, readily available to casual miners who dig pits in river beds and pan for diamonds much as one would pan for gold. Typically, this type of diamond extraction is a precarious, tedious, poorly-paid and unhealthy enterprise and one without a framework of regulations to protect miners, but it is one of the few non-agricultural employment options available to poorly-educated young men in isolated parts of Africa.[10] The miners tend to be manipulated by local landowners or by entrepreneurs who organize them into small groups – providing credit, food and basic equipment in exchange for stones. There are environmental as well as social and economic ramifications of this system: the convergence of diamond diggers, many producing holes up to 30ft deep, leads to soil loss, severe gullying and sometimes to the undermining of roads and other structures.[11]

Diamonds were first found in quantity in Sierra Leone in the eastern provinces of Kono and Kenema (see Figure 1). The initial exploitation was based on a tributary system whereby miners were given the right to prospect in specified areas by paramount chiefs; they then turned their trove over to the chief and were provided with a share of its total value.[12] At the same time the colonial government was looking for potential concessionaires to develop the main diamond areas, settling on the Sierra Leone Selection Trust (SLST), a De Beers subsidiary, in 1934. The SLST was given a 99-year lease and, shortly thereafter, the right to hire its own security forces to protect against intruders. When the SLST found itself in competition for access to diamonds with the local chiefs and miners, the region took on the complexion of a gold-rush frontier with substantial petty crime and smuggling.

The mining areas, in effect, provided a safety-valve for young men seeking a livelihood, and De Beers' efforts to keep out illicit miners was ultimately a losing one. In the 1950s, illegal diamond mining and smuggling expanded rapidly with most diamonds being sold for hard currency in

FIGURE 1

MAIN RESOURCE AREAS IN SIERRA LEONE

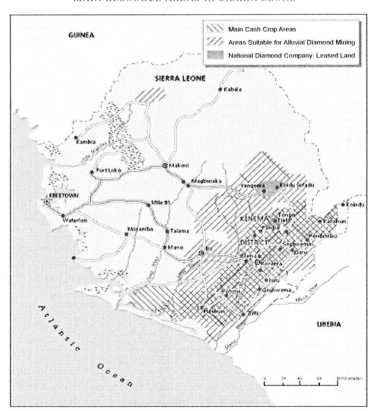

Liberia. The Lebanese community played a central role in this process, often with members of the same family covering both ends of a smuggling ring in Sierra Leone and Monrovia.[13] In order to bring this situation under control, the colonial government reduced the size of the SLST concession, provided a legal basis for local mining to function, and expelled 40,000 foreign miners who had flocked to the area.[14] Many Lebanese were able to obtain licenses, however, as they came to play a growing role in both the legal and illegal diamond trade. Gradually De Beers became disillusioned with this process and moved its regional headquarters to Monrovia.

Diamond riches came to play a more critical role in the political economy of Sierra Leone as the country moved towards independence in 1960 and then, as part of the patronage politics of the 1970s and 1980s. Taxes and fees associated with mining had contributed substantially to the national treasury during the colonial period, but even before the SLST completely pulled out in 1984, decreasing numbers of diamonds were being traded through official channels. Instead, profits were siphoned off by the leadership of the ruling party and its clients. Contacts with the international market continued to be made by Lebanese traders resident in Sierra Leone and at one point, the diamonds were actually contributing to each of the factions in the Lebanese Civil War.[15] By the late 1980s, smuggling had become so rampant that hardly any stones were still part of the legal exchange structure.[16]

The Process of State Collapse

The start of the war in Sierra Leone can be dated from March 1991, when a group of insurgents known as the Revolutionary United Front (RUF) crossed over from Liberia, but conditions favourable to the success of the RUF had been developing for decades. The role of diamonds in contributing to the enrichment of politicians and their followers has already been mentioned but diamonds provided just one of the sources of illicit wealth that sustained the political élite. Within a decade of independence, state operatives had come to profit from the taxes and fees associated with cash crops, from bribes and paybacks contributed by foreign companies seeking access to fisheries, rutile (titanium oxide) and bauxite, and the expropriation of property. Potential challengers to this systematic looting by the state were intimidated by the instrumental use of violence.

In the late 1980s, as the state became completely superfluous as well as predatory, sustaining its patrimonial structure became difficult. When the International Monetary Fund (IMF) called for fiscal restraint in exchange for continued loans, social services were all but eliminated and even the rice subsidies that had kept the Sierra Leone Army (SLA) in line were sacrificed.

A volatile combination of conditions were emerging in Sierra Leone: 1) increasing rural-urban migration that contributed to a growing cohort of young men lacking education, skills or job prospects, 2) a return to the subsistence sector by farmers discouraged by poor cash crop prices and by isolation from markets caused by deteriorating roads and petroleum shortages and, 3) as a result of 1 and 2 above, the need for expensive food imports that drained the state's limited supplies of hard currency. All that was absent from this brew was the potential for severe ethnic or religious conflicts. Politicians had manipulated ethnicity for their own purposes, particularly rivalries between the northern Limba and Temne people who had dominated the APC government in the 70s and 80s and the Mende of the south and east, but these antagonisms had not yet become the source of major confrontations.

When the RUF forces entered Sierra Leone, led by a former SLA corporal named Foday Sankoh, there was much speculation as to what factors had stimulated the invasion. It was widely believed that Charles Taylor wanted to both punish Sierra Leone for having worked against his interests with the regional peacekeeping group, ECOMOG, and to distract the SLA from fighting against him in Liberia.[17] A secondary factor, however, was the genuine disgruntlement on the part of dissident youths with a corrupt government, and for some, the breakdown of the patronage networks that had previously supplied them with some support. Certainly, what might be termed a rebellious youth culture had been forming for years on the edge of Freetown and other cities. Many unemployed and undereducated members of these groups worked part-time as thugs, enforcing government edicts.[18] Gradually, the youth culture had come to be influenced by students who railed against the APC regime and then by the efforts of Libya's President Ghaddafi to provide training for selected malcontents as a means of spreading his messages and expanding his network of allies.

When the RUF took shape as a loosely organized contingent of dissidents, it was initially based on a vague desire to replace the government in Freetown with a more egalitarian alternative, but it evolved into a less ideological and more wealth-seeking movement. From the beginning, Charles Taylor provided support for Sankoh and the RUF that included facilities for training in Liberia, instruction in guerrilla warfare, weapons, and fighters from Liberia and Burkina Faso (Burkinabe). It was undoubtedly part of the equation that the RUF would compensate Taylor with the proceeds from diamond sales when it was in control of the mines.

By the time of the RUF invasion, Sierra Leone had come to resemble its pre-colonial and early colonial counterpart in terms of spatial structure.

Before independence, African rulers had typically tried to control their core areas, accepting that authority would decline with distance and that it was more critical to dominate people and resources than territory.[19] Then, when Freetown emerged as a colony in the late 1700s, it included only the basic urban and peri-urban area; it was not thought necessary to politically dominate the hinterland. The independent state of Sierra Leone reflects this legacy in that it came to focus on a series of connected islands, each of which contributed income to the centre or served as a conduit for exports. Those areas that were not considered 'economically viable' functioned as labour reserves, much as during the colonial period. The RUF insurgency eventually mimicked this pattern.

The Regional Context

From its inception, the war in Sierra Leone reflected the country's position within a larger region. It is possible to identify a series of nested relationships in West Africa that are critical to the endemic warfare that has come to prevail in the area. At one end of the scale is the Mano River Union (MRU) which includes Liberia and Guinea as well as Sierra Leone. The borders between the MRU countries have always been porous; ethnic groups that spanned the border moved freely between countries and a legal and illegal trade has always taken place, especially in response to the presence of the US dollar in Liberia.

At the level of West Africa as a whole, there have been two competing contingents. First there are the Francophone states which include, among others, Burkina Faso, the Ivory Coast and Togo, countries that have often collaborated to further their mutual interests and which allied themselves both with France, as expected, and with Anglophone Liberia. Then there is Nigeria, the regional powerhouse that has ties with its own coterie of primarily Anglophone countries, including Sierra Leone. Ostensibly, all of these states are unified in an organization known as ECOWAS which promotes West African co-operation, but the reality is much more complex. A diplomat even referred to the political jockeying engaged in by these countries as West Africa's version of the 'Great Game'.[20]

Initially within Sierra Leone, and then within a wider context, the actual invasion by the RUF along the Liberian border had a definite geopolitical logic. Liberia had a long-standing claim to part of the boundary zone and so possessed a rationale for supporting the RUF as a means of possibly adjudicating this issue. Border areas in general are often gathering places for the socially and economically marginalized, where government authority is minimal and illegal activities are carried out with impunity. Along the Sierra Leone-Liberian border, for example, diamond diggers had formed villages where anti-government sentiment made the RUF a preferred alternative.[21]

One of the actual invasion sites, Kailahun province, had become increasingly isolated due to the closure of the railroad by the APC government. The other site, the south-eastern district of Pujehun, had been the scene of a chiefdom dispute that had resulted in strong local antipathy to the government. As a staging ground for the RUF insurgency, the east had one other advantage: it was the most resource-rich part of the country, the best area for growing valuable cash crops such as cocoa and coffee and the site of concentrations of alluvial and kimberlite diamonds (see Figure 1).

The Spread of the Conflict

The invasion at Kailahun and Pujehun was to be part of a pincer movement, with the two RUF brigades coming together further in the interior. The goal was to control a substantial, resource-rich territory within which an urban centre could serve as administrative headquarters – much as Gbargna in Nimba County had became the 'capital' of Taylor's Greater Liberia. Initially, the RUF incursion went according to plan. Having entered the country with just a few thousand fighters, the RUF expanded with impunity since the local population was unarmed and sometimes sympathetic. The invaders followed a strategy of occupying villages by either co-opting or eliminating the local chiefs, elders and educated élite and commandeering their food or other requirements. Fighting forces were expanded through the recruitment of individuals who fit the original RUF profile: school drop-outs, diamond diggers and general itinerants for whom the RUF promised the potential of easier access to the country's riches.[22]

The RUF had no revolutionary programme for relating to the peasantry, however. The rebels terrified most of the rural population and volunteer recruits to the RUF had to be supplemented by kidnapped children and young adults.[23] New members were inducted into the RUF ranks through a combination of initiation rites (an established practice in Sierra Leone's secret societies), material rewards (usually plundered from other villages), training (the bush camps were substitutes for non-functioning schools) and mandatory participation in raids. According to the RUF, once the new fighters were seen as the enemy by the local population, they were unlikely to be welcomed back in their home villages.

In order to counter this incursion, the government tried to mobilize its limited assets including foreign aid (a declining factor in the 1990s), taxes on cash crops (declining as well because of the war), remittances from citizens living abroad, taxes on rutile and bauxite, and fees and taxes associated with diamond digging and sales.[24] Even when the APC government was replaced in a military coup conditions remained much the same. The SLA units, never trained to repel an invasion, were at first only marginally effective. They were invariably poorly-supplied, erratically paid, and frequently immobilized because of impassable roads or petrol shortages. Under these circumstances, soldiers were known to participate in illicit activities of their own, including raiding villages for tribute and even co-operating with the RUF in dividing up the spoils of war.[25] They became infamously identified as Sobels, soldiers by day when they fought the RUF and rebels by night when they participated in looting.[26] They were gradually strengthened by new recruits, army regulars provided by the Guinean government and ULIMO fighters, anti-Taylor dissidents anxious to gain a foothold near the Liberia border.

During the initial year-and-a-half period of their insurgency, the RUF were able to survive and persevere because their resource base was diversified. Food and cash crops were cultivated, harvested and sold, often by forced labour, while diamonds were collected from dispersed alluvial sites as the RUF made their way closer to the major diamondiferous areas in Kono District and Tongo Fields in Kenema District. One Freetown correspondent identified the RUF approach as follows: 'Escapees from the rebel stronghold report that the intention of the invading force is to cut Sierra Leone, like Liberia, into two, taking the economically viable part which produces the nation's cash crops and minerals – they don't want any other part of the country'[27] By June 1991, the RUF was only 18 miles from Koidu, the district centre of Kono, but the threat of the loss of the diamond mining area caused resistance to stiffen and slowed the RUF advance.

By this point, the spatial structure of the expanding RUF political entity had taken on a definite form: The RUF territory could be divided into three parts which fluctuated over time: a) areas firmly under RUF control, mainly in Kailahun, Pujehun, and some of Kenema Districts, b) expansion/ contraction areas where RUF raids and the destruction of villages were sometimes followed by army counter-attacks and government reoccupation and, 3) more distant areas where the RUF propaganda machine spread rumours of an imminent attack (see Figure 2 – Strategy 1).[28] In effect, the RUF hoped to minimize confrontations by intimidating the rural population into rapidly deserting their villages even before an attack had taken place.

The rural population that stayed in place faced the risk of kidnapping, murder, theft or property destruction by both RUF fighters and government soldiers in turn. Some tried to disperse as widely as possible so as to avoid being a target, even going so far as moving out of villages during the day and returning at night. Such strategies required the ability to live off wild plants and limited hunting since cultivation was severely limited. Even

FIGURE 2

RURAL INSURGENCY: TWO STRATEGIES

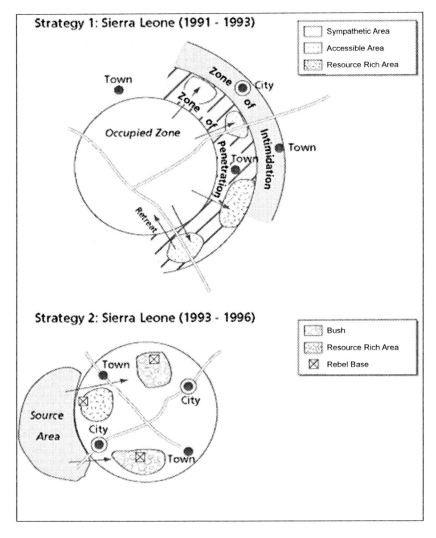

beyond the conflict zone, villagers refrained from burning vegetation so that smoke would not advertise the presence of a rural settlement.[29]

By early 1992, the SLA was able to sustain its counter-offensive and the RUF, were actually being pushed back. This was when the government began to engage in what might be termed the rhetoric of normalcy. It would declare areas to be rebel-free and encourage all IDPs to return home, particularly chiefs who were to set an example.[30] The Rehabilitation and Relief Committee was formed to provide returnees with seeds and tools and the repatriation of refugees was discussed. The residue of the conflict was referred to as a mopping up operation designed to eliminate the last vestiges of the rebellion.

Yet, in spite of the rhetoric to the contrary, the conflict was far from over. The government did not take into account the larger regional context, within which the struggle with the RUF was embedded. Since the RUF retained its Liberia connection, there would always be a source of new supplies, weapons and fighters, and setbacks would only be temporary. For example, when the government counter-insurgency made it too costly for the RUF to hold onto extensive territory, the rebels regrouped and transformed their spatial strategy. Rather than trying to defend towns and large villages against army attacks, the RUF dispersed to at least six major bases with about 5000 to 6000 fighters each, scattered throughout the national space.[31] The bases were typically hidden in areas of forest or dense bush, connected by bush paths, ideally suited for the new guerrilla 'war without frontlines'[32] (see Figure 2 – Strategy 2). Radio equipment was widely scattered as well, allowing for communication between bases as well as the broadcasting of frequent propaganda messages. The RUF also began to carry out the atrocities for which they were to become notorious, cutting off limbs and other body parts as a mechanism for both sowing terror and undermining the official economy.

No part of the country was immune from the expanding conflict as food production declined precipitously. IDPs flooded hastily built camps around major towns and refugees fled the country. In October 1992, the RUF finally infiltrated the Kono diamond district, in part because government soldiers were digging for diamonds themselves rather than maintaining a strong defence. The two remaining bulwarks of the Sierra Leone economy were captured later: the major rutile and bauxite producing areas. The RUF were not able to mine and process rutile or bauxite themselves, but they denied the government the opportunity to earn hard currency from mineral sales.

During the next three years, the relative circumstances of the protagonists fluctuated, although the RUF pushed ever closer to Freetown. This was also the period when the security situation became complicated by two additional elements. Firstly, there was the growing menace of armed bands, often former soldiers who had deserted and who survived by plundering the countryside. Secondly, there was an expansion of local militias, organized from secret societies and groups of traditional hunters that were originally meant to provide intelligence to the SLA on RUF infiltration. They were often referred to by the Mende term, Kamajors, although similar contingents were organized among other ethnic groups and eventually the term Civil Defense Forces (CDF) became standard. The Kamajors were more successful than the SLA at protecting villages against attacks and even reoccupying villages that had been abandoned. In time, the militias were as likely to confront the SLA as the RUF since the former frequently competed with the militias for influence, power and resources in the ongoing conflict.[33]

When morale in the capital had reached a particularly low point in June 1995, the government made a contract with Executive Outcomes (EO), a private South African security company, that was certainly more effective than the SLA in countering the RUF offensive. EO possessed both the technology and experience to locate and obliterate the RUF camps, they were very loyal as long as they were paid, and, critically, they allowed the government to retake the diamond areas and obtain a reliable source of income.[34]

The Election and Its Aftermath

In 1996, after considerable preparation and under difficult circumstances, a reasonably fair election was organized to replace the military government and Ahmed Tejan Kabbah of the Sierra Leone People's Party (SLPP) became president. This success initiated another period of optimism: a treaty was signed with the RUF, refugees began to return home, Executive Outcomes left the country, and numerous NGOs committed themselves to a crash development programme to resurrect the economy. There were, however, definite signs of trouble beneath the surface. Most disturbing were the indicators of ongoing RUF and even SLA control of selected areas of the country, combined with RUF and SLA clashes with local militias. There was even evidence that the new government was recreating the patrimonial-style system that had undermined Sierra Leone's economy in the first place.[35]

This experiment with democracy was cut short in May 1997 when the military, feeling increasingly marginalized by downsizing and by competition from the CDF, staged a coup and then invited its former enemies, the RUF, to join the new government. The RUF at this point was being supported by a vigorous trade in diamonds for arms. Liberia was playing a critical role in receiving the contraband diamonds but there were numerous intermediate points, such as Gambia and Burkina Faso, before the stones reached the markets in Antwerp. Some of the same countries were also intermediate points in the networks of arms dealers that originated primarily in the Ukraine, Russia, Slovakia and Bulgaria. No dent could be make in this complex structure until several NGOs, such as Partnership Africa-Canada and Global Witness, put pressure on the diamond industry and later the UN Security Council to change the insidious practice of allowing 'conflict diamonds', mined by rebel groups, to enter into the mainstream diamond market and be traded for weapons.[36]

The 1997 combination of the RUF and the Sierra Leone Army, known as the Junta, followed the coup with a rapid occupation of the cities while the Kamajor militias dispersed through the countryside to avoid detection. Civilians left Sierra Leone if they could or remained on the move as circumstances dictated. The economy continued to decline during the period of less than one year when the Junta was in control. This was in part the result of a boycott of the Junta by The West African Economic Community (ECOWAS) and its military arm, ECOMOG. ECOMOG also launched occasional military assaults from bases at the airport and just outside Freetown, where they had been placed earlier to protect the Kabbah regime. The Junta was also plagued by various acts of civil disobedience and competition for access to the diamond-producing areas, even between the co-conspirators, the RUF and the SLA.[37]

After considerable pressure from the international community, a treaty was finally signed by the RUF in October 1997. The treaty promised a return to the elected government, but a lack of progress in this direction led instead, in February 1998, to a renewed military assault by the Civil Defense Forces (CDF) and ECOMOG. This combination of forces pushed the Junta eastward from Freetown, west from the Liberian border, and out of virtually all the key towns and cities. By March, the fighting had become intense in Kailahun and the Kono diamond mining areas. The increasingly global character of this confrontation was exemplified by an illegal delivery that was made to the Junta: a load of weapons was conveyed in a Ukrainian-owned helicopter by an Indian national who was later arrested in Canada with the passport of a dead Slovak.

After the Kabbah government was restored the rhetoric focused on the portions of the national space (70 per cent, 80 per cent and then 90 per cent) that were under government control. These optimistic claims again hid an ominous reality: the RUF was retreating to the remote rural locations where it could gear up to resume its pattern of attacks and atrocities as soon as it was rearmed through its links with Liberia. In December 1998, not long after the countryside had been proclaimed safe, the RUF fighters retraced the route of their retreat – cutting a particularly destructive swath across the northern half of Sierra Leone and reaching Freetown by early January 1999 (see Figure 3). They were finally halted by ECOMOG and driven back from the city but it was clear that the Armed Forces Revolutionary Council (AFRC), which had been reconstituted by the Kabbah regime, had not stood up to the RUF threat and that ECOMOG had neither the capacity nor the motivation to vanquish the RUF on its own.[38]

FIGURE 3

THE WAR FOR SIERRA LEONE: SEPTEMBER 1988–MARCH 2001

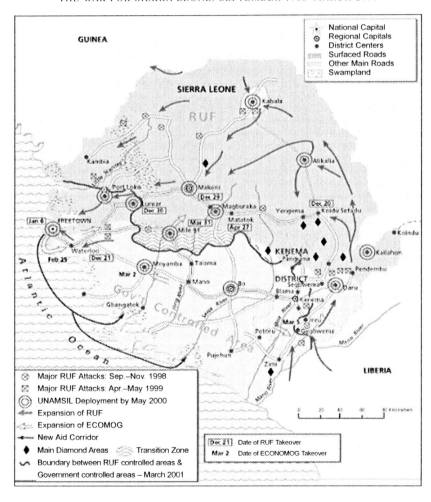

On 24 May 1999, the RUF agreed to a cease-fire and the Freetown government, despairing of receiving any outside assistance, signed the Lome Accord in July 1999 in which they accepted a mediated peace, demobilization and disarmament, amnesty for combatants, the deployment of peacekeepers and a design for a government of national unity that included Foday Sankoh in control of resources. The process of implementing the new treaty was arduous – the RUF was slow in complying, while many in the international community felt that the RUF had no place in a legitimate government. It was clear that the RUF lacked the motivation to engage in any real power-sharing.[39]

Sierra Leone at this stage was a fragmented country – more than half of which was a no-go zone dominated by the RUF and inaccessible to most NGOs and all government agencies[40] (see Figure 3). With no obvious solution to this problem given the lack of commitment on the part of the West, it was decided that a contingent of UN peacekeepers (UNAMSIL) would be deployed in government-controlled areas. Only after time-consuming negotiation was it possible for UNAMSIL to fan out from the south and east of the country into northern towns. A British Broadcasting Corporation (BBC) reporter visiting the RUF-occupied town of Makeni with the UN referred to the RUF zone as a 'state within a state demarcated by a roadblock, manned by armed soldiers and set apart with a simple string across the road'.[41]

The majority of peacekeepers were Nigerians and there is evidence that some of them arranged with the RUF to share diamond caches, a pattern that had surfaced when the Nigerian-dominated ECOMOG troops participated in the Liberian Civil War. Nigerian peacekeepers were finally accused of profiteering by the head of UNAMSIL, General Jetly, leading to a confrontation, the withdrawal of 3000 Indian soldiers from UNAMSIL, and a reduction in the effectiveness of the peacekeeping effort.[42]

Gradually, between February and April, the UN forces expanded into RUF-controlled territory, established their presence in Daru and finally in Kailahun (Figure 3). Throughout this process the RUF were never co-operative; they stole weapons and equipment from the peacekeepers, set up barricades and interrupted the delivery of food aid.[43] Then, in May 2000, at the time that the last of the ECOMOG forces were turning their posts over to the UN and the peacekeepers were about to establish an outpost in the Kono area, the RUF detained 500 newly arrived Zambian peacekeepers, totally derailing the peace process.

Fortunately, just as one more UN effort looked as if it were about to falter, a combination of UN perseverance and a British troop commitment saved the mission and eventually freed the captured peacekeepers. The RUF leader, Foday Sankoh, fled his home and was later captured, leaving behind evidence of substantial illegal diamond dealing. This information as well as anger at the RUF's abrogation of its treaty obligations finally led to the public denunciation of Taylor's ongoing role supporting the RUF and the EU suspension of $50m in economic aid to Liberia. Outraged, Taylor called for a commission of inquiry since 'he had only limited control over his porous border with Sierra Leone'.[44] In July, the Security Council voted to ban rough diamond purchases from Sierra Leone until the country had a certification programme and also named Liberia as the conduit through which diamonds were reaching the market.[45] In August Sierra Leone proposed a scheme to certify its own diamonds and by mid-September the first diamonds were being exported under this plan.[46]

Sierra Leone remained in limbo while negotiations with the RUF were renewed once again. Several factors conspired to make the RUF more compliant this time. First of all, the success of the boycott on non-certifiable diamonds from Sierra Leone eliminated a source of income for the RUF at the same time that Liberia, threatened with a boycott of its own exports, was not likely to assist its ally. Secondly, a contingent of British troops that had arrived to defend Freetown provided a strong deterrent to any RUF expansionary plans. Thirdly, the RUF suffered a reversal of fortune in Guinea. The RUF first joined with Liberians and Guinean dissidents to attack Guinea in early 2000, undoubtedly attracted by the prospects of looting plus proximity to additional diamond fields. However, the Guinean leadership reacted strongly to this threat, refusing to allow the situation to fester in the manner of the Sierra Leone government's reaction to the RUF's initial attack.[47] When Liberia had to pull back and Guinea, with Western aid, was able to utilize helicopter gunships and drop bombs from MIGs, the RUF suffered heavy losses. Finding all of their other options blocked, the RUF signed a peace treaty in April 2001, a year after their original confrontation with the UN.

The Reconstruction of a State

The challenge confronting all of the parties supporting a peaceful transition in Sierra Leone was how to put the country back together again so that any political or economic gains would be sustainable. A decision was made to proceed slowly and cautiously – giving the RUF a role in the process that would not be excessively disruptive but which was also not likely to provoke the rebels into resuming hostilities. This approach was time-consuming and costly, but proved to be more effective than alternatives tried in the past in other states consumed by conflict.

Step one in the process consisted of a series of meetings between the government, the RUF and the UN to determine the location of demobilization sites and the timing of the disarmament and demobilization process. Two districts were to disarm simultaneously so that an area dominated by the RUF would be paired with an area dominated by the government. This effort was often combined with the collection of civilian arms and the establishment of training centres for disarmed combatants. Disarmament and demobilization did not always go smoothly, especially in diamond-producing areas where the RUF were trying to stockpile stones for as long as possible. At one point, in Koidu, violence broke out, ending only when a buffer zone was established between the RUF and the CDC. About a month later disarmament was delayed when RUF fighters began once again to set up road blocks.[48] UNAMSIL referred to these and similar events as hiccups and patiently resumed negotiations until the process was again on track.

The next step in the sequence involved trust-building activities followed by the re-establishment of government authority in disarmed districts through the deployment of police or army personnel. Then, once state authority was in place, a newly constituted committee was asked to determine if a district was safe for the return of IDPs and refugees (see Figure 4). Unfortunately, plans to supply tools and seed to those being resettled fell short because of a scarcity of resources – funding was inadequate to support all the IDPs and refugees at a level that would have ensured a successful transition. Thus, most of the returnees faced daunting challenges: steep fees for delivery to a home site from the drop-off point, a shortage of inputs, home villages that were destroyed, a lack of services and a food supply likely to run out before any new crops were ready to harvest.[49] Because of these hurdles, it was not unusual for IDPs and refugees to reject the resettlement option, returning to the IDP camps that were scheduled to be dismantled or to the cities and towns that were already beset by unemployment and housing and food shortages.[50]

In spite of these circumstances, by the end of February 2002, all of the districts of Sierra Leone had been declared safe for resettlement except for 11 out of 13 chiefdoms in Kailahun District. This pattern was not surprising since the unsafe chiefdoms were located along the Liberian border – the area of the country most impacted by the RUF incursions (see Figure 4). Yet, there were signs that government authority was starting to return to the border region. By January 2002, the SLA was patrolling along the Liberian border, determined to try to control this vulnerable area. Efforts were made to stop the movement of diamonds in one direction and weapons in the other, but the soldiers were spread too thin to do more than monitor short stretches of the border at a time.

The resettlement process and the re-establishment of government authority was accompanied by preparations for national elections that were

FIGURE 4

THE RE-ESTABLISHMENT OF SECURITY, 2001–2002

held in May 2002. Attention focused on the RUF and the disturbing possibilities that the party might do well and, if not, that it would go back to the bush and resume the war. The RUF leadership were rumoured to be exchanging diamonds for supplies of rice and other consumables to curry favour with the electorate and to be registering under-age voters. In any event, the RUF were soundly rejected on election day, plagued by two related phenomena: 1) a tendency for the leadership to use party resources for personal expenditures and then desert the RUF for other parties and 2) a complete lack of appeal to voters given its record of atrocities.[51] Kabbah was confirmed as president in a relatively calm and incident-free election with a participation rate of over 70 per cent.

The Rebuilding of the Economy

As Sierra Leone made progress at reconstituting itself politically, the depressed economy remained a major source of concern. Loans and grants were designated for rebuilding Sierra Leone and some debt forgiveness was announced but not enough funds were being made available to resuscitate the economy. One focus of rehabilitation has been the cash crop sector. This will inevitably be a slow process based on infrastructure improvement combined with putting in place input delivery, marketing systems and extension services. Yet, besides agriculture, employment options remain scarce. The manufacturing sector is moribund, while the informal sector is reviving very slowly with some options opening up for local and longer distance trade. Jobs in the formal sector are limited, and many of these are linked to NGOs or the UN and thus will gradually be phased out. Sierra Leone has evolved into an AID-dependent state that has not been able to wean itself off foreign assistance. The economy grew about ten per cent from May 2001 to April 2002 and prices fell as well, but much of this phenomenon was the result of an unsustainable level of aid money.[52]

One of the key issues in the peace process is the fate of the former combatants of whom over 45,000 have turned in their arms. Many of the ex-RUF live in clusters at the edge of towns, lacking work or income and afraid of reprisals if they return home. Ideally, all of these individuals should receive some training, but there are not enough funds to support such an undertaking. Even when ex-fighters are able to participate in a special programme, there is a limited demand for workers skilled in such areas as carpentry, soap-making and tailoring. To circumvent this problem, some programmes are linked to public works projects, including restoring roads and providing clean water supplies. These efforts will serve as a stop-gap measure to help avoid excessive unemployment for up to two years, but eventually alternatives will have to be developed. Fortunately, skills related to farming will also be taught and these should prove useful if agricultural production can be revived.

Expectations are higher for the potential contribution of diamond mining to the national economy. The question here is very critical: can diamonds, the major stimulus to ten years of conflict, become the source of an economic recovery? The evidence to date is mixed but not particularly encouraging. The government's system for certifying diamonds has not proved to be effective for preventing smuggling. The extreme dispersal of the resource continues to complicate any efforts at centralized control; although the export statistics are encouraging, it is likely that more than half of all diamonds mined in Sierra Leone do not pass through the official system.[53] Most of the smuggling is on a small scale as miners, buyers and other entrepreneurs attempt to avoid the relatively modest government fees and three per cent tax. The government has been unable to attract a large, reliable corporation that could try to impose order on the current system, although that may be an option for the kimberlite dykes that are easier to control than the alluvial diamond deposits. Meanwhile, the international Kimberly process finally agreed on a mechanism for controlling the world-wide flow of diamonds from source areas to processing centres. Although several NGOs have referred to the monitoring mechanism as weak, a deadline of 31 July 2003 has been set for all diamond producers and traders to sign up for the certification system or be placed under a trading ban.[54]

If diamonds are going to be a centrepiece of effort to jump-start the economy, then a major challenge is to improve the prospects of the miners themselves who continue to work under unhealthy conditions for limited remuneration. Even as the peace process was under way, miners were digging for diamonds and expanding the landscape of deep pot-holes, yellow river-beds, and collapsed roads and houses that has characterized the environs of diamond centres such as Koidu.[55] Although miners in that area are now registered and forced to remain at a set distance from bridges and houses, the frontier areas are still unregulated. It will certainly be impossible to police the combined areas of the four original diamond concentrations plus the eight additional districts recently identified as diamondiferous.[56]

The most logical approach to improving the performance of the alluvial diamond sector would be to first provide alternative economic activities so as to slow inmigration, and then organize the miners in place so that they all prospect on assigned holdings. The World Bank recommends a model that has worked for gold miners in Peru: careful mapping of mineral areas followed by the allocation of specific sites (with a dispute adjudication system in place), the provision of small loans to buy equipment and, finally, training to improve extraction techniques.[57] The use of motor pumps or excavators would allow the miners to dig deeper holes where they might find more diamonds while damaging a smaller area.

The Sierra Leone government wants to move in the direction suggested by the World Bank but the situation is complicated by an entrenched lack of commitment to transparent processes, the result of several decades of illegal diamond dealing that pre-dates the war. Even the promise of returning 25 per cent of the diamond revenues to the local producing area has not changed this reality. In 2001, an American company attempted to establish a diamond diggers co-operative in Kono District whereby members would pool their finds, the company would take a percentage for having provided food and equipment and the rest of the profits would be split among the miners. The company has pulled out, however, discouraged by private sales of stones and by corrupt activities, including the selling of membership in the co-operative.

The Wider Geopolitical Context

The current efforts at recuperating from a decade of conflict cannot be divorced from the larger West African setting. The main source of confrontation, then as now, is the Liberian government led by Charles Taylor. There are four interwoven strands that currently constitute the Liberian dilemma, the first of which involves the Mano River Union. ECOWAS would like to revive the MRU as a mechanism for diffusing regional tensions. With this end in mind, meetings were arranged between ministers of Sierra Leone, Liberia and Guinea and even between the leaders themselves. Out of these discussions came agreements on strengthening the MRU and plans to arrange joint patrols along the common border. It would appear, however, that Charles Taylor is probably using the MRU negotiations as a ploy to demonstrate good intentions rather than as a genuine mechanism to achieve peace in the region.[58]

The second thread involves the Security Council sanctions imposed on Liberia in May 2001 as a result of its involvement in trading in diamonds and arms with the RUF. The sanctions were placed on arms shipments, on diamond sales and on international travel by selected government officials. The Taylor government has continued to engage in illicit exchanges, however. Weapons still reach Liberia by increasingly devious routes and have been seen openly in Monrovia and elsewhere.[59] Hard evidence of these transgressions appeared when a plane landed outside Monrovia, setting off explosions. The plane turned out to be owned in the United Arab Emirates (UAE), registered in Moldava, and destined for a central African location, and was undoubtedly carrying contraband weapons.[60]

As for controlling diamond exports from Liberia, this policy has become increasingly important since it was discovered that Al-Qaeda had been using Liberia as a conduit for diamonds mined by the RUF, the perfect commodity for hiding assets from public scrutiny. This connection between Liberia and world terrorism has not been insignificant; twenty million dollars worth of diamonds may have been purchased by Al-Qaeda operatives who travelled regularly to Monrovia after the African embassy bombings in 1998.[61]

Given Liberia's lack of compliance, the Security Council agreed to a renewal of sanctions in May 2002 and is pressing for greater international co-operation in enforcement. Many countries, including Burkina Faso and Guinea, have profited from their involvement in sanctions-busting.[62] There is also increasing pressure to expand the sanctions to include timber products. To date, the Liberian timber trade has been protected by France and China, the two major trading partners in this arena, but evidence is mounting that timber sales are financing Taylor's destabilization efforts in neighbouring states, as well as other illegal activities. The timber companies themselves are also complicit in breaking sanctions, especially with regard to arms purchases for Liberia.[63]

A third thread in the Liberian drama is an ongoing insurrection by a group known as Liberians United for Reconciliation and Democracy (LURD). Dissidents have been fighting Taylor since his election but the conflict intensified after February, 2000 when the LURD was formed from several elements of the old anti-Taylor coalition of the Liberian Civil War. The LURD has also recruited heavily among the former CDF in Sierra Leone at the same time that the Liberian army has absorbed former RUF. The LURD has supported itself in several ways including looting, selling diamonds, and trading cash crops and diamonds for arms with President Conte of Guinea.

The insurgents managed to capture much of north-western Liberia (Lofa County) after an offensive in late 2001. When, by March 2002, several towns within 40 kms of Monrovia had been captured, the government declared a state of emergency although opponents contend that Taylor exaggerated the threat as part of an unsuccessful strategy to avoid renewed sanctions.[64] The confrontations have generated new flows of refugees to Sierra Leone and Guinea, creating new problems for both countries.[65]

The government pushed back the LURD and the fighting abated during the summer rains but a second offensive was launched in October–November 2002 and this one has reached even closer to Monrovia. New waves of refugees have been created as even the IDP camps have been attacked and human rights violations have been documented for both sides in the conflict. Efforts have been made, particularly by ECOWAS, to negotiate an end to the fighting, but little progress was made at peace conferences held in November 2002 and February 2003 or during more recent efforts at mediation.

Finally, Liberia is linked to a conflict that erupted in the Ivory Coast in September 2002, when soldiers from northern Ivory Coast organized a failed coup and then retreated to the north. When civil war threatened, the French encouraged a negotiated settlement but during the discussions, a second rebellion began in the west in January 2003.[66] This movement, which advanced into the Ivory Coast from Liberia, has been closely linked to Charles Taylor and appears to have been sustained by Liberian army and RUF fighters.[67] The second group of rebels have identified themselves as belonging to two Ivory Coast-based groups: the Movement for Justice and Peace (MJP) and the Ivorian Popular Movement of the Great West (MPIGO), but evidence supports a strong link to Taylor's efforts to replace one more government with a more sympathetic alternative.[68] This replay of the invasion of Sierra Leone 12 years earlier has again resulted in atrocities against civilians and has transformed one region of a previously prosperous country into a zone too dangerous for most NGOs.[69] In any case, Liberia's militancy has now impacted negatively on all its neighbours, as well as on trading partners such as Mali which were isolated by the closing of the Ivory Coast's northern border.

The Prospects for Peace in Sierra Leone

Although the relatively smooth transition to peace and democracy in Sierra Leone has been impressive, there are many issues that still need to be considered as part of a prognosis for the future. In April 2002, The Country Indicators for Foreign Policy Projects (CIFP) issued a conflict risk assessment report for the Mano River Union and Senegambia states.[70] Based on an evaluation of nine issues relevant to the potential for conflict, and using a scale from 0 (low risk) to 12, the project identified Sierra Leone as having the highest risk of conflict with a total index of 7.2, and an especially high score for risk of economic instability (9.6).

Part of the CIFP analysis of Sierra Leone was a separate brief which focused on some of the negative factors impinging on the country's future options. These included several years of a negative growth in gross national product (GNP), almost continuous conflict for ten years and a displaced population of over one million.[71] On the other hand, Sierra Leone has not experienced population pressure or environmental degradation and most of those displaced have now been resettled. The researchers produced a worst and best case view of the future of the country but their most likely scenario was termed a fragile peace. Under these circumstances, the country would still be coping with illegal diamond trafficking and would only slowly be carrying out economic and social restructuring.

This cautious perspective is echoed in other sources.[72] Ongoing corruption and the lack of control over diamond deposits could lead to the emergence of criminal gangs which would once more threaten civilian security in such areas as Kono and Tongo Fields and deprive the government of needed revenue.[73] A dearth of economic opportunities could lead to the same result. Petty crime has already become a major source of insecurity, and looting, armed robbery, kidnapping and other income-generating criminal activity could become more pervasive. Those families not involved in crime might slip into subsistence where no obvious, lootable resource competed with agriculture.

Even more ominous is the instability of the region and the volatile regime of Charles Taylor. A report issued in April 2002 called on the international community not to relax its vigilance since Taylor's ambition to create a greater Liberia remained extant as did the resources necessary to sustain this vision.[74] Taylor's access to Guinean and Sierra Leone diamonds has been reduced, but he still can tap into the Liberian supply and supplement them with gold and forest resources that are being decimated at a prodigious rate.

The March 2003 report by Global Witness had even more damning points to make about Taylor's potential influence on Sierra Leone. Their prognosis is as follows: Taylor is supporting former RUF and Junta members already positioned in at least four cells in Sierra Leone. These infiltrators, who are allegedly being supplied with weapons by small coastal boats, have been trained to disrupt the war crime trials in Freetown.[75] Even if this plot is not acted upon, the current reality is grim: 1) the border with Liberia remains porous with little hope of controlling the flow of people and goods, 2) Liberian refugees and former soldiers in Sierra Leone could function as a destabilizing force, and 3) the UNAMSIL forces are gradually being phased out. The region remains insecure as LURD forces continue to expand (it is likely that in April 2003 they controlled more than half of Liberia's territory), as a new rebel group (The Movement for Democracy in Liberia) emerges in eastern Liberia, and as the Ivory Coast remains in flux in spite of a power-sharing agreement.

In late April 2003, an Ivorian rebel commander was killed by his own Liberian and Sierra Leonian followers when he demanded that they lay down their arms and go home in compliance with a recent treaty. In an ironic twist, the leader of the band of mercenaries and probable assassin was none other than Sam Bockarie, a controversial former leader of the RUF who is one of those indicted for war crimes. Charles Taylor has been informed that he will face prosecution if he does not turn Bockarie over to the Special Court in Freetown while Taylor, in turn, has denied that Bockarie is in Liberia.[76]

West African Geopolitics in a Wider Context

West Africa is now full of challenges to the widely accepted rule that the world is divided into states, each of which should control the territory within its own boundaries.[77] Individual states have surrendered sovereignty to a range of players: war-lords, mercenaries, transnational corporations as well as to other recognized states. Areas of temporary stability alternate with 'zones of chaos' or 'no-go' areas where the laws are not enforced.[78] Fighting can erupt at any time, funded by the sale of contraband goods or by diaspora communities and sustained by the free flow of armaments. To the UN Secretary-General, this is all part of the cycle of violence in West Africa which, once started, has a momentum of its own and is difficult to bring to a conclusion.[79]

The war in Sierra Leone has provided the perfect microcosm of this process, with a decade-long conflict which followed a cyclic pattern. The RUF rebellion expanded to threaten and overtake areas of resource concentration as well as political targets, then withdrew into remote rural areas. During the retreat phase, the insurgents remained hidden, often in dense brush, like viruses waiting to break out again once resources had been traded for arms and fighting forces had been replenished. These forces could never have expanded following the contraction of their territory without links to international business and criminal or terrorist elements, as well as government entities willing to break sanctions in order to further their own geopolitical and economic goals.

In this fluctuating situation, boundaries have taken on a whole new meaning. In Africa, boundaries were already areas beyond government control long before the spread of endemic violence.[80] Even after independence they were the sites of illegal and quasi-legal activities including resource exploitation and local smuggling. But in Sierra Leone and neighbouring states, border zones have become much more dangerous and threatening. They function as areas of infiltration and weapons exchanges where local civilian populations are replaced by armed bands.[81] Conventional border markers have been replaced by a pervasive landscape of fear that include hiding places for ambushes and arms caches, abandoned villages and sites filled with the detritus of brief occupations by bands of fighters.[82] Efforts to reclaim positions along the Sierra Leone-Liberia border have been costly and frustrating.

All of these circumstances make it very difficult to bring conditions of insecurity to a conclusion. Any impetus toward peace is going to be countered by those whose interests favour chaos as a cover for the capture of territory and resources. Sierra Leone may have been brought back from the edge of collapse by a combination of 17,500 peacekeepers, British troops and other committed parties, but it currently faces infiltration by subversives along its sea and land boundaries, a diamond industry which remains elusive in terms of government control, a cohort of displaced families and former soldiers whose economic prospects remain dim, and a government that cannot root out corrupt practices. It also cannot escape from a wider region where instability has now become the norm. It has proved much easier to undermine peace and recovery than to effectively re-establish centralized control and economic viability in an African state that has experienced resource-based violence.

NOTES

1. In 2000, approximately one-quarter of all the conflicts in the world were resource related. M. Renoir, 'Breaking the Link between Resources and Repression', in The Worldwatch Institute, *State of the World 2002* (New York: W.W. Norton 2002) p.149.
2. M. Klare, 'The New Geography of Conflict', *Foreign Affairs*, Vol.80, No.3 (May/June 2001), pp.60–61. See also, M. Klare, *Resource Wars* (New York: Metropolitan Books 2001).
3. G. O'Tuathail, 'The Postmodern Geopolitical Condition: States, Statecraft, and Security at the Millennium', *Annals of the Association of American Geographers*, Vol.90, No.1 (March 2000) p.166.
4. C. Clapham (ed.), *African Guerrillas* (Oxford: James Currey 1998) pp.7–8.
5. W. Reno, 'Reinvention of an African Patrimonial State: Charles Taylor's Liberia', *Third World Quarterly*, Vol.16, No.1 (Jan. 1995), pp.112–15. The phenomena of political entities like 'Greater Liberia' is discussed in T. Dietz & D. Foeken, 'The Crumbling of the African State System', in G. Dijkink and H. Knippenberg (eds), *The Territorial Factor: Political Geography in a Globalizing World* (Amsterdam: Vossiuspers, 2001), p.190–92.
6. M. van Creveld, *The Transformation of War* (New York: The Free Press 1991), p.203; and P. Chabel and J.P. Deloz, *Africa Works: Disorder as Political Instrument* (Bloomington, IN: Indiana University Press 1999) p.85. See also C. Allen, 'Warfare, Endemic Violence & State Collapse in Africa', *Review of African Political Economy* Vol.81 (1999), p.371.
7. J.F. Bayart, S. Ellis and B. Hibou, *The Criminalization of the State in Africa* (Oxford: James Currey 1999) p.41.
8. C. Nordstrom, *A Different Kind of War Story* (Philadelphia, PA: University of Pennsylvania Press 1997) p.38, p.42.
9. J. Barnett, *The Meaning of Environmental Security* (London: Zed Books 2001) p.4.
10. World Bank, *Conflict Diamonds*, Africa Region Working Paper, Series No.13 (Washington, DC: Word Bank 2001), p.45.
11. USAID, Office of Transition Initiatives (OTI), 'Sierra Leone: "Conflict Diamonds", Progress Report on Diamond Policy and Development Program', 30 March 2001, p.5.
12. J.L. Hirsch, *Sierra Leone: Diamonds and the Struggle for Democracy*, International Peace Academy, Occasional Paper Series (Boulder, CO: Lynne Rienner Publishers 2001) p.26.
13. L. Gberie, *War and Peace in Sierra Leone: Diamonds, Corruption and the Lebanese Connection*, Partnership Africa-Canada, The Diamonds and Human Security Projects, Occasional Paper No.6, 2002, p.11–12. See also, D.C. Fithin, 'Diamonds and War: Cultural Strategies for Commercial Adaptation to Low-Intensity Conflict', PhD dissertation, University of London, 1999.
14. Hirsh (note 12), p.27.
15. World Bank (note 10), p.7

16. Official exports of diamonds from Sierra Leone fell from 2 million carats in 1970 to 595,000 in 1980 and, to 48,000 in 1988. A.B. Zack-Williams, 'Sierra Leone: The Deepening Crisis and Survival Strategies', in J.E. Nyang'ora and T Shaw (eds), *Beyond Structural Adjustment in Africa* (New York: Praeger, 1992), p.153.

17. A. Alao, 'Diamonds are Forever ... but so also are Controversies: Diamonds and the Actors in Sierra Leone's Civil War', *Civil Wars*, Vol.3, No.2 (Autumn 1999), pp. 47–9.

18. There is a useful discussion of the rise of violent gangs in Sierra Leone in J. Kandeh, 'Ransoming the State: Elite Origins of Subaltern Terror in Sierra Leone', *Review of African Political Economy*, Vol.81 (1999), pp.358–61.

19. J. Herbst, *States and Power in Africa* (Princeton, NJ: Princeton University Press 2000) p.20, pp.64–9.

20. H. French, 'A West African Border with Back to Back Wars', *New York Times*, 25 Jan. 1998.

21. P. Richards, 'Are "Forest" Wars in Africa Resource Conflicts? The Case of Sierra Leone', in N. Paluso and M. Watts (eds), *Violent Environments* (Ithaca, NY: Cornell University Press, 2001).

22. A.B. Zack-Williams, 'Sierra Leone: The Political Economy of Civil War, 1991–1998', *Third World Quarterly*, Vol.20, No.1 (Jan. 1999), p.146.

23. I. Abdullah, 'Bush path to Destruction: The Origin and Character of the Revolutionary United Front/Sierra Leone', *Journal of Modern African Studies*, Vol.36, No.2 (March 1998), p.231. See also, R. Joseph, 'The International Community and Armed Conflict in Africa –Post Cold War Dilemmas', in G. Sorbo and P. Vale (eds), *Out of Conflict: From War to Peace in Africa* (Uppsala, Sweden: Nordiska Africkainstitutet 1997), pp.19–21 for a concise discussion of the nature of African insurgencies.

24. M. Kaldor, 'The Structure of Conflict', in L. Wohlgemuth, S. Gibson, S. Klasen and E. Rothschild (eds), *Common Security and Civil Society in Africa* (Stockholm, Sweden: Nordiska Afrikainstitutet 1999), pp.127–8.

25. S.P. Riley, 'Liberia and Sierra Leone: Anarchy or Peace in West Africa', *Conflict Studies*, Feb. 1996, p.17.

26. I. Douglas, 'Fighting for Diamonds – Private Military companies in Sierra Leone', in J Cilliers and P. Mason (eds), *Peace, Profit or Plunder: The Privatization of Security in War-Torn African Societies* (South Africa: Institute for Security Studies, 1999), p.178.

27. 'Fighting for Diamonds', *West Africa*, 24–30 June 1991, p.1034.

28. For example, in Bonthe District, reports of rebel threats were rife. Rebels were said to be distributing 'we will come soon letters', and residents were living in fear, in spite of SLA troops stationed in Bonthe town. 'Rebels Attack Kono', *West Africa* 4242, 22– 24 July 1992, p.1216.

29. A. Richards, 'Rumours of War', *Focus on Africa*, Vol.2, No.3 (July–Sept. 1991), p.13.

30. 'Interview with Abdulai Conteh, 1st Vice President', *West Africa* 3737, 23–9 March 1992, p.496.

31. M Butcher, 'Hard Road to Democracy', *West Africa* 3734, 2–8 March 1992, p.374.

32. I. Abdullah and P. Muana, 'The Revolutionary United Front of Sierra Leone: A revolt of the Lumpenproletariat', in C. Clapham, *African Guerrillas* (Oxford: James Currey, 1998), pp.183–4.

33. 'Sierra Leone: the Threat from the East', *Africa Confidential*, Vol.35, No.7 (April 1994), p.6.

34. W. Reno, 'Privatizing War in Sierra Leone', *Current History*, May 1997, p.228–9.

35. Douglas (note 26) p.187.

36. H. French, 'West African Surprise: Suddenly Peace Takes Root in Sierra Leone', *New York Times*, 5 May 1996.

37. 'RUF, Soldiers Clash', *West Africa* 4170, 15–19 Oct. 1997, p.1616.

38. Y. Bangura, 'Strategic Policy Failure and State Fragmentation: Security, Peacekeeping and Democratization in Sierra Leone', in R.R. Laremont (ed.), *The Causes of War and the Consequences of Peacekeeping in Africa* (Portsmouth, NH: Heinemann, 2002), p.152. Most rehabilitated soldiers proved disloyal in the battle in 1998 for control of the North. In Makeni, some of these troops attacked the Nigerians of ECOMOG rather than the RUF.

39. Ibid., p.155.

40. M. Duffield, 'Post-Modern Conflict: Warlords, Post-adjustment States and Private Protection', *Civil Wars*, Vol.1, No.1 (Spring 1998), pp.70, 79.

41. BBC News, M. Doyle, 'Riding Sierra Leone's Roadblocks', 9 April 2001.
42 G. Campbell, *Blood Diamonds* (Boulder, CO: Westview Press 2002) pp.92, 95.
43. N. Onishi, 'Sierra Leone Poses Test for UN's Africa Policy', *New York Times*, 5 April 2000, p.A10.
44. 'Liberia Slams Unfair EU Aid Blockade', *Agence France Presse*, 15 June 2000.
45. B. Crossette, 'Singling Out Sierra Leone, UN Council sets Gem Ban', *New York Times*, 5 July 2000, p.A8.
46. C. McGreal, 'Sierra Leone: Children Dig Gems', *Mail and Guardian*, 26 May 2000.
47. L. Gberie, *Destabilizing Guinea: Diamonds, Charles Taylor and the Potential for Wider Humanitarian Catastrophe*, Partnership Africa-Canada, The Diamonds and Human Security Project, Occasional Paper No.1, 2001, p.6.
48. A. Kposawa, 'Disarmed Combatants Flood Tongo as RUF Rebels Mount New Checkpoints', *Standard Times* (Freetown), 12 Dec. 2001.
49. A Blackwood and S Nyce, 'Food Security for Sierra Leone: Returnee Communities in Jeopardy', *Refugees International*, 22 April 2002.
50. J. Charney, 'The Global Response to Internal Displacement: Still Struggling for Effectiveness', *Refugees International*, 25 April 25 2002.
51. D. Farah, 'Once Mighty Rebels are Biggest Losers in Sierra Leone Vote', <http://www.washingtonost.com>, 16 May 2002, p.A20.
52., A. Zavis, 'Peace in Sierra Leone Just Beginning', *Associated Press*, 20 May 2002.
53. US Government Documents, 'Testimony of Joseph H. Melrose, Jr., Ambassador in Residence, Ursinus College, Former US Ambassador to Sierra Leone', 13 Feb. 2002; see also, BBC News, 'Sierra Leone in Diamond Struggle', 22 March 2002, which included a discussion with Peter Kuyembeh, the Finance Minister of Sierra Leone. Diamond production did expand as shown by the following figures, but official exports were still well below total exports: $1.2 million (1999), $10 million (2000), $26 million (2001), $41 million (2002).
54. K. Akosah-Sarpong, 'The Dawn of the Kimberley Process', *The Concord Times* (Freetown), 5 Feb. 2003; see also, BBC News, 'Blood Diamond Deadline Set', 30 April 2003.
55. BBC News, M. Doyle, 'Sierra Leone: Memories of War', 19 Jan. 2002, p.4.
56. F. Awako, 'Twelve Districts Declared Diamondiferous', *Freetown Print Media Highlights*, 20 Feb. 2003.
57. World Bank (note 10) p12.
58. J. Dalieh, 'Another Rabat Summit in the Making as MRU Foreign Ministers Meet', *The News* (Monrovia), 9 April 2002.
59. BBC News, M. Doyle, 'Liberia Sanctions Reviewed', 18 April 2002.
60. 'Report of the Panel of Experts Appointed Persuant to Security Council Resolution 1395, Paragraph 4, in Relation to Liberia', UN Security Council, New York, April 2002.
61. D. Farah, 'Diamonds: 2 African Leaders are Linked to a Scheme', *The Washington Post National Weekly Addition*, 6–12 Jan. 2003.
62. A. Dukale, 'The U.N., Taylor and Kaddafi', *The Perspective* (Smyrna, Georgia), 8 Nov. 2002.
63. Global Witness, *The Usual Suspects: Liberia's Weapons and Mercenaries in Cote d'Ivoire and Sierra Leone* (London: Global Witness, 2003).
64. M. Tostevin, 'Rumor and Plot Theories Bubble in a Tense Liberia', *Reuters*, 14 Feb. 2002.
65. 'The Plight of Liberian Refugees in Sierra Leone Requires Urgent Response', *Refugees International*, 28 April 2002.
66. L. Fofana, 'Politics-Liberia: Tension Mounting on the Sierra Leone Border', *One World Net*, 7 March 2003. See also, J. Paye-Layleh, 'Military: Fighters Attack in East, West of Troubled Liberia', *Associated Press World*, 12 Feb. 2003.
67. L. Gberie, 'Resolving the Linked Crises in West Africa (part 1)', *Concord Times* (Freetown), 22 Jan. 2003.
68. Global Witness (note 63) pp.29–31.
69. U.N. High Commissioner for Refugees (UNHCR), 'Hundreds Flow Back to Cote d'Ivoire amid Liberian Conflict', 10 April 2003. See also, 'Situation Deteriorating in "No-go" Areas of Western Cote d'Ivoire, UN Envoy says', U.N. News service, 12 Feb. 2003.
70. S. Ampleford, C. Wakaba, and D. Carment (principal investigator), 'Conflict Risk

Assessment Report for West Africa: Mano River Runion and Senegambia', Country Indicators for Foreign Policy (CIFP), April 2002.

71. K. Marriott, L. Kettlewell, M. Luong, and C. Yoshitomi, 'Sierra Leone: A Risk Assessment Brief', CIFP, Carleton University, 1 Feb. 2002.

72. A. Zavis, 'After Decade of Horror Building Peace in Sierra Leone has Just Begun', *Associated Press*, 20 May 2002.

73. R. Dowden, 'Sierra Leone Locked in Shackles of Corruption', *The Guardian*, 12 Oct. 2002.

74. International Crisis Group (ICG), 'Liberia: the Key to Ending Regional Instability', Executive Summary and Recommendations, 24 April 2002.

75. Global Witness (note 63) p.7.

76. BBC News, 'Liberian Leader Warned over Fugitives', 1 May 2003.

77. A. Murphy, 'National Claims to Territory in the Modern State System: Geographical Considerations', *Geopolitics*, Vol.7, No.2 (Autumn 2002), p.194.

78. T.Luke and G. O'Tuathail, 'The Fraying Modern Map: Failed States and Contraband Capitalism', paper presented at the annual meeting of the Association of American Geographers, 19–28 March 1999, p.23; Duffield (note 40) p.88.

79. Kofi Annan, 'The Threat to Peace', Sierra Leone Web, <http://www.sierra-leone.org/slnews.html>.

80. Hirsch (note12).

81. K. Dodds, 'Political Geography II: Some Thoughts on Banality, New Wars and the Geopolitical Tradition', *Progress in Human Geography*, Vol.24, No.1 (2000), p.123.

82. For a discussion of changing boundary narratives, see D. Newman and A. Paasi, 'Fences and Neighbours in the Postmodern World: Boundary Narratives in Political Geography', *Progress in Human Geography*, Vol.22, No.2 (1998) pp.186–8.

Identity, Space and the Political Economy of Conflict in Central Africa

KEVIN C. DUNN

The ongoing conflict in the Great Lakes region – manifesting itself in the current Congolese 'civil war' – is both a perplexing case study for traditional international relations (IR) theory and a source of rich insights for alternative theorising about the nature and causes of conflict. The current conflict involves a besieged repressive regime, a fragmented rebel movement with dubious claims at legitimacy and popular support, several neighbouring countries directly involved in the fighting, and a bevy of small and mid-level political and economic actors. The causes of the 'civil war' are historically rooted and regional (and global) in scope.

The existing literature on the conflict tends towards two explanatory poles. On the one hand, there have been substantial arguments that fit into a 'politics of greed' explanation. This school of thought largely explains the causes and continuation of the violence in the region as a battle over control of the Congo's natural resources: mainly diamonds, cobalt, timber, gold, etc. A second school of thought casts the conflict as being rooted in issues of ethnicity. The basic tenet of these explanations is that conflict in the region is caused by longstanding tribal hatreds. Western media coverage of the conflict is particularly representative of this second approach.

The purpose of this essay is to offer a more nuanced explanation of the conflict by exploring how identity and space shape the political economy of violence in the region. The current conflict (sometimes referred to as a 'civil war') was initiated by the Ugandan and Rwandan regimes and their Congolese allies in August 1998. I explicitly link this war with what I refer to as the larger (and longer) crisis in the Great Lakes region. I regard this crisis – manifested in such recent events as the 1994 Rwandan genocide and the 1996–97 war to overthrow the Zairian dictatorship of Mobutu Sese Seko – as a historically socio-political crisis of governance in the region. As this essay argues, this larger crisis is regional in scope, affecting all the nation states in the area, but not reducible to any given one. This crisis reflects the economic, political, social and discursive interconnectedness of the region.

This essay argues that existing explanations overemphasise the supposed greed of the actors involved, without sufficient attention paid to the discursive aspects of the conflict. These discursive elements, particularly discourses on identity and space, are integral to understanding the conflict. For that reason, the goal of this essay is to construct a theoretical approach which integrates the material and the discursive. Within this framework, I incorporate perspectives from the fields of international political economy (IPE), identity studies and critical geopolitics. The strength of this approach is its integration of existing perspectives into one unified and sustained interrogation of the crisis in the Great Lakes region. The goal is to provide a more nuanced explanation of the causes and continuation of the conflict than is currently found in the existing literature.

This essay is divided into three sections. The first section provides a brief historical account of recent events in the Great Lakes Region. Given the space limitations, this account will necessarily be perfunctory and not without controversy. The second section introduces the essay's theoretical approach. A 'political economy of violence' perspective will be explained, then augmented with insights from the fields of identity studies and critical geopolitics. The third section provides an explanation of the crisis in Central Africa utilising this framework and organised along local, regional and global levels of analysis. This final section represents a 'first cut' analysis to illustrate the usefulness and necessity of a framework that combines material and discursive dimensions.

A Brief Review of the Conflict in Central Africa

The events behind the recent instability in the region have a long history and claiming an originary moment is often impossible and arbitrary. For the Democratic Republic of the Congo (DRC, formerly Zaire), the past decades were characterised by increasing state collapse[1] and continual resource extraction to the enrichment of President Mobutu and his political aristocracy. Bending to pressure, Mobutu held a Sovereign National Conference in 1991, which had the unforeseen effect of exposing the numerous tensions in Zairian society. For example, the representatives from North and South Kivu provinces in the eastern part of the country used the National Conference as a forum to attack the Kinyarwanda speakers in the regions, referred to as Banyarwanda and Banyamulenge, respectively. The Kivu representatives sought to rescind the citizenship of these groups and force them to return to Rwanda and Burundi. By 1993, armed groups began attacking Banyarwanda in North Kivu. Soon, the killings were in full swing, paralleling actions in neighbouring Rwanda. By mid-1994, thousands were dead in North Kivu and thousands more had sought refuge in Rwanda and South Kivu.[2]

On 6 April 1994, a plane carrying President Habyarimana of Rwanda and President Ntaryamira of Burundi was shot down over the Rwandan capital of Kigali. This provided the spark for several months of killing and fighting, now commonly referred to as the 1994 Rwandan genocide. The 100-day killing spree resulted in the murder of around 800,000 Rwandans, the overthrow of the Rwandan government by Paul Kagame's Rwandan Patriotic Front (RPF), and the exodus of over 2 million Rwandans to refugee camps inside Zaire. These refugees were a mix of civilians, Interhamwe (the militia largely held responsible for the genocide), and members of the defeated Rwandan army (Forces Armées Rwandaises, FAR). The refugee camps quickly became controlled by the Interhamwe and FAR. Over the next two years, these groups (with the blessing of Mobutu's central government) reorganised and rearmed. Soon, they began launching attacks from the camps into neighbouring Rwanda and against the Banyamulenge in South Kivu. After their requests for assistance were ignored by the international community, the Rwandan government and local Banyamulenge decided to take matters into their own hands by attacking their attackers.

The rebellion in eastern Zaire slowly began to take shape in August and September 1996 with the rebels launching a multi-prong attack against the refugee camps, Interhamwe and Zairian army (Forces Armées Zaïroises, FAZ). Orchestrated and assisted by the RPF regime in Kigali, the rebels quickly moved from south to north, gaining control of the 300 miles of Zaire's eastern frontier. The refugee camps were attacked and disassembled. By November, the rebellion had acquired a name, Alliance des Forces Démocratiques pour la Libération du Congo/Zaire (AFDL), and a leader, Laurent-Désiré Kabila. Kabila seems to have been plucked out of relative obscurity by the Ugandan and Rwandan regimes in order to give a 'Zairian' face to the rebellion.

As the rebels moved westwards, they were joined by other anti-Mobutists. Their external supporters included the regimes in Rwanda, Uganda and Burundi (and some logistical support from the US). As the rebels moved towards Kinshasa, Angolan government troops poured across the border to assist them in the overthrow of Mobutu, who was being aided by the Angolan rebel group UNITA (Uniao Nacional para a Independência Total de Angola). By 17 May 1997, Kinshasa had fallen and Mobutu and his entourage had fled. Soon afterwards, Kabila proclaimed himself the new president; renamed the country the Democratic Republic of the Congo (DRC); reintroduced the flag and the currency unit originally adopted at independence; banned political parties; and began to consolidate his power.

Within a year of Kabila's victory, his relationship with his regional allies, as well as the international community, had soured. His relationship with the regimes in Rwanda, Uganda and Burundi had become increasingly hostile. On 2 August 1998, a new rebellion broke out in the eastern part of the country, exactly where the original rebellion had occurred. However, it quickly became apparent that the rebellion was being directed by the regimes in Uganda, Rwanda, and (to a lesser extent) Burundi. Kabila's regime was rescued by the governments of Angola, Zimbabwe, Namibia, and to a more limited extent Sudan and Chad. After several months of fighting, it appeared a military solution was untenable for either side. Negotiations began, but by the summer of 1999, the rebel front had splintered into three groups backed by different foreign sponsors and fighting had broken out between the Rwandan and Ugandan contingents occupying different portions of the Congo. The country was effectively divided in half, with Ugandan and Rwandan troops and their Congolese allies occupy the east and the Kinshasa government holding on to the west with the help of Zimbabwean, Angolan and (to a much lesser extent) Namibian soldiers.

In the context of that stalemate, President Laurent-Désiré Kabila was assassinated by a bodyguard on 16 January 2001. In the immediate aftermath of the assassination, Joseph Kabila, the army chief of staff and the murdered president's twenty-nine-year-old son, was appointed the new president of the Congo. Joseph Kabila's ascendancy seemed to breathe fresh life into the beleaguered peace process. By the end of December 2002, a peace deal was hammered out, aimed at removing the foreign troops and creating a transitional government of national unity. After several false starts, the interim government, which included portfolios for members of rebel groups and the political opposition, was named in June 2003. The main rebel leaders were sworn in as vice-presidents the following month. At the time of writing, fighting still continued in the eastern part of the Congo, especially in the Ituri province, despite the presence of United Nations peacekeepers (MONUC). Moreover, allegations continue that Uganda and Rwanda have not removed all of their troops from within the Congo. Yet, there seems to be cautious optimism that the war that has killed an estimated 2.5 million people, either as a direct result of fighting or because of disease and malnutrition, may be nearing an end.

Towards a Critical Theoretical Framework

Actors are engaged in the Great Lakes crisis for at least two reasons: the material opportunities it offers and the performative and discursive possibilities it provides. On the one hand, armed conflict in Central Africa has been used in part as an instrument of enterprise and violence as a mode of accumulation.[3] On the other hand, the resort to violence is also a performance and discourse.[4] The performative and discursive components of the conflict are utilised by socially excluded actors, as well as groups seeking to reify their dominance. In fact, it is impossible to maintain a distinction between practice and discourse. For that reason, this essay bridges material and discursive approaches to the ongoing conflict by interweaving three strands: an examination of the 'political economy of conflict', an exploration of the politics of identity and identity construction, and a critical geopolitics dimension that explores the spatial practices and representations at work in the conflict. These three strands are complimentary and reinforcing.

For an understanding of the material dimensions of the war, I find a 'war economies' approach most useful. This sub-field of IPE examines the economic and political agendas and interests of various actors within the conflict. It is specifically concerned with how these interests and agendas are defined, as well as the material ramifications of the actions engendered by them. Perhaps the greatest insight from this perspective is that in a war economy, the goal of the conflict is not necessarily the defeat of the enemy in battle, but the continuation of fighting and the institutionalisation of violence for profit.[5]

The case of the war in the Great Lakes region illustrates that there are at least four material opportunities offered by a war economy. First, a war economy provides certain actors (whether they be individuals, social groups, nation state regimes or international businesses) the possibility to accumulate wealth. Violence often represents not a problem but a solution for many groups, creating new opportunities for profit for many of those involved.[6] These profits are usually achieved through theft or predation. In the case of theft, primary resources are usually the desired goal. When large quantities of primary resources (namely diamonds, gold, coltan, timber, ivory, etc.) are stolen, these goods are frequently smuggled out of the country and entered into the regional and global markets via neighbouring territories.

Second, involvement in a war economy also provides opportunities for removing a rival. The case of Central Africa illustrates how this is played out on different levels. For example, the war provides opportunities for certain ethnic groups aggressively to combat rival ethnic groups. The conflict in Central Africa also provides nation state regimes the possibility of removing rival regimes or insurgent groups. On the international level, it provides global powers the opportunity to remove their rivals, whether they be political or economic powers. Third, a war economy enables certain actors (individuals, social groups, governments and international economic actors) to increase their relative power through the accumulation of social and/or economic capital. This is most clearly seen in the case of the rise of regional hegemonic actors, which will be examined later.

Fourth, a war economy enables certain actors to capture strategic physical positions. The Central African war illustrates that the desire to acquire control over specific spaces is usually related to the desire of increasing one's 'security'. However, how that 'security' is defined varies between individuals. For some actors, the land acquired will provide important resources for their economic security. For others, the land will be strategically important for providing a physical buffer between themselves and their dangerous rivals.

Taken together, these four aspects of a war economy help constitute an actor's 'interests' or 'agenda'. However, 'interests' and 'agendas' are not self-evident, inherent or given. Neither, for that matter, are 'danger' and 'security'. Rather, they are created discursively. Therefore, there is a need to integrate discursive perspectives within this theoretical framework. For example, it is important to examine critically the definitions of 'danger' and the practices that are legitimated to provide 'security' against that 'danger'. Thus, the material aspects of a war economy are intrinsically linked to its discursive production. Structural approaches mistakenly privilege prescriptive norms of conduct and specific resource allocations – both of which are discursively constructed. Social interaction must be explained in relation to its discursive context. This essay will examine the conflict in the Great Lakes region within a framework that combines discursive and material approaches. Within the Central Africa case, 'interests', 'agendas' and 'security' are intimately linked with conceptualisations of people and place. Therefore, a critical framework must incorporate a discursive analysis of identity and space.

Recent theoretical works on *identity* have moved beyond static conceptions that focus on supposed inherent ethnic or cultural conflict tropes, as represented in the recent works of such scholars as Samuel Huntington and Robert Kaplan.[7] Instead, identities can be understood as the product of multiple and competing discourses, which construct unstable, multiple, fluctuating and fragmented senses of the self and other. Identities are socially constructed, conditional and lodged in contingencies that are historically specific, intersubjective and discursively produced.[8] Within Central Africa, group and ethnic identification historically has been dynamic. The long history of loose and flexible alliances in Central Africa further undermines the assumption that ethnic groups are homogenous.[9] As such, an explanation of the ongoing conflict in Central Africa should explore how ethnic identification has been recruited for social and political purposes. Achieving this goal entails an examination of the historical narratives and social myths that construct identities.[10]

The case of Central Africa illustrates that discourses on identity perform at least two important tasks. First, they produce the categories of 'us' and 'them'. Identities of groups – ethnic, racial or national – are often produced through narrativity.[11] The process of narrativisation entails taking on, creating, assigning or performing a story of some sort that captures the central elements and characteristics of what it means to be a member of the specific community. Narratives of identity are formed by a gradual layering on and connecting of events and meanings, usually through three steps: the selection of events themselves; the linking of these events to each other in causal and associational ways (plotting); and interpreting what the events and plot signify.[12] These narratives of identity create a sense of 'us', while simultaneously constructing 'them' or the 'other'; they help define who is considered a 'rival' or 'enemy', and why. Identity in international politics helps shape the hierarchy of social positions of power, influences how actors are perceived and treated by others, and affects how actors view and understand the world around them.[13] The next section illustrates that these identity narratives play a crucial role in the creation and continuation of the conflict.

Second, narratives of identity also provide the discursive frameworks through which accumulation of economic, social and political capital is enabled. Discourses are not simply words or ideas, they are also the actions and practices that enact the idea, that make it 'real'. Certain paths of action become possible within distinct discourses, while other paths are made 'unthinkable'.[14] A discourse informs rather than guides social interaction by influencing the cognitive scripts, categories and rationalities that are indispensable for social action.[15] The accumulation of wealth, as well as social and political capital, is generally performed within discursively constructed frameworks that enable not only its accumulation, but the means by which it is accumulated. This framework provides the narrative by which the accumulation of wealth, and the means through which it is established, are 'justified'. This approach rejects the view held by (neo)-realism and (neo)-liberalism that actors are motivated by inherent universal interests, rational means–ends preferences, or by internalised norms and values. Social action and agency result because people are guided to act in certain ways, and not others, largely 'on the basis of the projections, expectations, and memories derived from a multiplicity but ultimately limited repertoire of available social, public, and cultural narratives'.[16]

In addition to identity, the case of Central Africa also illustrates the need to interrogate critically the discursive production of *space*. Recent works from the field of critical geopolitics have helped integrate the concept of space into IR theorising.[17] These works recognise the plurality of space and the multiplicity of possible constructions of space. Importantly, they explore the interconnectedness of spatial practices and the representations of space. The term 'spatial practices', according to John Agnew and Stuart Corbridge, refers to 'the material and physical flows, interactions, and movements that occur in and across space as fundamental features of economic production and social reproduction'. Representations of space 'involve all of the concepts, naming practices, and geographical codes used to talk about and understand spatial practices'.[18] As Gearóid Ó Tuathail has noted, spatial practices and representations of space are inherently intertwined because it is unsustainable to maintain a distinction between practice and discourse.[19]

Discourses on space, as we shall see, are often closely connected to the construction of identities. The narratives that help construct group identities are often grounded in specific definitions of space: whether they be the 'homelands' of social groups or the territorial delineations of a nation state. The next section illustrates that discourses on space/land are intimately related to the (often violent) attempts to reify group identity, usually at the ethnic and state levels.

Finally, the desire to capture strategic physical positions is grounded in discursive understandings of space, namely the strategic mapping of space. How is security defined? By whom? For what ends? What constitutes a 'security zone'? What determines a 'strategic' position? These discursively produced definitions are inherent, though often overlooked, elements to the construction and maintenance of armed conflict. A critical geopolitics approach explores the power used to define 'dangers', as well as the power used in constructing a vision of the world in ways that specify political behaviours in particular contexts to provide 'security' against those 'dangers'.[20] Such an approach is vital to understanding the dynamics of the crises in Central Africa, where 'danger' and 'security' have been defined within specific spatial discourses. Indeed, the crises are directly linked to different and conflictual spatial practices and representations of space employed in the region.

The next section examines the conflict in the Great Lakes region to illustrate how actors engage in a war economy both for the material opportunities and as a performance and discourse. What makes this approach unique is its attempt to connect the material and the discursive in its theoretical framework. In terms of the material side of the conflict, the essay will pay particular attention to the accumulation of wealth, the removal of rivals, the accumulation of social and political capital (power), and the capturing of strategic physical positions. In terms of the discursive side of the conflict, the essay will pay particular attention to discourses on identity and space. The next section will examine the connections, as well as the disjunctures, between the material and discursive aspects of the war in the Great Lakes region.

People, Place and Fear in Central Africa

A central element of my methodological approach is the employment of a 'thick description' model, which contextualises actors and events in space and time. However, this approach must also account for the complex and conflictual dynamics created by the myriad actors involved in Central Africa. A simple top-down approach that only examines nation state actors would paint an extremely partial and misleading picture. For that reason, this approach is conceptually framed within local, regional and global levels of analysis. Thus, the discussion of the conflict in Central Africa will be structured along these three levels. However, it is impossible adequately to understand the dynamics within one level in isolation from the other two, and this essay will strive to illustrate the intersections of the levels.

Local Level

The emergence of a war economy in Central Africa has enabled many actors to engage in wealth accumulation that they otherwise would not have been able to achieve. In fact, at the local level, the ongoing conflict in the DRC has completely altered the productive and (formal and informal) trade networks in the eastern provinces of the DRC.[21] Much of these changes can be traced to the actions of intervening forces. Now, resource-deprived neighbours of the DRC export gold, coltan, cobalt, timber, palm oil, coffee and elephant tusks. These goods have become a major source of foreign exchange for regional actors. While the economy of eastern DRC has traditionally been part of a regional trade area extending eastwards to the ports of the Indian Ocean and north to the Sudan, recent changes have affected the local economic dynamics and patterns of trade. The emergence of a war economy has made local traders and peasants targets as well as objects of control to armed combatants. In the case of the DRC, local peasants have been exploited by armed groups seeking to establish their monopolistic control of resources and trade. These armed groups use violence or the threat of violence to acquire resources as cheaply as possible. Yet, the discursive production of identity is intimately involved in defining who and what are 'objects of control', and why. Moreover, the dominant definitions of 'danger' and 'security' in the region have long been framed by discussions of identity.

Within Central Africa, group and ethnic identification historically has been dynamic; largely shifting in response to threat perception.[22] This illustrates not only the constructed and contingent nature of identities, but also the mobilising forces of fear and anxiety, which are discursively produced. The region's evolving and socially constructed ethnicities have been grounded in social myths and historical narratives. Much has been made of the often violent struggle between Hutu and Tutsi in the region, particularly in the wake of the 1994 Rwandan genocide. René Lemarchand has pointed out how ethnically defined social memories have produced different historical myths and conceptual frameworks between the region's Hutu and Tutsi.[23] The remembrance of genocides (past and future) has served as a formative element for social cognitive maps, especially since there has been a tendency by many to substitute collective guilt on behalf of an entire social group for individual responsibility. The resulting Hutu and Tutsi identity discourses have narrated a sense of 'us' versus 'them' within a distinctly violent context. While these categories of identification are neither fixed nor stable, they have provided the 'script' through which violence has been utilised to reify identity boundaries between Hutu, Banyamulenge, Mayi Mayi and other social groups. It should be remembered that the collective memories of genocide and past wrongdoings inform the perception of many actors involved in the ongoing conflict.

Within the Central African war economy, narratives of identity are intertwined with material struggles over resources. For example, trade in a war economy becomes more monopolistic and the scope of rent-seeking predation on trade increases.[24] Violence and the threat of violence become the dominant capital in these situations. Such use of violence is not uncommon historically, especially in poverty-stricken areas where the use of arms and the threat of violence provide economic and political opportunities unavailable in the course of 'normal' daily life. At the local level, individuals and social groups acquire arms to protect as well as enrich themselves (economically, socially and politically). Such activities occur not only between rival rebel factions and their foreign patrons, but between historically competitive social groupings such as the Mayi Mayi and Banyamulenge. The interests and agendas of these groups are frequently constructed around claims to land, as the narratives of group identities reflect longstanding regional competition between agriculturists and pastoralists. The narrativisation of Mayi Mayi and Banyamulenge identity, for example, have been formed by a gradual layering on and connecting of events and meanings that often have specific spatial dimensions. Distinctions between the 'self' and 'other' within these narratives are often related to differing understandings and utilisations of land: agriculturists versus pastoralists, natives versus invaders, and so forth. In the current conflict, violence is often used as a performative act by rival social groups to stake a claim on land, within the discursive frameworks constructed by the narrativisation of their group identities.

The link between identity, land, and power illustrates that conceptions of social identities are not tied exclusively to nation states. Labels 'Zairian/ Congolese' and 'Rwandan,' for example, have often been relatively meaningless at the local level where the spatial practices of everyday life maintain a place-specificity that defies assumptions of state-centric approaches. Social groups and local identities have been constructed in the Great Lakes Region without *a priori* reference to the territorial nation state. Thus, other geographically-contingent forms of identification are evident within the historical narratives and social myths used to construct and reify identities in the region.[25] In North and South Kivu, 'ethnicity has an institutional underpinning in the continuing presence of a parallel, exclusive and mono-ethnic, traditional land tenure system. This system not only excludes that part of the population with a different ethnic origin from equal access to land but also from participating in the existing power structure.'[26] This linkage between land and identity was one of the primary factors in the effort during the 1980s and 1990s to drive the Banyarwanda and Banyamulenge out of Zaire as 'non-citizens'.

The continuing fighting taking place in Ituri province between Hema and Lendu militias underscores this point. International attention increasingly turned to the violence in Ituri, especially after it was reported that 250 civilians were killed in the town of Tchomia in June 2003.[27] Growing concern led to the deployment of a UN peacekeeping force (MONUC) in the provincial capital of Bunia. While the competition between the local Hema and Lendu populations has been complicated by external involvement, mainly from Uganda, Rwanda, and western economic interests such as Heritage Oil and Gas Company, the underlying tension continues to revolve around access to land. At the local level, definitions and understandings of space, access to land, and the institutionalization of ethnic identities through spatial representations and practices are integral parts of daily life. As such, competing definitions and understandings of space have been at the root of many of the local conflicts in the Great Lakes Region, illustrating the interrelatedness of land, identity, and power. However, understanding the politics of space has been an overlooked aspect of existing literature on the conflicts in Central Africa.

It has been wisely suggested by several scholars that one needs to understand recent African developments through an appreciation of 'the politics of borderlands'.[28] There has recently been much insightful scholarship in this direction, particularly in addressing issues of 'deterritorialisation' (the selective coverage of a territory by a government), the loss of governmental control and political loyalty in borderlands, and the cultural and political implication of Africa's porous borders.[29] As such, an image of Central Africa emerges as a region without 'meaningful' state borders: the flow of people, weapons, goods and resources is largely unrestricted. Yet, we need to move beyond considering only state borders and engage in examinations of other forms of boundaries.[30] Taking another perspective, Central Africa is a region enmeshed in a complicated web of socially constructed borders: linguistic, political, ethnic, cultural, economic, and so forth. At the end of the twentieth century, these boundaries were more important than the borders of so-called sovereign states. As such, a theoretical framework for understanding the crises in Central Africa must consider the construction and political implication of those boundaries. To a certain extent, most Central Africans live in a 'borderland' where, as Christopher Clapham has noted, the two major factors are conflicting sources of authority and the unequal distribution of resources.[31]

Regional Level

Yet, the interests and agendas of local actors have largely been overshadowed (at least in popular discourses of the war) by those of the regional actors, namely the interests and agendas of the governments involved in the conflict. At the outset of the conflict, the regime of Laurent Kabila[32] discursively portrayed the rebellion as a Rwandan/Tutsi invasion.[33] However, Kabila's subsequent actions illustrate the underlying logic of a war economy: the continuation of fighting and the institutionalisation of violence for profit. Laurent Kabila and his government used cease-fires as chances to re-equip and reorganise their forces. Although Kabila signed the Lusaka agreements in 1999, he quickly announced that the deal was flawed and unacceptable.

Kabila's intransigence can be explained in part by the fact that he had established economic ties with his regional allies in order to accumulate wealth for himself and his associates. On 23 September 1999, for example, Zimbabwean Defence Minister Moven Mahachi announced that Zimbabwe and Congolese defence forces had set up a joint diamond and gold marketing venture to help finance the war in the DRC. The venture associated Osleg, a company 'owned' by the Zimbabwean army, with the Congolese company Comiex, reportedly representing the interest of the Congolese army.[34] It appears, however, that Osleg is in fact owned by private military interests, including Zimbabwean General Zvinavashe. Zvinavashe also owns a private trucking company, Zvinavashe Transport, that supplies Zimbabwe's troops in the DRC. Moreover, Comiex is reportedly a creation of the late President Kabila, with his fellow ministers as private shareholders.

The Kabila regime also extracted resources from the diamond-producing corporation MIBA (which is 80 per cent owned by the state and 20 per cent owned by the Belgian corporation Sibeka). *African Business* reported that Kabila wasted no time helping himself to the company's coffers. In April 1997, the company was ordered to transfer $3.5 million from MIBA's account to Comiex, whose main shareholder is Kabila himself. Other 'voluntary' contributions followed. On 23 February 2000, MIBA was ordered by the Kabila government to hand over its Tshibwe kimberlitic concessions to a company named Sengamines. Sengamines was created the month before and is controlled by Kabila's Comiex, Zimbabwean General Zvinavashe's Osleg, and a Cayman Islands-registered company called Oryx Zimcon Ltd.[35] This illustrates Kabila's strategy of 'selling off' the DRC's resources to his external protectors while simultaneously enriching himself. The creation of a conflict economy has had the effect of transforming the DRC into an 'economic colony' of the numerous intervening forces, from Angola and Zimbabwe to Rwanda and Uganda.[36]

President Robert Mugabe of Zimbabwe has discursively framed his country's involvement in the DRC within the principles of international law and solidarity among the Southern African Development Community (SADC, of which the 'new' Congo became a member after Kabila's victory). Highly unpopular at home – the casualty figures are a state secret and the cost is estimated to be around $1 million a day – Mugabe's intervention can be explained in part from the 'political economy of conflict' perspective. Rebel leader Wamba-dia-Wamba has referred to Mugabe's interest in the Congo as 'basically a mercantilist intervention'.[37] This economic enrichment appears solely to benefit the ruling elite. By late 1998, it was revealed that members of Mugabe's ruling party, top military officers and member's of the president's own family had lucrative contracts with the Kabila government.[38]

Yet, the aforementioned joint venture between Zimbabwe's Osleg and Kabila's Comiex illustrates the Zimbabwean elite's need to find new ways to exploit their country's intervention in the DRC. The war in the Congo is not turning out to be the cash cow many originally expected. It was earlier thought that the appointment of Zimbabwean CEO Billy Rautenbach as the head of the Gecamines copper and cobalt parastatal might benefit Zimbabwe. This hope was furthered when a contract was signed between Gecamines and Rautenbach's Ridgepointe Overseas Ltd for an 80 per cent interest in Gecamines' Central Group operations. However, Gecamines is going through the worst crisis of its history, with its cobalt output 40 per cent below that of 1998.[39]

In addition to Zimbabwe, the MPLA (Movimento Popular de Libertação de Angola) government of Angola has been one of the DRC's strongest allies. It had originally backed Kabila's rebels against the Mobutu dictatorship, in part due to the MPLA's longstanding resentment of Mobutu. Not only had Zaire (backed by the US and apartheid South Africa) invaded Angola in the 1970s, the Mobutu regime had continued to provide invaluable assistance to the UNITA rebel group, even after the end of the Cold War. Over the years, UNITA had established itself as a 'shadow state' whose existence greatly relied on Mobutu's support and on Zaire as a conduit for arms and the smuggled diamonds used to bankroll its war.[40] With Kabila's rebel forces rapidly moving westwards, the MPLA regime saw an opportunity to rid itself of Mobutu and strike a (hopefully) fatal blow against UNITA's base and supply lines inside Zaire. As Kabila moved closer to Kinshasa, MPLA troops poured across the border and aided in the final capture of the capital.

When the anti-Kabila war broke out, Angolan government troops quickly responded to the initial rebel threat in the west by all but annexing Kitoni, Matadi and the Inga Dam hydroelectric power plant. This has proven to be fortuitous for the Angolan government, as it has helped the country's economy and given them *de facto* control over the Congo River basin (and hence control over the small Congo oil output). Within a 'political economy of conflict' approach, the MPLA's support can be traced to two related factors: the government's desire to advance its own strategic position against the UNITA rebels; and Angolan elites' desire to exploit further the economic profits of conflict, namely control over the diamond trade. At its core, Angolan involvement (by both the MPLA and UNITA) in the DRC war has served further to enlarge the scope of their own war economy, where defeat of the other is less important than the institutionalisation of conflict for profit.

Originally, the Rwandan regime of Paul Kagame was the primary force behind Kabila's AFDL and their victory over Mobutu.[41] However, relations between Kabila and his Rwandan backers soon soured, particularly after the Kabila government failed to achieve its anticipated goal of bringing security to the eastern part of the country. More important, he denied the Rwandan and Ugandan regimes the latitude to create the kind of 'security zone' they wanted. The rebel groups attacking the regimes of Uganda, Rwanda and Burundi had not been completely wiped away. Ironically, the 1996–97 rebellion had succeeded in driving many of these armed groups *into* those countries, heightening the levels of violence and insecurity. Viewing their erstwhile ally as ineffective and increasingly hostile, the regimes in Rwanda and Uganda decided to try again. Though Kagame's regime in Rwanda initially denied any involvement, it was the primary force behind the anti-Kabila war. Its motivations were similar to its motivations in 1996. Facing increased attacks by Interhamwe and FAR, as well as the growing hostility of the Kabila regime, the Rwandan government acted to strengthen its power in the region and, thus, its own security.

In addition to these political interests, the Rwandan government's involvement in the DRC war has also been shaped by an economic agenda. As Michael Dorsey has argued, the RPF regime has been using the war to create an economic base that would free it from Western economic dependency.[42] As a result, RPF leaders and associates have become deeply involved in the DRC's war economy, particularly in establishing monopolistic control of the economic trade in the areas they control, as well as extracting primary resources from the DRC.[43] Yet the RPF's economic area in the DRC is much smaller than that of Uganda's. Moreover, the RPF is not faring as well as Uganda in terms of accessing precious minerals, controlling trade, and raising revenue through the taxation of local populations.

Like the RPF in Rwanda, Yoweri Museveni's Ugandan regime was initially drawn into the anti-Mobutu war because of what it defined as its strategic interests. By aiding Kabila's AFDL rebels in Zaire, Museveni hoped to increase his own regime's security against Ugandan rebels groups – namely, the Allied Democratic Forces (ADF) – that were using Zairian territory as rear bases for the destabilisation of Uganda. Supporting the AFDL in their drive to Kinshasa would also remove Mobutu, a continuing thorn in his side.[44] Museveni, and the leaders in Rwanda and Burundi, hoped that a central government headed by their ally Kabila would prove to be more friendly and capable of exerting control in the eastern part of the country. At the very least, they hoped Kabila would be willing to look the other way while they were doing the job themselves.

After a year in power, however, Kabila had failed to provide Uganda and Rwanda with safe and secure borders. Thus, Museveni's regime intervened a second time for strategic reasons, this time to remove the man it had originally helped place in power. The policy of intervention was sweetened for the Museveni regime by prospects of tapping into, if not controlling, resources in north-eastern Congo, from gold mining to the smuggling of coffee, timber and minerals.[45] Moreover, part of Museveni's frustration with Kabila stemmed from the latter's refusal to consider economic integration eastwards, as well as the retraction of advantageous concessions to Salim Saleh, Museveni's half-brother.

By late 1998, the anti-Kabila rebellion began to fragment.[46] The presence of Ugandan and Rwandan troops supporting the rebels has turned many Congolese towards Kabila. In rebel-held areas, the local population resented the presence of Rwandan and Ugandan soldiers, their reported brutality, and their hijacking of the local economy.[47] Both countries engaged in strategies of harassing local farmers and businessmen in order to establish monopolistic control of the trade in their occupied zones. The gold, coltan, timber, palm oil, coffee, and elephant tusks that they extract from eastern DRC have become a major source of foreign exchange. In fact, it was reported that Uganda exported three times more gold in 2002 than it produced, suggesting the bulk of that gold was actually pilfered from the Congo.[48] The rift between the rebels and their Ugandan and Rwandan patrons was primarily motivated by competition over the exploitation of Congolese mineral resources.[49] In fact, some of the fiercest fighting of the war has taken place between Ugandan and Rwandan troops for control over Kisangani, the focal point of the diamond trade in eastern DRC. The plundering of the Congo's resources by the Uganda n and Rwandan armies has been rampant and well-documented.[50]

Thus, the actions of the various regional players can be understood in part by their self-defined economic and political interests. Many of the neighbouring states initially became involved in the conflicts because of what they considered to be their strategic interests. Primarily, these regimes were concerned with establishing safe and secure borders in order to ensure their regime's survival (as was the case of Rwanda, Uganda, Burundi and Angola). However, as a war economy emerged, these regional actors became increasingly interested in the continuation of the conflict for profit. The war in the DRC became a source of much needed resources and capital for many of the ruling elites in the region. While the general populaces of the states involved are not benefiting economically from their government's involvement, certain regional elites have used the emerging war economy to enrich themselves.

Yet these regional agendas have been authored with significant identity and spatial dimensions. For example, the DRC war has not provided key players like the Zimbabwean regime with the benefits many had expected. From a purely materialist perspective, Zimbabwe's involvement in the conflict is irrational since it is losing money at an alarming rate. However, focusing on identity discourses introduces two valuable dimensions to the explanation. On one hand, Zimbabwean elites are re-employing and re-articulating an age-old trope that defines the Congo as a resource-rich land waiting in fallow for exploitation and development. By buying into and reproducing those discourses, Zimbabwean elites are further drawn into Congo, just as colonial Belgium and Cold War era economic actors were. The discourse of Congo's vast, untapped wealth continues to be a powerful motivating force in the twenty-first century.

At another level, Zimbabwe's self-defined identity as regional power and hegemon has been an important aspect to its involvement in the DRC. Mugabe has used the situation to promote himself as a regional leader, pushing South Africa's Nelson Mandela into the background. More interestingly, Mugabe has rhetorically constructed Kagame and Rwanda as small-time players who have overstepped their boundaries. For example, Mugabe has justified his intervention by claiming that Zimbabwe could not let 'little' Rwanda push it around.[51] Prestige and hegemonic aspirations appear to be primary motivators for Uganda and Rwanda as well. It is clear that each country's initial involvement in the anti-Mobutu rebellion was tied to their construction of Zairian identity and their own self-perceptions. Moreover, the growing rift between the Museveni and Kagame regimes is primarily motivated by each one's desire to play the role of regional hegemon.

Regional narratives have employed and exploited ethnic identification and alterity in other ways as well. For example, the Ugandan-backed rebels within the DRC have resorted to anti-Rwandan speeches and representations in order to fan the flames of xenophobic hostility while diverting attention from their own foreign backing.[52] Perhaps most important, there have been interesting regional identity discourses being authored in Central Africa. Perhaps most crucial is the ongoing construction of Bantu identity and the narrative of 'Bantu solidarity'. The popularly held myth in the region holds that Tutsi are invaders from the north, who have usurped land and power from the region's original Bantu inhabitants. This has become a central thesis in regional identity discourses and has become a visible element of the socio-political dynamics in the DRC, as well as in Uganda, Rwanda, Kenya, Angola and Congo–Brazzaville.

Regional governments have also been active in employing nationalist-based narratives in the construction of regional identities. In the case of the Congo, there has been an important and powerful evolution of narratives. Initially, President Mobutu defined the Kabila-led revolt as one pitting 'Zairians' against 'Tutsi foreigners'. As such, Zairian identity was defined through the exclusion of ethnically defined easterners. Upon coming to power, Kabila articulated a 'new' Congolese identity grounded in the construction of shared social memories; that is, the shared suffering of the 'people' under Mobutu's neo-colonial dictatorship. However, after his split with Museveni and Kagame, Kabila increasingly defined 'Congolese' identity by articulating shared ethnic hatreds against Tutsi and Rwandans. The conflict has provided valuable discursive and performative opportunities for the definition and reification of national identity narratives by the ruling regimes in the Congo, Rwanda, Uganda and Zimbabwe. Usually, the resulting nationalist identities have become increasingly defined via xenophobic and violent alterity.

Spatial practices and representations have also been an important aspect of the regional dimensions of the ongoing crises. For example, it has often been suggested that the Rwandan RPF's involvement in the two Zairian/Congolese rebellions were based in an attempt to ensure the security of the Rwandan sovereign state. Yet such an argument is misleading and obscures some important spatial assumptions. First, it is difficult to speak of the sovereign integrity of the Rwandan state when the RPF's authority barely stretched beyond Kigali, the capital. Moreover, the Kagame regime was not motivated by the protection of the Rwandan population – many of whom were incarcerated or wanted for their role in the 1994 genocide. Rather, the RPF was interested in the preservation of the 'Tutsi' community writ large – a community whose boundaries did not correspond to recognised state borders. Protection of 'sovereignty' referred not to states, but ethnically defined communities. Tellingly, RPF troops have become known locally as '*soldats sans frontières*'.[53]

Taking a critical geopolitics approach to the conflict allows one to see that multiple and conflictual spatial representations and practices are at work.[54] The numerous external regimes involved in the current DRC conflict have defined their strategic interests, danger and security with specific, and conflictual, spatial dimensions. This can partly be understood by the fact that many actors conceive the political space of the region as concentric circles of diminishing political control – that is, as MPLA-controlled space, UNITA-controlled space, Zimbabwean-controlled space, and so forth. Indeed, the ongoing feud between the Museveni and Kagame regimes is, at its core, a violent disagreement over spatial representations and practices. These spatial practices employed by regional actors are intertwined in the self-representation of their identities. The fact that non-neighbouring Zimbabwe can justify its involvement in the DRC war through the rhetoric of 'self-interest', 'danger' and 'security' underscores the need for a critical understanding of the spatial dimensions of the conflict.

The integration of material and discursive elements at the regional level can be illustrated by the hegemonic aspirations of the Zimbabwean, Ugandan and Rwandan regimes. All three regimes have constructed identities for themselves as regional powers, based on narratives of prestige and hegemonic aspirations. These constructions of self-identity create cognitive maps that enable the actors to 'know' and to act upon what they 'know'. Certain paths of action become possible, while other actions are regarded as 'unthinkable'. In short, their narratives of identity enable them to engage in militarised adventurism outside their territorially defined borders. This intervention is intimately tied to spatial representations. The Congo is regarded as a space into which one can project/perform regional power. Recall that the RPF regime defines itself as the protector of a 'Tutsi' community whose boundaries cross the recognised borders of the Congolese state. Likewise, both the Zimbabwean and Ugandan regimes define Congolese space in such a way that engenders their physical occupation of territory, as well as their continuing economic extraction/predation within that space. This is informed by the performative aspect of hegemonic claims. Hegemonic claims engender specific sets of actions that produce material effects which serve to reinforce claims of hegemony (and the cognitive maps scripted within that discourse). Hegemony is not a singular act, but a reiteration of a norm or set of norms through repetition. Within Central Africa, the regimes of Zimbabwe, Uganda and Rwanda are engaged in producing competing and (violently) conflictual discourses of hegemony, identity, space, security, interest and danger. Yet these regional events do not take place in isolation from the local and global levels. As the discussion of globalisation will illustrate, the three levels are intimately intertwined.

Global Level

With regard to the Congo's emerging war economy, there appear to be at least two dynamics at work on the global level. On the one hand, there has been a high level of complicity among international companies, offshore banking, and Western governments in the development of the region's war economy. On the other hand, it can be argued that local and regional actors are reacting to – and exploiting opportunities provided by – the process of globalisation.

There is a long and sordid history of 'international' (namely, Western) involvement and intervention in Zaire/Congo, from its origins in King Leopold II's economic exploitation to the CIA and Belgian-backed assassination of Patrice Lumumba and the installation of Mobutu's 30-year-plus dictatorship. Within the immediate scope of the ongoing DRC war, foreign intervention has remained high. The rise of Kabila was facilitated by the US (acting through its Ugandan and Rwandan allies).[55] The break between Kabila and his original Rwandan and Ugandan backers had global dimensions as well. As Thomas Turner notes, 'In 1998, the US apparently accepted the assurances of its allies that Kabila could be overthrown quickly and easily.'[56] Given the US' backing of the Museveni and Kagame regimes, many Central Africans believe that the US either initiated or encouraged the rebellion against Kabila. The US' actions behind the scenes of the Lusaka cease-fire agreement illustrate its support for Museveni and Kagame. It favours a regional solution, particularly one that benefits Uganda and Rwanda. Moreover, the involvement of Sudan and Libya on behalf of Kabila has been a major source of concern for the US.[57]

Issues of identity and space have played an interesting role with regard to French involvement in the region. France's governments had long sought to establish a *chasse gardée* (private estate) in post-colonial Africa. This *chasse gardée* provided these French governments with an arena to act as a global power. After 1975, Paris actively incorporated the former Belgian colonies into that sphere of influence.[58] Central Africa became a space into which France projected its own self-identity through the performance of its diplomatic, economic and military strength. In the late 1990s, France portrayed the Kabila-led rebellion as part of an 'Anglo-Saxon' conspiracy.

The French government and many French newspapers argued that the US and its proxies in Uganda and Rwanda were attempting to spread their hegemony into France's *chasse gardée*.[59] As Jean-Claude Willame has noted: 'France's behavior and its "reading" of Zairian evolution was based less on actual dynamics than on France's obsession with the supposed American ambition to supplant French influence.'[60]

France's image of recent events in Central Africa has largely been shaped by this 'Fashoda syndrome', with the region depicted as 'a cultural, political and economic battlefield between France and the Anglo-Saxons'.[61] Following the rift between Kabila and his American, Ugandan and Rwandan backers, France has used the collapse of the supposed 'Anglophone' alliance as an opportunity to reintroduce its influence in the region in the hopes of redefining the space as a restored *chasse gardée*. It has been suggested that the involvement of Chad and the Central African Republic on behalf of Kabila is due in part to France's attempt to regain influence in Kinshasa.[62]

In addition to Western governments, Western economic actors have also been actively involved in the DRC conflict, at least initially. With the collapse of Mobutu's regime, Western economic interests were quick to respond. While US Secretary Albright spoke of 'unlocking the Congo's vast potential', *Newsweek* proclaimed that the Congo 'offers a bonanza to US investors'.[63] Foreign gold and diamond mining corporations, such as American Mineral Fields Incorporated (AMF) and mineral giant De Beers (which enjoys longstanding domination of diamond purchasing in the country), engaged in what some saw as another 'scramble' for Congo's wealth.[64] As one observer wryly commented, war made good business sense for the mining corporations.[65]

However, explanations of the DRC war that focus predominantly on international/Western exploitation tend to overstate foreign involvement and ignore recent developments. In point of fact, recent events have illustrated that, as Erik Kennes has argued, the DRC government has not been able to link up with recent changes in the global economy.[66] Most of the world's major mining companies have chosen not to engage in the DRC, in part because of Kabila was not dependable and because the situation on the ground became unstable. As Kennes notes, the real economic actors in the anti-Kabila war have been traders, small fraudulent companies and those involved in military commercialism, all of which operate under the logic of predation.

This is not to suggest that Western economic interests have not been involved in the development of the DRC's war economy. In fact, as the work of Reno, Mwanasali, and others have noted, Western economic actors helped lay the groundwork for the emergence of a war economy.[67] Kennes is correct in noting that, once the violence became institutionalized at a level that no longer made 'business sense,' many major economic actors shifted their focus to more stable and profitable areas in Africa (such as Tanzania and Mali). Yet, it would be a mistake to assume that western economic interests simply walked away from the Congo. As Ian Taylor has observed, international business, through its contracts, deals and provision of all manner of means, served to finance and sustain many of the actors involved in the conflict.[68] For example, it has been reported that the Heritage Oil and Gas Company has signed an oil deal that will allow them to drill in the Ituri province, thus increasing the stakes in the conflict between the local Hema and Lendu populations, as well as the central government.[69] Western economic actors with interests in diamonds, gold, coltan, and small arms also remain factors in the conflict, either directly or indirectly.

However, it needs to be recognised that much of the West's response to the ongoing conflict has been framed by representations of regional identities. In fact, recent events have transpired within a global context shaped by Western representations of the region.[70] Specifically, the identities of local and regional actors have been situated within a Western-scripted genocide discourse. This discourse – with its use of rigid dichotomies (such as victim/victimiser, Tutsi/Hutu, etc.) – has been partly constructed by outside observers, namely the Western media. For example, in the midst of the 1994 genocide, the Western media portrayed all the people who were seen crossing over to Zaire from Rwanda as Hutu who were collectively responsible for genocide. They all automatically acquired a Hutu identity in the eyes of the 'international community' even if they were not self-defined as Hutu.[71] These Western representations are not simply innocuous images, but have powerful ramification.

In his discussion of the Great Lakes crises, David Newbury observed: 'This is a region not well known in the west, but one nonetheless enveloped in a century of powerful imagery – ranging from the "Heart of Darkness" to the "Noble Savage". In other words, it is an area that outsiders feel they "know" well.'[72] The 'knowledge' constructed in Western discourses is of a land of AIDS, the Ebola virus, inherent savagery and barbarism; an apolitical chaos beyond the rational comprehension of the 'civilised' West.[73] This (re)constructed trope has become known as the 'New Barbarism' thesis and has been applied to numerous African contexts, including the Great Lakes region. The basic tenet of this thesis is that Africa is an inherently wild and dangerous place, plagued by politically meaningless violence brought about by culture and the environment.[74] In the rhetoric of 'New Barbarism', Africa simply cannot sustain basic elements of civilisation. Such representations have important policy implications. As Paul Richards notes, 'Insulation rather than intervention is the rational response of the major powers.'[75] Western, particularly American, responses to the events in Central Africa have been largely informed by this trope – employing the rhetoric of 'chaos', tribalism and irrational African violence. At the heart of this rhetoric is the image of an African identity too inherently savage and backwards to progress towards 'modernity'. It is, to a certain extent, a renunciation of the 'civilising mission' – 'You Africans are beyond hope; we give up.' Western discourses on Central African identities have a direct relationship to Western policies, which further underscores the important link between discourse and action.

Yet the conflict in the Congo also stems from local and regional actors reacting to – and exploiting opportunities provided by – the process of globalisation. The process of globalisation is best understood as the emergence of new patterns of flow, transfers and interactions. The global restructuring engendered by globalisation has involved 'the social, economic, and cultural transformation(s) of the old order into a new one'.[76] While Western multinationals may have shifted their focus away from the DRC, local and regional actors have responded by exploiting the emergence of these new patterns of flow, transfers and interactions to increase their own economic standing. For example, the dynamics of globalisation have enabled Ugandan and Rwandan economic actors to smuggle primary resources out of eastern DRC and into the global markets. The growing global trade in 'blood diamonds' is a further example of the complex effects of globalisation.

While globalisation has provided new opportunities and agency to local and regional actors, it has also had a simultaneously disruptive effect. As Mark Duffield has argued: 'Market deregulation and declining nation state competence have not only allowed the politics of violence and profit to merge, but also underpin the regional trend toward protracted instability, schism, and political assertiveness in the South.'[77] That is to say, emerging war economies are tied to local and regional survival strategies in the face of global restructuring.

At the global level, the discourses surrounding globalisation have important spatial dimensions. As Agnew and Corbridge observe, 'along with the changing ways in which the international political economy operates ... come new representations of the division and patterning of global space'.[78] The changing political economy and restructuring of trade flows in Central Africa, for example, are linked to altered perceptions of the division and patterning on local, regional and global space. These changes are often in response to externally authored changes in the regulatory landscape. As Alan Hudson writes, 'the politics of globalisation, then, is all about who has the power to draw boundaries around places and peoples, at what scale such boundaries are drawn, and what the boundaries signify'.[79]

Clearly, authorship within the processes of globalisation is not equally distributed across the globe. Rather, the hegemonic Western powers retain primary authorship over the dividing and patterning of global space. With regards to the current DRC war, one can easily recognise the discursive power of Western-authored representations of space. For example, the continuing mantra from Western (that is, US, Belgian) governments and media that the Congo is 'too big to be governed as a single state' dramatically alters the regulatory landscape of the region. Through this representation of Central African space, foreign intervention, control and exploitation of the 'Congo' becomes justified and necessitated.

This portrayal of the Congo as being too big a space to be self-governed is tied to a larger and persistent theme in Western discourses on Africa. This theme is the geographical projection of a bifurcated world, based on a backward–modern dichotomy. Western images of the Great Lakes region as 'backwards' and 'modernising' inform discourses that narrate the recent events in one of two ways (though they are by no means mutually exclusive). First is the portrayal of recent events as part of a 're-tribalisation of politics' in Africa. Second is the portrayal of the conflict as part of a 'state-building process', similar to evolutions that purportedly took place in pre-modern Europe.[80] The implication of the latter is that these events are a necessary stage of 'development', while the implication of the former is that Africans are too savage and tribal truly to 'develop'.

Both manoeuvres are important because they place Central Africa in a temporal and geographical position separate from the Western observer. These discursive constructions effectively separate the crises of Central Africa from their global economic and political contexts, and thus erase any culpability. These Western representations of global space 'write off' the Great Lakes region. This act occurs simultaneously while Western economic (and political) actors benefit from the conflict, especially via access to cheapened natural resources (such as diamonds, coltan and ivory).

Conclusion

Traditional approaches to international relations and conflict assume that actors are motivated by inherent (universal) interests, rational means–ends preferences, or by internalised norms and values. As such, they tend to produce explanations that are both limited and limiting. This essay, however, argues that social action and agency result because people are guided to act in certain ways, and not others, on the basis of the projections, expectations and memories derived from a multiplicity but ultimately limited repertoire of available social, public and cultural narratives.[81] These narratives have a material dimension, but are intimately linked with discursive constructions of identity and space.

The purpose of this essay has been to outline a theoretical framework that adequately reflects the material and discursive dynamics of the crisis in Central Africa, and to present a 'first cut' analysis to illustrate the usefulness and necessity of that framework. Perhaps one the greatest insights provided by this study is the realisation that it is impossible to separate the material from the discursive. For example, local-level agents engage in the current conflict for material gains, defined through the lens of identity and space. The identity narratives of Hutu, Lendu, Hema, Mayi Mayi, Banyamulenge and other social groups are grounded in specific spatial practices and representations. The narratives held by these actors help give meaning to the world around them, while making certain courses of action possible and others unthinkable. To argue that Lendu and Hema militias are solely engaged in the war for profit from predation ignores the important roles that social identity narratives and spatial understandings play.

Likewise, regional governments are engaged in the conflict for multiple reasons. For certain, many of these regimes are interested in accumulating wealth and power. Yet these desires, and the means by which they seek to realise them, must be understood within their discursive contexts. For example, spatial and identity discourses are important elements in Zimbabwe's engagement in the DRC. At work are identity discourses concerning Mugabe's personal character, Zimbabwean national self-identity, SADC brotherhood, and Rwandan and Ugandan 'otherness'. Equally important are the spatial discourses in which the region is understood as a legitimate arena for the projection of Zimbabwean hegemony and the Congo as a territory open for economic extraction. Approaches that ignore the importance of identity and space provide overly simplistic understandings of the situation. For that reason, the 'politics of greed' explanations of the conflict in Central Africa are somewhat lacking. By interweaving a 'political economy of conflict' perspective with discursive analyses of identity and space, one can get a deeper understanding of the processes at work in the conflict.

Yet the proposed framework opens important methodological and theoretical paths of inquiry. For example, a focus on spatial representations and practices requires an examination of the lived experiences of actors. Such examinations should be historical in scope and include local-level research. Doing so allows for a deeper understanding of how spatial representations and practices create and reinforce hierarchies. Such research may also provide fertile ground for the study and theorising of resistance.[82] This is equally true for an examination of identity discourses that resist hegemonic representations. Merely focusing on the dominant discourses of identity and space has the effect of reifying hegemonic representations and practices. In employing this framework, one should examine the coincidences and disjunctures of the three perspectives employed, as well as across the local, regional and global dimensions. As such, I offer this essay as a 'first cut' in the introduction and utilisation of a theoretical framework that I believe will lead to deeper and more fruitful insights in the study of conflict in Africa.

ACKNOWLEDGEMENTS

This is a revised and updated version of an article that originally appeared in *Geopolitics*, Vol.6, No.2 (Autumn 2001), pp.51–78.

NOTES

1. Many authors speak of the 1980s and 1990s as a time of Zairian 'state collapse'. Yet it is more illuminating to talk not of 'state' collapse, but of the alteration of discourses on 'stateness' (both at the international and local levels). What occurred during this time was the removal of the guise of the 'sovereign state' and the exposure of the complexities of Zairian 'realities'.
2. Gérard Prunier, 'The Great Lakes Crisis,' *Current History* 96/610 (1997) p.195.
3. William Reno, 'Shadow States and the Political Economy of Civil Wars', in Mats Berdal and David M. Malone (eds), *Greed and Grievance: Economic Agendas in Civil Wars* (Boulder, CO: Lynne Rienner 2000) pp.57–8.
4. Paul Richards, *Fighting for the Rain Forest* (Oxford: James Currey 1996).
5. Berdal and Malone (note 3) p.2.
6. David Keen, 'Incentives and Disincentives for Violence', in Berdal and Malone (note 3) p.25. As Keen has noted, there are six economic functions of conflict. First, the conflict is used to supplement and/or replace the salaries of the combatants. In the DRC, government forces, officials, rebels and members of the interventionist forces all engage in this practice. Second, violence is used to acquire protection money from elites, foreign companies and local traders. This is the case in the DRC where mining companies in the south and traders in the east pay protection monies to various combatants. Third, violence is used by combatants to gain and protect their monopolistic control of trade. In the 'rebel'-held areas of eastern DRC, the conflict between the Ugandan and Rwandan regimes (and their Congolese allies) can be seen as a conflict over the monopolistic control of trade and resources. Fourth, the conflict is used to exploit local labour. In the DRC, this has enabled combatants to get resources cheaply, especially through the exploitation of peasants. Fifth, the conflict enables certain elements to extract from international aid. Finally, violence in a war economy is used to stake a direct claim on land.
7. Samuel Huntington, *The Clash of Civilizations and the Remaking of World Order* (New York: Simon and Schuster 1996); Robert Kaplan, 'The Coming Anarchy', *The Atlantic Monthly* (Feb. 1994) pp.44–76, and *The Ends of the Earth: A Journey at the Dawn of the 21st Century* (New York: Random House 1996).
8. Stuart Hall, 'Fantasy, Identity, Politics', in E. Carter, J. Donald and J. Squires (eds), *Cultural Remix: Theories of Politics and the Popular* (London: Lawrence and Wishart 1995) pp.63–72, and 'Who Needs 'Identity'?' in S. Hall and P. Du Gay (eds), *Questions of Cultural Identity* (London: Sage 1996) pp.1–17; Wendy Brown, *States of Injury: Power and Freedom in Late Modernity* (Princeton, NJ: Princeton University Press 1995).
9. Ruddy Doom, 'Changing Identities, Violent Conflict and the World System', in R. Doom and J. Gorus (eds), *Politics of Identity and Economics of Conflict in the Great Lakes Region* (Brussels: VUB University Press 2000) p.60.
10. D.C. Martin has argued: 'The identity narrative channels political emotions so that they can

fuel efforts to modify a balance of power; it transforms the perceptions of the past and the present; it changes the organization of human groups and creates new ones; it alters cultures by emphasizing certain traits and skewing their meaning and logic. The identity narrative brings forth a new interpretation of the world in order to modify it.' See D.C. Martin, 'The Choices of Identity', *Social Identities* 1/1 (1995) p.13.

11. Margaret Somers observes that 'it is through narrativity that we come to know, understand, and make sense of the social world, and it is through narratives and narrativity that we constitute our social identities'. Margaret R. Somers, 'The Narrative Constitution of Identity: A relational and Network Approach', *Theory and Society* 23 (1994) p.606. Identities (however multiple and changing) are formed by being located or locating themselves within social narratives.

12. Stephen Cornell, 'That's the Story of Our Life', in P.R. Spickard and W.J. Burroughs (eds), *We Are a People: Narrative and Multiplicity in Constructing Ethnic Identity* (Philadelphia: Temple University Press 2000) pp.41–53.

13. Marysia Zalewski and Cynthia Enloe, 'Questions about Identity in International Relations', in K. Booth and S. Smith (eds), *International Relations Theory Today* (University Park: Pennsylvania University Press 1995) pp.279–305.

14. Roxanne Lynn Doty, *Imperial Encounters: The Politics of Representation in North–South Relations* (Minneapolis: University of Minnesota 1996) pp.2–3.

15. Jacob Torfing, *New Theories of Discourse: Laclau, Mouffe and Zizek* (Oxford: Blackwell 1999) pp.81–2.

16. Margaret R. Somers and Gloria D. Gibson, 'Reclaiming the Epistemological "Other": Narrative and the Social Constitution of Identity', in Craig Calhoun (ed.), *Social Theory and the Politics of Identity* (Oxford: Blackwell 1994) p.614.

17. John Agnew and Stuart Corbridge, *Mastering Space: Hegemony, Territory and International Political Economy* (London/New York: Routledge 1995); Gearóid Ó Tuathail and Simon Dalby (eds), *Rethinking Geopolitics* (London: Routledge 1998); Gearóid Ó Tuathail, *Critical Geopolitics* (Minneapolis, MN: University of Minnesota Press 1996); and David Newman (ed.), *Boundaries, Territory and Postmodernity* (London: Frank Cass 1999).

18. Agnew and Corbridge (note 17) p.7.

19. Ó Tuathail, 'Postmodern Geopolitics? The Modern Geopolitical Imagination and Beyond', in Ó Tuathail and Dalby (note 17) p.18.

20. David Campbell, *Writing Security: United States Foreign Policy and the Politics of Identity* (Minneapolis: University of Minnesota 1992) and Joanne P. Sharpe, 'Hegemony, Popular Culture and Geopolitics: The Reader's Digest and the Construction of Danger', *Political Geography* 15/6 (1996) pp.557–70.

21. Musifiky Mwanasali, 'The View from Below', in Berdal and Malone (note 3) p.143.

22. René Lemarchand, 'Preface', in Doom and Gorus (note 9) p.10.

23. René Lemarchand, 'Genocide in the Great Lakes: Which Genocide? Whose Genocide?', *African Studies Review* 41/1 (1998) pp.3–16.

24. Paul Collier, 'Doing Well out of War: An Economic Perspective', in Berdal and Malone (note 3) pp.101–3.

25. Anssi Paasi, 'Boundaries as Social Processes: Territoriality in the World of Flows', in Newman (note 17) pp.69–88.

26. Koen Vlassenroot, 'Identity and Insecurity: The Building of Ethnic Agendas in South Kivu', in Doom and Gorus (note 9) p.274.

27. Emmy Allio, 'Lendu kill 250 Hema in 3 Hours', *The New Vision*, 2 June 2003. p. 1.

28. Christopher Clapham, 'Boundaries and States in the New African Order', in Daniel Bach (ed.) *Regionalisation in Africa: Integration and Disintegration* (London/Bloomington: James Currey/Indiana University Press 1999) pp.53–66; and Paul Nugent and A.I. Asiwaju (eds), *African Boundaries: Barriers, Conduits and Opportunities* (London: Pinter 1996).

29. Filip De Boeck, 'Postcolonialism, Power and Identity: Local and Global Perspectives from Zaïre', in R. Werbner and T.O. Ranger (eds), *Postcolonial Identities in Africa* (London: Zed Books 1996) pp.75–106; Daniel Bach, 'Frontiers versus Boundary-lines: Changing Patterns of State–Society Interactions in Sub-Saharan Africa', paper presented at the APSA Annual meeting, Chicago 1995; and Basil Davidson, *The Black Man's Burden: Africa and the Curse of the Nation-State* (New York: Times Books 1992).

30. See Michael J. Shapiro and Hayward R. Alker (eds), *Challenging Boundaries* (Minneapolis:

University of Minnesota Press 1996); Trevor J. Barnes and James S. Duncan (eds), *Writing Worlds: Discourse, Text and Metaphor in the Representation of Landscape* (London: Routledge 1992); and David Morley and Kevin Robins (eds), *Spaces of Identity: Global Media, Electronic Landscapes and Cultural Boundaries* (London: Routledge 1995).

31. Clapham (note 28) p.62.
32. This essay was written shortly before President Laurent Kabila was assassinated. Throughout the essay, I use the term 'the Kabila regime' to refer specifically to his reign.
33. Kabila's nephew, Justice Minister Mwenze Kongolo, stated on BBC radio: 'This is a Rwanda invasion and Rwanda and Uganda are spearheading the invasion of the Congo.' Kabila's spokesman Didier Mumengi added: 'Rwanda and Uganda are criminal states that have meddled in foreign affairs while drawing on a feeling of pity from the international community after the 1994 Rwandan genocide'. Quoted in Milan Vesely, 'Carving up the Congo', *African Business* (Oct. 1998) p.12.
34. François Misser, 'The Carpet-bag Generals', *African Business* (Dec. 1999) p.31.
35. François Misser, 'Kabila Turns Diamonds to Dust', *African Business* (July/Aug. 2000) pp.31–2.
36. It has been suggested that Namibia's involvement in the war can largely be explained by the fact that President Sam Nujoma's brother-in-law, Aron Mushimba, reportedly has mineral interests in the DRC through Quanto Holdings. See Doom (note 9) p.61.
37. Ernest Wamba-dia-Wamba, 'Interview: "Kabila cannot be allowed to win a military victory"', *New African* (Feb. 1999) p.14.
38. See *The Economist*, 7 Nov. 1998, p.46; *MRB*, Feb. 1999, pp.1–5; *Le Monde*, 13 Jan. 1999; and *Africa Confidential*, 20 Nov. 1998.
39. Misser (note 34) pp.31–2.
40. Jakkie Cillers and Christian Dietrich (eds), *Angola's War Economy: The Role of Oil and Diamonds* (Pretoria: Institute for Security Studies 2000).
41. Not only did Rwanda provide troops, logistical support and material, but many of the Banyamulenge fighters had received their training when fighting with the RPF in Rwanda since 1990.
42. Michael Dorsey, 'Violence and Power-Building in Post-Genocide Rwanda', in Doom and Gorus (note 9) p.312.
43. For example, it has been reported that Paul Kagame has personal interest in at least five companies operating in eastern DRC. See Reno (note 3) p.58.
44. It should be noted, however, that this hostility was somewhat tempered by the convergence of mutual economic interests between the Zairian and Ugandan regimes. Uganda had long proved itself willing to be an important transit point for illicit exports of Zairian coffee, gold and ivory carried out by members of Mobutu's entourage, with Ugandan officials receiving financial 'compensation' for their assistance.
45. *New Vision*, 18 April 1999, 14 Dec. 1998 and 18 Dec. 1998; *Africa Confidential*, 20 Nov. 1998.
46. In November, a new group (Mouvement pour la Libération du Congo, MLC) headed by businessman Jean Pierre Bemba, surfaced in the Equateur province of north-eastern Congo, an area controlled by the Ugandan army (UPDF). In April 1999, the RCD split into two with Wamba-dia-Wamba leading a splinter faction in Kisangani (also the headquarters of the UPDF) and the Goma group led by Emile Ilunga. The division within the RCD reflected a growing rift between the Museveni and Kagame regimes, with the former supporting Bemba and Wamba-dia-Wamba and the latter Ilunga.
47. Mwanasali (note 21).
48. David Musoke, 'Uganda Exports More Gold Than It Produces?', *The East African*, 23–29 June 2003. p. 22.
49. *Africa Confidential*, 10 Sept. 1999; Colette Braeckman, 'Carve-up in the Congo' (trans. Barbara Wilson), mimeo (1999).
50. United Nations Security Council S/2001/357, *Report of the Panel of Experts on the Illegal Exploitation of Natural Resources and other Forms of Wealth of the Democratic Republic of Congo*. New York: United Nations, 2001; Stephen Jackson, 'Fortunes of War: Structures and Dynamics of the Coltan Trade', London: Overseas Development Institute, 2001; Human Rights Watch, *Covered in Blood: Ethnically Targeted Violence in Northern DR Congo*, Vol.15, No.11(a), July 2003. In the wake of the UN Security Council's report, the Ugandan

government launched its own inquiry that eventually led to the dismissal of Army Commander Maj. Gen. James Kazini. While Kazini is probably guilty, most observers consider Kazini a 'fall-guy' whose dismissal protects more well-placed guilty parties.

51. For instance, Mugabe asserted: 'Do they think a country as vast as the [Congo] could ever be subject to the wiles and guiles of little Rwanda, or even Uganda? It's absolutely stupid.' Quoted in Howard Barrell and Iden Wetherell, 'Rebels Advance after Fall of Kindu', mimeo (16 Oct. 1998).

52. Dorsey (note 42) pp.346–7.

53. Carole J.L. Collins, 'Congo/Ex-Zaïre: Through the Looking Glass', *Review of African Political Economy* 75 (1998) pp.112–13.

54. While the 'carving up' of the Congo clearly offers rich insights into the spatial dimensions of the conflict, it is important to recognise the fallacy behind some observers' assumptions that the events in Central Africa would lead to a redrawing of the map of Africa. See Clapham (note 28) and Makau wa Mutua, 'Redrawing the Map along African lines', *The Boston Globe*, 22 Sept. 1994. This cartographic change has not (and probably will not) come to pass precisely because the existing state borders have long been regarded less as barriers than as conduits and sources of opportunities.

55. During the early stages of the anti-Mobutu rebellion, the US was one of its clearest supporters. As François Ngolet writes, 'these links were evident when an American diplomat, Dennis Hankins, the political official in Kinshasa, went to the rebel headquarters in Goma. Hankins's visit was followed by the US ambassador in Kigali, Peter Whaley, who frequently visited Kabila in Goma, at a moment when the rebels' strategy moved from a regional insurgency to the drive to overthrow Mobutu.' See François Ngolet, 'African and American Connivance in Congo-Zaire', *Africa Today* 47/1 (2000) p.70. The US sent other officials to visit Kabila as well. At a time when the AFDL was still seen as suspect by most Zairians, the head of the US Committee for Refugees, Roger Winter, visited Kabila in eastern Zaire and praised the rebels, suggesting that they were being warmly received by the local population. See David Aronson, 'Mobutu Redux?', *Dissent* 45/2 (Spring 1998) p.21.

56. Thomas Turner, 'War in the Congo', *Foreign Policy in Focus: Columbia International Affairs Online* 4/5 (1999).

57. Mwayila Tshiyembe, 'Ambitions rivales dans l'Afrique des grands lacs', *Le Monde Diplomatique* (Jan. 1999) p.9.

58. Theodore Trefon, 'French Policy toward Zaïre during the Giscard D'Estaing Presidency', *Les Cahiers du CEDAF* (1989) pp.1–103; Stephen Smith and Antoine Glaser, *Ces Messieurs Afrique: Le Paris-Village du continent noir* (Paris: Calmann-Levy 1992); Roland Marchal, 'France and Africa: The Emergence of Essential Reforms?', *International Affairs* 74/2 (1998) pp.355–72; and Daniel C. Bach, 'France's Involvement in Sub-Saharan Africa: A Necessary Condition to Middle Power Status in the International System', in Amadu Sesay (ed.), *Africa and Europe: from Partition to Interdependence or Dependence?* (London: Croom Helm 1986) pp.51–70.

59. Asteris C. Huliaras, 'The "Anglo-Saxon Conspiracy": French Perceptions of the Great Lakes Crisis', *Journal of Modern African Studies* 36/4 (1998) pp.593–609; Gérard Prunier, *The Rwandan Crisis: History of a Genocide* (London: Hurst 1995). French claims were seemingly supported by the fact that the US had trained many of the officers in the Ugandan army and the RPF, including Paul Kagame, in the early 1990s. Furthermore, as soon as the RPF seized power, it immediately sent 114 officers to the US for training. See Milton Allimadi, 'The US Connection', *West Africa*, 21 Dec. 1998, p.914. See also *Jeune Afrique*, 20 Nov. 1996, pp.18–25, 16 Dec. 1997; *Le Monde*, 11 Feb. 1997.

60. Jean-Claude Willame, 'The "Friends of the Congo" and the Kabila System', *Issue: A Journal of Opinion* 26/1 (1998) p.27.

61. Prunier (note 59) pp.104–8. See also Huliaras (note 56) and Glynne Evans, *Responding to Crises in the African Great Lakes*, Adelphi Paper 311 (Oxford: Oxford University Press 1997) pp.63–4.

62. Ngolet (note 55) p.79.

63. Madeline Albright, 'A New Chapter in US-Africa Relations', *US Department of State Dispatch* 9/1 (Jan./Feb. 1998) p.2; *Newsweek*, 12 May 1997, p.41.

64. See Collins (note 53); William Reno, 'Mines, Money, and the Problem of State-Building in Congo', *Issue: A Journal of Opinion* 26/1 (1998) pp.14–17; Howard W. French, 'The Great

Gold Rush in Zaïre, Mining Concerns Court Rebels Even Before Mobutu's Ouster', *New York Times*, 18 April 1997; and James C. McKinley Jr, 'Zaire's New Troops: Mining Executives Wielding Briefcases', *New York Times*, 17 April 1997. Even before Kinshasa had fallen, Kabila's Finance Minister Mawampanga Mwana was meeting with dozens of businessmen in Lubumbashi, including representatives from Goldman Sachs, First Bank of Boston, Morgan Grenfell and other economic investors. See *Wall Street Journal*, 13 May 1997. Indeed, North American mining corporations were quick to reach out to Kabila. American Mineral Fields (AMF), a mining firm based in Hope, Arkansas (the hometown of then-President Bill Clinton), approached Kabila and organised contacts. Given the rebels' advance into mineral-rich areas, Kabila was able to reap the benefits of new and pre-existing agreements. The AMF and Canadian-owned Tenke Mining Corp. reportedly began supplying millions of dollars to the AFDL, along with transport for Kabila's troops. See Ngolet (note 55) pp.70–71.

65. Christopher Gray, 'Multinational and Human Rights Promotion: A Role for Mining Companies in the Democratic Republic of Congo?', paper presented at the African Studies Association Conference, Chicago, 31 Oct. 1998.

66. Erik Kennes, 'Le secteur minier au Congo: "déconnexion" et descente aux enfers', in Filip Reyntjens and Stefaan Marysse (eds), *L'Afrique des Grands Lacs: Annuaire 1999–2000* (Paris: L'Harmattan 2000) pp.231–72

67. See Reno (note 64) and Mwanasali (note 21).

68. Ian Taylor, 'Conflict in Central Africa: Clandestine Networks and Regional/Global Configurations', *Review of African Political Economy*, Vol.30, No.95, March 2003, pp.45–55.

69. See Allio (note 27) pp.1–2.

70. This illustrates Somers and Gibson's point that 'Which kind of narratives will socially predominate is contested politically and will depend in large part on the distribution of power.' Somers and Gibson (note 16) p.73. There clearly exists an asymmetric power relation between the West and Africa with regard to access and control of discursive space.

71. Cyprian F. Fisiy, 'Of Journeys and Border Crossings: Return of Refugees, Identity and Reconstruction in Rwanda', *African Studies Review* 41/1 (1998) p.18.

72. David Newbury, 'Understanding Genocide', *African Studies Review* 41/1 (1998) p.76.

73. Recently the mayor of Toronto joked about cannibalism among African Olympic athletes, while the head of the US Agency for International Development seriously asserted that Africans 'don't know what Western time is. Many people in Africa have never seen a clock or a watch their entire lives', *New York Times*, 10 June 2001.

74. One of the foremost proponents of this perspective has been Robert Kaplan, particularly in his 1994 *Atlantic Monthly* article 'The Coming Anarchy'. Kaplan paints a picture of the world going to hell-in-a-hand-basket, often using Africa as his 'evidence'. The continent, he suggests, is undergoing a breakdown of its social fabric because, well, it is Africa. If his subtly racist stance is missed in his article, it is clearer in his follow-up book where he proclaims that Africa is sliding back to the 'dawn' of time. In one memorable passage, Kaplan asserts that 'Africa's geography was conducive to humanity's emergence, [but] it may not have been conducive to its further development'. See Kaplan (note 7) p.7.

75. Richards (note 4) p.xiv.

76. Marianne Marchand, 'Reconceptualising "Gender and Development" in an Era of Globalisation', *Millennium* 25/3 (1996) p.577.

77. Mark Duffield, 'Globalization, Transborder Trade, and War Economies', in Berdal and Malone (note 3) pp.72–3.

78. Agnew and Corbridge (note 17) p.7.

79. Alan Hudson, 'Beyond the Borders: Globalisation, Sovereignty and Extra-Territoriality', in Newman (note 17) p.92.

80. For example, many Western observers have dubbed the DRC conflict 'Africa World War One'. Others have compared it to Europe's Thirty Years War, which preceded the Peace of Westphalia and the formation of the modern sovereign state system.

81. Somers (note 11) p.614.

82. Paul Routledge, 'Critical Geopolitics and Terrains of Resistance', *Political Geography* 15/6 (1996) pp.509–31.

Notes on Contributors

Phillipe Le Billon is Assistant Professor of Geography, University of British Columbia, Room 216, 1984 West Mall, Vancouver, BC, V6T 1Z2, Canada, <lebillon@geog.ubc.ca>.

Richard M. Auty is Professor of Economic Geography, Lancaster University, Lancaster LA1 4YB UK, <r.auty@lancaster.ac.uk>.

Michael Watts is Director of the Institute of International Studies, University of California, Berkeley, California, USA, <mwatts@socrates.berkeley.edu>.

Thad Dunning is a PhD student in the Department of Political Science, University of California, Berkeley, CA 94720-1950, USA, <tdunning@socrates.berkeley.edu>.

Leslie Wirpsa is a PhD student at the School of International Relations, University of Southern California, Los Angeles, CA, USA, <wirpsa@usc.edu>.

Fouad El Khatib isa former UN arms inspector in Iraq and currently Deputy Director of the Policy Planning department at the International Affairs Directorate (DGA/DRI) of the French Ministry of Defence. His contribution is made in a personal capacity and does not represent the view of his department or that of the French government. <fouadelkhatib@csi.com>.

Sarah L. O'Hara is Professor of Environment and Society, School of Geography, University of Nottingham, Nottingham NG7 2RD, UK, <sarah.o'hara@nottingham.ac.uk>.

Shannon O'Lear is Assistant Professor of Geography, Department of Geography, MC 150, University of Illinois at Urbana-Champaign, Room 220 Davenport Hall, 607 South Mathews Avenue, Urbana, IL 61801-3671, USA, <solear@uiuc.edu>.

Susanne Peters is a Habilitation Fellow , Political Science Department, Giessen University, Karl-Gloeckner-Strasse 21/E, D-35394 Giessen, Germany, <susanne.g.peters@sowi.uni-giessen.de>.

Marilyn Silberfein is Professor of Geography and Urban Studies, Temple University, Philadelphia PA 19122, USA, <pawling@astro.temple.edu>.

Kevin C. Dunn is Associate Professor of Political Science, Hobart and William Smith Colleges, Geneva, NY 14456, USA, <k-d-@mekons.com>.

Index

Printed in the United Kingdom
by Lightning Source UK Ltd.
106395UKS00001B/13-21